THE UNITED NATIONS UNIVERSITY

STUDIES ON PEACE AND REGIONAL SECURITY

EUROPE
DIMENSIONS OF PEACE

THE UNITED NATIONS UNIVERSITY

STUDIES ON PEACE AND REGIONAL SECURITY

The United Nations University project on Peace and Regional Security was a special study carried out under the programme area on Peace and Global Transformation. Focusing on the Third World and Europe, the project attempted to analyse the trade-offs between the conflicting conditions in these regions of vulnerability and security and competition and solidarity. Five regional seminars were held in Africa, Asia, Europe, Latin America, and Oceania and the Pacific on themes related to conflicts over natural resources and security and human rights in determining global, regional, and national development. The results of these studies are part of the United Nations University's contribution to the United Nations International Year of Peace.

Project Co-ordinator: Janusz W. Golebiowski

TITLES IN THIS SERIES

Africa: Perspectives on Peace and Development
Edited by Emmanuel Hansen (1987)

Europe: Dimensions of Peace
Edited by Björn Hettne (1988)

Asia: Militarization and Regional Conflict
Edited by Yoshikazu Sakamoto (1987)

Latin America: Democratization and Economic Crisis
Edited by J.A. Silva Michelena (1988)

The Pacific: Peace, Security and the Nuclear Issue
Edited by R. Walker and W. Sutherland (1988)

Peace and Security in Africa: A State of the Art Report
Emmanuel Hansen (1988)

This book must be returned immed-
iately it is asked for by the Librarian.

THE UNITED NATIONS UNIVERSITY

STUDIES ON PEACE AND REGIONAL SECURITY

EUROPE
DIMENSIONS OF PEACE

EDITED BY BJÖRN HETTNE

The United Nations University

Zed Books Ltd.
London and New Jersey

Europe: Dimensions of Peace was first published in 1988 by:

Zed Books Ltd., 57 Caledonian Road, London N1 9BU,
United Kingdom and 171 First Avenue, Atlantic Highlands,
New Jersey 07716, USA

and

The United Nations University, Toho Seimei Building,
15–1 Shibuya 2-chome, Shibuya-ku, Tokyo 150, Japan.

Copyright © The United Nations University, 1988

Cover design by Adrian Yeeles
Printed by Biddles of Guildford

British Library Cataloguing in Publication Data

Europe: dimensions of peace. ——— (United
Nations studies in peace and regional security;
v. 2)
1. Reconciliation   2. Europe ——— Foreign
relations ——— 1945–
I. Hettne, Bjorn   II. Series
327.1'72'094   D1058

ISBN 0-86232-714-8
ISBN 0-86232-715-6 Pbk

Contents

Introduction   1
European projects for peace and development   1
The structure of the book and its contributions   6

PART 1: EUROPE IN THE NEW COLD WAR   13
1. **Europe in the Global Strategic Game** *Silviu Brucan*   15
   Post-war political developments in Europe   16
   Military pacts and the war system   18
   Superpower rivalry and Europe in the mid-1980s   19
   The challenge from the Pacific Rim   23
   The strategic significance of reform in the East   24
   Conclusion   25

2. **European Unity and its Implications for the Interstate System**
   Immanuel Wallerstein   27

3. **East–West Economic Cooperation and the Demise of Détente**
   Y. V. Andreyev   39
   On interrelations of economics and politics   39
   Evolution of trade and economic relations of the USSR with
     the West   41
   Current problems of economic relations of the USSR with
     Western countries   49
   Conclusion   53

4. **Europe and Star Wars: Security Dependence or Independence?**
   Hans-Henrik Holme   55
   The quest for European security   56
   SDI and Europe   68
   European reactions: should dependency be welcomed?   71
   SDI: Security-dependence or independence?   76

PART 2: EUROPE AND THE THIRD WORLD   85
5. **Europe and Centre–Periphery Conflicts: Lessons From the Global**
   Crisis *Tamas Széntes*   87

6. **East–West Rivalry and Regional Conflicts in the Third World**
   Raimo Värynen   101
   Introduction   101
   Regional orders in the Third World   103
   Modes of great-power involvement   105
   Transformations in the international system   110
   Conflicts in the period of US predominance   113
   Conflicts and fragmentation in the international system   118

7. **East–West, North–South Conflict: Interrelationship:**
   Western Europe's Role *Lothar Brock*   127
   Introduction   127
   Global dimensions of the East–West conflict   129
   Western Europe in global politics   134
   Conditions favouring and limiting an independent role for
     Western Europe   140
   Global détente and the interest and capabilities of
     Western Europe   146

8. **A Keynesian Global Strategy for Employment and Peace**
   Angelos Angelopoulos   150
   A world economy out of control   150
   A plan to face the debt crisis and promote world economic
     growth   155
   Toward a Keynesian approach on a world scale for a new
     Marshall Plan   158

9. **Peace and Poverty: Europe's Responsibility** *Louis Emmerij*   161
   The interrelationship between peace and development   161
   Evolution towards basic needs   163
   Conclusion   176

**PART 3: BEYOND THE COLD WAR: EUROPE IN SEARCH OF A
   NEW ROLE**   179
10. **Transcending the European Model of Peace and Development**
    Björn Hettne   181
    The nation state and the state of anarchy   181
    The modernization imperative in the Third World   186
    Transcending the European Development Model   188
    An alternative security for Europe   192
    A Europeanized Europe   196
    Concluding remarks on voluntarism   201

11. **Transforming the State. An Alternative Security Concept for**
    Europe *Mary Kaldor*   204
    Introduction   204

Long political and economic cycles 204
The role of deterrence 210
The role of military technology 213
The European peace movement and alternative security
  concepts 215

12. **Economic Aspects of the Politics of Peace and Security**
    Alfred Bönisch 221
  Armament and the functional mechanism of the
    economy 222
  International economic cooperation as an instrument for
    the stabilization of peace 226
  Expansion of economic relations with the developing countries
    on a democratic basis 230
  Conclusion 232

13. **In Search of Peace and Security: The Potential of Neutrality**
    Josef Binter 235
  Introduction 235
  The concept of neutrality, definition, features and
    characteristics 235
  Neutrality as strategy for conflict resolution 239
  The contribution of neutrality to world peace and the role of
    European neutrals 243
  Conclusion 247

14. **The World Economy, International Relations and the European**
    Challenge *Andre Gunder Frank* 249
  Recent developments in transatlantic and intra-European
    relations 258
  Prospects for East–West Pan-European rapprochement 262

15. **A Culture of Peace or Exterminism: Socio-cultural Alternatives**
    Miroslav Pečujlić 266
  New militarism 267
  The crisis of modernization 269
  Disarmament and development 277

Index 281

Tables

3.1 The USSR trade turnover by groups of countries 42
6.1 Great power involvement and regional orders in the
    Third World 107

8.1 External debts of the developing countries: 1977 and 1984   152
8.2 Latin America countries: foreign debts servicing and exports   153
8.3 Projected public debt service   154

List of Contributors

Y. V. Andreyev, Institute for World Economy and International Relations, Moscow, USSR.

Angelos Angelopolous, Member of the Academy of Athens, Former Governor of the National Bank of Greece.

Josef Binter, Austrian Institute for Peace Research and Peace Education, Stadtschlaining, Austria.

Lothar Brock, Peace Research Institute, Frankfurt, Federal Republic of Germany.

Silviu Brucan, University of Bucharest, Bucharest, Romania.

Alfred Bönisch, Akademie der Wissenschaften der DDR, Zentral-institut für Wirtschaftswissenschaften, Berlin, GDR.

Louis J. Emmerij, Institute of Social Studies, The Hague, Netherlands. From January 1986 President of the OECD Development Centre, Paris, France.

Andre Gunder Frank, Institute for the Socio-Economic Studies of Developing Regions, University of Amsterdam, Netherlands.

Björn Hettne, UNU Project on European Perspectives, Dept of Peace and Development Research, University of Gothenburg, Sweden.

Hans-Henrik Holme, Institute of Political Science, University of Aarhus, Denmark.

Mary Kaldor, Science Policy Research Unit, University of Sussex, England.

Miroslav Pečujlić, Faculty of Law, University of Belgrade, Yugoslavia.

Tamas Széntes, Karl Marx University of Economic Sciences, Budapest, Hungary.

Immanuel Wallerstein, Fernand Braudel Center for the Study of Economies, Historical Systems and Civilizations, University Centre at Binghamton, State University of New York, USA.

Raimo Väyrynen, Dept of Political Science, University of Helsinki, Finland.

Introduction

European projects for peace and development

In the current European situation the peace issue and the development issue are both under debate, but the relationship between the two is a matter of some confusion since the two debates are carried out in different contexts: military security and economic crisis management. Without denying the relevance of these debates in their own terms, important new dimensions could be added by relating them under the 'peace and development' umbrella. The rationale behind this argument is that there must be a consistency between development model and security arrangements. The common denominator of the articles published here is their comprehensive approach to security. In the introduction to these contributions we shall briefly consider three models of peace and development and, derived from these, seven European social projects for solving problems of security and crisis management.

By a 'social project' we mean a specific course of action that contains a vision of the world, a strategy for realising that vision and a number of actors having a political base. There must of course be a sufficient number of actors in order to speak of a 'social project'. If we don't believe that history unfolds itself in accordance with some hidden law, we must understand the European future as shaped by the struggle between different social projects, as well as the possible alliances between them. To assess the possibilities of alliances it is important to consider the paradigmatic compatibility or non-compatibility between the general models described below.

The *Conventional Model* pictures the world as an interstate system, each state being a sovereign unit and constituting a national economy. For each state the rest of the world is an anarchy both in terms of the free play of market forces and in terms of lacking overall political order. Economic competition and efforts to maintain a balance of power through armaments thus characterise the international behaviour of nation-states.

The *Reformist Model* contains three crucial elements. First, the level of armaments must be lowered but with the balance of power maintained. Thus the actual conception of security is not much different from that of

1

the *conventional model*, but security is maintained through 'minimum deterrence'. Secondly, the resources released by disarmament, or rather armament's decrease, should be transferred to developing countries so that the purchasing power of these countries can be increased. Thirdly, the growing demand resulting from this massive transfer of resources will create growth and employment in crisis-ridden industrial countries. Thus, management of global interdependence will be a more stable foundation for peace.

The *Alternative Model*, in contrast, is a fundamental reinterpretation of current peace and development concepts. Here development means creating a sustainable society where basic human needs are fulfilled and the relationship between society and nature is non-exploitative. Such a society would also be more secure, in the broader sense of the term. It would be self-reliant, less vulnerable, and ecologically balanced. The role of the nation-state will be minimized or transformed.

The first model is identical with the traditional (or 'mainstream') European approach to peace and development. Serious dysfunctions have emerged, and the world order organized in accordance with the conventional model seems to be breaking down.

The reformist model tries to tackle some of the negative symptoms: The excesses of armaments, economic stagnation, rising unemployment, and polarization between rich and poor within nation-states and within the world-system. So far these attempts have not succeeded. Instead this – basically social democratic – position is becoming increasingly marginalized. Many call this position 'utopian' today.

Would it be less utopian to call for a transcendance of the European model, in accordance with the third model? There are of course several possible European scenarios and their peace relevance differs, according to one's viewpoint. I will here consider the following seven social projects:

The Atlantic Project	
Peaceful Coexistence	} Conventional
A European Superpower	
The Trilateral Project	} Reformist
Global Interdependence	
Fortress Europe	} Alternative
The Green Project	

Atlanticism and *Peaceful Coexistence* are in fact rather similar in content. However, the points of departure are, in the first case, US interests and, in the second, USSR interests with Europe playing a more or less subordinate role in both cases. Both projects are within the realm of the conventional model and imply continued superpower dominance (and competition) in world politics. The recent discussion on strengthening the conventional defence of Western Europe is certainly a response to criticism of this subordination, but essentially an effort to save the Atlantic alliance with the role of Europe somewhat upgraded. This would, in fact, be welcomed by the US since her defence burden would, relatively speaking, be reduced.

As for 'peaceful coexistence', the concept presupposes the existence of two camps with contradicting socio-economic systems. However, this socio-economic contradiction must not be allowed to manifest itself on the politico-military level, particularly not in the nuclear age. The contradiction has, at least in theory, to be solved through the ultimate victory of the socialist socio-economic system. In order to protect this system, so long as it remained vulnerable, the Warsaw Pact was established.

The third conventional project, and a more ambitious one as far as the role of Europe is concerned, is the prospect of *Europe as a Superpower*, which was very much discussed in connection with the first enlargement of the EEC in 1973 (when Britain, Denmark and Ireland joined). The later enlargements (Greece, Spain, Portugal) have, significantly, not led to similar concerns.

In order to achieve true independence within the framework of the conventional model, there would be a need for a European nuclear force which could at least guarantee minimum deterrence. It is easy to see great complications in British-French military cooperation so long as Britain maintains her Atlanticist orientation. The project also depends on a strong Franco-German axis. The closeness that has developed between these two old arch-enemies is truly remarkable although the Green Party and the strong peace movement in West Germany are now complicating matters.

France is also worried by the American SDI (Strategic Defense Initiative) which is meant to consolidate the Atlantic alliance and the predominance of the US within that alliance. President Mitterand has therefore initiated the so-called Eureka project, an all-European research project with partly the same R and D (Research and Development) elements as SDI but with a clearer civilian orientation. All West European countries (including the neutrals) have responded favourably to Eureka, revealing the extent to which the 'Pacific challenge' now worries Europeans. However, the content of Eureka is still very much in the air.

The *Trilateral* and *Global Interdependence Projects* are of a more reformist nature. They both stress the development problem which they define in terms of decreasing demand and fragmentation of the world market and they see disarmament and detente, together with economic liberalization, as political preconditions for development, albeit of a rather conventional kind. The concern for disarmament is more pronounced in Project Global Interdependence, articulated, for instance, in the Brandt Commission's reports. In the Trilateral philosophy, the management of interdependence is the key concept and here the socialist world is explicitly included, although 'peaceful coexistence', of course, implies convergence of the two systems rather than the ultimate victory of socialism.

The Brandt Commission's reports, on the other hand, were rather silent on the role of the socialist world, while assigning a strategic function (as a Keynesian demand raiser) to the South. In both projects, Europe figures prominently and takes a rather autonomous role. Global Interdependence is very much a contribution of European Social Democracy to the struggle for a New International Economic Order.

Disarmament as the main means of transferring resources is crucial to the Brandt Commission philosophy, although this problem is more fully dealt with in the report of the Palme Commission on Disarmament and Security Issues, as well as in the reports of the United Nations' Expert Group on Disarmament and Development. All these reports constitute the basis of the reformist model.

Finally, two alternative social projects depart substantially from mainstream solutions: one red and one green. The red or *Fortress Europe* is, in many respects, conventional left Keynesianism, but departs radically from conventional wisdom by its vision of a regionalized world. The idea behind this project is to take advantage of the 'domestic' market and combined productive capacity of a unified Europe, that is, the Common Market and nations of the European Free Trade Association (EFTA) and, in a longer perspective, possibly also the Eastern European countries. This would create a large economy which, like the US and Soviet economies, could be basically self-sufficient. Protectionism, on the European level, seems to be the only way to save a unique European achievement – the welfare system – since the alternatives, protectionism on the level of the nation-state or monetarism à la Thatcher, are paving the way for economic anarchy, destabilization, social conflicts and, ultimately, political tensions that could escalate into war.

This is a project of the European left, rejecting monetarism, but also going beyond conventional Keynesian policies. The weakness in Keynesianism is its exclusive focus on demand management while leaving the supply side wholly to private initiative. The keys to European recovery, according to the 'out of crisis' project of the European left are three: reflation, restructuring and redistribution and these policies have to be carried out on a European level. Unilateral expansionism will defeat its own purpose, as the French socialist experiment shows.

It is necessary to pinpoint the differences between the Global Interdependence perspective of, for instance, the Brandt reports and the European Fortress approach since adherents of both projects are found among European socialists. It could, perhaps, be said that the former are Keynesian towards the South while being moderately monetarist at home, while the latter have reservations about increasing trade as a means of combating the crisis, as long as this increasing trade is not accompanied by changes in the structure of supply and demand, changes which are compatible with social justice. From the point of view of social justice, a global Marshall Plan, transferring resources from North to South, would be premature unless major structural reforms are undertaken in the Third World.

The *Green Project* also avoids too much interdependence and goes even further in terms of decentralisation and local self-reliance. There are Green parties in West Germany, Belgium, France, Ireland, Sweden, Austria,

Luxemburg, Switzerland, Holland, Britain and Finland. Die Grünen in West Germany are obviously the most active and articulate. However, to a much larger extent than other political parties, the Greens constitute a transnational phenomenon due to the two main issues involved. The first is *environmental protection* which, according to the Green view, is incompatible with the modern industrial system, whether socialist or capitalist. Rudolf Bahro, who has experience of both, borrows E.P. Thompson's concept 'exterminism' as a general characterisation of western civilisation. A worldwide industrialisation would in his opinion destroy life on earth, but before that happens the competition for dwindling resources would increase the level of political tension in the world system to the point when a nuclear disaster could destroy the world. Thus, the second issue mobilising the Greens is *peace*. Ecology and peace are linked but their realisation needs a complete transformation of society. In Green politics these two issues constitute the fundamental starting points and are not mere points in a party programme.

In view of the rather insignificant number of votes the Green parties in different parts of Europe have up to now received, it can, of course, be doubted whether they really represent a force for change. However, the appearance may be deceptive. The change to power structures is usually a subtle process in which many small changes have an aggregate effect.

Logical and coherent solutions belong to the world of abstractions. The future will be a more or less stable outcome of the struggle between competing social projects. What are the global implications of these social projects?

One unfortunate burden Europe has imposed upon the rest of the world is a development model that is unviable in economic and political terms. In this era of uncertainty, however, there are some possibilities for Europe to take on a new role as a global actor in the promotion of peace and development. The first priority must be to not make things worse. This implies a withdrawal from projects that block Third World development and endanger world peace. Continued Atlanticism and so called 'peaceful coexistence' have a rather low peace relevance, since the dual global power structure implied in these social projects gives the superpowers too free a hand in their respective spheres of interest. The realization of the potential role of Europe as a third superpower, aggressively competing with the others, would also make things worse. At present, this does not seem a likely development.

Assuming that Europe does not make things worse, how can she make things better? Obviously, by trying to reduce East-West tension which manifests itself in a tragic and artificial division, concretely expressed in the Berlin Wall. However, closure of the gap could, in accordance with the conventional model, be interpreted as a security risk by each of the superpowers, since a 'europeanisation' of Europe implies reduced superpower control and a movement towards the other camp. The superpowers tend to identify national security with bloc stability.

What radical and far-reaching alternatives could then be possible, given political realities and the implications of the various alternatives for peace and security in other regions?

The conventional model is utopian because of its long term unviability. This is due to the inherent contradictions of the model rather than its political support, which is not lacking. On the other hand, the non-conventional solutions (the reformist and alternative models) may be more viable in terms of their modes of operation but here the accusation of utopianism rests instead on a lack of visible political support. However, the previously much secluded issue of security has, in the last 5 to 10 years, become a problem of more general concern and broadening debate. This means that different options with varying political support can be articulated. Furthermore, it will be increasingly difficult to separate the security issue from the development issue in this emerging debate. It is significant that in the alternative solutions discussed here the two issues are inseparable. The reformist model sees disarmament as a precondition for development, whereas the alternative model conceives security as an integral part of new patterns of development with emphasis on sustainability in ecological terms, invulnerability in socio-economic terms and transarmament towards defensive defence in military terms.

Only projects relating to either of these two models have a peace relevance but the reformist projects, while being politically more realistic, do not in fact guarantee stable peace. Why? Because the development model is, in itself, conflict-generating both on the domestic scene and for international relations. Therefore, the reformist model can at best provide a model of transition.

The structure of the book and its contributions

The articles in this volume originate from a UNU sponsored seminar in Austria in May, 1985. The aim of the seminar was to discuss the various interrelated issues of peace, security and development in Europe within the context of Europe's role in world peace and global transformation and with special emphasis on the interlinkages between the regional and global problems of peace and development. The seminar also tried to identify emerging positive counter trends and to raise new ideas on problem solution, conflict management, development alternatives, mutual confidence building, peaceful cooperation and disarmament. Furthermore, the Schlaining meeting also provided an opportunity to summarise three previous meetings on regional security in Latin America, Africa and Asia. Therefore, the theme chosen was 'Europe's Role in Other Regions' Peace and Security'. In spite of this theme, it must be admitted that the discussion was somewhat Eurocentric. For instance, the SDI and its effects on Europe was intensively discussed, whereas issues of this kind were conspicuously absent in the Latin American and African meetings where the debt crisis and the starvation catastrophe were more in focus. It is obvious that the peace and development problematic is conceived differently in different parts of the world and that a bridging of this gap in itself has major peace relevance.

Eurocentrism apart, a European meeting in which European issues are discussed is of great importance. The first section of this book deals with the current scene in Europe in the context of the new cold war.

Silviu Brucan provides a macroscopic overview of the development of a bipolar war system centred on Europe and the role of Europe in the global strategic game dominated by the two superpowers. Brucan points to the double function of the military pacts, one outward-directed, the other inward-directed, the latter having the function of maintaining bloc stability. He also, however, emphasises the different intra-bloc dynamics of the process of loosening up. What is usually called 'liberalization' in western literature with reference to the East should rather be seen as assertion of national culture and the remaking of socialism along national paths. Like several other authors in this part, Brucan points to the importance of the Pacific challenge for the future role of Europe.

Immanuel Wallerstein's contribution deals precisely with Europe's room for manoeuvre in the new cold war and in the current restructuring of the world system. Europe has been the most politically stable area in the post-war period simply because of deep superpower involvement. Wallerstein believes that this relative stability will be shaken in the future due to a number of structural, economic, political and ideological changes. The most spectacular European contribution to a reorganisation of the world-system would be continental unity, an ambiguous concept to which many of our contributors address themselves. The main opening for this unity, according to Wallerstein, would be a global realignment, with a US-Japan-China alliance stimulating closer cooperation between Western and Eastern Europe and the Soviet Union. Thus Europe's scope for action will depend both on global developments in the world system at large and the internal process of integration.

European integration may take many different forms. *Y.V. Andreyev* discusses the Soviet view of the fate of East-West economic relations in the post-detente era and stresses the continued peace relevance of East-West economic cooperation. Andreyev thinks that such cooperation by no means is excluded by the fact that the parties represent antagonistic forms of property. On the contrary, when the international situation as a whole has been aggravated, economic relations acquire a special importance. The political context of this is détente or the road back to détente, defined as a complicated interlacing of political, military and economic components. However, there is an independent dynamic 'objective necessity' in economic relations. Andreyev points out the difference in approach between the 'linkage strategy' of the US and the 'interdependence' view of the world prevalent in Western Europe. The latter view rejects 'economic war' as a means of solving external political problems.

Hans-Henrik Holme asks the question: Is independence of the superpowers the way by which Europe can achieve security? He does so in the context of the current debate on SDI. For Western Europe, SDI means a continued dependence on the United States at a time when there is a strong desire for a more independent role for Europe. Holme describes European security independence as 'a powerful dream'. The agony of national decision-makers is therefore very visible. Far from simplifying the issue, Holm makes a careful analysis of both the rather contradictory SDI initiative and its implications and concludes that, although the SDI offer should be rejected, there can be no regional European security in an insecure world. Europe cannot achieve its security without involving itself directly in the security of other regions.

As many seminar participants pointed out, the SDI is a symbol of many things: of the cohesion of the Western alliance, of the belief in US leadership, of the permanence of the conventional security doctrine, and of the belief in the unlimited possibilities of science and technology. In fact, SDI embodies the very essence of the mainstream model of peace and development. To say no to SDI is to question conventional wisdom in development and peace. That is why the French are designing a European version: the Eureka project.

The second part of this book takes up the relationship between Europe and the Third World, starting with the impact of the East-West divide, then considering some more constructive solutions.

Tamas Szentes starts from the premise that peace and security are complex and multidimensional concepts which imply that the effects of European direct or indirect involvement in other regions' peace and security are manifold. Apart from political and military effects, one must also consider what Szentes calls the two 'invisible wars': misery and hunger, and deterioration of the environment. Among the direct effects of East-West struggle are the excessive role of state and army as well as the phenomenon of clientism leading to 'over-radicalisation' of both leftist and rightist regimes and the creation of obstacles to regional integration or cooperation. Instead the result is increasing disintegration, instability and outward-orientation. Among the indirect effects, Szentes particularly emphasises the role of Europe, East or West, in providing 'models' that distort the development patterns in many developing countries. No model can be successfully copied and even original models are subject to critique or changes of reality. On the other hand, there are no solutions that can disregard the basic interdependencies of the world system.

Raimo Väyrynen argues for more analytical emphasis on the autonomous dynamics of regional subsystems and how changes in these subsystems interact with changes in the world-system as a whole. He stresses that there is an erosion of the overall bipolar power constellation at the same time as the potential of regional power centres and regional socio-economic formations is on the increase. For these reasons, regional conflict formations constitute appropriate units of analysis and a theoretical and conceptual approach to such studies. Väyrynen points out that the outcome of regional conflicts most often is a result of superpower politics and that conflict-resolution mechanisms, indigeneous to the regions, are more incipient than established. This is most problematic since the ongoing fragmentation of the international system seems to multiply manifest conflicts in the Third World.

Lothar Brock calls for a truly global détente (the détente of the 1970s was never global while the East-West conflict was global from the beginning) and asks what Western Europe can do to bring it about. It is quite evident that all Europe has much to gain from a resumed détente and much to lose by any horizontal conflict escalation. This can be seen in the emerging European Community's Central America policy, which (although not always with one voice) emphasises regional non-military solutions, external aid and internal reforms. The search for a European identity is limited, (because it cannot ignore the intra-European differentiation of problems, potentials and interests) and real because Western Europe has a genuine interest in widening its options for adjustment to the global crisis. It is the existence of such options which constitutes the main difference between industrialized and developing countries. However, Brock warns us not to expect anything spectacular concerning Europe's role in other regions' peace and security, since the capacity or willingness of people to act according to their objective or long-term interests is rather limited.

Such cautiousness should perhaps also be observed in the case of the strategy of a massive transfer of resources discussed, for instance, in the Brandt Commission reports. This strategy is, as *Angelos Angelopoulos* explains, closely linked both to the conception of the world economy as interdependent and the theory of Keynesianism applied on a world scale. Angelopoulos makes the point that the arrangement of existing debts is a precondition for the revival of economic activity, not only in the Third World but also in industrial countries. In Angelopoulos' view, Europe is destined to play a more autonomous role between the superpowers and contribute to the reinforcement of détente, leading to a reduction in military expenditures and the realization of resources necessary for a worldwide economic recovery.

Louis Emmerij reminds us that the poverty problem no longer captivates the minds and the attention of people, although it has been argued that 'poverty anywhere is a threat to peace and prosperity everywhere'. Why not launch a campaign to wipe out absolute poverty within one generation, Emmerij asks. The strategy he proposes, and analyses in detail, is a basic needs strategy with which he has been closely associated. Europe's role in the realization and implementation of such a strategy could be vital, although Brock's warning quoted above also applies in this case. It is thus obvious that the potential global role of Europe is far from realized, as will be even more evident when we listen to the voices of the Third World.

The third part deals more explicitly with Europe's new role or roles, already referred to by some of the other authors. Björn Hettne's paper exemplifies current rethinking about the European model. He argues that the nation-state and the inter-state world system originated in Europe and moulded the rest of the world through the creation of colonial empires and that a dominant factor in world development has been the politico-military imperatives implied in the process of nation-building.

Europe has now reached the limits of the mainstream model of peace and development and the transcendence of this model has begun. A new pattern of development must, however, go together with an alternative system of security, based on sustainability, invulnerability, legitimacy and trans-armament. A Europeanised Europe finally implies a retreat from the European development model, the dissolving of bloc politics and the convergence of what is called Third System politics.

Mary Kaldor puts particular emphasis on the possibility that the peace movement may dramatically change the political landscape of Europe and the world. She argues that the only shield against nuclear war is not SDI, but human consciousness. She disagrees with analyses that reduce the role of the State as primarily functional to the economy and outlines an approach that provides a more independent analysis of the state. The historical role of the peace movement, Kaldor writes, is to bring about a fundamental transformation of the social relationships that constitute the State and the inter-state system away from reliance on physical coercion towards more democratic state forms, just as the historical role of the labour movement was and is a transformation of economic relationships.

Alfred Bönisch, in general agreement with Andreyev's article in Part I, underlines two main reasons for the socialist states to expand international economic relations:

- to materialize the process of political détente, to stabilize it economically and to develop it further;
- to stimulate one's own economic development.

He finds the first reason presently more important since the primary concern must be to prevent an atomic war. He particularly focuses on the relations between armament and economy and argues that high military expenditure erodes and deforms the material basis of society. This is especially evident in the field of employment effects. Thus reduced armament expenditures, coupled with a programme of job creation which, at the same time, serves to save energy, to increase development aid and to use non-polluting technologies, would be an effective contribution towards the policies of détente. Not only increasing East-West but also North-South economic cooperation and trade would fulfil this purpose, and the latter should take place within the framework of a new international economic order.

Turning from the economics to the politics of peace, it can also be argued that neutrality has been and still is a positive factor in reducing tensions and promoting détente. However, there are complications to be analysed. *Josef*

Binter provides a thought-provoking essay on the concept of neutrality and the role of the European neutrals (Austria, Switzerland, Sweden and Finland). Neutrality remains an amorphous concept containing different varieties and policies, one major distinction being between neutralised countries (Austria) and countries that practice neutrality due to a unilateral political decision (Sweden). In the latter case, the country can unilaterally change its status of neutrality if it so wishes. Neutralization, on the other hand, must be based on an agreement by the superpowers to leave a country or a certain area outside of their competition. It has great potential as a peace strategy but has so far not been used outside Europe. As for unilateral changes towards a neutral position their peace relevance depends on the way they effect the power balance or rather the perceptions of balance. It should, therefore, be kept in mind that neutrality in this way presupposes and even forms part of the East-West division.

André Gunder Frank combines the economics and politics of peace in his call for a Pan-European Entente for Peace and Jobs, instead of nationalism in the form of protectionism and isolationism or, as another alternative, 'global keynesianism'. Frank departs from the current discussion on extended European protectionism but would like to see larger European economic cooperation to include also Eastern Europe and the Soviet Union. This 'greater Europe' should also form ties to the Middle East and Africa. When there is a real mutual economic interest basis for such a rapprochement, and when the alternative is a possible nuclear destruction, there is more than enough reason to make the political effort. It would not lead to utopia but offer greater hope for the achievement of important and widely shared desires – maintenance of world peace or at least avoidance of nuclear war, greater possibilities for economic growth in Western Europe, wider opportunities for national independence and political liberalization in Eastern Europe, and increased political bargaining power and room for manoeuvre for socialist and nationalist liberation movements in the Third World.

Miroslav Pečujlič opens up even more far-going prospects away from 'exterminism' against which concept he puts what he calls 'radical emanciption'. One horizon is empty and closed; the other open and crowded with creative possibilities, mainly expressed in mass-scale social movements and peace movements taking a central place among them. Pečujlič thus takes up the theme introduced by Kaldor and emphasises emancipatory projects rather than government strategies. He warns against 'closed regionalism' and a 're-feudalization' of the world at a planetary level. Instead Europe should strike through the chain of armaments and find a third way of bringing political and material reinforcement to the strategy of non-alignment and affording more space to Third World nations to pilot their own course of development. But any new relationship with the Third World presupposes a qualitative change in our own type of development.

Björn Hettne

Part 1: Europe in the New Cold War

1. Europe in the Global Strategic Game

by Silviu Brucan

Although Europe no longer plays the predominant role in world affairs it did in the 18th and 19th centuries, when the European powers were virtually running the world, it is still a continent of considerable importance in many respects. In the 1970s, its economic potential surpassed that of any other continent; with a population totalling one-fifth of the globe's, Europe produced roughly 47% of the world's income and nearly 55% of its industrial goods. Traditionally, Europe has led the way in international trade, accounting in the 1970s for 54% of world exports. UN data show that nearly half of the world's scientists work in Europe. However, in the 1980s, a challenge to that predominant position is coming from the Pacific Rim and the paper will examine its dimension and chances of success.

It was in Western Europe that capitalism originated and expanded all over the world, and it was in Eastern Europe that the Russian Revolution made the first crack in the international system. Therefore, the stakes in Europe are very high and there are authors who hold that it is here that the issue of 'where is our world going' will be decided. Small wonder that Europe is the last continent where the postwar bipolar structure of power, with the US and the USSR as protagonists, has been stubbornly preserved. It is sharply divided into two military blocs and economic groupings, and it shelters right in its midst the highest concentration of armed forces and conventional and nuclear weaponry on our planet.

With the emergence of China as a world power, Europe has become not only subject but also object in the big strategic game. Moscow has been warning Western Europe not to sell modern weapons to China whilst Washington is attracted to embark on a triple alliance with Japan and China that would inevitably affect its primary commitment to Europe and certainly its relations with the USSR. Overlapping and intersecting the big strategic game, the economic war over markets, resources, and balance of trade between the US, Japan and Western Europe makes a leading American columnist wonder what is actually the present danger for the US: 'Is it a military threat from the Soviet Union or an economic threat from some of our allies who are out-working and out-producing us?'[1]

The reason I mention these aspects is to point out the host of factors and contingencies that make up world politics these days. It is in this broad context that I propose to examine the role of Europe in the global strategic game.

Post-war political developments in Europe

Political developments after World War II in Europe can be divided into two historical periods. The first, beginning in 1945 and extending till the end of the fifties, was dominated by the division of Europe along ideological lines into two opposite and hostile camps tightly lined up behind the US and the USSR. It was the extension into Eastern Europe of the revolutionary process under the Soviet military umbrella that led the US and its Western allies to counter with the containment policy, the North Atlantic Treaty Organization, the Marshall Plan, the Truman Doctrine etc. *Class conflict* and the *ideology* that goes with it were pushed to the forefront of world politics. The Cold War was the virulent expression of that priority in international affairs.

With the halting of the wind of change in Europe at the end of the 1950s the thrust of revolution shifted toward the underdeveloped continents, with the Third World looking for 'a place in the sun'. National resurgence permeated world politics. In the West, General de Gaulle came out against American domination; in the East, the Sino-Soviet polemic broke out. Against this background, the US and the USSR discovered their common interest in maintaining the nuclear strategic lead in their hands; the two nuclear treaties (Test-ban and Non-proliferation) jointly drafted by Soviet and American experts reflect this basic common policy. Briefly, a new stage opened up in world politics in which *national-strategic* considerations overrode ideological ones.

Implied in this analysis are two theoretical assumptions: it is the aggregation of men according to *class* interests or *ethnic* ties that conditions their behaviour and thinking whenever they engage collectively in large-scale movements. As one or the other motive force expands on a sufficiently large international scale, it may well become predominant in the whole international system. Hence, modern history, beginning with the French Revolution, has been marked by periods of intense national competition alternating with periods of sharp class-ideological conflict. I call this historical interplay the seesaw of class and national motive forces in international politics; for, as one comes to prevail, the other goes down, diminishing its impact on foreign policies.

My contention is that during these two periods in post-war Europe, the relations between the superpowers with their partners in Western Europe and Eastern Europe respectively bear a certain resemblance. Major political developments in both parts of Europe, though different inside because of their socio-economic system, have run parallel, displaying striking similarities. During the Cold War, both Western and Eastern nations were tightly aligned behind their respective leaders. The position of the US and the USSR was similar: undisputed authority monopoly in the formulation of policy and strategy, complete subordination to the goals set in Washington and Moscow. As national-strategic reasons prevailed over ideology in both East and West, nations gaining strength within both alliances began to assert themselves to promote national interests, gradually demanding a say in the formulation of policies and military doctrines. In the West, France led the way towards political emancipation, followed by West Germany's *Ostpolitik.* In the East, the trend is reflected in such events as 1956 in Hungary and Poland, later in Romania's independent stance and, last but not least, Czechoslovakia. Truly, the phenomenon is stronger in Western Europe, where the asymmetric structure of the alliance is less overwhelming than that in the East where the Soviet Union's power exceeds by far that of all its allies together.

To be sure, the social content of national self-assertion in the East is different from that in the West. Here, what has been wrongly called in the Western literature 'liberalization' is actually the attempt of local revolutionay forces to *remake socialism in their own way,* according to national conditions and political traditions. One must recall that, in the aftermath of the war, the Soviet Union was the dominant power in the region, enjoying the glory of liberator from Nazi oppression. To both the Soviet Communist party and the local communist parties of Eastern Europe, the mechanical adoption of the Soviet model seemed the best and safest course, particularly in view of the vigorous assault of the imperialist powers seeking to disrupt and destabilize the infant political regimes. Whereas in the Cold War period, international conditions were conducive to subordination within the bloc and to close imitation of the Soviet model, now international conditions favour the reverse trend – that is, self-assertion of national revolutionary forces, emphasis on national equality and cultural identity, rejection of forms and methods in building socialism that are ill-suited to the given nation. In Romania, where servile mimetism had gone as far as declaring Romanian language and culture as chiefly Slavic, the country's latin heritage was restored to recognition. The Prague Spring was essentially a drive to remake socialism consonant to national conditions. Czechoslovakia had been, even before the revolution, an industrial state with a high level of culture and a tradition of political democracy. It was actually the only Eastern country that was ripe for socialism, according to Marx's paradigm. Surely, such a nation could hardly assimilate the Soviet model which had been tailored in a backward country.

Now, if we only translate some of the notions used in the East into Western terms, and consider the whole process within a capitalist milieu, we shall easily discover the resemblance. Change USSR to USA, and you will have in the West a trend toward national emancipation, increasing insistence on participation in the making of NATO strategy, promotion of an independent trade and monetary policy coming into conflict with American supremacy. While nationalism has bad connotations in both

Washington and Moscow, the moment it is monitored in the rival camp, the pejorative adjectives are suddenly replaced by terms of praise and encouragement. De Gaulle was scorned in Washington and praised in Moscow; and so was Romania in reverse.

This is not to say that class interests have vanished all together in the making of foreign policy. Even de Gaulle, when he perceived the Cuban missile crisis as a test of power with an underlying ideological component, immediately assured President Kennedy of France's support. Also, whilst pulling French troops out of NATO, France remained in the Atlantic alliance because de Gaulle realized that capitalism could not be maintained by France alone. Class interests and the ideology that goes with them have remained to this day the cement that keeps NATO together.

Military pacts and the war system

Originating in the ideological climate of the Cold War, NATO and the Warsaw Treaty have survived the centrifugal forces of nationalism through a stabilizing system that feeds its own dynamic as the institutional framework of the bipolar structure of power. At the heart of this system lies the mutual distrust inherited from the cold war which is continually reinforced by the mutual fear that any 'lowering of the guard' may pose a challenge to the very bases of society as it exists in both the West and East.

Thus, military pacts with an ideological underpinning have two major functions: one, openly proclaimed, is directed outward; the other, well disguised, is directed inward. The former is meant to protect pact members against an external threat; the latter, to secure the perpetuation of the system of relations inside the alliance, its structure of power. Between the two functions, a self-adjustment mechanism is at work. When the external threat of aggression is imminent, the outward function takes precedence while the inward one recedes into the background. When the external threat diminishes, the inward function prevails. If need be, the military pact is used to restore order inside, that is to deal with challenges to the system. The external threat is then only a pretext or a cover-up for the internal operation. Dubchek with his Prague spring simply ignored the second function of the Warsaw Treaty and so did the leadership of Solidarity in Poland. In the West, Kissinger's warning against communist participation in Italy's government (described as a threat to NATO) and more recently, US public displeasure with Mitterand's decision to bring three communist ministers into his cabinet fall within the same conception of NATO's dual role: safeguarding the capitalist system inside is no less important than repelling external aggression. Actually, the relations between NATO and the Warsaw Treaty constitute the matrix of the world-wide war system.

As a result, the arms race has been kept on an ascending line in Europe, irrespective of the fluctuations in the political climate, whether the spirit of détente prevailed or subsided. Direct military expenditures in both NATO and the Warsaw Pact have kept rising unperturbed by the Nixon-Brezhnev accord on détente and by SALT I or II, the quadripartite agreement on West Berlin, *Ostpolitik* and the Helsinki Conference on European Security and Cooperation. There is but one conclusion: the war system, originating in the competitive nature of the interstate system, works no matter the political climate or the socioeconomic system. The main theoretical point here is that a subsystem cannot behave differently from the global system of which it is a part. Socialist nations, in their external relations, have to adjust to the patterns of relations prevailing in the international system which continues to be fed by central capitalism. Up to now, socialist nations have failed to display either the necessary strength or the political will to change the interstate system or, for that matter, to oppose the war system. And as the saying goes: 'if you can't beat them join them'.

Superpower rivalry and Europe in the mid-1980s

Ronald Reagan came into the White House at a time when the decline of American power was visible. In economic terms, compared with 1950 when the US accounted for half of the gross world product, its share in 1980 was down to 25%; in world trade, Western Europe had outstripped the US, becoming the biggest world exporter, while Japan was gaining ground even on the US domestic market. The sheer impotence shown in the case of the hostages held at the US embassy in Teheran, following the American debacle in Vietnam, illustrated the limits of US military power. *La classe politique* was divided, according to an American author, between 'those who believe that we must adjust our interests and behaviour to the more modest position we now occupy in the world and those who believe that we can and must recapture the position and leadership we once enjoyed'.[2] As leader of the latter, Reagan was confronted with the asymmetric structure of US power (financial predominance, military parity, economic decline). Hence, his strategy to use the formidable financial assets of the US to upgrade its military power so as to overcome its economic weakness vis-à-vis Western Europe and Japan, while mobilizing all the resources of world capitalism to reduce the power and influence of the USSR. Nevertheless, this strategy has a strong ideological component, for only by reasserting its leading role in the capitalist world can the US expect its Western economic competitors to fall in line. The question is whether such an asymmetric structure of power can make for a successful strategy with aims so ambitious?

As for the Soviet Union, its panoply of power assets is much poorer. Therefore, ideology notwithstanding, the Soviet response to the Reagan challenge has been to rely chiefly on its formidable military power. Paradoxically, though in a different way, the weak point of the Soviets is also its economic performance. So, we are dealing with two superpowers having an economic problem. The two giants, having concentrated for too long on military competition, are now discovering that they have neglected the very core of their economic power, and implicitly of their military preponderance.

The US, though in the midst of an economic upturn, is faced with an alarming budget deficit coupled with a chronic balance of trade deficit caused by its dwindling industrial competitiveness on world markets; its long-term effect is a shrinking industry – the deindustrialization of America.

The USSR is struggling with an outdated and inefficient economic system that does not and cannot assimilate the scientific-technological revolution. As a result, the Soviets have been lagging further and further behind central capitalism and are threatened with being pushed to a lower rank in the world economy.

The great irony of history is that the most critical domestic problem confronting the US can be solved only by state intervention while the most critical problem confronting the USSR can be solved only by integrating market mechanisms within the planning system. But, ideologically, neoconservatism is opposed to state intervention while neostalinism is opposed to market mechanisms. The two species of modern conservatism have been reinforcing each other's determination to maintain the military-strategic priority in their relationship and in the world at large.

With the change of guard in the Kremlin and a new leader, Mikhail Gorbachev, with his hands on the tiller of economic reform, the question arises whether a shift is possible in Soviet-American relations away from the frantic race for military superiority to non-military areas of conflict and cooperation. One can hardly provide a quick answer at a time when the US thrust toward recapturing a hegemonic position in world affairs goes hand in hand with domestic policies favouring the rich, particularly the defence industries. Indeed, the superpowers have never been so conspicuously working at cross-purposes as now.

What role can Europe play in the big game?

First, one must recall that in the early 1980s Western European countries provided the kind of support that enabled Reagan to carry out successfully his strategy in Europe. The crucial political act in that direction was the 1979 NATO decision to produce and deploy in Western Europe by 1983 Pershing-2 and Cruise missiles that could reach major targets in the European part of the USSR.

In retrospect, however, it was the Soviet initiative to deploy the new medium range SS-20 missile that set off Western Europe's action. Whatever the military reasoning or motivation behind the Soviet decision, the fact is that the SS-20s were directed against Western European targets and not American ones. Therefore, it is only natural that those who were directly implicated by that Soviet decision should have reacted in kind. It is not accidental that the initiative for that reaction came from Chancellor

Schmidt of West Germany.

Militarily, the new generation of medium range missiles has created the possibility of early nuclear destruction coming from the European theatre itself; this amounts to the nuclearization of military hostilities in Europe based on the theatre's self-contained capabilities. Secondly, what appeared in Europe as an issue of theatre deterrent has resulted, in overall strategic terms, in a US advantageous position: whereas the Soviet SS-20 could reach only Western Europe but not American territory, the new US missiles deployed in Western Europe could destroy essential targets in the USSR with higher accuracy than ICBMs and very little warning. This destabilizing situation brought the strong Soviet reaction, on the one hand, and the massive demonstrations staged by the peace movement particularly in West Germany – the main target area for nuclear bombs.

Most interestingly, a totally different evolution has characterized East-West economic exchanges in Europe during the years of high US-Soviet tension. Trade between the two parts of Europe has remained relatively high at $80 billion annually. To assess the importance of East-West trade in Europe, one must recall that it jumped from roughly $10 billion in 1970 to well over $80 billion in 1980. At a time when world markets for Western industrial exports have been dwindling, resulting in rising unemployment, Soviet and East European eagerness to buy industrial equipment and modern technology is an important factor in West and European trade policy. It is estimated that more than one million jobs in Western Europe depend on Eastern industrial orders. This is why Reagan's attempt to embargo the building of the Soviet gas pipeline to Western Europe was categorically rejected by West Germany, France, Italy and Britain, and so was his overall policy to restrict East-West exchanges.

Briefly, military developments in Europe worked at cross-purposes from economic ones. The reason why the USSR in its European policy has emphasized politico-military means rather than economic ones may be found in a global perspective. In the world economy, the USSR holds an inferior position being subject to unequal exchange in its trade with the West and having to protect its currency through a high rate of exchange. However, in the politico-military sphere, the USSR has succeeded in building a force equal to that of the United States which allows the Soviets to display political and military initiative on the world scene, affecting for better or for worse the international political climate. Surely, the USSR could do nothing of that sort in the world economy where its actions are adaptive rather than disruptive. Hence, the emphasis on politico-military means in trying to influence world developments seems to have been a more convenient choice of strategy.

Now, it is Washington's turn to set Europe in motion with Reagan's Strategic Defense Initiative, popularly called 'star wars'. Despite Washington's professed policy of 'close consultation with our allies', Reagan's dramatic March 1983 announcement of his defence initiative took Western governments by surprise. Mitterand came out sharply against star wars as 'overarmament' and called for a moratorium on space weapons. Responding to the intensive US pressure to lend their support to America's position in the Geneva talks, Bonn, London, and Rome offered a conditional backing to the research stage of SDI, warning that any step further would have to be discussed seriously within NATO. In the meantime, the British Foreign Minister made public his government's reservations on the military merits of SDI and expressed the fear that it may destabilize present deterrence strategy; in West Germany, officials warned that Star Wars could decouple fatally West European defence from US defence. Indeed, for all Washington's efforts to reassure its allies and to buy their support with promises to involve them in research for new technologies, the SDI clearly means that the US nuclear guarantee of Western European security would become neither credible nor feasible for the very simple reason that it is designed 'to make America safe leaving Europe vulnerable', as one West German author put it. Naturally, the SDI has generated in Western Europe a serious preoccupation for the setting-up of a joint effort to take care of specific defence needs in the case of a superpower race in space weaponry.

The politico-strategic issues which are most likely to offer Europe the opportunity of asserting its own views and interests are Central America and the Middle East. In general, Reagan's view of the Third World as a battlefield for East-West competition is not shared by European countries, although the ideological whip manipulated by Washington has more often than not prevented them from saying so. In particular, Washington's emphasis on military methods in dealing with Latin America has aroused grave concern in European capitals. Such scandalous actions as the mining of Nicaraguan ports early in 1984 were widely criticized, and, of course, Reagan's cynical admission that America's aim in Nicaragua is the overthrow of the leftist government produced consternation. The neo-conservative spokesman, Irving Kristol, apparently irritated by Western criticism of US policy in Central America went as far as warning that 'The US is not going to remain committed to the defence of Western Europe, at the risk of nuclear annihilation, if Western Europe is not equally committed to the defence of America's interests. In the debate over Central America, the very existence of NATO itself is at stake.'[3] Indeed, America's position as the leader of the West is the issue at point and this is the very core of NATO's existence.

In the Middle East, America's strategy of turning the region into an anti-Soviet fortress is contrary to Western European interests. The net result of that strategy has been the arming with modern weapons of all conflicting parties either by the US or by the USSR. And as the experience of the Iraq-Iran war has shown, the objective of military hostilities in the region is the destruction of oil deposits – precisely what the West is vitally interested to protect and preserve. However, up to now Washington, has succeeded to discourage every political or diplomatic initiative of the EEC in the region.

The challenge from the Pacific Rim

Earlier, assessing the importance of Europe as the continent with the greatest economic potential, I noted a formidable challenge from the Pacific Rim, threatening to remove the centre of world politics from the Atlantic to the Pacific. In one of his most perceptive anticipations, Marx spoke of such a prospect: 'The Pacific Ocean will then play the same role as at present the Atlantic and that of the Mediterranean in classical antiquity'.

Indeed, Japan is already the fastest growing industrial economy while the middle-income countries of East Asia and Pacific (South Korea, Taiwan, Singapore, Hong Kong, and coming from behind Thailand, Malaysia, Indonesia and the Philippines) achieved a much higher rate of GDP growth than that of Europe (8.6% between 1973–79 and 5.2% between 1980–83).

The most dramatic turnabout in the Pacific Rim is, however, China's radical reform introducing market mechanisms into its socialist economy. Were China's modernization programme to gather momentum and its one billion people to become the workforce of a dynamic economy, its impact on the global economy would be truly revolutionary.

At a time when world trade is stagnant, the value of merchandise moving across the Pacific has increased more than ten fold in the last decade. With its most competitive industry, Japan's trade surplus with the EEC rose from $0.25 billion in 1970 to $12 billion in 1983 and even more so with the United States.

The critical issue, however, is whether the US would incline toward the Pacific instead of the Atlantic, for in that case the large Pacific Rim would account for 60 per cent of the world gross product. In May 1984, the French premier noted that US trade with the Pacific countries had out-stripped that with Europe and exclaimed: 'A new geography is being born': $183 billion compared to the $113 with the Atlantic.

More important, from 1979 to 1983, US investment in the Pacific region grew annually by about 20%, three times as fast as in EEC countries. In its turn, Japan's investments in America grew even faster: by 1982 they had reached $8 billion and, by a last count, the Japanese influx of capital now runs at a rate of $25 billion to $50 billion, surpassing by far US investments in Japan. The rapidly growing economies of the Pacific Rim are pulling the United States and Canada ever more deeply into the region in contrast with the sluggish European economies or the debt-ridden countries of Latin America facing years of austerity.

The basic condition for regional cooperation is already there. Most Pacific nations trade more with one another than with the rest of the world. Modern technology – the single greatest factor working for integration – is working its way through communication, transportation, flow of information, ideas and people. Satellite transmission of radio and TV programmes, for example, have broken the shells that isolated many areas in the Pacific Rim. Conversely, an economic war is going on between the US and Japan while socialist ideology sets China apart from the rest of the Pacific Rim.

Therefore, economic cooperation in the Pacific Rim is gaining ground but a more compact form of regional integration is not on the cards in the foreseeable future because of great discrepancies in wealth and differences in culture and ideology.

The strategic significance of reform in the East

With Hungary, Bulgaria and, at the other end of the socialist spectrum, China having embarked on radical economic reforms with startling results in agriculture, the cutting edge of the issue now confronting all socialist countries is market mechanisms. How to integrate market mechanisms in the central plan while keeping market forces under control, and how to achieve this without altering the basic political structure – these are the problems Communist governments will have to wrestle with for the rest of this decade.

Clearly, the old Stalinist command-type planning and management system is outdated and a striking conclusion comes out of a thorough analysis of Soviet economic performance: this system does not and cannot assimilate the scientific-technological revolution. Every small techno-logical progress requires gigantic extra-economic efforts coupled with an immense waste of resources. As a result, ever since the technological revolution modernized industry and agriculture, the East-West economic gap has been widening. From 1955 to 1980, the East-West gap increased in absolute terms of per capita GNP from $4000 to $7730. The share of CMEA (Comecon) in world industrial production that had risen in 1950–60 with 10.6 points (reaching 28.4% of the total) rose only 3.6 points in 1960–70 and a mere 1 point in 1970–82.

The strategic position of the Comecon in the world economy can be defined by three figures: roughly 30% share of world industrial production while its share of world trade is roughly 11% and that in world financial transactions only 9%. In other words, radical economic reform is required not only by domestic needs but also by strategic considerations. Let us recall that because of historical conditions with socialist revolutions starting in backward or less developed countries, the fundamental strategic task of the USSR and other socialist countries has been, and remains, to catch up with central capitalism in economic-technological terms, without which socialism cannot function as a post-capitalist society. If the USSR and East Europe are to play a significant role in the global strategic game of tomorrow, military force is not enough. In fact in the nuclear era, the use of force ceases to be the final arbiter of international conflict, and, implicitly, the decisive factor in changing power relations in world politics. Truly, it may take some time for political institutions and leaders to grasp that new reality and adapt to it.

To sum-up, a radical reform that would put East Europe back in the economic race at the world level may have a direct bearing on the place and weight of Europe in the big global game. It may also open up new opportunities for East–West interchanges in Europe that would revitalize the European economy and technology.

Conclusion

The global strategic game for the rest of the 1980s will be dominated by the East–West conflict and by West–West economic competition with the main actors: USA, USSR, Western Europe, Japan, and China clashing on the world scene on various lines of conflict; in regional terms, the principal dispute will involve Europe and the Pacific Rim. Consequently, the North–South conflict and the strategy of development will be further pushed on to a secondary plane in world affairs until the Third World succeeds in overcoming its lack of unity and in organizing its forces into a political factor with a strategy of its own.

The process of capital accumulation driving the world economic system and the pressure of modern technology, as the specific way in which the productive forces emanating from national societies operate in world politics, will compel nation-states to regulate the increasing activities that transcend national boundaries and eventually to integrate into larger units than the nation-states. Experience shows that geographical and ideological factors determine the process of globalization to proceed first on a regional basis (e.g. EEC, Comecon).

Yet, because of class struggles inside societies and rivalries among nations, the drive of modern technology does not operate as a one-directional sweep, but as a dual and contradictory motion. The effect is a dialectical interplay between the factors that make for cohesion and integration and those making for division and conflict with the former prevailing only in the last analysis. In Europe we can see this in the vacillating evolution inside the EEC and the COMECON; in the Pacific Rim, in the partnership and rivalry so characteristic of US–Japanese relations, as well as in the relations between the ASEAN group and Japan.

The remaining years of this century may go down in history as its most critical and explosive period for never before have so many social and political contradictions requiring structural changes converged in a world so small and so capable of destroying itself.

Notes

1. James Reston, 'US Defense: The Present Danger', *New York Times,* 18 November 1978.
2. See S. Brucan, *The Dialectic of World Politics,* Free Press Macmillan, 1978.
3. NATO Review 1976 and 1977; and SIPRI Yearbook 1976 and 1977.
4. Robert Tucker, 'The Purposes of American Power', *Foreign Affairs*, Winter

1980/1981, p. 242.

5. See *Economic Survey of Europe in 1982*, United Nations, 1983.

6. Irving Kristol in *Encounter*, March 1985.

7. *World Development Report*, World Bank, Oxford University Press, 1984.

8. *World Paper*, special issue on The Pacific, Boston, March 1985.

9. Ibid.

10. Extrapolated from the data calculated by the World Bank for the years 1955 and 1980; see also World Development Report, Washington DC, 1982, p. 22.

11. *Narodnoie Hozeaistvo SSSR*, 1922–82, Moscow, 1983.

2. European Unity and its Implications for the Interstate System

by Immanuel Wallerstein

One of the most remarkable features of the contemporary world is that the continent which, since 1945, has seen the least amount of violence (interstate or intrastate) is Europe. There has been some violence of course, but compared to Asia, Africa, and Latin America very little. And yet the two world wars of 1914–1918 and 1939–1945 were fought largely on the European landmass and resulted in enormous physical destruction, loss of lives, and political upheaval there.

If one asks why this is so, there is no doubt that to a considerable extent Europe has been in the shelter of the Cold War. This may sound paradoxical. However, the reality of 'mutual deterrence' has meant that both the US and the USSR were frightened that any small outbreak of violence in Europe could escalate rapidly into full-scale nuclear war. They have clearly been less frightened that this would happen if violence occurred elsewhere. I cite four arenas in which violence has occurred or is occurring without (as yet) such escalation: Iran-Iraq, Cambodia-Vietnam, Ethiopia-Somalia, Honduras-Nicaragua. The explanation for the violence in each arena is different. The degree of direct influence of the US and the USSR varies greatly. I wish in no way to suggest that these conflicts are the same, or even similar, except in one respect: they have gone on for some length of time without resulting in nuclear war. It is hard to believe this would be true in the very unlikely case that armed conflict were to commence between for example West Germany and Czechoslavakia.

On the other hand, of all the regions of the world, Europe has also experienced the least political change since say 1947, by which time the present political arrangements seemed more or less to have been consolidated. To be sure, Greece, Spain, and Portugal have undergone some important constitutional changes. But even so, it would not be hard to defend the case that Europe has been more politically stable than Asia, Africa, or Latin America. If one asks why this is so, once again a large part of the explanation lies in the Cold War. By 1947, it was clear on which side of the Cold War various governments were located. This has been institutionalized in NATO and the Warsaw Pact. There are some states outside these frameworks, but in each case there are tacit understandings about the ways in which these states will conduct both their foreign and internal affairs. When we use the code word of Yalta, we are referring to this reality, whatever was or was not actually agreed upon at the Yalta meeting itself.

Elsewhere, more political change has occurred. In part, this has been because the US and/or the USSR was not always able to block such changes. Vietnam represents the most stunning example of the limits of US power. But it would falsify analysis if we only considered the variable of indigenous roots of change. A second factor was that, for all the verbiage of their leaders, the US and USSR governments have shared one geopolitical assumption: in Europe was located the vital core of their 'interests'. They might 'tolerate' changes elsewhere, however reluctantly, but they could not tolerate them in Europe.

Their devotion to Europe has not been a source of unmitigated joy to Europeans, either west or east. But it has been a fact of life, with which Europeans have learned to live and from which they have drawn certain advantages. At the same time, they have squirmed under the disadvantages of this *mise en tutelle,* for it has been nothing less, but thus far we have seen no real rebellion. In a recent article in *Le Monde,* André Fontaine, who is always judicious, wrote:

> The French disagree amongst themselves about many things, but there are some points, and more than is generally realized, on which they all agree. The management of the country's affairs in the light of the international crisis and the dedicated selfishness of our American ally is increasingly an element in this consensus.

The 'sacred egoism' of the superpowers is a heavy burden for Europeans to bear. Europeans chafe under them, demonstrate against them, but suffer them largely because they have no real choice. I do not wish to exaggerate. Many west Europeans are happy to think of themselves as the allies of the US and many east Europeans think likewise of the USSR. But presently there is no real way by which to measure how large a group would remain happy were all constraints to disappear. Since they will not disappear in any near future, perhaps we will never know.

One last reality about Europe should not be ignored. The UNU conference on European security took place in May 1985 on the eve of the 40th anniversary of the defeat of Europe's then most powerful, most centrally-located country, Germany. One lasting legacy of that defeat was the creation of two German states, each attached very firmly to a different side of the Cold War. German reunification has been only a minor issue in post-war politics. Perhaps careful studies of the collective psychology of Germans in the two states would find that reunification was not even a high priority for many of them. But it is such a powerful latent rallying-point in this present epoch – the heyday of nationalisms – that it will again be on the political agenda in the near future. If, however, once again one asks why this has has not yet been the case, again the main explanation must be the Cold War. Neither superpower would tolerate for a moment the possibility that 'their' ally would be swallowed up by the other side's ally. And probably neither would they tolerate even the idea that their 'ally' would be the one doing the swallowing, since it would then become a much more powerful and intractable ally – a fear shared by most other European countries. Hence everyone throws cold water on any thought of German reunification, and the Germans thus far have had no choice but to go along as graciously as possible. (This is not to deny that there are not many Germans who themselves are opposed to reunification, fearing its political implications.)

The relative absence of violence in Europe, combined with the relative political stability, makes Europe the exception rather than the rule of the post-1945 world. Will this continue? Since I have explained these phenomena as being in large part a consequence of the Cold War, the question is whether the Cold War will continue for much longer. Reading the newspapers of the last five years, one has the impression that the Cold War, after having flagged somewhat in the late 1960s and 1970s, has been revitalized and determines more than ever the course of European history. And yet, of course, we know that there are a number of objective factors underlying this conflict which are in the process of changing radically.

One is economic conjuncture. Since 1945, the capitalist world-economy has been in one of the expansive phases of its regular long cycles – indeed the biggest single economic expansive period in the history of the world economy, in terms of absolute production, productivity, mechanization, urbanization, and proletarianization worldwide. We are wont to talk of an industrial revolution in the late eighteenth century. But, in fact, if ever there were a moment to be called an 'industrial revolution', meaning by that making the manufacturing sector the central pivot of world economic activity, it is probably this post-1945 period which really merits the title. During it, manufacturing became so widespread that it ceased to be the mark *per se* of economic advantage. Manufacture has become common-place in the world economy.

This extraordinary expansion was, however, able to sustain itself no longer in fact than previous such expansions, that is, circa a quarter of a century. It was to be followed, as had happened so many times before, by a long period of relative economic stagnation (the so-called 'crisis' of popular denomination), in the middle of which we find ourselves at present. Europe, both west and east, had flourished in the period of expansion. From the ruins of war a phoenix-like reconstruction and technological transformations took place. We talk of 'economic miracles' in Western Europe and of very high growth rates in Eastern Europe. The basic reality was not all that different between the two parts of Europe, although the level of economic activity and well-being was higher in the west. No doubt other areas of the world experienced the advantages of economic expansion as well, but none (except for Japan) quite to the extent of Europe in the 1950s and 1960s. This economic well-being certainly did not disturb the relative political tranquillity of which I have been speaking.

There was a second structural feature to this first postwar period. Within the framework of an expanding capitalist world-economy, the role of US economic enterprise was at first overwhelming. In 1950, the US could outproduce all other zones of the world-economy in all domains. And on this basis American enterprises were able not merely to dominate world trade but to expand individually in size and space (that is, transnationally) to an extraordinary degree. Of course, when one produces so very well, one is sometimes caught short by a lack of customers. The US had to create customers, concentrating on Western Europe (and Japan). This was so for purely economic reasons; but it was also for political reasons – once again the Cold War. Thus it was, however, that by 1970, when the world economy had already entered its B-phase of stagnation, the greatly expanded basic productive plant of western Europe and Japan had in many ways caught up to, and in some ways passed beyond, US structures. The overwhelming US economic advantage of 1950 had become much slimmer by 1970.

These two changes – the shift of the world-economy from an A to B phase, and the shift from a situation in which the US was economically a giant amidst Lilliputians to one in which she was one strong power among several – were part of the same process, the normal entropy of monopolistic advantage within capitalism.

The fact that such a relative economic decline of the US in the world-economy was in some sense normal did not make it less a shock for the world-system. America's role in the world-system from 1945 to circa 1967 was special. It was the hegemonic power. Its unquestioned economic competitive advantage in all fields, plus its exceptional military power allowed it almost always to obtain its will in the political arena. To be sure, the USSR was able to carve out what might be called a zone of non-interference. And some national liberation movements in the peripheral areas were able to pursue their paths despite fierce US opposition – most notably, in China and Vietnam. Yet, by and large, US word was fiat in this period.

With the ending of the expansionary phase, and the frittering of the US monopolistic advantages (especially vis-à-vis Western Europe and Japan), this ceased to be true. The automatic US majority in the United Nations was transformed virtually into the opposite, an automatic anti-US majority. US ability to contain national liberation movements it considered unfriendly was severely undermined. Iran provides the most spectacular example. And less obviously, but perhaps more importantly, US political leverage in Western Europe declined considerably. No doubt the Reagan foreign policy was designed to reverse this political downturn, but it has at most only slowed the process. From the standpoint of the US, the halcyon days of the 1950s and early 1960s are gone, never to return.

There is a fourth factor of structural change, a change in the ideological structures, the mentalities, of the world system. At a purely ideological level, the Cold War was the culmination of a 19th century intellectual battle between 'liberalism' and 'Marxism'. The real history of these two ideologies is rich and complicated. What is to be noted is that one correlate of the early Cold War was the crystallization of each ideology into a particular, relatively simplified, form which was dogmatic (in the sense that intellectual variance was not well-tolerated politically), rigid (in the sense that intellectual activity was largely confirming rather than reorganizing activity), and consequently brittle.

That which is brittle is bound to crack. There were two big cracks, which reinforced each other, and which can by symbolized by two dates: 1956 and 1968. 1956 was the year of the XXth Party Congress of the CPSU. Kruschchev's report had a major impact not so much because of what it said, but because it was said at all. This self-criticism, however limited, not of an individual, but of the leading party in the communist world movement, reversed long-standing truths and apologias, and therefore permanently legitimated scepticism. The corrosive effects of such scepticism on the internal social structures of the USSR, on the relations between the USSR and other socialist states (China, eastern Europe), on the functioning of the world communist movement have been great and are far from exhausted today. One half of world verity had been opened to reorganization.

The other half could not be too far behind. What 1968 represented was the institutionalization of a deep scepticism about the liberal consensus that had previously dominated all the cultural, intellectual, and political institutions of the Western world, and indeed of large parts of the periphery. There too what was important was less what was said than that it was said. What had been self-evident became debatable, and the group who had the right to enter the debate was no longer restricted to a small group of specialists. Debate had become open to informed 'amateurs'.

In all these arenas – economic, political, ideological – it would be a mistake to exaggerate the structural changes of the last 15 years. But it would be a mistake as well to underestimate them. For it is in the nature of these structural changes that they will continue, and will have greater import as the years go by. Eventually they should shake the relative stability of the European scene, the phenomenon with which we began this analysis. In each of the three arenas, an element has been set in movement, whose outcome is uncertain.

Economic reorganization is going on in the world-economy. The 1970s and the 1980s mark the period in which considerable reshuffling – of location of economic activity, of sectoral profitability, of world economic structures – is occurring. The real question, however, is where this re-shuffling is going to come out in the 1990s and beyond. We may anticipate that it is likely that the world-economy will enter into a new expansionary phase, perhaps not quite as spectacular as the last but quite real nonetheless. We may anticipate that informatics, biotechnology, and new energy forms will serve as the leading industry sectors. But who will be able to gain monopolistic edges that will guarantee the direction of flows of surplus? This is not at all certain, but clearly it must be of concern to

Europe that she might come a poor second in the race. We see this in the current manoeuvring concerning the SDI.

There is a reorganization underway also in the interstate system. The principal political structures of the Cold War still stand – the two military alliances. But important elements have changed. China is no longer a Soviet ally. The political leverage of Western Europe and Japan vis-à-vis the US has increased enormously. And the actual military strength of a number of countries in Asia, Africa, and Latin America is more significant than it once was. Instead of a crisp bipolarization, there is a fuzzy one, with many players more equal to each other. This means that a reshuffling of alliances is a political possibility, which it was not before. Were there to be a reshuffling, it is not clear who would end up where. What is clear is that there is no advantage in being the last to move. And this must be of concern to Europe.

Finally, if the crystalline versions of the two nineteenth-century ideologies have been cracked, they have not been shattered. Several ideological developments are possible. Both ideological systems could take advantage of the new flexibility forced upon them and reproduce themselves in more sophisticated forms. Or, only one of the systems might do this. Or, neither would do it, and then we would have one of two main possibilities: a long period of confusion and the erratic emergence of new mysticisms; or a more rational *Aufhebung* of the ideological superstructure. Europe, which gained an ideological monopoly on world thought four centuries or so ago, is under severe and efficacious attack from the multiple civilizational renewals elsewhere. Once again, Europe's concern is no doubt whether it will put itself in a purely reactive position (and hence ultimately a marginal position) or whether Europe can participate actively in the new processes of intellectual analysis.

What are the chances, therefore, that Europe will take significant initiatives in the process of economic, political, and ideological reorganization of the world-system, initiatives in the next 25 years or so? The most spectacular initiative would be a move in the direction of European unity, one that would heal the division of Europe which is a fundamental legacy of the second World War. Is this in the realm of the possible, or mere *kaffeeklatsch* fantasy?

It is easy to see the factors which make this seem remote, indeed fantastic. There are two fundamental ones. The first is that there are genuine, deep-seated ideological and political differences between Western and Eastern Europe. If one has doubts about this, one has only to look at how people and governments thought about, talked about, and reacted to the rise and fall of Solidarnosc between 1980 and 1983. By post-1945 standards, the struggle between Solidarność and the Polish government was a relatively civil and muted one – in terms of violence and ideological screeching. Yet the issues were clearly drawn and strongly felt, and that throughout Europe. These differences will not disappear suddenly. The ability of the US and the USSR, as the official champions of the contending ideologies, to utilize calls to ideological basics as tactical weapons in controlling their allies has repeatedly been shown to be real and efficacious. That is to say, both these countries have power beyond the strictly economic, military, and political realms. There are still many people in other countries who act in terms of these internalized ideologies, and accept the legitimacy of the ongoing ideological leaderships the US and the USSR give. In hard ideological terms, unity between Western and Eastern Europe seems to imply that one or the other or both yield serious ideological ground, and on both sides this breeds very strong resistance.

There is a second fundamental difficulty about European unity. I have stressed previously certain economic parallels (seen from a world perspective) of European economic developments in the 1950s and 1960s, but we should be careful not to overstate these similarities. At the moment, the unification of Europe into some common economic structure would pose the same problem, multiplied several times, of the incorporation first of Greece, now of Spain and Portugal, into the EEC. We have seen the political stability of the EEC very stretched in this process. It is not clear it could survive an attempt to widen membership further, especially as long as the world-economy remains in its stagnation phase.

Frankly, the two factors – the ideological rift and the economic disparities – are enough for most analysts to dismiss further discussion of European unity as politically irrelevant. I wish however to pursue the subject at least one step further, speculating on what kinds of developments might alter the situation sufficiently that the present barriers to unity would weigh less in the picture. I think the initial shock would probably have to come from outside.

Suppose, first, that US-Japanese relations changed suddenly from their present carefully articulated minuet of fierce but gentlemanly economic competition, combined with the political low posture of the Japanese, to one in which there was open, dynamic economic collaboration, to the exclusion of Western Europe. This would involve interlocking directorates of US and Japanese transnational corporations, and relatively coordinated investment processes. This no doubt would be politically dangerous and fly in the face of deep cultural resistances. But look at some of the economic advantages of such an economic flight forward. From a situation in which the countries with the two leading R & D loci for the leading industries of the 1990s are cutting each other's throats, and therefore their eventual profits, the two combined could quickly gain that kind of unquestioned transitory monopoly on the world-market that would make possible a quite extraordinary capital accumulation. It would give the Japanese instantly an economic lead they might otherwise have to struggle hard for with less certain, more partial results. It would, however, give American corporations a cushion that would guarantee a long period of lucrative activity, with the side bonus for the ordinary American of making economic decline much slower and less perceptible. Certainly, US corporations (and corporate executives) might feel they were accepting an eventual formally junior role, but this could be hidden for quite a while. Such executives have already learned how to accept their greying hair by combining it with slim bodies and a little *dolce vita*. This lesson could be applied to new world economic alliances. Furthermore, such a scenario is not pure invention. The arrangements between Toyota and General Motors, for example, are the first steps in this direction.

Of course, such an alliance between transnationals would have very clear political consequences. One would be over relations between the US and Japanese states. The latter would probably have to play a bigger military role than it does now. It would be reluctant to do so, first because of the internal political tensions this might stimulate, and secondly because this is expensive and, in the short run, economically damaging. It is exactly for this reason, however, that the US government would be pressing it to play (and pay) its 'fair share', since this would then relieve the US burden, with consequent world economic and internal political advantage.

The second political consequence might be to shift the internal political balance within the US establishment. There has been a long-standing debate about geopolitical strategy in the US between Europe-firsters and advocates of a Pacific Rim strategy. This is a complicated picture of strange internal alliances and motivations. The key fact however is that the US establishment – industrial, financial, and political – have, for the most part and for obvious reasons, been Europe-firsters. This has been therefore US strategy, and we have already spoken of its consequences for Europe. A genuine intermesh of American and Japanese transnationals could alter the US internal political balance and make possible, for the first time, the triumph of a Pacific Rim strategy.

Finally, China might have to precipitate decisions in matters about which she has wanted to move slowly. China's geopolitical strategy since 1949 – whoever has been in power – has been very long-run. The main emphasis has been on pursuing an internal structural transformation within relative isolation until the economic base would become strong enough for China to play the world role that seems appropriate to her. But a Japanese-American flight forward could upset the calculations of such a prudent strategy. Both the temptations of joining such a winning alliance early and the economic risks of holding back might lead to a decision that an early commitment might optimize China's ability to rise within the new alliance, and vis-à-vis its partners, with relative rapidity.

Suppose then – we are only speculating, I remind you – the US-Japan-China triumvurate (of say 1995 or 2000) were to reason, with some plausibility, that the optimal policy to pursue in the interstate system vis-à-vis the peripheral zones of the world – the 'South' – was not the repressive one of opposition to their national liberation movements, but a *selective* cooperation with such movements in power in the stronger Southern semiperipheral states, or even just with some of them. This would have to involve some redistribution of world surpluses, but given that I am postulating a significant increase in the accumulation of capital, there would be plenty of profit to spread around. One does not even have to assume that this policy would succeed everywhere in defusing political explosions. A partial and limited success might be seen as sufficient justification for such a policy.

Now look at such a picture from Europe's standpoint. Threatened by economic retrogression vis-à-vis a new multi-state, multi-national network which would seem to have 'harnessed' the market potential of China and, perhaps increasingly, of some large, important, politically solid (because nationalist) zones of the South, western Europe might conceivably come to feel as does the USSR that it was 'surrounded' by a potentially hostile world. And Eastern Europe might feel in danger of becoming the backwater of a declining world zone. Attitudes could conceivably drastically change in western Europe, eastern Europe, *and* the USSR.

Let me postulate one last hypothetical possibility. For quite different reasons, it is conceivable that both the US and the USSR could see a steep increase in internal disorder. Again we do not need to exaggerate. I am not postulating civil wars, or even overthrows of governments. I am merely suggesting the existence of social unrest sufficient for the two governments to be forced to concentrate considerable energy and money in resolving these internal situations.

The course of such unrest in the US is quite clear. In fact, in some sense the social unrest has already begun. The two central stimulants of such US unrest are the 'Third World within' and the victims of economic reorganization. The existence, repression, and rebellion of the 'Third World within' is an old story in US history. There is one difference today. The present main groups involved (Blacks and Hispanic-speakers) represent for the first time a really large demographic mass, concentrated in the major urban centres, more politically sophisticated than ever before, and somewhat linked emotionally (and even politically) to a world-wide network of liberation movements.

The US already had a major explosion in the 1960s which was defused only by some political concessions and considerable economic transfers. Economic decline, however, makes further economic transfers unlikely. And it even makes political concessions more difficult. This is because the decline, while no doubt disproportionately hurting the minorities, also hurts important segments of the ethnic majority. The latter also demand state action on their behalf, and increasingly see state action in favour of minorities as competitive with their own demands. We could conceivably, therefore, see in the US both 'left-wing' and 'right-wing' strong social movements, each fighting the establishment and each other.

The position in the USSR is of course quite different. Politically, the great problem is the heavy hand of a complicated set of bureaucratic structures (state plus party) which is resistant to streamlining and processual change. Furthermore, this is not merely a matter of mentalities but of economic interest. The inefficiencies of this structure are rewarded by excessive privileges. No doubt various leaders at the top of the structure are aware of these problems and, supported by certain cadres, want to reform the situation. But will they be able to do so? The world economic situation also places constraints on the USSR in terms of how much surplus is at their disposal to reallocate. Furthermore, the Cold War (especially in its current renewed intensity) places enormous economic constraints, as well as constraints of human energy, on the USSR.

Two further elements complicate the picture. Nationalism within the USSR has been remarkably well contained over the past 60 years. In that sense, the Soviet system has worked relatively well. Still there are strains that are not negligible. The currents of 'Muslim' nationalism are very strong in the world today and diffusion across the frontiers cannot be discounted. Western-zone and Caucasian nationalism may well be fed by strains coming from eastern Europe. And finally there is the sleeper of Russian nationalism, the one nationalism thus far most suppressed in the USSR.

This is compounded by the absence of genuine workplace trade union rights which, in the advanced industrial structures of the USSR, cannot but mean that they are a hotbed of latent protest If, in the interest of streamlining these structures, some pressure is placed on the extensive featherbedding which is today one of the chief rewards of the Soviet industrial working class, the situation could breed still more discontent and consequently unrest. And this unrest could then take the form of either of tradeunionism or Russian nationalism, either of which could be explosive.

In any case, I am not trying here to examine in detail the internal structures of either of the superpowers. I merely want to suggest some reasons why extensive social unrest is possible. And the significance of this for our purposes is that such unrest would normally force the governments to turn inward, and therefore to some extent away from Europe. I realize it is more complicated than this. First of all, one classic solution for internal social unrest is external aggressivity. Secondly, in the case of both the US and the USSR, especially the latter, neglecting external situations could permit developments on their frontiers which could stimulate still further internal social unrest. Nonetheless, Europe might acquire more autonomous 'space'.

What I have done is try to develop a series of circumstances that are not too implausible and which might create conditions in which steps towards European unity, west and east, might seem one viable political option. Consider, given the circumstances I have been outlining, how the situation might look from the point of view respectively of Western Europe, the Soviet Union, and Eastern Europe.

For Western Europe the advantages in some kind of economic arrangement among these three zones would be several. They could see it as strengthening their position in the world-economy in important ways. It would directly enlarge their market at a moment when our presumed Japanese-US temporary monopolistic advantage was excluding them from much of the world. Indirectly, if western Europe were to get the political support of the USSR, it might then have greater political success in getting access to some markets in the periphery from which the Japanese-US combine was seeking to exclude them. And politically, Western Europe might see this as a big step in 'recuperating' Eastern Europe in cultural terms, since the political 'liberalization' of the Eastern European countries might be considered to be part of the package.

The Soviet point of view would be quite different from that of Western Europe. The USSR might also see, however, various kinds of advantage in the arrangement. First, loosening the ties of Western Europe and the US (even if NATO were not disbanded) has long been a major objective of Soviet foreign policy, and they might see this as one inevitable side-effect of new economic arrangements with Western Europe. Secondly, the USSR wants some guaranteed access, at least over the next 20–30 years, to various kinds of advanced technology, and such an arrangement would offer such a guarantee. Third, the USSR might feel that one way to contain internal unrest would be both to improve the immediate economic situation and to obtain the political umbrella of a link with Western Europe, thereby undermining some of the 'radicalism' of the opposition. Fourth, the USSR might entertain the hope that this would help the long-range prospects of political parties sympathetic to her.

As for Eastern Europe, such an arrangement might be almost all gain. It would permit an 'opening' to the west which would not be interpreted as 'opposition' to the Soviet Union. They would draw many of the same economic advantages as the Soviets. It would contain their own internal unrest. In any case, Eastern Europe has no better alternative to its present impasse than such a development.

Finally, the one advantage all parties to such an arrangement might see in common would be that it could provide an elegant 'solution' to the division of Germany, permitting a sort of informal reunification that, from the point of view of neighbours, west and east, would seem non-threatening.

All this has been an exercise in geopolitical speculation. I have not yet indicated whether and for whom this is good or bad. From the perspective of the world-system as a whole, I see one enormous negative to the whole development compensated perhaps by three positives.

The negative is that, if everything I have described were to occur, this would breathe considerable new life into the existing capitalist world-economy by creating relative stabilities where they do not now exist and by recreating a relatively even balance of forces in the world-system. Of course, for some this would not be a negative. But for me, one must realize, that, in the reworked system I have been picturing, a large portion of the world's population would still be outrageously exploited, perhaps more than ever.

Nevertheless, I offer my three positives. First, such a reorganization of the interstate system would reduce the likelihood of nuclear war, both by creating a better balance of forces, and, paradoxically, by dethroning

Europe from its position as the key arena of the Cold War. Europe's stability has since 1945 always been under the sword of Damocles. This might cease to be so.

The second great advantage is in the realm of ideology. What I have described as possible is ideologically absurd. Remember, I am *not* positing any change in the dominant ideology of any significant actor in this situation. Coming in the wake of all the scepticism that already exists about the traditional dominant ideologies, this 'theatre of the absurd' might be the culminating blow in forcing a genuine intellectual *Aufhebung* which, in my view, is desperately needed – the dethronement not only of nineteenth-century social ideologies but of Baconian-Newtonian physical science as well.

The third great advantage is that such an intellectual revolution might make possible a genuine re-evaluation by the world's antisystematic movements of their strategic options so that they might get out of the historic cul-de-sac in which they have found themselves more and more in the post-1945 period, which is that the seizure of state power by these movements is simply not a sufficient condition to permit the passage from a capitalist world-economy to a socialist world order. It will take time, energy, and thought to rework fundamental strategy. The postulated shifts in the interstate system might provide the time, and, by the intellectual dethroning, the incentive to organizational rethinking. And all this together might make possible the genuine fundamental change these movements have been seeking, thus far with only partial success.

3. East–West Economic Cooperation and the Demise of Détente

by Y.V. Andreyev

On interrelations of economics and politics

Economic relations between countries constitute an important part of the whole system of international relations and economic and political elements in this system are always interrelated in the closest way. This interrelation and mutual influence manifest themselves distinctly in a complex of relations between East and West. And just here their economic relations are especially politicized which is conditioned primarily by a coexistence and struggle of two antagonistic forms of property – the socialist or public one, and the capitalist or private one. It should of course be stressed that this struggle by no means excludes the progress of cooperation between countries of different social systems.

The interrelation of economics and politics in East-West relations has acquired special importance in recent years when the international situation as a whole has been aggravated by the US administration's policy of undisguised confrontation with the USSR and other socialist countries. At the end of the 1970s the aim of breaking the military-strategic parity formed between the USSR and the USA, and between the Warsaw Treaty Organization and NATO, and of achieving a military superiority over the socialist countries came to the forefront of the strategy of the US and its NATO allies.

In such an aggravated international situation, the foreign policy of the Soviet Union is based on the necessity of preserving the gains made by détente and of augmenting what was achieved and agreed upon in Helsinki because only the easing of international tension can produce the fruitful cooperation of states. Détente is the main way towards a mutual confidence between countries, towards averting any war whether it be small, big, limited or total.

Détente is a complicated interlacing of political, military and economic components. It represents a way of connecting these three factors, with economic cooperation constituting the material tissue of political and military détente, and giving a positive impulse for further progressive development.

Such a course of events took place in the first half of the 1970s. The 1975 Conference on Security and Cooperation in Europe was the peak of political détente. The Final Act signed in Helsinki is a code of peaceful coexistence and cooperation of states of different social systems, in other words, it is a code of détente.

Certain measures on the realization of military détente agreed upon during negotiations between the USSR and the USA in the 1970s exerted a beneficial influence upon the whole complex of relations between East and West. Therefore, there were formed favourable conditions for progress on economic cooperation between the USSR and Western countries.

From the end of the 1970s however, political and military détente declined. The struggle between the opposite trends in world politics was aggravated sharply. Under such conditions, the Soviet Union and Warsaw Treaty member-states have tried everything possible for a radical improvement of the international situation, using the Programme of Peace for the 1980s adopted by the 26th Congress of the CPSU and the programme documents of fraternal parties. Owing to the efforts of the socialist countries, the opponents of détente could not gain the upper hand in this struggle because détente was deeply rooted.

The basis of the whole system of détente is formed by numerous agreements and treaties achieved in political and military fields in the 1970s and still in force at present, in spite of the complexity of the international situation as a whole. However, a complicated world and European situation does not negate the results of the Conference in Helsinki, the tenth anniversary of which we are celebrating this year; on the contrary, the more complicated international conditions, the more evident their significance. Nevertheless, the military and political situation at present remains strained and this is reflected in the sphere of economic relations between East and West.

Another important circumstance should be noted at this point. The United States administration is pursuing an aggressive policy against East-West economic cooperation. Actions have included almost continuous sanctions, embargoes and other hostile actions against the USSR since the end of the 1970s intended to achieve a sharp curtailment of economic relations.

But in Western countries where the governments confine themselves to the policy of peace and cooperation, economic relations with the USSR are progressing successfully. And even in numerous countries where the leadership supports the USA policy in general, the view prevails that economic relations with socialist countries should be developed, that these relations exert a positive influence upon peace and international security.

Their positions in coordinating economics and politics do not coincide with that type of coordination which prevails in the 'strategy of linkage' sermonized by the most conservative forces in the USA. According to this strategy, the economic relations of the West with the USSR should be subordinated to achieving the military and political objectives of the West and to achieving a superiority over the Soviet Union. As former secretary of state, Alexander Haig, noted:

> Our trade and economic relations in a broader aspect should support our efforts to neutralize an accumulation of the military potential of the Soviet Union... Although, undoubtedly, we have commercial interests which should be taken into account, considerations of security should still play a dominating role.[1]

The 'linkage strategy' includes economic aggression (embargoes, sanctions, etc.) as important components widely used by the American administration.

In Western Europe there is an inclination not towards 'linkage strategy', but to the concept of 'interdependence'. This concept proceeds from a recognition of the principles of peaceful coexistence, from a necessity of broad progress of economic relations between different social systems (intersystem relations) in order to raise the level of the economic interdependence of East and West, and ensuring peace and international security in such a way. The 'interdependence strategy' rejects an 'economic war' as a means of solving external political problems. All these ideas are present in the works of numerous scientists from West European countries in which they analyse East-West economic relations. Some examples are the French economist M. Lavigne, and the West German scientists P. Pissulla and J. Nötzold. It is possible to argue that in the West there is an acute clash of concepts over the relationship between economic and political aspects of East-West relations, particularly between the USA and Western Europe. At present, US aggressive policy in this sphere is on the increase and directed at a restriction of intersystem economic relations.

Summing up the analysis of the connection between economic and political aspects of East-West relations in the contemporary period, it is possible to conclude that political conditions for intersystem relations are complicated and unfavourable in general. How have these relations developed to such a condition?

Evolution of trade and economic relations of the USSR with the West

The progress of the foreign trade of the Soviet Union with all industrially developed capitalist states is described in Table 3.1.

First, it is necessary to emphasize that there has been continuous growth in the USSR foreign trade turnover with all industrially developed capitalist countries. In spite of the fact that this growth is to a certain extent conditioned by changes in prices, the calculations in comparable prices also show the growth of USSR's trade turnover with Western countries. In this respect, the 1980s are of a special importance as this has been a period characterized by some bourgeois representatives as one of stagnation constituting a crisis of intersystem relations.

The data in Table 3.1 show that even during the 1980s the USSR's trade

Table 3.1 The USSR Trade Turnover by Groups of Countries

Groups of countries	1960 M.roub.	%	1970 M.roub.	%	1980 M.roub.	%	1981 M.roub.	%	1982 M.roub.	%	1983 M.roub.	%	1984 M.roub.	%
Developed capitalist countries	1,917.3	19.0	4,694.2	21.3	31,583.1	33.6	35,358.7	32.2	37,741.4	31.6	38,371.7	30.1	40,923.5	29.3
Socialist countries	7,370.8	73.2	14,403.1	65.2	50,552.5	53.7	57,933.9	52.8	64,952.0	54.3	71,409.7	56.0	80,326.3	57.5
Developing countries	783.0	7.8	2,981.3	13.5	11,961.7	12.7	16,446.6	15.0	16,882.6	14.1	17,698.4	13.9	18,461.2	13.2
Total:	10,071.1	100	11,078.6	100	94,097.3	100	109,739.2	100	119,576.0	100	127,479.8	100	139,711.0	100

Source: *Vneshnyaya torgovlya SSSR* (International Trade of USSR) for corresponding years.

turnover with all industrially developed capitalist countries was continuously growing. It should be especially emphasized that in 1983 there was a considerable fall in prices of crude oil which led to a deterioration in the terms of trade of the USSR with Western countries in particular. Therefore, the growth of the turnover in 1983 and 1984 is conditioned by an appreciable increase in the volume of trade with this group of countries.

Certainly, nobody denies the existence of problems, sometimes very serious ones. In addition to well known difficulties, another came to light – the rates of growth of the USSR's trade turnover with Western countries decreased in the 1980s in comparison with the 1970s. However, the growth of the USSR's trade turnover with all industrially developed capitalist countries was in progress although with lower rates against the background of a considerable absolute decrease in world trade in 1981 and 1982. An unprecedented absolute decrease of world trade during those years was conditioned by a deep economic crisis which gripped the capitalist world in 1980–82 and reflected itself also on intersystem relations. It reduced the demand for Soviet export products and engendered a wave of protectionism. A prevalent trend of high interest rates in the money markets and a coordinated policy of Western governments in the field of giving state export credits, directed in general against the USSR, create difficulties in credit and consequently in the economic relations of the USSR with capitalist countries. All this means that in the 1980s the economic 'environment' was also unfavourable for intersystem relations.

Why are the economic relations of the USSR with the West progressing with such an enviable stability in spite of a complicated international situation, radical system contradictions, dissimilar management and organizational systems and other difficulties?

The progress of East-West economic cooperation is based on two fundamentals: the objective necessity of these relations and their mutually beneficial character. Lenin wrote the following on the necessity of economic relations: 'There is a greater force than the wish, will and decision of even hostile governments or classes, which makes them embark on the path of relations with us'.[2]

Progress of productive forces of society, the international division of labour, internationalization of the economy engendered by the division of labour and enhanced by the scientific and technological revolution growing apace on the world scale – all this is included in the foundations of objective necessity of economic relations between states of different social systems.

The international division of labour, and the internationalization of the economy conditioned by it, raise the question of the nature and genesis of this process. A majority of Western economists who appraise positively the progress of economic cooperation between East and West corroborate this division of labour, internationalization of the economy and consequently the inevitability of East-West economic relations in general with postulates of the 'theory of comparable advantages'. Without going into its critical analysis, it should be noted that this theory describes adequately one trend in the international division of labour related to a unique distribution of non-renewable natural resources and different environmental and climatic conditions of economic life. Those countries which have a surplus of raw materials and energy resources by virtue of natural peculiarities, like the Soviet Union, for example, may exchange these commodities for the products of other industries in countries where there is a shortage of raw materials and energy resources as is the case in many countries of Western Europe. Interindustry specialization and exchange which are developing on such a basis constitute an important direction of the international division of labour, both at present and in future.

Such a trend in the international division of labour cannot, however, be a principal one, and what is more, a single one. Greater possibilities for exchange and relations open up through intraindustry specialization. This is now a characteristic feature of international economic relations and foremost in the relations between industrially developed countries. The Soviet Union and its Western partners are highly developed countries in economic and industrial respects, with machinery construction, chemicals, electronics and electrical engineering constituting the basis of their industry. From the viewpoint of the theory of international division of labour, it objectively opens new opportunities for East-West economic cooperation along the lines of an intraindustry exchange, in addition to an interindustry exchange.

Finally, at this stage of the scientific and technological revolution, the division of labour has acquired a special importance and has become an objective basis and impulse of production cooperation including an intersystem one. A close interaction of the division of labour occupies now a decisive place in both interindustry and intraindustry reproduction proportions, and exerts a significant influence upon East-West economic cooperation.

The Finnish researchers, Reinikainen and Kivikary, used an interesting method in one of their works – they assumed a hypothetical situation of a complete autarchy of two world economic systems and analysed it. According to their appraisal, the absence of intersystem relations would mean an impossibility of the global, and, consequently, optimum international division of labour, a duplicating of R&D, enormous expenditures to replace resources which are at the disposal of counterparts, a waste of time, a restriction of exchange of information and useful ideas, and a restriction of the internationalization of economy in general. In the end, all this would reflect on the level of welfare of peoples. The authors came to a conclusion on the necessity and mutually beneficial character of East-West economic relations.[3]

The second important basis of economic relations is the interest of both parties based on the mutually beneficial character of cooperation. Western countries derive considerable economic benefits from economic cooperation with the USSR and other socialist states mainly through an expansion of opportunities for marketing their products. For example, in 1981 the share of the Soviet Union was 25% of exports of certain types of steel and a considerable part of metal-cutting machine tools from West Germany. Between 1974–1980 our country signed eight per cent of contracts on exports of French machinery and equipment. Up to 16 per cent of products of the British textile industry are sold in the Soviet market. The Soviet Union takes approximately 5% of Italian exports of inorganic chemistry products and also of synthetic and artificial fibres.

These are especially important as the orders of the USSR and other socialist countries ensure employment for about two million people in industrially developed countries. In its turn, Soviet supplies of a number of commodities are of a considerable importance in satisfying import demands of developed capitalist states. For example, in the beginning of the 1980s, Great Britain satisfied 60–85% of the demand for ores, 23% for chromium compounds, 20% for coniferous saw-timber, 14% for undressed furs. The Soviet Union has become a large supplier of cotton and a number of chemical products to France. According to data for the beginning of the 1980s, West Germany satisfied its demand for coniferous saw-timber by 13% and for phosphates by 14% with Soviet supplies. In addition, the Soviet Union is one of the leading suppliers of a number of precious metals.

Energy resources are of a great importance in the contemporary world. The supplies of Soviet natural gas to West Germany now constitute 17% of gas imports to this country, and this share is growing as a result of the realization of a new 'gas-pipeline' project. The share of supplies of natural gas from the USSR to France is 15% (it will be increased in 1990), and the share of supplies of oil and oil products 20–30%. Numerous West-European countries attach serious political significance to an expansion of economic relations with our country as well as being an important factor of détente.

East-West economic cooperation ensures substantial benefits to our country too. Imports gives an opportunity to solve numerous scientific and technological problems, accelerating progress in a number of industries, raising the efficiency of the national economy which leads in the end to considerable time-saving. Therefore, economic relations of the USSR with developed capitalist countries play their fruitful role in accomplishing the economic programme of our country.

The position of the Soviet Union with respect to progress in East-West economic relations was clearly formulated at the 26th Congress of the CPSU:

> The Soviet Union stands, as before, for stable and mutually beneficial relations with capitalist countries, for their expansion on the basis of a strict observance of mutual obligations... Our external economic activity should to a greater extent promote satisfaction of demands of the national economy for equipment, technology, raw materials and resources, and also the demand of the population for consumer's goods... The course of the Soviet Union to large scale

improvement of international economic cooperation remains unchanged because it is our principal course reflecting a purposeful direction of the Soviet foreign policy in international economic relations towards preserving peace and promoting détente and mutual understanding between peoples.

The course of the USSR and other socialist countries was confirmed at the economic summit conference of CMEA member-states in June, 1984. In the declaration 'Consolidation of Peace and International Economic Cooperation' adopted at that conference, it was emphasized that

in the sphere of international economic relations, life requires mutually beneficial and equitable cooperation of all countries. A solid material basis for the consolidation and promotion of détente cannot be created without this.

CMEA member-states suggested a broad programme for furthering international economic cooperation where the necessity was emphasized for the realization of agreements reached at the conferences in Helsinki and Madrid, for an exclusion of economic aggression, for compulsory observance of principles of international relations agreed upon. The socialist countries proposed to develop economic relations at both the state and firm level, in bilateral and multilateral ways.

The United States of America adheres to another approach to intersystem relations seemingly directed at their radical curtailment. During the 1980s the US administration repeatedly used sanctions, embargoes and boycotts against the Soviet Union, for example, the embargo on the sale of grain to the Soviet Union imposed by President Carter in 1980. According to calculations of American experts, losses for the United States came to 22 billion dollars. As a result, President Reagan had to cancel this embargo in 1981.

However, attempts to pursue an economic policy inflicting damage to all participants of intersystem relations have not stopped. A distinctive feature of the US course in this sphere is to draw their West-European allies into participation in hostile actions against the USSR. The tactic of imposing adventurist sanctions against the Soviet Union were cancelled after pressure from allies and domestic business circles, but the general level of discrimination against the USSR in trade is still becoming higher. Events around the orders for the Urengoy-Western Europe gas-pipeline in the West exemplify such tactics. As is known, sanctions directed against the USSR and our West-European partners were in force for only five months (June–November, 1982) and then were cancelled. However, they did make representatives of West-European business circles more reserved in concluding large-scale deals with the East.

The offensive operates in many directions. The main intention is to isolate the USSR from world achievements in science and technology. With this aim in view, the Western countries put on the agenda the question of extending COCOM lists. Several closed meetings of this agency have been held on the initiative of the USA since the end of 1981. And in spite of the fact that virtually all West-European COCOM member-states are against an extension of lists of 'dual use commodities', as it would considerably cut down their exports to the USSR and other socialist states, the principal agreement on a certain extension of these lists was achieved and was realized in the summer of 1984.

The USA is also trying to control trade between the USSR and countries of Western Europe which are not COCOM member-states. Under the threat of including West European firms on 'black lists' and using an appeal for the unity of all countries of the 'free world' in the struggle against communism, the American government forces foreign companies to refuse to sell products prohibited for export by COCOM to socialist countries.

The next direction of USA policy is to attempt to curtail the supplies of so-called strategic commodities, especially energy resources, from the USSR with the aim of reducing a so-called 'dangerous' dependence of Western countries on the USSR in this sphere. However, such arguments are rejected in Western Europe because the share of supplies of Soviet energy resources for the consumption of these countries is far from a 'critical level of dependence' as calculated by the Americans themselves.

Still another goal of US contemporary foreign economic policy is discrimination against socialist countries in the credit sphere. Minimum rates on state and subsidized-by-state export credits given to the Soviet Union by the member states of the Organization for Economic Cooperation and Development (OECD) were substantially increased in 1982. The American administration managed to secure the assent of a number of Western countries not to give preferential state credits to the USSR.

In addition, a detailed monitoring of all transactions in East-West economic relations was started within OECD, the decision being adopted in June, 1982. From 1981, East-West economic relations have been one of the main items on the agenda at annual meetings of leaders of the 'Big Seven' (the USA, West Germany, Great Britain, France, Japan, Canada, Italy).

It should be especially noted that there are differences, and often considerable ones, in the views of the USA and the countries of Western Europe on virtually all aspects of East-West economic relations. These manifested themselves strikingly when economic sanctions against the USSR were imposed in June, 1982. An attempt to extend American jurisdiction beyond the limits of the United States was unanimously rejected by all governments of Western Europe. The differences are conditioned by the fact that, due to economic, political, historical and geographic reasons, West-European countries are interested in maintaining and developing economic relations with the USSR and have no intention of using them as an instrument of political struggle in general.

As already mentioned, the Soviet Union attaches great importance to a consolidation of economic cooperation between countries of different social systems including an expansion of the treaty and legal basis of economic cooperation. Such a basis introduces elements of stability into the progress of economic relations. The political importance of economic agreements which improve the general climate of interstate relations is also great. A treaty and legal infrastructure of East-West economic relations is characterized by complexity and wide ramifications. It includes different international legal documents and also organizations established by partners in order to develop economic relations. The international legal documents include trade treaties and agreements on economic, scientific, technological and industrial cooperation, and on the formation of intergovernment commissions, etc. A large group of documents is composed of programmes of economic cooperation.

The documentary infrastructure is characterized by the following distinctive features. First, by a great number of documents. For example, some 100 treaties and agreements regulate the economic relations between the USSR and Finland. Second, by long-term periods. Thus, the agreement signed in 1978 by the USSR and West Germany on the development and promotion of cooperation in the sphere of economy and industry was for a 25-years period, and a long-term programme of the main directions of cooperation elaborated on this basis defines the prospects of economic relations between the Soviet Union and West Germany up to the 21st century. The programme of development and promotion of trade, economic, industrial, scientific and technological cooperation between the USSR and Finland is long-term. Third, the documentary infrastructure embraces a broad circle of problems. Agreements and programmes exist now between countries to regulate the whole complex of economic relations, that is trade, economic and industrial cooperation, scientific and technological exchange.

It is necessary to single out intergovernment commissions on economic, scientific and technological cooperation within the treaty and legal infrastructure. These commissions and working groups are doing extensive work on programming and control over the realization of the whole complex of interstate economic relations. Joint trade and industrial chambers, representations of firms and banks, and other organizations have also developed useful activity. In short, a firm treaty and legal basis for USSR economic cooperation with developed capitalist countries has been formed. However, the existence of such a basis does not automatically ensure a favourable trade and political climate of cooperation. In this respect, it is important how exactly and successfully agreements signed are realized in practice. In addition, it is necessary to take into consideration the existence of international legal documents and agreements which exert a negative influence upon relations of the USSR with developed capitalist countries.

Taking into account these considerations, it should be stated that in the external economic policy of a number of Western countries there is a process of preservation and sometimes an expansion of discrimination against the USSR. Let us recall the existing and expanding list of 'strategic commodities' in force in the NATO member-states (excluding Iceland and Spain) and Japan.

The 'most favoured nation' status in trade with the USSR is violated to a greater or lesser extent by virtually all industrially developed capitalist countries. Discriminatory quantitative restrictions in the imports from the USSR to numerous Western countries are also in force. The customs regime applied to Soviet exports is also discriminatory especially in EEC member-states and the USA. There are other forms of trade discrimination against the USSR.

Taking into account these considerations, it should be stated that, at the beginning of the 1980s, unfavourable political and economic conditions formed in regard to the promotion of the USSR's economic cooperation with developed capitalist countries. However, negative factors, and this is the most important, could not stop all cooperation because of the enormous economic potential of the USSR, its objective necessity, its mutual interest and its mutual benefits.

Current problems of economic relations of the USSR with Western countries

Here we consider those problems which, for one reason or another, were or are in the centre of attention of the scientific and non-scientific communities.

1. *Credit relations.* From 1960 the USSR's trade balance with industrially developed capitalist countries was negative virtually every year (except for 1967, 1974, 1980, 1983 and 1984). The net cumulative negative balance of trade of the Soviet Union with this group of countries during the period from 1960 to 1984 was about 12 billion roubles. An excess of imports over exports, which was considerable from the beginning of the 1970s and was related to no small extent to the development of new forms of cooperation, was paid off in general by credits. Just at that time credit relations between the USSR and Western countries became especially active.

As is known, the most important items of Soviet imports from Western countries include machines, equipment and means of transportation. Over two-thirds of world trade in these commodities are realized now on the basis of credit, and therefore credit terms have become one of the most important premises for establishing relations between partners.

The USSR was given credits for purchasing machines and equipment and other commodities. It is important to note at this point that supplies of machinery were to a considerable extent realized on the basis of compensation transactions, that is, credits were paid off mainly with the products of those enterprises where the equipment purchased on credit was mounted. It ensured additional guarantees of a reliability of credit relations with the Soviet Union. Furthermore, the balance of its trade with developing countries is permanently active, the main part of which is expressed, as is known, in hard currency. Certain circles in the West, and especially in the USA, do everything possible to break credit relations with the USSR and to torpedo East-West economic relations as a whole.

As already noted, in 1982 the US managed to force the OECD member states to raise considerably the rate of interest for state credits to the Soviet Union and not to give preferential state credits to the USSR. Let's mention, by the way, that preferential credits form only one-quarter of borrowings of the USSR and other CMEA member-states in the Western credit markets while the other three-quarters are credits with market rates of interest. As for preferential rates themselves, both Soviet and objectively inclined Western specialists consider them a normal instrument in the competitive struggle for markets.

The American administration has started to put credit questions forward very actively during recent years. This took place at the summit meetings of seven leading capitalist powers. Although the American representatives could not juggle the proposal on the establishment of an organization which would strictly control all East-West credit relations, the progress of credit relations of the USSR with the Western partners was curtailed. It was shown by the fact that the USSR preferred to pay France for the equipment for the Astrakhan gas-condensate plant in cash without credit on an excessive rate of interest although projects of such a kind are the best objects for credit relations.

However, in spite of all obstacles and as a result of the USSR's import policy, the trade balance of the Soviet Union with the West was settled with an excess of almost 1 billion roubles and the net debt of the USSR to Western commercial banks was reduced to four billion dollars in 1983. In 1984 there was again a positive trade balance which the USSR had with the Western countries amounting to 1.8 billion roubles. The total net debt of the CMEA member-states to the Western governments and commercial banks has also been reduced during recent years and amounted to 57–59 billion dollars at the end of 1983.

All the above-stated gives grounds to a conclusion that the Soviet Union and other socialist countries have a strong and solid position as reliable partners in East-West trade and credit relations. Any obstacles created in the West in this sphere turn in the end against those who create these obstacles.

2. *Compensation projects.* The large-scale, complex and long-term character of East-West economic cooperation in the 1970s is to a considerable extent related to the emergence of new forms of economic relations beyond the limits of foreign trade. Their main features are joint investment, production, scientific and technological activity. Economic cooperation or a joint investment activity occupies a leading part among new forms of economic relations of the USSR with industrially developed capitalist countries. It stipulates a joint construction or expansion and modernization of different national economic enterprises. Compensation

projects play a special role in the development of economic cooperation. They constitute a complex form of foreign economic relations which includes an allocation of financial and material resources (usually in the form of target crediting), a creation of productive capacities and a payment off (compensation) of credits with supplies of products produced by these capacities or with similar products of other enterprises. At this point it is necessary to mention two aspects. First, the basis of a compensation cooperation is capital construction, that is, a specific form of production and not an exchange. Second, compensation ensures directly a paying off of credits through such transactions.

In total, over 100 compensation agreements have been concluded between the CMEA member-states and Western firms, at the same time over 60 enterprises were, and are being, constructed under conditions of the conpensation in our country. According to UN calculations, the share of compensation supplies in the whole trade turnover of the CMEA member-states with the countries of the West is 25–30 per cent.

The following types of economic cooperation are practised on the largest scale: a joint extraction and utilization of natural resources in the USSR; a joint construction of industrial enterprises for production of semi-manufactured goods and components in our country.

The compensation 'gas-pipes' project stated in the 1960s is an example of the first type of economic cooperation according to which pipes for the construction of the gas-pipeline were supplied to the USSR, and natural gas was exported from the USSR. Austria, Italy, West Germany and France participated in the realization of this project.

Soviet-Japanese large-scale compensation projects also belong to this type of transaction, including the following: extraction of South-Yakut coal, an expansion of development of timber resources of our Far East, an additional prospect for the Yakut deposits of natural gas.

Such projects are realized with the participation of small countries. Austria has already been mentioned. Elements of compensation are included in the project for the construction of the iron ore concentration combine in Kostomuksha (Karelia), according to which concentrates will be exported to Finland as partial compensation of the participating Finnish partner.

Economic cooperation, mainly on a compensation basis, in the chemical pulp and paper, and metallurgical industries of the USSR belongs to the second type of cooperation. Firms from numerous West-European countries, including Great Britain, France, West Germany, Italy and a number of small countries, were and are participating in the construction of enterprises of these industries, and a part of their product is supplied to the Western market as a payment for services of our partners.

In the late 1970s, adversaries of new forms of cooperation enhanced their activity in the West. The struggle against non-traditional forms of relations is one of the main features of the American 'linkage' strategy. According to this concept, new forms of relations, and compensation transactions especially as well as production cooperation, connected with supplies of advanced technology to the Soviet Union, reinforce the USSR's military-economic potential, on the one hand, and deform the Western market with reverse supplies of Soviet commodities, on the other, and lead to an enhancement of competition in it and even to a growth of unemployment. Such criticism is made on a rather large scale in Western Europe. For example, the West German economist, Schüller, argues that compensation transactions wind an 'anti-market interventionist spiral' and exert a negative influence upon employment.

It is unnecessary to say that a country like the Soviet Union cannot make its military-economic potential dependent on the import of techniques and technology from Western countries in particular. It does not tally also with an often used thesis on the 'military superiority' of the USSR over the USA.

As for the influence of compensation transactions on employment in Western countries, the calculations of Soviet specialists show that the production of machinery and equipment supplied by Western firms to the USSR acccording to compensation transactions is characterized by higher requirements in labour than the production of commodities in fuel and chemical industries supplied to the market of the West as a compensation in general. Therefore, participation in compensation cooperation increases employment as a whole in developed capitalist countries.

Similar calculations are made by Western specialists. The West German economists Betkenhagen and Wessels also came to the conclusion that compensation transactions ensure a considerable macroeconomic effect by both the growth of welfare achieved and the growth of employment with its interindustry shift.[4]

Research works of other West German specialists like Altman and Clement have shown that compensation transactions do not undermine market relations, and that they have a great future.[5] A similar position is shared by the French economist Paleologue and the West German specialist Schröder.[6]

The project of the century, the new gas-pipeline project for which the first agreements were concluded in 1981 is a brilliant example of the vitality of the compensation idea. In spite of attacks by opponents of East-West economic cooperation in general and opponents of compensation agreements in particular, this project has been successfully realized. The main principle of such a cooperation is traceable to its mutual benefits. Our Western partners obtained a large (several billion dollars) market for their products – pipes, compressor stations etc. They will also get natural gas badly need by them. The Soviet Union, in its turn, obtained assistance in construction of the pipeline and will get several billion dollars annually from the sale of natural gas.

It should finally also be emphasized that compensation transactions have recently been used on a broader scale in economic relations between the Western countries themselves too.

Conclusion

In the 1970s in connection with the promotion of détente, an important new period of economic relations of the USSR with all industrially developed capitalist states began. First, the amount of mutual trade grew at accelerated rates, while, side by side with imports, exports from the USSR to developed capitalist countries increased. Second, economic relations between countries made a transition to a solid and long-term institutional basis almost everywhere. Third, new forms of economic cooperation passing beyond the limits of routine trade made broad progress; these include economic cooperation, production cooperation, scientific and technological cooperation. Fourth, the whole system of credit and financial securing of economic relations made a step forward. Fifth, an appreciable success was achieved in the field of cooperation on a multilateral basis.

At the end of the 1970s some Western economists and politicians began to speak about an emergence of another stage of economic relations between the USSR and the West, namely, about the stage of crisis, stagnation and curtailment of economic relations. However, in spite of a deterioration of political and business conditions for economic cooperation, it continues its progressive development. The powerful resource potential of our country, an objective necessity of this cooperation, and the mutual interests of partners are the basis of it.

Certainly, there are serious problems and difficulties in the way of progress in economic relations. They include radical system contradictions, different management and organizational systems, negative aspects of foreign economic policies of Western countries etc. The presence of these problems enhances even more the significance of political factors and political will which is necessary for realizing existing premises for economic cooperation.

The summit conference of the CMEA member-states confirmed the principled course of socialist economic diplomacy. As was stated in the Declaration on main directions of further progress and expansion of the economic, scientific and technological cooperation of the CMEA member-states, the socialist states are still further ready to develop mutually beneficial trade, economic, scientific and technological relations with developed capitalist countries, and with all the states of the world. There was also confirmed the conviction that the promotion of these relations would favour the consolidation of mutual understanding between peoples and détente.[7]

Both détente and economic cooperation are deeply rooted in the whole world.

There is no doubt that when the present page of world history is turned, all reasonable people will ascertain that the building of peace and détente was due to not a small extent to the solid foundation formed by economic cooperation between different countries.

Notes

1. A. Haig, 'Statement by Secretary of State before the Subcommittee on international trade of the Committee on Finance', 28 July 1981, Washington, D.C., 1981.

2. V.I. Lenin. *Collected Works*, Vol. 44, pp. 304–5.

3. V. Reinikainen and U. Kivikari. 'On the theory of East-West Economic Relations', in *Finnish-Soviet Economic Relations*, Macmillan Press, 1983, pp. 3–20.

4. DIW, Wochenbericht, B., No. 13, 1981, pp. 158–159.

5. F. Altman, H. Clement. 'Die Kompensation als Instrument im Ost-West Handel', München, 1979, pp. 192, 202.

6. E. Paleologue, 'Les nouvelles relations economiques internales', P., 1980. K. Shröder. 'Der Einfluß der Ost-West Kooperation auf die Export Structur der RGW-Länder und auf die Beschäftigung in den westlichen Economien', in *Sozioökonomische Probleme der intersystemaren Wirtschaftsbeziehungen*, Nijmegen, 1979.

7. *Pravda*, 16 June 1984.

4. Europe and Star Wars: Security Dependence or Independence?

by Hans-Henrik Holme

Is independence of the superpowers the way in which Europe can achieve security? Does the political quest for European security have any prospect of success or is European security tied to and dependent upon the respective superpowers?

European security has since the conclusion of the Second World War in many respects been a mere function of the relationship between East and West. To some the European problem is in itself a contributory cause of the adverse relationship between East and West. The Second World War, whether by design or default, created a Europe divided between East and West, and in Germany created a symbol of the new division. In this context European security was nothing but reflections of policy and perceptions on either side of the superpower divide.

To individual European states, security policy was based on a choice between a non-aligned stance and superpower alignment. Non-alignment was chosen by the non-combatants in World War II (Sweden, Switzerland) or by the countries neutralized by the superpowers (Finland, Austria and to some extent Yugoslavia). To the great majority of European countries, superpower dependence was the way to achieve security. In Western Europe, massive arms aid and the creation of the NATO alliance instituted this dependence. In the East, ideological control secured the same objectives and later resulted in the creation of mirror image institutions (Warsaw Pact, Comecon).

European security could not be achieved in isolation and the security policy of the individual states revolved around the ensuing dilemma: How do you reduce dependence (and increase your freedom of action and self-determination in security policy) without jeopardising your security? The true irony of the situation is that the same situation exists for the superpowers. The institution of the East-West conflict in Europe meant that the superpowers became hostages to their own clients. Confrontations and differences between European countries in East and West immediately became objects of superpower conflict, and this automatic escalation in itself endangered superpower security.[1]

Some fundamental questions arise from this dilemma and they appear in many of the debates on changes in security policy. The latest example is the proposal for a fundamental change of strategy as envisaged by President Ronald Reagan in the Strategic Defense Initiative, otherwise known as 'Star Wars'. The proposal to create a defensive system has once again brought up the issue of Europe's role in East-West relations and posed the question to European governments and publics: Does dependence assure security?

The quest for European security

How may European states (East and West) individually and collectively provide their own security? Around this fundamental question a number of security policy debates have revolved since the institution of the fundamental division of Europe between East and West.

Though many shades can be found in this debate, it is obvious that there are two fundamentally different positions confronting each other: Some argue that Europe needs the superpower commitment – European security *is* the superpower guarantee. The security policy of the aligned states must try to uphold and strengthen that commitment in the face of the other superpower's attempt to break it down and in the face of centrifugal factors created by economic, technological and political developments within the countries.[2] Others (the independence movement) argue that the superpowers no longer provide security for the European countries. On the contrary, they inject instability into the European system. The superpowers are the ones that prevent East-West trade from developing its natural course. They are the ones clamping down on internal movements towards reforms that could produce tension-reducing changes in the individual countries. And they are the ones to introduce new weapons into an already overarmed Europe.

The fundamental threat to European security, it is argued, emanates from the superpowers and their conflict. Europe must achieve independence in order to increase its own security.[3] These two views are so fundamental that they merit a closer look.

European security *is* the superpower guarantee
This school of thought argues that without the security guarantee from the USA and from the USSR, both Eastern and Western Europe would exist under the constant threat of blackmail, intimidation and even invasion from the other superpower. The US nuclear umbrella and its extension over the NATO members of Western Europe is seen as a cornerstone in the security policy both of the Western European countries and of the US. This 'coupling' between the USA and Western Europe has consequently been a fundamental problem for the security policy relationship between these countries.[4]

The nuclear guarantee fundamentally rests on the willingness of the US to initiate a nuclear war with the Soviet Union over the defence of Western

Europe. This commitment obviously is a worrisome policy both to the Europeans and to the Americans. To the Americans it means, first, that the United States may be drawn into a conflict with the Soviet Union that is not of its own making, and, second, that the US puts its own population at risk in order to couple its security to that of the NATO countries. To the Europeans, it is a worrisome policy in that it has required the introduction of US nuclear weapons on European soil. Coupling requires the European countries to tie their security policy in with that of the US, and consequently reduces their freedom of action.

The limitations have been accepted due to the perceived beneficial effects for European countries. The nuclear guarantee has introduced an element of stability into the post-war world, and has helped reduce the internal disagreements between various Western European countries by moving fundamental security policy decisions out of Europe. The problem of German rearmament, for instance, would have been a major conflict, had it not been for the US presence and influence. European security dependence has also reduced the pressure for conventional armaments and made it possible for some NATO countries to keep the superpowers' arms race at arm's length.[5]

The European policy choice to base security on the US nuclear guarantee, however, has not been the result of a weighing of advantages and disadvantages of coupling, but rather the result of a perceived lack of alternatives. In the face of an aggressive and powerful Soviet Union, the Western European nations have not considered themselves capable of providing their own defence. In the immediate postwar years the American guarantee was needed to counter the powerful Red Army, which never demobilized to the same extent as was done in the West. Following the development of Soviet nuclear capabilities, the nuclear guarantee was needed to prevent the Soviet Union from using its power to put pressure on the Western European countries. With the advent of nuclear parity between the superpowers, new nuclear weapons are perceived to be needed in Europe. The new INF-weapons threaten the Soviet Union directly from European soil. Thus, the Soviet Union is prevented from driving a wedge between the US and her Western allies due to the reduced credibility of US-based strategic forces. In this argument for coupling between the US and Western Europe lies the rationale of introducing the new INF systems into Europe: the Pershing II and the GLCM.[6]

The fundamental political rationale of introducing these weapons was based on the necessity of providing a coupling between the strategic American forces and the European theatre. To the proponents of the INF decision, that is also what has been achieved. The alliance is now claimed to be in better shape than ever, and the INF decision and its implementation are seen as contributing to the present favourable state of affairs within the alliance.[7]

This school of thought argues that to Western Europe there is no viable alternative to the dependence on the US nuclear guarantee, and despite the costs associated with this guarantee, coupling is necessary and provides Western Europe with a security that it would be difficult, costly and maybe even impossible to achieve in any other way. These arguments have increasingly been challenged by the movement for a more independent Europe.

European security: the independence movement

Concurrently with the development of the NATO alliance and the reinforcement of the US commitment to Europe, the inherent tensions and costs associated with being dependent on US security policy and interests created the motivation for the growth of support for a more independent European security policy. Moreover, the existence of a non-aligned Europe (Sweden, Finland, Austria, Switzerland and Yugoslavia) meant that an independent security policy was present as an alternative. To a number of European countries, the choice was between alliance with the US and some sort of independence, either alone or together with others. The negotiations over a Scandinavian defence pact in 1948–49 is a case in point. But even after the individual European countries made their choice of alignment (our discussion is limited to Western Europe – the situation of the Eastern European countries is quite different and will not be discussed here), the impetus was present for a more independent European role in providing for their own security.

The construction of the Brussels treaty (and the subsequent transformation of it into the Western European Union (WEU)) was to some of the participating countries one of the first vehicles for the expression of an independent European security policy. The plans for a European Defence Community (EDC) (1951–54) were ambitious attempts to create an independent security forum corresponding to the economic forum created through the European Coal and Steel Union. However, the plans for the EDC fell, first and foremost because of the reluctance of the major European countries to relinquish national control (especially France, but also Great Britain). Later attempts to reinvigorate the security cooperation within Europe proved no more successful than the failed EDC.[8]

None of these policy attempts had much success in creating independent European security policies until the advent and consolidation of détente strengthened the Europeans' feeling of increased freedom of manoeuvre vis-à-vis the US. Détente, US involvement in Vietnam, Watergate and US economic decline reduced the US hegemony and allowed the growth of an independent European security policy in embryo. The breakdown of détente from the end of the 1970s increased the pressure for an independently formulated European policy. The US demands for alliance solidarity clashed with the interest created in Europe during détente for a more peaceful relationship with the Soviet Union and Eastern Europe. The foreign policy differences over Iran, the Middle East, Afghanistan and Poland occurred together with the difficulties created by the INF decision and created strong and consistent demands from both left and right of the

European political spectrum for an independent European security policy. The political consultations under the European Political Cooperation (EPC) were used by the European countries as a mechanism for voicing their collective concern with developments in US policy deemed detrimental to European interests. The revival of the WEU and increased bilateral contacts between West Germany and France are current examples of this tendency. Finally the growth of the peace movements in many of the Western European countries, and the involvement of new groups in the security debate meant that an independent European security policy was a constant and major demand in the re-vitalised national security debate.

Fearful of this new tendency, European governments in the allied countries have made demands for increased consultation between the US and her European allies, for increased participation of the European defence industries in NATO procurement, and for an independent European voice in dealings with the Soviet Union. Despite agreement on this, the difficulty in achieving European agreement on matters of substance means that a European security policy is still a dream. Nevertheless European security independence is a powerful dream, and the political forces supporting policies aimed at making the dream come true seem to be growing in strength.

There are several different versions of independence within what I have here labelled 'the independence movement'. Independence in the least radical form is to see Europe as unified within an Atlantic framework. Europe has to be one pillar of the alliance, and the USA the other. In order to achieve true interdependence between Europe and the USA, Europe needs to be more unified than it is today. This conception of independence is one that conforms easily to American plans of reducing European reliance on the US, thus alleviating some of the burden that the USA is carrying today.

The other version is to see an independent Europe as a counter to superpower control and dominance. This version has long been a concern of the French, and also a driving force behind many European integrationists.

Finally some regard an independent Europe as a delinked, all-European system where Western Europe is detached from NATO and Eastern Europe from the USSR. This Europe has been enjoying widespread support among the peace movements, and among some politicians, but has had less support on the state level.

In terms of the debate on single issues like that on the SDI, these different versions of independence become mixed. Here I shall concentrate mostly on the state, as the SDI debate is over the policies of various European states, either one by one or coordinated in common policies.

Central to many of the proposals aired for an independent European security policy is the notion of Europe as a Third Force in the antagonistic relationship between the USA and the USSR. Europe has to play the role as a balancer that can reduce the antagonism between East and West and create an all European security system.[9]

According to some, Europe has become a battlefield of the hegemonial conflicts of the superpowers. Consequently the allies have to reconsider their policy of 'subordinance to American supremacy'. This subordinance no longer guarantees European security, either to the allies or to the non-aligned. Western Europe has to play the role of the mediator, both in political terms and in developing a different defence posture in Europe through a non-provocative conventional defence. The goal is an all European security system based on cooperation and mutual acceptance of the adversaries' right to exist.[10]

A number of institutional suggestions and proposals have been aired. Some argue for the reconstitution of the EPC, others think that the WEU is the best forum. Finally, some regard Franco-German cooperation as the best possibility of increased European cooperation.

In all of the issues that form the substance of the present security debate in Europe, its parameters are determined by the discussion between the proponents of relying on the guarantee of the superpowers and the independence movement. The differing views on the Geneva arms control negotiations, on the CSCE negotiations and even on trade and technology policy are reflections of the different views on how European security is best achieved. This debate takes place between different states in Europe, but, perhaps more importantly, within various states. This internal and external debate over the costs and benefits associated with dependence and independence in the European context is very clearly visible in the debate over the proposed new Strategic Defense Initiative (SDI). This new programme will fundamentally affect the debate on the costs and benefits associated with European security dependence. Two questions need to be raised here: How does SDI affect European security dependence, and does SDI enhance or reduce European security?

SDI: what is it?

President Reagan's speech on defence spending and defensive technology on 23 March 1983, introduced a new initiative into the strategic discussion. The Strategic Defense Initiative (SDI) has since then grown in importance both in the priorities of the Reagan administration itself and in the international security debate.

When SDI was introduced, it was as much of a surprise as the feared 'bolt from the blue'. Very few in the administration were aware of the initiative before they saw the President on TV, and experts, allies and adversaries alike were taken by surprise.[11]

Certainly SDI had antecedents, but they were of little importance and virtually unnoticed both by the strategic community and by the public at large. Research into Anti-Ballistic Missile (ABM) technology had been going on in the US for quite some time. In the Joint Chief of Staff's United

States Military Posture for FY 1983, the ASAT (Antisatellite) programme was described as 'vigorously pursued'. The Ballistic Missile Defense was described as heading toward a decision on providing options for the defence of ICBMs through 'Low Altitude Defence (LoAD), future systems and overlay defence'. The research was claimed to be conducted within existing treaties and purported to be a hedge against Soviet treaty abrogation and as a counter to specific Soviet threats (e.g. against US-satellites).[12]

Lobby groups existed who tried to argue for an increased use of space and high-energy technology to create a 'High Frontier' that could give the USA a strategic advantage in the competition with the USSR.[13]

Very few, however, took any of this seriously. The potential economic and political costs and the technical difficulties associated with the schemes marketed in Washington, together with the failure of the previous ABM scheme (the Safeguard ABM system was dismantled in 1976 for cost effectiveness considerations) meant that very few anticipated that strategic defense would be the new focus of the strategic debate.

Yet, that is exactly what Ronald Reagan proposed in his March 23 speech. Reagan in his own words 'launched an effort which holds the promise of changing the course of human history. There will be risks, and results take time. But I believe we can do it.'[14]

What is it that is to change the course of human history? What are the goals of this new initiative and what are the envisaged means to achieve it?

The SDI goals

The goals as President Reagan explained to the public in his 1983 speech were all ultimately directed towards rendering nuclear weapons 'impotent and obsolete', and this should be done by 'eliminating the threat posed by strategic nuclear missiles'. In his inaugural speech in 1985 he stated the further goal of totally eliminating the threat of nuclear war. Considering the important roles played by nuclear weapons, ICBMs and nuclear war planning in present US policy, this is an ambitious goal. However, the mere utterance of long-term goals of this type would probably not in and of itself have produced a major reaction, since it might be regarded as yet another example of political hyperbole and hypocrisy when, at the same time, more nuclear weapons were being constructed, deployed and used as threats.

But SDI contained other goals. The goal was also to do away with offensive weapons. As the technology for the new defensive system is developed and deployed, offensive nuclear weapons may be dismantled so a stable balance is maintained between offensive and defensive weapons with a final goal of removing all offensive weapons.[15]

Secretary of Defense Casper Weinberger was even more explicit and presumed that a move in the direction of defence on the part of the US would create a corresponding move in the USSR: 'I would hope and assume that the Soviets with all the work they have done and are doing in this field, would develop a similar defense, which would have the effect of totally and completely removing these missiles from the face of the earth'.[16]

In later statements on SDI, the removal of offensive weapons has, however, been stressed less and mentioned only as a result of potential arms control, arms reduction talks between the two superpowers.[17]

This reinterpretation of original goals is in the process of radically transforming SDI from what it was originally conceived as and into something quite different. This is especially evident in the overall goal that the President raised of doing away with deterrence as the basis for US and allied security. The President in his speech stressed that it is necessary to break out of a future that relies solely on offensive retaliation. 'Wouldn't it be better to save lives than to avenge them?', asked Ronald Reagan, and a number of his senior counsellors and advisers echoed that question in speeches and statements of their own since his speech. Secretary of Defense Weinberger expressed it clearly when he said that SDI ' . . . is an attempt to devise a system that protects our people instead of avenging them', (speech to Pittsburg World Affairs Council, 30 October 1984).

A lot of his advisers, however, have also begun to question this assumption of their President. Undersecretary of Defense Fred Iklé, for example, has asserted that blaming SDI for overturning the existing policy of strategic nuclear deterrence, is just plain wrong. SDI would not scrap a policy of deterrence, on the contrary, it would enhance deterrence by making it harder for the Soviet Union to reach its goal. To prevent the split between the different views of the role of deterrence within SDI, the argument has been developed that by destroying attacking missiles the deterrent (e.g. US's own ICBMs) is protected and at the same time the population is protected because a Soviet first strike becomes impossible. The protection of the US is, of course, the central goal of SDI.

Protection is the ultimate goal of SDI, but also a very elusive goal. What is it that is going to be protected? To the President it is 'our own soil and that of our allies'. It is the goal of total defence against strategic ballistic missiles, since the removal of fear in the population is the underlying political objective.[18] Technology should be developed that would make it feasible to achieve a high degree of defence against the threat of a nuclear strike from the Soviet Union or anybody else. The ultimate goal is a 100 per cent effective defence. 'The defensive systems the President is talking about are not designed to be partial. What we want to try to get is a system . . . that is thoroughly reliable and total. I don't see any reason why that can't be done', said Caspar Weinberger, (NBC's 'Meet the Press', 27 March 1983).

Even as a goal this is not realistic. The perfect defence is not possible. Even disregarding the problem of circumvention, the SDI system as presently imagined would not be capable of shooting down all the missiles directed at the West. Director of the SDI office, Lt. Gen. James Abrahamson has stated several times that a perfect astrodome defence is 'not a realistic thing', (*Science,* 10 August 1984). But a defence which is less than perfect (e.g. 90 per cent success rate) would all the same be beneficial, it is argued, compared to the situation that we are in now where there is no defence except through deterrence by the posing of counter-threats. The sheer fact that a 100 per cent population defence is an unrealistic goal, however, distracts considerably from the political benefits associated with the original vision of the President. As critics have pointed out, a system with a 90 per cent success rate would still leave enough missiles coming through to inflict unacceptable damage on the US (e.g. the destruction of 10 major US cities).[19]

Consequently, more attention has focused on the ability of the proposed systems to achieve point defence. The objective here is to defend the US ICBMs or other essential military targets from incoming missiles, and thus it is a continuation of the already ongoing research on BMD. Achieving this goal is technically more realistic, it is argued, and it would restore the credibility of the land-based ICBM-deterrent. Even this goal is probably difficult to achieve due to the foreseen Soviet countermeasure (overwhelming the defence etc.). But, it is argued, the defence will be beneficial anyway by complicating Soviet planning and making a Soviet first strike more difficult to achieve.[20] The defensive system would 'complicate and frustrate aggression' and would thereby enhance the US deterrent. The 'window of vulnerability' would be closed by this combination of offensive and defensive forces.[21]

Edward Teller illustrates this argument clearly in outlining the necessity for a combination of offence and defence.

> ...Their (the US and the USSR) armaments at present include only swords. A combination of swords and shields represents a considerable improvement, which would increase with the proliferation of shields. Such a situation does not make it possible to throw away swords, but if shields are much less expensive than swords, peace will tend to become more stable.[22]

Disregarding the cost considerations – on which there is considerable uncertainty – this is a far cry from the President's goal of changing the course of human history.

Goals of a less ambitious nature include considerations on creating a thin defence against small attacks. An ABAM defence constructed to handle nuclear missiles launched by accident from the USSR or missiles launched by one of the smaller nuclear capable states. The construction of a 'thin' defence either in the terminal or in the boost phase would, however, require the same technology needed to develop a full system and therefore be very cost inefficient. Furthermore, terrorist nuclear attacks through other means of transporting nuclear bombs (suitcases, freightships, etc.) could not be prevented with such a system. The problem of dealing with accidental launching could be solved more simply in other ways. The goal of a thin defence has, however, not been a central one for the administration even though it does figure in certain arguments advanced for the current research expenditure.[23]

Apparently, a central goal of the SDI has been to ensure that the allies should also be covered by the new defensive system. The protection should cover also their soil. Even though the concern for the allies was added on in small sentences in the original drafts of the President's speech, it does nevertheless figure there, and a major preoccupation of the administration since the launching of the initiative has been to calm allied fears of this new initiative. The President underlined that: 'Proceeding boldly with these new technologies, we can significantly reduce any incentive that the Soviet Union may have to threaten attack against the United States or its allies.' The protection envisaged for the allies is based partly on a protective shield and partly on reducing Soviet ability to threaten the use of nuclear weapons. SDI is supposed to develop a capability to provide a shield against theatre weapons like the SS 20.

But more important than the theoretical ability to defend against the SS 20, is the postulated effect SDI will have on increasing Soviet uncertainties in planning an ICBM attack on the US. If the USSR is no longer certain that it can penetrate US defences, the credibility of the US deterrent force is enhanced. This should then increase the credibility of the extended deterrent. This, it is argued, is in the interest of the allies.[24]

As SDI has developed and been elaborated, other goals have evolved, and more are sure to come. Most of these are arguments constructed to support the development of SDI and are not central goals to the programme. It is argued, for instance, that the advent of the powerful peace movements underlines the need to find an alternative to deterrence. Policy cannot be executed unless there is some element of public support. 'Policies have to be in harmony with what is commonly held as proper behavior.'[25] If nothing is done to ensure greater harmony, unilateral disarmament may present itself as a solution, and that, it is argued, should be avoided. Others have stressed that even though SDI could not provide a perfect defence, it could ensure that the number of nuclear explosions in a nuclear exchange could be reduced to a number that would not trigger the climatic catastrophes associated with the so-called nuclear winter. In any case, it is argued, damage limitation is in itself a more moral goal than the threat to retaliate.[26]

All of the goals of the SDI programme are present in the ongoing discussion in a highly confused and mixed manner, and the inherent contradictions between many of these goals are papered over by claims that what appear as contradictions are merely differences between short and long-range objectives. By claims that there are multiple objectives, or by saying that so far it is only research and nobody will be able to foresee what is going to be discovered tomorrow, the inconsistencies are disregarded.

The debate over the various goals of SDI has been going on within the US administration and has created confusion and uncertainty as to what SDI constitutes. SDI seems to exist in at least four different versions within the administration:

The first stresses that SDI is only a research programme. The 'object is to provide the basis for an informed decision, sometime in the next decade, as to the feasibiity of providing for a defense of the United States and our allies against ballistic missile attack.' (Paul Nitze, Special Advisor to the President, speech to the IISS, London, 28 March 1985). According to this view, deterrence is and will continue to be the basis of US-USSR strategic relations for the foreseeable future, and the preservation of the ABM treaty is very important.

The second also stresses that SDI is a research programme, but here the goal is to create the perfect defence. The Defensive Technology Study under the chairmanship of James Fletcher concluded in their first study that 'the scientific community may indeed give the United States "the means of rendering" the ballistic missile threat "impotent and obsolete" '. Through a 10–20 year research programme with emphasis on detection and boost-phase programmes, the study foresees a final, low-leakage system created.[27]

This conception of SDI is supported by i.a. George Keyworth, the President's Science Advisor, and by Ronald Reagan.[28] This plan will only involve testing permitted by the ABM treaty, and the decisions on compliance and deployment are pushed into the future. The demonstration test necessary will, of course, despite what the advocates of this form of SDI say, subject the ABM regime to severe challenges.

The third type of SDI enjoying support within the present administration places the emphasis on intermediate defences. The idea is that research is conducted on all aspects and that deployment is undertaken as you go along and discover new possibilities in the various phases of defence. The fundamental assumption is that some defence is better than none. Deployment of an intermediate defensive system is useful because it will solve the security problem while full systems are being developed. This argument is presented in the so-called 'Hoffmann Report on Ballistic Missile Defenses and US National Security'. This study was undertaken at the request of the President to assess the role of defensive systems in security strategy. It thus complemented the Fletcher report that reviewed the technological feasibility of the SDI programme. The study advocated concentrating on the ABM option, the development of sensors (CONUS) and a limited boost-phase intercept option. These options if chosen and pursued now will 'contribute to reducing the prelaunch vulnerability of our offensive forces'.[29]

The final version of SDI sees it as a programme to protect missile silos, and to reduce the vulnerability of the ICBM. Consequently, terminal defences that may intercept incoming warheads should be deployed now, either under the ABM treaty ceiling of a hundred launchers, or through a reneging on the ABM treaty. Neither Caspar Weinberger nor Richard Perle are ABM-treaty supporters, and, through stressing Soviet non-compliance with the treaty, some observers see the administration as gearing up for termination of the ABM regime. 'I am sorry to say it (i.e. the ABM treaty) does not expire. That is one of its many defects', (Richard Perle, House Armed Services Committee Hearings, 23 February 1982). According to reports, this option of deployment of terminal defences is now supported especially in the US army.[30]

With all of these differing versions of SDI being advocated by different branches of the administration, the confusion was complete. Everybody had their own favourite version of SDI, and a need was felt for a central unifying strategic concept that could tie all these many versions together in one formula.

Formulated by Paul Nitze, four sentences summarized the common SDI concept:

> During the next ten years, the US objective is a radical reduction in the power of existing and planned offensive nuclear arms, as well as the stabilization of the relationship between offensive and defensive nuclear arms, whether on earth or in space.
>
> We are even now looking forward to a period of transition to a more stable world, with greatly reduced levels of nuclear arms and an enhanced ability to deter war based upon an increasing contribution of non-nuclear defenses against offensive nuclear arms.
>
> This period of transition could lead to the eventual elimination of all nuclear arms, both offensive and defensive.
>
> A world free of nuclear arms is an ultimate objective to which we, the Soviet Union, and all other nations can agree.

As a result of this strategic concept, three criteria were developed that have become fundamental for the administration when outlining the case for SDI. Defensive technologies must be effective, they must be survivable (the Soviets cannot easily shoot them down or render them ineffective in some other manner), and finally they must be cost-effective at the margins. As Nitze put it in his speech to the Philadelphia World Affairs Council: ' . . . that is, it must be cheap enough to add defensive capability so that the other side has no incentive to add additional offensive capability to overcome the defense'.[31]

According to Nitze, these criteria are demanding and deployment is conditioned upon meeting these standards.

SDI: How to do it

The SDI programme is premised on the technological ability to destroy ballistic missiles before they reach their target. The flightpath of the ballistic missiles may be divided into four phases: The boost phase where the first and the second stages of the engines are burning. In the post-boost phase the 'bus' (the projectile of the missile, containing guiding systems, fuel and MRV (individual nuclear warheads called multiple reentry vehicles (MRV)) has separated from the engines and launches the MRV on their separate flight paths. The midcourse phase describes the now individual flight paths of the warheads. The final phase is the terminal phase where the warheads and decoys along with them reenter the atmosphere.

SDI is designed to engage missiles in all phases of their flight (a four layer defence). Attacking the missiles in the final phases of the flight involved well-known technology corresponding to existing ABM technology. The new aspects of SDI have primarily to do with the capability to hit missiles in the boost and postboost phases. However, technological developments have been underway for some time that may enable the development of new systems in all of the phases.[32]

The SDI programmes require global full-time surveillance (the increased importance of satellites has put ASAT programmes on the SDI agenda) and defensive technologies of its own to prevent the new battle stations from being hit. Furthermore, the programme also aims for defence against shorter range ballistic missiles whether ground or submarine launched.

The development of a defensive system should produce an incentive for states to do away with nuclear weapons presently in their arsenals. It should also make it possible for arms control to succeed because the threat of destruction is reduced in importance. In presenting this argument (during the election campaign), Reagan proposed that the US should share the result of the development of these new technologies with the Soviet Union so that they, too, would do away with offensive weapons.

Obviously, in a situation with no offensive weapons and no threat, there is no need for, or basis for, a nuclear deterrence policy. However this situation is certainly not around the corner, the technology is not even developed yet, the Soviet Union has not accepted the idea and the costs of getting there are unknown.[33]

The interim period is therefore of more immediate importance. This was also underscored in the President's SDI speech: 'As we proceed we must remain constant in preserving the nuclear deterrent and maintaining a solid capacity for flexible response.' This, according to the President, requires continuing modernization of the present offensive strategic forces, both ballistic missiles and bombers and other missiles. In Europe, in particular, it requires an increase in conventional armaments. In terms of arms control policy, it means that negotiation from a position of strength is still the US favoured arms control approach.

Apart from some of the more esoteric technology, SDI does not in the foreseeable future change the present arms, defence, and strategic policy of the US nor of the alliance. The original version of the President was at best futuristic, and even he saw no change in the short or medium term. The subsequent presentation of the problem underscores that SDI is more an expanded and updated ABM programme than a fundamental revision of Mutual Assured Destruction (MAD). Even in terms of funding, the $26 billion requested for SDI for the period 1985–1989 is only an increase of $9.5 billion of what the outlay for this research would have been anyway, (Report to Congress, 1985, p. 77).

Why then spend so much time discussing SDI as if it was something totally revolutionary, and why bother with the importance that these changes may have on the US-European relations? SDI shows the fundamental problem in the security dependence of Western Europe on the US in that SDI is internally generated, but with strong external effects. The mere fact that the US proposes a system like this has political and strategic effects. It changes the arms control negotiation situation betwen the US and the USSR and it changes the situation between the US and its Western European allies.

The question is how.

SDI and Europe

The presentation of the SDI was certainly to the allies also a bolt from the blue. Nobody had been informed beforehand, they were not even given the usual advance notices that the President was going to present a major new policy. The presentation of the SDI decision was a clear example of what is usually a major gripe from the Europeans: The US does not treat the rest of the NATO alliance as equals. It expects support for US policies, but does not bother to consult with the allies before making major decisions that affect their security. As Helmut Schmidt expressed it once: A major problem in US-European relations is that the Americans' understanding of consultation is to say to the Europeans: 'Do as we ask – and please do it within the next two days'.[34]

The President's speech mentioned the need for closer consultation with the allies, but also said that '*I am* directing an effort . . .' This is what the Europeans resent. Asking the Europeans to back something they had not been part of conceiving is to create scepticism and resentment in Europe at the outset. Some argue, as indeed administration officials have done, that this new initiative is 'a generous offer'. The President offered a new programme to achieve the protection of not only the US but also the allies from London to Tokyo. The research programme is offered with no demands for allied financing and no demands that the allies should do anything active to receive this generous US offer. Their safety and ours are one, the President said, and hoped presumably to alleviate any fears that the US was retreating into a fortress America position.[35]

The way the President presented SDI created questions and fears among allies that the concern for allied safety was an add-on rather than an integral part of the initiative. The President said that he wanted to eliminate the threat posed by strategic nuclear missiles, thereby excluding tactical, theatre, cruise missiles and bombers. These are the types of weapons which are of primary concern to the Europeans. How is the President going to render nuclear weapons obsolete, if the programme concentrates on strategic missiles?

In the period following the President's speech, his advisers tried to explain these contradictions in two ways: One, that the SDI system – concentrating on boost-phase defence – would offer global protection against strategic missiles. There is no way to detect the target of a launched missile, and, consequently, all launched missiles would be shot down. His advisers have further said that, in reality, the President meant that all ballistic missiles would be covered, and, through this, improved air defence and terminal defences in Europe, the SDI could offer protection of Europe too.

This is, however, far beyond the scope of SDI, and would for sure involve huge European costs.

The other argument used is that if the US ICBM force is protected, deterrence is enhanced because the US threat to use them becomes credible. The reduction of the vulnerability of the land-based leg of the strategic triad will itself increase strategic stability because the risk of being pushed into a 'lose-them-or-use-them dilemma' is reduced. According to Iklé, SDI 'envisages and would include deterrence against theatre-range missiles targeted on Europe'. Arms control negotiator Max Kampelman argued that a two-tier strategic defence capability would protect US missiles, thereby making the US counter-threats more credible to the Soviets. Thus, the credibility of the deterrence would be enhanced, which would be of value to the Europeans.[36] Even if we regard the goal of providing population defence both for the US and for the allies as unrealistic, SDI could, according to administration arguments, increase the security of Europe by reducing the counter-force threat and by making the US capable of retaliating by protecting their ICBM force from a Soviet first-strike.

An unstated, but it seems increasingly important, goal of the SDI vis-à-vis the alliance is to strengthen the alliance by demonstrating unity on SDI. The 'generous' offer from the President to the allies becomes a symbol of alliance cohesion and solidarity. As the programme matures and develops in the American system, the arguments for costsharing, for sharing of responsibility and the sharing of political obligations will undoubtedly be raised on both sides of the Atlantic. In Europe by those that fear the effects any differences in view between the US and Europe may have on the alliance. In the US demands for solidarity may be raised both by the right wing advocates of strong leadership and strong military, but certainly also by the isolationist liberals that accept commitments unwillingly and have a low tolerance for upholding US commitments and programmes that are unwanted. The Nunn, Glen, Roth and Warner amendment to the FY-86 defense bill is a case in point. The amendment provides incentives for cooperative research and development projects between Europe and the US on defence equipment. As part of this incentive, Senator Nunn stressed that it is required that 'the Europeans are prepared to cooperate with us using their own funds'.[37]

It has been argued that SDI is being marketed with so much fervour and commitment that it is turning into an implicit alliance-loyalty test. Allied governments are becoming obliged to pledge their support to the initiative since any expression of doubt connotes contempt. Terence Todman, US Ambassador to Denmark, expressed it in terms of coupling. He referred to the European criticism of the SDI programme for decoupling the US from Europe, and said that when invited to participate in the research some of the European countries refuse. 'Noting some of the allied reaction one might ask who is decoupling from whom?'[38] The presentation of SDI, furthermore, came in the midst of the deployment of the INF missiles in Europe. That decision also had turned into a test of alliance solidarity and mutual purpose. The decision is of course still in the process of being implemented, but the difficulty in getting everyone – or at least almost everyone – in the alliance to back this decision, means that the absorptive capacities within the alliance for disagreement and disunity have been spent to the limit. The US demands for new symbols of solidarity through SDI present the alliance with new and grave challenges at a time when it is not very well equipped to handle them. European reactions should be seen in this light.

A central argument in presenting SDI to the Europeans has been that SDI at its present stage is a guard against Soviet breakout from the provisions in the ABM treaty. The treaty allows modernisation and research on ABM systems, and, as such, the new US programmes are presented as hedges against sudden Soviet breakthroughs in technology that would present the West with a *fait accompli*. SDI is claimed as consistent with the obligations contained in the ABM treaty, and even though this is disputed by some with reference to violations on both sides, the central problem with SDI in relation to the ABM treaty is that the envisaged deployments will certainly undermine the ABM regime and possibly create an offensive-defensive race among the superpowers.[39]

It is this possibility that itself is the basis of the other argument that SDI is useful because it provides the allies with leverage over the USSR in arms control negotiations. The present ABM treaty was not concluded, despite USA offers to negotiate ABM systems in the sixties, before the US started developing its own ABM systems. In the same way, it is argued, that SDI is today a major force behind the Soviet willingness to negotiate in Geneva. SDI is then presented as a bargaining chip that may eventually be negotiated away in the Geneva talks between USA and USSR. Even though the bargaining chip argument is disputed – among the critics you find Ronald Reagan – it is used especially in the American marketing effort in Europe. The statement that Caspar Weinberger made to the *Christian Science Monitor*, (29 October 1984) is illustrative: 'It's not a bargaining chip. If we can get it, we would want to have it, and we're working very hard to get it. It is not a chimerical thing out there on the margins to try to influence them to make reductions in offensive systems'. Compare this with the statement made by Abrahamson the same day: 'We may even do some trading. We might say, OK, we won't put something up for three years if you take out 500 warheads'.[40] European support for the programme is becoming a priority US concern, and consequently the US has offered the Europeans participation in the research programme under SDI. Cooperation will assume the form of cooperative scientific research and allied bidding on SDI contracts and political consultations through existing mechanisms.[41]

SDI would, it is argued by the proponents, increase coupling between the US and Europe. The gradual reduction of American strategic vulnerability would make the US threat of nuclear retaliation more credible, because strategic defence would solve the problem of choosing between Boston and

Bonn. The USSR would be deterred from attacking the US by the existence of the defensive systems, and the threat to answer any Soviet attack on Europe with a blow against the USSR would be more credible.

Some have argued that SDI might eventually require some sort of basing in Europe (Laser ground stations etc.), which would in itself be an expression of commitment to Europe parallel to the basing of intermediate range nuclear offensive systems. To provide the needed protection for Europe, the deployment of a modernised air defence system (the Patriot) to defend missiles stationed in Europe has been mentioned, but the costs and effectiveness of this system are still unknown.[42] Stationing of modernized versions of air defence missiles to hit incoming missiles is, however, a likely future prospect. This will reopen the entire debate on Europe's defensive-offensive role and the debate on the coupling between Europe and the US. SDI proposals have already stirred a controversy both within Europe and between Europe and the US. So much so that an observer has argued that the political costs associated with getting SDI accepted and implemented by far would outweigh the military and strategic benefits that it may eventually produce.[43]

SDI as a new transatlantic strategic concept has created yet another discussion over the relative costs and merits of equating basing NATO policy with US policy and the US' conception of interests.

The SDI programme may potentially further increase Europe's dependence on US policy. The technology of the programme would have to rely heavily on US developments, and the strategic rationale and even the arms control policy use of this new programme would underline European dependence.

European reactions: should dependency be welcomed?

When the SDI was presented to the world in 1983, the initial European reaction was one of disbelief. Traditional US supporters maintained an embarrassed silence and maintained that the SDI was just something for domestic US consumption and had nothing to do with strategy between East and West. The Soviets reacted immediately and denounced the US initiative. Because it would violate the ABM treaty, they argued, it would lead to a new arms race. It reflected the US ambition to achieve superiority through a first strike capability. The USSR followed with a series of proposals for bans on weapons in space, and a declaration of no-first-deployment on the part of the USSR. Andropov said that the USSR would not place ASAT weapons in outer space before the US did so, and he also proposed a mutual ban on deployment and testing of all space based weapons.[44]

The superpower public negotiation game was regarded as yet another indication that SDI was a propaganda ploy, and there was no need to take it seriously. German newspapers called it 'Ein Traum – kein wirkliches Programme'. Other papers warned that this would complicate the arms control negotiations and make it more difficult to get public support for NATO's ongoing modernization. Others, however, evaluated the US initiative on its moral goals and expressed approval of the underlying ambition to do away with MAD and the preference for defensive technologies. Furthermore, it was seen as a counter to perceived Soviet dominance in ABM and ASAT research and technology. The first reactions from Europe were based more on pavlovian reactions and there were few that considered it necessary to enter into more reflective analysis of the new proposal.[45]

The US, however, slowly began detailing the programme and began pressuring the Europeans for political support. When the NATO nuclear planning group met in Cesme in April 1984, Caspar Weinburger asked the Europeans for some sort of political support for the programme but was met with opposition from several countries, including the Federal Republic of Germany. The communique from the meeting registered allied agreement, but later in public both Defence Minister Wörner and Chancellor Kohl voiced their opposition. At a series of meetings in 1985, the United States tried to get allied endorsement, but except for the NATO defence minister meeting in Luxembourg in March, no common endorsement was forthcoming.

The criticism also came from the German opposition where both the SPD and the Greens voiced strong resistance to the plans. Towards the end of 1984 and in early 1985, the US launched, as a consequence of this criticism from the allies, a major effort to convince the Europeans about the merits of the US proposal and added a carrot to the package: European participation in the SDI research programme.[46]

The results were increased awareness on the European side of the priority that the US accorded this programme and also that the Europeans began to give reluctant support – support that was filled with fine print and double meanings, but these could be and were disregarded by the US administration. The SDI programme began acquiring a major role in Western discussions.

The European reaction can be exemplified through an analysis of the four points agreed upon by Reagan and Thatcher at their Camp David meeting in December 1984. The agreed points were: 1) the purpose of the West is to maintain balance. It is not to achieve superiority; 2) the new strategic defences cannot be deployed without negotiation in view of existing treaty obligations (i.a. the ABM treaty); 3) the overall aim is to enhance and not to undermine deterrence; 4) the aim of negotiations between East and West is to reduce the arsenal of offensive arms on both sides.

In presenting the agreement, Thatcher stressed that she supported the SDI plan as a research and not as a deployment plan, and that it was a long-range programme.[47] The support is qualified with a lot of fine print, and the four points of 'agreement' reflect some of the fundamental worries that the Western European governments have.

The first point reflects the worry that the US will use the defensive systems to press for superiority as indeed some US commentators have been arguing that the US should.[48] SDI as an ABM defense plan to protect the ICBMs will increase the Soviet fears that the US is planning a first strike and therefore induce them either to increase their offensive arms or to create their own ABM and a new arms race would result.[49]

The second point illustrates the fear that SDI would increase the already existing pressure for abrogating the ABM treaty. The research and the testing will in itself create pressures for Soviet actions which will constitute violations of the treaty and there will be a race in order to prevent the other party from breaking out.

The third of the agreed points was that the purpose was to enhance deterrence, and the underlining of this reflects the European fear that research on SDI will destroy deterrence. People will be deluded into believing that we are moving away from MAD and into a situation of MAS (mutual assured security). In the transition period, first strike is a very likely policy – indeed, perhaps the only possible one. Furthermore, the French and the British deterrent will be reduced in effectiveness. NATO's flexible response strategy would be impaired in that the nuclear deterrent would be incredible against a conventional Soviet attack.

Finally, the building up of defence increases the incentive to increase offences and the fourth point of the agreement, that offensive armaments should be reduced, reflects this. The Soviets have already made clear that they will increase their offensive weapons as a result of the proposed plans. Since no limitations on offensive nuclear arms are in place in Europe, they may do so most easily here. Furthermore, SDI would create a race between creating new space systems and systems to hit these systems, and systems to defend the defensive systems etc., etc.[50]

Underlying the presentation of these 'agreed' four points were fears that arms control would be impaired rather than helped by this new plan, and the economic consequences would be so great that the Europeans would be left in the cold because they could not afford it. The costs would also increase the already existing domestic pressure in the US to reduce its military presence in Europe.

Behind the agreement between the US and the allies, serious and widespread concern about the proposal linger on. Sir Geoffrey Howe, the British Foreign Secretary, in a speech to the Royal United Services Institute outlined the concerns explicitly. He said that concerns about not fuelling a new arms race should be brought into consideration during the research stage, rather than after. He also voiced concern over the defensibility of these new systems, and the ability of politicians to maintain control over important peace and war decisions.[51]

Finally, he said, as members of the Atlantic Alliance, we must consider the potential consequences of this unique relationship. 'We must be sure that the United States' nuclear guarantee to Europe will indeed be enhanced not at the end of the process, but from its very inception.'[52]

The misgivings and fears presented by the British reflect wide-spread sentiments in Western Europe and are, with minor differences, also present in France and West Germany. The French have worried in particular over the credibility of their own deterrent, and have been working on the possibility of developing their own space defence. Mitterand explicitly spoke about a European space community as the best answer to tomorrow's demands and military realities.[53]

The French have reacted negatively to the American SDI proposal. Due to the enticing effect that the promise of participation in a high technology programme might have on the European states, France has proposed a cooperation programme designed to strengthen European technological capability in the areas where SDI will also concentrate. The programme named Eureka (ironically also the motto of California) has met with support both from Britain and from the Federal Republic. Owing to the strong pressures in Europe and especially among the WEU countries for a common European position on the SDI offer, the French proposal has met with general approval. The US has recognized this and is trying to stress the compatibility between the SDI and Eureka programmes. So far, however, the Eureka proposals seems to be doing what the French intended it to: reinforcing the strong scepticism against SDI in Europe. The French have been very outspoken in their criticism of the SDI proposal. Defence Minister Charles Hernu called it dangerously destabilizing, and France proposed to the Committee on Disarmament that a treaty banning the militarization of space should be adopted. This should limit ASAT systems, prevent energy weapons, whether deployed in space or on land, and guarantee that each state may use and orbit satellites without fear of them being taken out.[54]

It could have been expected that the West Germans would react more favourably than Britain and France since they do not have a deterrent of their own to protect. And, indeed, the Federal Republic has expressed support with the SDI plans on several occasions. Defence Minister Manfred Wörner has said that 'We support the SDI Research Programme', and Chancellor Kohl has on several occasions expressed support for the SDI programme. He has stressed that Western Europe should not be 'technologically decoupled' from the United States. At the same time, reservations are expressed by Hans Dietrich Genscher and his spokesmen. Jürgen Möllmann (State Secretary in the Foreign Ministry) has said that 'The Bundesrepublik takes a wait-and-see attitude'.[55] Despite the obvious differences within the present CDU-FDP government, even the CDU has qualified its support for the SDI programme with a number of provisions: SDI research should be seen as an attempt to deter a new research competition between USA and USSR. The research should not replace deterrence. Europe must have full insight and full participation in the programme, and the effects on the ABM treaty must be carefully considered. Given the fact that these considerations come from the CDU caucus, they highlight the widespread scepticism against SDI in the Federal Republic.[56] Defence Minister Wörner said as an early comment on the SDI plan:

> Protection or trap for Europe. That is the theme for the coming years. There is anxiety regarding the destabilization of the East-West equilibrium and the decoupling of Western Europe from the US, as well as a split in the Western alliance.[57]

Despite the present ideological compatibility between West Germany and the USA, and despite the fact that nobody wants to create another INF-débâcle within the Alliance, the Kohl government has, in fact, reacted quite reluctantly to all but the suggestion that mutual research be done. The reluctantly favourable response to the US research proposal may be explained by pointing to the fact that this is the only way to gain some influence over the programme. Since research in itself may create potential benefits for Europe economically or technologically, the Europeans have satisfied US demands for solidarity by giving a positive response to the research cooperation proposal.[58]

It does not mean, however, that the SDI programme is supported. The West German government fears public reaction to this new proposal, and they fear that détente between East and West will be destroyed as a consequence of this new initiative. It may also lead to decoupling, as Wörner pointed out. Both in the sense of the nuclear guarantee but also in the sense that economic and research competition between Europe and the US would be intensified as a result of SDI.

The European reaction has been critical, and even on the proposals for research cooperation, sceptical voices now appear, in part from some of the smaller European countries: Norway, Holland, Denmark, but also from groups within the major European powers. Who is going to cooperate on this new research – corporations, scientists or governments? (The United States rejected an offer from the Soviet Union to have a team of scientists from both countries work out the potential consequences of the new technologies by arguing that such an evaluation had to be done through governmental negotiation). What sort of influence will Europeans be accorded if they enter into this research? Does this mean that they will have an independent voice in the determination of strategy?[59]

What will it all cost, and how is it to be financed? If through public financing, is the money going to be diverted from other arms programmes or are additional funds needed? Finally, some Europeans worry whether the cooperation would actually involve any transfer of knowledge. The cooperation between Europe and the US on the Columbus project has lead many to regard US offers about mutual research with a high degree of suspicion.[60] The critical voices have, however, so far not prevented the Europeans from entering into agreements with the USA on space research projects. The Germans and the Italians have concluded agreements with the US on the Columbus project, and have left the French standing in the cold with their proposal for a common European effort. Some French commentators have speculated that this is a case of the losers of the Second World War trying to gain influence over nuclear weapons through the backdoor and without the participation of France and Great Britain.[61]

Far-fetched as this may be, it does reflect the divisive influence that the SDI initiative already has had on the Europeans. The differences in relationships of these countries to the US and their differences in national security policy seem to be exacerbated through the SDI proposal and the US research offer.

This in and of itself has made it increasingly difficult to reach compatibility in goals which is the substance of coupling between the US and Western Europe. The SDI proposal has increased and sharpened the debate in Europe on whether to follow along with the American initiative in order to reduce its negative effect and to ensure political coupling, or to fight the SDI plans since they will endanger European security.

By highlighting the European dependence on the US in the field of security policy, the SDI proposal has strengthened the wish for an independent European policy. Independence as a set-off to increased dependence, as a counter-attempt to reduce the divisive influence that SDI has on the inter-European relations, as a necessary foundation for a domestic consensus on security policy in Europe, and in order to prevent SDI from placing further obstacles to the development of a better relationship between East and West.

SDI; security-dependence or independence?

SDI fundamentally focuses on defensive weapons. The object of the research programme, the interallied consultations, and the long range vision of the US President, all focus on defensive weapons. Simultaneously, the US is modernizing its offensive weapons. The MX is, in the President's own words, 'a long overdue modernization. We are sitting here with our land-based missiles out-dated by anything and any comparison with the Soviet Union'.

We are in a situation where the US and the Soviet Union are modernizing their offensive missiles and other types of offensive weapons (the cruise missiles, the stealth bomber etc.), and a future consisting of a mix between offensive and defensive systems resulting from the new research seems the most likely prospect. Reagan obviously envisages this situation too. In an interview with Newsweek he was asked: 'Is there anything that suggests to you that the Soviets will not try to build up offensively while we are researching Star Wars, or that they will not try to match the program?' In reply, he said:

Oh, I think they're trying to match it, and as I say, I think they started ahead of us. If we're right in our suspicions that they are expansionist and they already outnumber us greatly in the offensive weapons, and then they alone developed a defensive weapon before us, then they wouldn't have to worry about our deterrent – a retaliatory strike. Then they could issue the ultimatum to the world. So if there's any thought of that, then it would make it all the more necessary that we have a defensive weapon, too.

Obviously the Soviets will have an identical view of US intentions behind SDI and consequently we are likely to enter into a defensive – offensive arms race. What are the consequences for Europe of this situation? What happens if defensive systems are developed at different paces in different countries? Four scenarios are imaginable: Defence is developed 1) only in the USA; 2) only in the USA and Europe; 3) only in the superpowers, but not covering either of the allies; 4) only in the USSR.

Defence only in the USA
Development of the defensive systems to cover the US alone (not giving total security but at least enough to make the leaders feel more confident about the ability to withstand an all-out nuclear attack) is, in essence, for what SDI is primarily designed, and the political add-ons about extending it to cover Europe and sharing it with the Soviets are political commitments that may change from one situation to the next.

If the defensive systems protected the United States, two situations might occur: One is that the US would decouple from the European scene. Their interests, economically, politically and strategically, in preventing others from dominating Europe would naturally be the same as they are today. But with the existence of a defensive shield, the Soviets would have only Europe to direct a retaliatory blow against in a situation of nuclear exchange between the super-powers. However unlikely this situation may seem in military terms, the political realities of foreseeing such a situation are more than enough to produce strategic instability and alliance insecurity. European governments will worry in such a situation that the US may be more prone to reckless behaviour vis-à-vis the Soviet Union, because of its own feeling of security against attack.[62]

The opposing argument is that since the risk to the US of fighting a war in Europe is reduced as the American homeland is protected, the threat to retaliate with offensive nuclear weapons against the USSR becomes more credible. As a result, deterrence is enhanced. Consequently, one coud argue that increased strategic stability will result. This situation, besides assuming perfect defenses and political leaders willing to risk their populations to achieve political ends, also foresees limiting war to Europe – which, of course, is completely contrary to any definition of European security, and therefore no marketable alternative in Europe.

Defence only in the USA and in Europe
The SDI initiative contained from the start a stated commitment to extend the 'shield' to cover the allies. In Europe this will involve a combination of boost-phase defenses from the overall systems and a series of terminal

defenses based in Europe. The political coupling problem that besets the present relationship between the US and Europe will remain the same. The European reliance on US decisions will even increase. The employment of the defensive systems would involve a US decision, and the US may be reluctant to make this decision in a situation where the attack is directed only against Europe. Furthermore, the European feeling of security under the defensive shield, however unrealistic, may itself create problems in the relations between the US and Europe. The final element keeping European and US security interests on line has been the common threat from the Soviet Union. Furthermore, internal differences within the European countries will resurface, and we are already seeing the beginning of this in the French fears of German and Italian participation in SDI research.

Defence covering only the superpowers
A scenario that brings out fear, insecurity and political anxiety is the prospect of both superpowers having some sort of defensive shield covering themselves but nobody else. In this situation deterrence between the superpowers is devoid of meaning, British and French nuclear deterrence will be useless against the Soviet Union and the demands for conventional deterrence will increase dramatically. Security in Europe will be tied to the possibility of Europe defending itself against conventional attacks, and it will be impossible to do anything about a nuclear threat. Europe will, in this situation, become a hostage to the superpowers' differences, and will be the true theatre for confrontation. The superpowers will feel secure and accordingly play out policy differences openly in the European scene. The situation will be highly unstable and will involve strong pressure towards an independent European security policy and probably European attempts to devise their own defensive systems.

Defence only in the USSR
Finally, one could imagine the unlikely, but possible, situation that only the Soviet Union possessed a defensive system. Obviously this scenario is part of the motivation behind the present American effort. In this situation, the relationship between Europe and US will be under strong pressure for change. The present US guarantee and escalation dominance will be reduced, and Europe will have to provide for its security more independently. The situation will be highly unstable. Given the composition of the strategic forces, a Soviet capability to destroy incoming ICBMs would be less of a threat to the US nuclear force than the US threat is to the USSR strategic force. The latter have 70 per cent of their warheads on ICBMs whereas the corresponding US figure is 21 per cent. The possibility of the West placing Eastern Europe at risk and the possibility of circumvention plus the vulnerability of the USSR to embargo means that a Soviet defensive system would not, in itself, give the security background for achieving political goals through intimidation. The demands for substantial rearmament in Europe would, however, present themselves

very strongly. Furthermore, the divisive effects on the NATO alliance would probably be very serious.

These scenarios are relevant to the present discussion in so far as they explain the fear that motivates discussions between the Europeans and between Europe and the U.S. A defensive scenario with the continuing existence of offensive weapons is more unstable than any other scenario imaginable including one where offensive weapons are continuously developed and deployed.[63]

Evaluating the effect of SDI on European security would include an assessment of the effect the SDI proposal has on the present East-West climate. How does SDI affect the arms control negotiations and the mutual attitudes between the superpowers? How does the SDI proposal affect the European perceptions of US interests and commitments vis-à-vis Europe, and what is the reaction from the public at large in the face of these prospects?

The research programme that is started will have effects on the direction of research. The research funds allocated for other purposes will decrease or other governmental expenditures will suffer. The research programme and the discussion of SDI plans in itself also affects the relationship between different groups internally in different states. The internal discussion within the US e.g. between the various branches of the armed services over the SDI proposals is a case in point. Similar cleavages will develop in Europe. Finally, the cost of the SDI proposal has already presented itself in terms of strain on the domestic consensus that was slowly being rebuilt inside European countries, and between the US and Europe. The potential benefits are, at present, more imagined than real, seen from a European perspective. It is possible that the SDI proposal induced the Soviet Union to return to the negotiation table in Geneva, but it will not induce them to arms control agreement when SDI is non-negotiable. The political costs of SDI are clearly seen. The benefits are hard to find. SDI has already made Europe more dependent on the US and that, in and of itself, is part of the problem with the proposal.

Is, as many Europeans are now arguing, European independence an alternative to this situation?

It may appear more attractive to opt for European independence than it actually is. In the present situation the possibility for the Europeans to influence the direction of the strategic development between East and West is very small. The increase of European independence may further decrease European possibilities to influence the East-West debate. There is not a third way, and there is no such thing as regional European security in an insecure world.

However laborious and difficult the process may be, the only true solution to the European security problem is common global security. The only definition of European security interests which will, in the end, be able to increase European security, is a definition building on global security. Europe can not achieve its security without involving itself directly in the security of other regions and first and foremost in the East-West relationship.

One of the possible ways that Europe may follow is the assertion of pressure that reduces superpower confrontation, and such a possibility may exist in firmly rejecting the SDI offer. The rejection itself will be difficult in that it runs counter to a long tradition. But acceptance will, as pointed out, increase Europe's dependence and increase strategic instability. The offensive-defensive race is not on yet, and may be stopped. Europe has a responsibility to the security of other regions, to the security of the global system to help stop a new arms race. The Nordic countries may be the place to start such an initiative due to the different affiliation of the Nordic countries. Since part of the rejection of SDI obviously involves restraining the USSR from pursuing similar research and development, the Nordic countries may also present a bridge between East and West. SDI, at present, is a stumbling block to arms control and confidence-building discussions, and, if Europe removed itself from SDI, the enthusiasm in both of the superpowers for an enormously expensive and probably ineffective space defensive system would probably wane.

What Europe should not do is choose dependence once again. Dependence does not assure security, but neither does isolated independence in a strategically interdependent world.

Notes

1. Michael Smith's overview in *Western Europe and the United States, The Uncertain Alliance*, London: George Allen and Unwin, 1984.

2. Andrew J. Pierre, "Can Europe's Security be 'Decoupled' from America?", *Foreign Affairs,* 1973, pp. 761–777; and Alan Sabrosky, 'NATO: A House Divided?', *Atlantic Quarterly,* Vol. 2, No. 2, summer 1984, pp. 97–118.

3. See for one of many expressions of this Horst Ehmke, 'Eine Politik zur Selbstbehauptung Europas', *Europa-Archiv,* Folge 7, 1984, pp. 195–204.

4. Hans-Henrik Holm, *U.S. and European Security: The Troublesome Coupling,* mimeo 1984.

5. Defence expenditure as a percentage of GNP varies substantially within the NATO alliance. In 1982 Canada, Denmark, Italy, Luxembourg and Spain spent under 3 per cent of GNP; Belgium, the Netherlands, Norway and Portugal spent between 3 and 4 per cent; France and FRG spent between 4 and 5 per cent; Britain, Greece, Turkey and the USA spent more than 5 per cent of GNP on defence. See *The Military Balance 1984–1985*, IISS, London, 1984.

6. Hans-Henrik Holm, Nikolaj Petersen (eds.), *The European Missiles Crisis: Nuclear Weapons and Security Policy*, London: Frances Pinter Publishers, 1983.

7. Secretary of State George Schultz in his speech at a Rand Conference, 19 October 1984 made this point. He said that harmony and confidence has been restored. Increasing consensus and widening agreement is what characterizes the alliance today.

8. The US provided a strong external pressure for European independence.

From the Marshall Aid and through the Atlantic partnership of the Kennedy administration to Kissinger's year of Europe various US administrations have themselves pressed for a united Europe. See Michael Smith, op. cit., pp. 103–116.

9. For a list of various of the proposals see *Bulletin of Peace Proposals*, Vol. 15, No. 1, 1984.

10. Peter Schlotter, 'Reflections on European Security 2000', loc. cit., pp. 5–6.

11. Laurence I. Barrett gives in *Time*, 11 March 1985 an account of 'How Reagan Became a Believer'. According to this story is was the combination of Robert McFarlane and Edward Teller that made Reagan a believer.

12. *United States Military Posture for FY 1983*, Washington D.C., 1982, p. 77. Accounts of the development of defensive technologies may be found in Union of Concerned Scientists, *The Fallacy of Star Wars*, New York: Vintage, 1984. And in David Baker, *The Shape of Wars to Come*, New York: Stein and Day, 1984.

13. Daniel O. Graham, *We Must Defend America and Put an End to Madness*, Chicago: Conservative Press, 1983.

14. President Reagan's speech on Defense Spending and Defense Technology, 23 March 1983.

15. See testimony before Senate subcommittee on 22 February 1983 by the Director of the Strategic Defense Initiative, James Abrahamson.

16. Caspar Weinberger, 27 March 1983. (Emphasis added).

17. A good example is the interview with Ronald Reagan published in *Newsweek*, 8 March 1985.

18. Ronald Reagan's 23 March 1983 speech.

19. McGeorge Bundy, George F. Kennan, Robert S. McNamara, Gerard Smith, 'The President's Choice: Star Wars or Arms Control', in *Foreign Affairs*, winter 1984-85, Vol. 63, No. 2, pp. 264–278.

20. Zbigniew Brzezinski, Robert Jastrow, Max M. Kampelman, 'Search for Security: The Case for the Strategic Defense Initiative', *International Herald Tribune*, 28 January 1985.

21. The window of vulnerability debate refers to the critique against the SALT II accord that it gave the Soviets an advantage in landbased-ICBMs. President Reagan started his term by arguing for the necessity to change this. However, the START proposals and the Reagan approval of the Scowcroft commission report closed the window – until it resurfaced in the SDI-debate. See Strobe Talbott, *Deadly Gambits*, New York: Alfred A. Knopf, 1984, pp. 304–305.

22. Edward Teller, 'The Role of Space and Defense in the NATO Alliance' in *NATO's Sixteen Nations*, Nov. 1984, pp. 14–16. Gen. Edward Rowny, American START-negotiator, in his fight against the ABM treaty used the same metaphor: 'Two adversaries arm themselves with shields and spears, then agree to throw away the shields. But if one side starts making more and longer spears, then sooner or later the other side has to think seriously about retrieving its shields'. Here quoted from Strobe Talbott, op. cit., p. 319. He points out that the trouble with this analogy is that shields can never deflect nuclear spears, and given the absence of limits or the number of spears the development of shields become fruitless.

The reuse of old analogies reflects that the SDI has turned into a continuation of the old ABM debate.

23. Sidney D. Drell, Philip J. Farley, David Holloway, *The Reagan Strategic Defense Initiative: A Technical, Political and Arms Control Assessment*, A Special Report of the Center for International Security and Arms Control, Stanford University, 1984, pp. 70–72.

24. Lawrence Freedmann, 'NATO and the Strategic Defense Initiative', *NATO's*

Sixteen Nations, Nov. 84, pp. 17–20. See also *Report to the Congress on the SDI,* April 1985, p. A-7.

25. Edward Teller, op. cit.
26. Paine and Gray, 'Nuclear Policy and the Defensive Transition', *Foreign Affairs,* vol. 62, pp. 819–42, in particular p. 840.
27. The Strategic Defense Initiative, *Defensive Technologies Study,* DOD, March 1984.
28. George A. Keyworth, *The Case for Strategic Defense: An Option for a World Disarmed,* Issues in Science and Technology, Vol. 1, No. 1, pp. 30–44, and Ronald Reagan, *Remarks of the President to the National Space Club Luncheon,* 19 March 1985.
29. Fred S. Hoffman, *Ballistic Missile Defenses and U.S. National Security,* FSSS, 1983, p. 3.
30. IISS, *Strategic Survey,* 1984–85, London 1985, p. 14.
31. Paul H. Nitze, *On the Road to A More Stable Peace,* Speech to the Philadelphia World Affairs Council, 20 February 1985.
32. Holger H. Mey, 'Technologie der Raketenabwehr', *Osterr. Milit. Zeitschrift,* 6 Heft 1984. See also a series of articles in the *International Herald Tribune: Weapons in Space,* March 1985.
33. For a technical assessment see Sidney Drell et al., op. cit., pp. 39–63.
34. Helmut Schmidt, 'Saving the Western Alliance', *The New York Review of Books,* 31 May 1984, pp. 25–27.
35. Lawrence Freedman, op. cit.
36. Zbigniew Brzezinski et al., op. cit. The argument that deterrence is also protection and therefore there is no difference between the two views is false. Obviously Ronald Reagan by protection means a protective shield covering the 'soil' not just the weapons.
37. The NATO debate is summarised in Stanley Sloan, 'In Search of a New Transatlantic Bargain'; William Wallace, 'European Defence Co-Operation: The Reopening Debate' both in *Survival,* Vol. 26, No. 6, Nov. 1984. And Phil Williams, 'The Nun Amendment, Burden Sharing and US Troops in Europe', in *Survival,* Vol. 27, No. 1, Jan. 1985.
38. Joseph Kraft, 'Observe the Fine Print in the SDI Support', *The International Herald Tribune,* 23–24 Feb 1985. And Terence Todman, *The Reality Behind 'Star Wars',* Address to the American Club, Copenhagen, 8 May 1985.
39. *Arms Control Today,* Vol. 14, No. 6, July–August 1984. See also Report to the Congress: S.D.I., 1985, App. B. Here it is stressed that the US may withdraw from the treaty, and that an agreement on offensive arms limitation is a precondition for maintaining the ABM-regime.
40. Ibid., pp. 8–9.
41. *The Economist,* 16 Feb 1985, 'Europe is reluctant to reach for the stars'.
42. *The Economist,* 'A Patriot for Europe', 12 Jan 1985.
43. Lawrence Freedman, op. cit.
44. *Keesing Contemporary Archives,* 1983.
45. See the account in Jürgen Scheffran 'Schutzschirm oder Falle für Europa? Zur Debatte in der NATO über Weltraumsrüstung und Raketenabwehr', *Blätter für deutsche und internationale Politik,* No. 6, 1984, pp. 657-677.
46. *The NATO Communique,* NPG, 4 April 1984.
47. *International Herald Tribune,* 22 Feb. 1985.
48. Colin Gray, Keith Payne, 'Victory is Possible', *Foreign Policy,* No. 39, 1980, pp. 14–28.

49. The defensive system capability obviously increases if command and control facilities and ICBMs are hit in a first strike. This makes the SDI provocative and therefore increases the incentive of the USSR to preempt in a situation where war is likely. See Bernd Greiner, 'Zwanzig Argumente gegen den 'Krieg der Stein'', *Blatter fur Deutsche und Internationale Politik*, 1985, Nr. 3, p.275, and Peter A. Clausen, 'SDI in Search of a Mission', *World Policy Journal*, Vol. II, No. 2, pp. 249-270.

50. Peter Jenkins, 'Star Spangled Banner', *Guardian,* 27 Feb. 1985.

51. The warning time will be so short that the defensive systems will have to be triggered automatically without any political decision-making.

52. *The International Herald Tribune,* 16 March 1985, and *The Guardian,* 16 March 1985.

53. See Mitterand's speech to the Parliament in Den Haag, 7 Feb 1984.

54. *Politique Etrangére*, no. 2, 1984, pp. 377–380.

55. *Der Spiegel,* Nr. 15, 1985, pp. 21–23.

56. Jonathan Dean, *Will NATO survive Ballistic Missile Defense?* mimeo, Washington, March 1985, pp. 13–15.

57. Jürgen Scheffran, op. cit.

58. See Kohls statement in his speech to the Annual Congress of the Christian Democratic Party, 20 March 1985.

59. Theo Sommer, 'Der Wink mit dem Raketen-Zaunpfahl', *Die Zeit,* 22 Feb 1985. See also E.P. Thompson, 'The Ideological Delirium which strikes chords in the worst traditions of American Populism', *The Guardian*, 18 Feb. 1985.

60. Jürgen Scheffran, 'Ist die Militarisierung des Weltraums noch aufzuhalten', *Blätter für deutsche und internationale Politik*, No. 10, 1984, pp. 1167–1183. And *Der Spiegel,* 1985, Nr. 15, p. 21.

61. Pierre Lellouche, 'The Star-Crossed Star Wars Plan', in *Newsweek*, 4 March 1985.

62. Sidney Drell et al., op. cit.

63. Charles Krauthammer, 'Will Star Wars Kill Arms Control', *New Republic,* 21 Jan 1985, pp. 12–16. In Paul E. Gallis, Mark M. Lowenthal and Marcia S. Smith, *The Strategic Defense Initiative and United States Alliance Strategy,* CRS report 85–48F, Washington 1985, three different scenarios are discussed: A U.S. lead in SDI, a Soviet lead in SDI, and a close mutual cooperation.

Part 2: Europe and The Third World

5. Europe and Centre – Periphery Conflicts: Lessons From the Global Crisis

by Tamas Széntes

The concepts of peace and security have been interpreted in contemporary peace research literature as complex and multi-dimensional, i.e., not simply as the absence of war or military threat. Therefore, the role of Europe in other regions' peace and security has to be assessed far beyond the cases of direct involvement in world conflicts, local wars and militarization. It must be assessed also in the context of all direct and indirect effects Europe has exerted on life conditions and development patterns outside Europe. In this short chapter I cannot deal with all the manifestations of such effects. Nor can I present a historical balance sheet of the European interventions in other regions' internal affairs and development. As explained in another paper of mine,[1] the world role of Europe in the last five centuries has been outstanding both in a positive and a negative sense. It has given birth to two social systems, capitalism and socialism; initiated several revolutions in science and technology the results of which have strengthened European dominance, or influenced the development of other regions; it has created internally integrated notational economies and societies while preventing via colonialism or other means their rise in other regions; it has contributed much to the development of human culture, as well as to culturally damaging other societies; it has witnessed the rise of bourgeois democracy, as well as fascism, the birth of socialist democracy as well as its early deformations; it has caused two world wars and a cold war, while also establishing the first rules and institutions of peaceful cooperation, the first international organizations and peace movements, and so on . . .

Here we focus on the main consequence of European development after the Second World War on the Third World's peace and security.

In general, its peace has been disturbed or endangered by global militarization and the arms race on the world level, by foreign military interventions, local wars, regional arms races, internal militarization, and two 'invisible wars'; the first one manifested in mass misery and hunger causing permanent losses and damage to human life, and the other that waged between human society and nature resulting in the deterioration of the environment, ecological imbalances, and exhaustion of non-renewable natural resources. Since peace is meaningless under the conditions of oppression, terror, discrimination and exploitation, obviously all those forces, internal and external alike, which act against social progress, democracy and national sovereignty are, by definition, a danger to peace in the Third World, too. Security is endangered also by external military threat, political subversion and destablizing effects induced from abroad. Other security threats come from interventions in the economy, pressure based upon the asymmetrical dependence relations of the world economy, the uncertainties in food, energy and technology supplies, the impact of foreign hostile propaganda and misinformation, the dominance or massive demonstration effects of alien cultures etc.

No doubt, many of the above factors and conditions disturbing or endangering peace and security in the Third World are the products of Europe's past role. European colonialism made such a lasting impact on the colonized territories of the Third World that many local wars and regional conflicts have their roots in the colonial legacy particularly those stemming from boundary problems[2], separatist movements, and manipulated nationality problems or religious divisions. Cultural colonialism was responsible for the erosion of many valuable and progressive cultural traditions and, thereby, for the loosening of intra-societal cohesion forces, as well as for the anachronistic counter-reaction of forcefully revitalizing some obsolete, reactionary ones, causing additional conflict. The 'invisible war' of poverty and hunger[3] is mainly the consequence of the Third World's socio-economic structures which are peripheries of the capitalist world-economy whose sectorally imbalanced, 'dualistic' nature has undermined local demographic equilibrium, reduced the self-sustaining capacity of local communities, and caused an expanding marginalization of rural masses.[4] It has also produced a substantial loss of local control over the economy, creating opportunities for foreign powers to intervene in their favour in the local decision-making process as well as exacerbating vulnerability, throughout trade, financial and technological ties of dependence.[5]

Without exempting Third World countries from some responsibility of their own[6] we need also to see how the post-war division of Europe into two blocks with opposite socio-economic systems influenced the situation in the Third World from the point of view of its peace and security, and how the resulting East–West conflicts interact with the global North–South conflicts of the world economic centre and its periphery. When speaking about the interactions of East–West and North–South relations it must be noted, that the concept North–South, unless used only as a terminological simplification of the otherwise correctly interpreted concept of centre-periphery relations, may conceal and largely falsify the latter, while the concept of East–West relations does not correctly express the historical competition of two social systems.

It is obvious that neither the terms North–South nor East–West are used by journalists and scholars to refer to geographic regions but as terms expressing the differences in both levels of economic development and between social systems.[6] This ambiguous interpretation, by applying different criteria of classification to the various parts of the same world, conceals system specificities within both the North and the South (as well as 'sub-system' specificities within the global macro-system) and development differences within both the 'East' and the 'West' (as well as their 'sub-system' specifities within the global macro-system of the world-economy). Another vagueness is manifested in that usually the East does not include all the socialist countries but only the countries of the Warsaw pact, while the West is applied to all the developed capitalist countries of Western Europe (whether NATO members or not), North America and often even Japan, Australia and New Zealand.

In the discussion on European East-West relations we have to take into account also the incongruence which appears in that only one of the two leading powers is a European country. This makes not only the meaning of a military power balance even more uncertain and ambiguous than what follows from the differences and uneven development of weapon systems, but also the pattern of European interests and East-West interactions very asymmetrical.

Though our topic suggests a focus on intra-European East–West relations and their interaction with North–South centre-periphery relations, inevitably it includes the United States too, not only in regard to centre-periphery relations but also in regard to European East–West relations.

Centre-periphery relations can be reduced neither to colonialism nor to the development gap, expressed in quantitative terms, between advanced and underdeveloped countries existing side-by-side. They involve functional relations of asymmetrical economic dependence in various forms, which are then complemented by foreign political, military, technological and cultural influences. Since the centre-periphery dichotomy stems from the inherent spontaneity and uneven development of the capitalist world economy, and is rooted in the unequal structures of the world's social relations of production, those conflicts resulting therefrom, both between the centre and periphery and within the latter, cannot be solved fully without structural and institutional changes, without a substantial restriction of spontaneity and unevenness in world-economic development and without a substantial modification of production relations on a world level.

Centre-periphery conflicts occur between countries or groups of countries. The crucial issue in these conflicts is national sovereignty. The struggle of the periphery is aimed at achieving national liberation (not only in political, but also in an economic and cultural sense) and emancipation. Though *national* interests seem primarily to confront each other, the fact that in both the centre and the periphery different class forces stand for or against, and benefit or lose from, the relationship, conflicting social interests are also manifested.

The historical contradiction between capitalism and socialism originates in the capital-labour antagonism inherent in the world capitalist system, i.e.

from the dominance of accumulated 'dead' labour, capitalized by a class, over the 'live' labour of another, which manifests itself in the dual rules of the distribution of social roles and incomes for the capital-owners (according to ownership), and for the labourers. Socialism arose for the social liberation and emancipation of labour, i.e., to eliminate the dominance of capital and to introduce a single rule of distribution in the whole society. As a consequence of uneven development and the centre-periphery nature of the world capitalist system, socialist transformation has started in single and less developed peripheral or semi-peripheral countries. It has necessarily involved elements of the struggle for national emancipation. And since the rise of the socialist system within a national framework implies also changes, but only partial ones, in the global system of the world, the dialectics of mutual effects necessarily modifies the operation of both systems.

Though European East–West relations appear as a conflict between socialism and capitalism, represented by two groups of countries, i.e., as a basically class conflict centered around the issue of social emancipation, in reality, despite all the system-differences, the procapitalist or prosocialist forces of society are not allocated according to the geographical country or bloc frontiers, and besides, national interests are largely interfering with, reinforcing or weakening the conflicting social class interests. Thus, the identification of the historical struggle between capitalism and socialism with the conflict of two groups of countries or, particularly, with the two military blocs, is, indeed, an inadmissible oversimplification.

Europe has become the main source and sphere for the interactions between system conflicts and centre-periphery conflicts, with a great many consequences for European and Third World development as well as for peace and security. These interactions, with the concomitant interferences of social class and national interests or movements, can bring about cumulatively positive and negative results alike. The former can be illustrated by the example of the short period after the defeat of Nazi Germany and before the Cold War when we witnessed a constructive cooperation of the big powers of different social systems, committing themselves to eliminating the conditions and dangers of war, to safe-guarding the state sovereignty of all nations and to promoting the process of decolonization and national liberation in the Third World as well as the democratic transformation of Europe, and, when the various anti-fascist and democratic forces helped each other in the world-wide struggle against oppression, discrimination and aggression, respecting the endeavours and interests of each other concerning national and social emancipation. The latter, i.e., the cumulation of adverse consequences has been widely demonstrated by the Cold War period which has given birth to many tendencies, as well as false ideologies, acting or often influencing actions which harmfully affect peace and security in the Third World. No doubt, even in this period, there were possibly or actually many positive effects which accompanied the most negative tendencies. One can refer, e.g., to the final defeat of colonialism which, however, would have come anyway, perhaps even sooner, without the Cold War, to the rise of the non-aligned movement which was a reaction only to the Cold War bipolarism and block policies; to the break-up of the nuclear monopoly which can already be valued in the context of the preparation for war and then only relatively; to the acceleration of the social or national emancipation process in some periphery or semi-periphery countries but often artificially detached from local social reality; to the Cold War-induced support and politically motivated financial assistance to Third World countries or movements, but often for military purposes and for manipulating them against each other; to the stimulus of the scientific and technological revolution by cold war militarization, with a tremendous cost however, such as largely diverting research and development from basic needs problems of the Third World; to the rapid progress in regional integration, gaining impulse from cold war cohesion, in Western and Eastern Europe, but at the expense of blocking cooperation with each other and the Third World; or to the results of the structural transformation in the Eastern European economies under the conditions of cold war isolation which, however, often entailed very high social costs and sacrifices, etc. On the whole, and despite the above, during the Cold War a sort of negative-sum-game developed of which the arms race was but one, though undoubtedly the most decisive, element.

While the Cold War itself was neither initiated nor developed in the context of centre-periphery relations, the East–West confrontation has directly or indirectly affected the development, peace and security of the Third World. First, by the externalization of this confrontation to the Third World, and, second, by the spread and reinforcement of militarization. In addition, the transplantation attempts or demonstration effects of development patterns arising in the two Europes under cold war conditions have caused or reinforced tensions and conflicts within and between Third World societies. The East–West arms race and the cold war-influenced changes in the structure of the European economics and their trade relations have also made an impact, a mostly unfavourable one, on the world market position of developing countries and their structural role in the international division of labour, thereby also on the life and development conditions of their society.

It would, of course, be too easy, but hardly well-founded, either to relate all the aggravated tensions, intra-society and inter-state conflicts, militarization tendencies, regional wars and arms races etc. to the East–West confrontation as the manifestation of the struggle of the two world-systems in the arena of the Third World, or to present not only the latter but also Europe itself as the victim of the 'superpower game'. The former is suggested by the paradigm of bipolarism, this very product of the Cold War itself, which identifies the historical struggle of the two social systems with the confrontation of the two military blocks (attributing a messianic or evil role to each respectively), while the latter is suggested by the paradigm of the 'superpower-twins', this curious ideological reflexion of the contradictory period of a limited, partial and temporary détente with an ongoing arms race, which accuses both superpowers of being equally evil for all the conditions endangering peace and security, for all international conflicts, for oppression and militarization in the world, thereby exempting every other actor from responsibility.

These paradigms are misleading not only because of the oversimplification of the historical contradiction of social systems and the actual differences between the two superpowers in their roles in the world process of social and national emancipation, but also because of the neglect of the very interactions between East–West and North–South relations and those which the internal changes and political actions within the Third World are exerting also on superpower relations and policy.

As a consequence of the Cold War confrontation, practically all political changes in the Third World have been seen in the context of a bipolar world, as shifts in East–West power relations, and thereby calling forth reactions by the major powers. This explains why those tendencies to militarization and political polarization stemming from the local specificities of the socio-economic structure and from the historical conditions of national liberation[8] have been reinforced by those resulting from the transfer of the East-West confrontation to the Third World, and why, at the same time, they have also contributed to the sharpening of the East–West conflict.

In so far as the centre-periphery conflicts get absorbed in East–West conflicts, or interpreted as part of them, both the traditional colonial powers and the post-war neo-colonial ones have had to resort to the support and military forces of NATO, while any support from the East to national movements of the Third World has been conceived by NATO as serving the spread of communism.

Owing to the real or assumed linkages of domestic political forces with external, world political ones, the chance for minority groups to seize or keep state power in several Third World countries has certainly increased. This refers not only to those puppet regimes established in the process of decolonization by neo-colonial forces, but also to many other regimes arising as products of coups-d'état. The external relations of internal political forces have become a part of the domestic power game so much so that the governing forces, as well as the opposition have often adjusted their political-ideological face accordingly and declared, irrespective of their original political philosophy and real social class background, a political goal identical with that of the supporting foreign power, thereby pleasing and obliging the latter and irritating its adversary.

What is worse is that, under the protection of foreign powers, the leadership of political regimes feels much less the need for a domestic alliance policy than the necessity to come to terms and make constructive compromises with the forces of opposition, and often shows a decreased tolerance vis-á-vis the opposition or even neutral domestic elements. This gives rise to the tendency of over-radicalization, which, in many cases, may also follow from an external military threat, from permanent pressure caused by the real or assumed danger of military intervention of the opposite foreign power, and leads, as a rule, to unrealistic economic policies, to the over-politicization of social and cultural life, to coercive, administrative ways of conflict management, to an overgrowth of security forces and an excessive role of the state and the army. Besides inducing an increasing militarization of society, it often also generates or aggravates conflicts with foreign powers and neighbouring countries, particularly the allies of the former.

In the social content of over-radicalization there are, of course, substantial differences between left and right regimes. In so far as the former try to reach goals beneficial to the people without its democratic participation and contrary to the given conditions of reality, the result is an organized violence applied against the people. Not to mention how easily an over-radicalized leftist regime, by becoming increasingly anti-democratic and aggravating the social tension, can actually pave the way for a rightist radical regime and vice versa. Though the over-radicalization of some regimes may, paradoxically, widen the manoeuvring opportunities for others, and though the major powers, no doubt, often try to moderate their own protected clients in this over-radicalization, on the whole it is one of the important sources of conflicts and dangers for peace and security on national, regional and international level alike. This reflects the impact of the East–West confrontation in the Third World.

Polarization, according to Eastern or Western orientation, often extends over the given region, too, which may generate new conflicts in the latter and set new obstacles to regional integration or cooperation, in addition to those stemming from the colonial legacy. Those marked asymmetries and disproportions characterizing the former pattern of international trade and communication relations of the developing countries, namely the heavy bias for long-distance, overseas relations with the metropolitan partners and against intra-regional cooperation (which have not only cost a lot for them but also reduced their security in many ways) have been partly replaced or rather complemented by a pattern hardly less asymmetric. True, such a reorientation of trade and communication of some countries in a given region towards the East for political or other reasons, demonstrating the chance for the others to do the same, undoubtedly reduces the economic dependence of the periphery on the dominant centre of the capitalist world-economy, and also contributes positively to the diversification of international relations, widens the manoeuvring opportunities for developing countries, improves their bargaining position and may actually provide a way out of the economic blackmail and political pressure put on them by the West. In so far as it also implies, however, a disproportionate share of the uneconomic long distance transport and communication as compared to the intra-regional ones, we can conceive it only, and at best, as a temporary restructuring of the international relations and division of labour, which may cause additional conflicts or difficulties in intra-regional cooperation.

The Eastern or Western orientation of the regimes of a region can produce regional conflicts and a loss of internal cohesion. Parallel with all the benefits the recipient developing countries may gain from European technical assistance, and despite their undoubtedly improved bargaining position given the end of the technical assistance monopoly of the metropolitan countries, the presence and the influence of foreign experts and the training by foreign scholarship of the first generation of intelligentsia, may prove to be of a disintegrating effect on local or regional society. The divergence of education of the elite in a given region does not promote the strengthening of cohesion forces.

Polarization, if merely or primarily resulting from external effects and not rooted in the social reality, hinders rather than promotes the inherent tendencies of social transformation to come to force. The result is increased disintegration, instability and outward-orientation.

The divided, heterogeneous and outward-oriented nature of domestic political forces has provided good opportunities for foreign powers to manipulate them against each other, even independently of the East–West competition, for the sake of *divide et impera* or possible economic benefits. An obvious example of the latter is the rather frequent case when a European or other major power sells armaments to both the government and rebellious forces in a developing country. It is also worth mentioning that support to opposition or rebellious forces in Third World countries has often been related to the rivalry within the West itself, rather than to the East–West confrontation.

Under the conditions of the manifold inter-state and intra-societal conflicts of the Third World, partly inherited from the past as a colonial legacy, partly generated or reinforced recently by the externalisation of the East-West confrontation, the projected or accelerated polarization, and the manipulations of various local forces against each other by foreign powers, it is, of course, easier for the tendency of *militarization* to come into force and for the military conflicts and arms race to spread, particularly if peaceful conflict-management is hindered by external influence and outward orientation, or its appropriate mechanism has not yet developed.

Since the Second World War there have been many regional or local wars in the Third World, linked with the East–West confrontation in Europe, either in the sense of having been induced or stimulated by European powers and arms exporters, or in the sense that armed conflicts were shifted from Europe, where a direct military clash would cause a nuclear holocaust, to the Third World. Due to the enormous losses and damages to productive capacities, infrastructure and natural environment, the gravest consequences of militarization are suffered by Third World countries, particularly the least developed ones. Due not only to the smaller load-bearing capacity of the poorer and less developed countries in general, but also to the structural specificities of their underdeveloped, peripheral economies, the relative size of the military burden and the adverse effects of militarization on economic growth and equilibrium are greater in the South than in the North.

The waste of scarce resources such as qualified labour, land, capital, research capacities etc. by military use is most disastrous in countries where the basic needs of population are not yet satisfied. The growth of the military sector tends to intensify and deepen those structural distortions reproducing economic disequilibria in developing countries and thereby also reinforcing the external dependence of their economy, accompanied by a regular income drain, a balance of payments problem, cumulative indebtedness and inflation. In so far as militarization is associated with the growth of the modern enclave sector only, it contributes to the reproduction of disintegrated socio-economic structures in these countries.

The Cold War confrontation has left its marks also on the development patterns of many developing countries. Their orientation towards the East or the West often implies the adoption of the model that Eastern or Western Europe presented (in theory or practice) to them during the Cold War. These models showed not only a certain contradiction between theory and practice but also the impact of the abnormal conditions of Cold War itself. Western Europe, imitating the American way of life and intending to demonstrate the superiority of the private economies of the West over the collectivized ones of the East, built up a consumer society after the Second World War which, despite its internal contradictions, was attributed to the unlimited freedom of individual enterpreneurship, *laissez-faire* capitalism and market spontaneity. The new technologies which resulted from the post-war, or rather the war-induced, revolution of science and technology, reflected the prevailing conditions and factor endowment in the most advanced countries of the West, and were praised as beneficial and applicable to all countries of the world. The euphoria of consumerism and technologism was complemented by West-European integration which was welcomed as the success of trade liberation, despite its built-in protectionism versus outsiders.

There is no need to explain in detail here[10] how disastrous the efforts to copy this false model in the Third World have been, particularly in countries where the demonstration effects of Western consumerism induced the local elite to increase its import demands for luxurious items or to implement a policy of import-substitution industrialization. The consequent economic disequilibrium manifested in high inflation and progressing indebtedness, the widening of the rural-urban gap, the acceleration of social differentiation, the increasing marginalization of the masses and the alienation of a narrow elite etc., have led to such an explosive accumulation of social tensions in several cases as to give rise to ever more oppressive regimes.

The Eastern European model has reflected the early stage of socialist transformation in Eastern Europe in the 1950s, characterized by cold war isolation, an autarchic economic policy, over-centralization, forced industrialization with a priority to heavy industry, an artificially high rate of accumulation and quantitative growth, an excessive restriction of market forces, detailed central planning, growing bureaucracy and overall state control in all fields of social life etc., not to mention the massive violation of the law, restrictions of human rights, the humiliating personal cult and spirit of suspicion also prevailing in that period.

Though social reality has substantially changed since that time in Eastern Europe, many features of it have survived or influenced the ideology and political practice of some socialist-oriented developing countries leading to even more unfavourable consequences than in Eastern Europe, such as serious bottlenecks, the growth of a state bureaucracy and administrative regulations without real economic development. In fact, difficulties which threaten to undermine the social basis or *raison d'être* of the regime.

Responding to the above by attributing all Third World problems to the East or the West is no less sterile or irrelevant, or by turning back to obsolete traditionalism, parochial fundamentalism and isolationism can cause additional intra-societal conflicts, violence and oppression, particularly in the simple substitution of a North–South bipolarism for the East–West one.

Such a substitution, i.e., the idea of another bipolar world implying an antagonism between the 'rich North' and the 'poor South', irrespective of the differences in social systems within each and the actual heterogeneity and distribution of world social forces, also neglects the very interactions between North–South and East–West relations, and ignores the differences and the interlinkages between centre-periphery conflicts and system-struggle.

Despite all the positive features in the Declaration and Action Programme to establish a *New International Economic Order,* these documents reflect such neglect and ignorance. Besides some other weaknesses and inconsistencies in the NIEO idea and programme,[11] the one-sidedness leaves out of proper account the problematique of East–West relations and this partly explains the failure of NIEO.

On the other side of the coin, the relatively short-lived and no less inconsistent process of *détente* has remained limited to the North, or rather only Europe, with hardly any implications for the South. In this case the treatment of East–West relations has involved a neglect of the problematique of North–South relations, despite the obvious interactions.

Though there were, of course, exceptions trying to establish a link between the improvement of East-West relations and that of North–South ones (such as e.g. the Soviet proposal to devote to development assistance a part of the financial resources to be released by a reduction of military expenditures or the reports of the Brandt Commission, etc.), in general the separation of the North–South and East–West issues has remained characteristic.

No doubt, détente has brought about many changes, some irreversible.

The 'iron curtain' between the two Europes has been gradually lifted, East–West diplomatic relations (including the two Germanies) have been normalized, tourism has developed, and, in many fields and forms, economic, technological, scientific and cultural cooperation between Eastern and Western European countries has made progress, etc. This may explain why even the dramatic worsening of relations between the United States and the Soviet Union in the late 1970s and early 1980s has not led Europe back to the Cold War.

Détente has failed however, to induce a more realistic approach to national movements in the South. So long as political changes originating in the context of centre-periphery relations are seen as shifts in the context of East–West relations, and while all endeavours of national liberation or emancipation in the Third World are viewed as a success for, or a subversion by, the Soviet Union, then North–South relations will continue to undermine a Soviet–American détente. For example, while the North has viewed the NIEO as an East-backed attack against the West, the South has tended to perceive détente as a sign of the Unity of the North against it. Rather than zero-sum games, in reality negative sum-games have developed. The symptoms and consequences of the latter have clearly appeared in the light of the global crisis of the prevailing world economic and political order, which has also dispelled many old illusions and misconceptions.

The empirical lessons and theoretical analysis of the global crisis[12] have revealed that:

- large-scale and intensive *interdepencies* exist in the contemporary world upon which the peace and security of regions mutually depends;
- there is only one, single world-economy implying an organic system and not merely a sum or juxtaposition of individual national economies, and, if any one part of it is 'sick', no other part can be spared the consequences;
- even the most developed capitalist economies of the dominant centre are vulnerable to the adverse effects of the concerted unilateral actions of other, less developed countries, as the oil embargo and subsequent price explosion showed;
- such unilateral actions do not damage only, or even primarily, those targeted but also others, often including their initiators;
- despite their substantially different socio-economic systems and one-time isolation, socialist countries are also part of the same world economic order whose crisis affects them also, while their economic difficulties also aggravate the world economic system;
- East–West confrontation can paralyse the work of important international organizations and global negotiations reducing further their abilities to cope with global problems, and contributing to the institutional nature of the crisis;
- global militarization and the expanding arms race have not only

increased the direct dangers for peace and security but, by playing a decisive role in the initiation and perpetuation of the economic crisis, have also endangered human life conditions;

- the prevailing pattern of the world division of labour, particularly the markedly unequal and imbalanced structure of the division of labour between industrial centres and the primary-producing peripheries has led to massive indebtedness which contains the germs of crisis and a restructuring would be in the interests of all nations;

- the mass misery, poverty and unemployment of the Third World and the increasing inequality of the world distribution of income will not only cause growing tensions and explosive conflicts in the South but will affect the security of the North and its East–West relations, as well as limit the marketing facilities and export growth of developed countries;

- no country in the world, not even the biggest, and no group of countries, not even the most coherent, can isolate itself from the world successfully, and all attempts of single countries to escape from the crisis at the expense of others are doomed to fail, at least in a longer run;

- no 'model' can be successfully transplanted to, and copied by, other societies;

- the squandering wastefulness of acquisitive consumerism in Western society has not only caused resource problems, imbalances, increasing import dependence (particularly in energy supply) and a relative deterioration of the quality of life in the West but, by its demonstration effect, has induced similar tendencies in the South and aggravated their economic difficulties. Clearly there is a need for a general reorientation of production and consumption towards the real human needs of the masses in the most developed economies;

- over-centralized management and planning systems with their focus on quantitative growth and forced accumulation which developed in the East under the conditions of cold war isolation have proved to be inappropriate not only for these countries but for the development of economic cooperation with the West and the South, as well as a model for the latter;

- protectionism, discrimination and other barriers to international economic relations between North and South or East and West are harmful to all, even those applying them;

- neither détente, East–West *rapprochement* and disarmament or armaments' limitation agreements can bring about lasting and irreversible results for world peace and security unless accompanied by definite progress in establishing a new international economic order and effective assistance to developing countries, nor can the idea of NIEO be put into practice if the East–West confrontation and arms race continues.

It follows as a final conclusion that the so called East–West and North–South relations cannot be isolated from each other; that the complexity and interactions of the world processes of social and of national emancipation make the ideology and policy of bipolarism unrealistic and self-defeating; and that the assumed zero-sum-games in economic and political power relations in both the East–West and North–South context necessarily turn out to be negative-sum-games.

Thus, if Europe wishes to contribute positively to the peace and security of the Third World, its task is not simply to return to the path of Helsinki, but to return to the path of a new world order, i.e., to promote not only peaceful intra-regional cooperation between countries of different social systems and the mutual disintegration of the two military blocks but also the gradual elimination of centre-periphery relations, the process of national emancipation and social progress in the Third World, and the establishment of a really new, democratic and demilitarized world order.

Notes

1. T. Szentes, 'World Peace, Security and Global Transformation: the Role of Europe' Paper delivered to *UNU Conference on Human and Social Development in Europe within Interregional and Global Perspectives.* Warsaw, 4–8 June 1984.
2. See Carl Gösta Widstrand (ed.) *African Boundary Problems.* The Scandinavian Institute of African Studies. Uppsala, 1969.
3. See Rajni Kothari, 'Peace, Development and Life', paper for the *UNU Consultative Meeting on Global and Regional Aspects of Peace.* London, 28–29 June, 1984 (Mimeo).
4. For a more detailed explanation see T. Szentes, *The Political Economy of Underdevelopment.* Akadémiai, Budapest, 1983, part two, ch. 3.
5. Szentes, op. cit., part two, chs. 1–2.
6. It is only an extreme version of the 'dependency school' and a vulgar Marxist critique of imperialism which attributes all the phenomena and causes of underdevelopment and the periphery position of Third World countries exclusively to external factors, ignoring both local collaboration with the latter or their voluntary choice of peripheral development as manifested in foreign direct investments. For a Marxist analysis on the role of 'internal' factors in periphery development in a capitalist world economy see A. G. Frank *Lumpen-bourgeoisie and Lumpendevelopment. Dependency, Class and Politics in Latin America.* New York, Monthly Review Press, 1972. For an analysis on the dialectical interrelationship of external and internal factors of underdevelopment see T. Szentes, op. cit., 1983.
7. For an interpretation, in a systemic sense, of the geo-economic region of Eastern Europe and an analysis of its role in the world economy see M. Simai, 'The Role of the Socialist Countries of Eastern Europe in the World Economy', *Trade and Development: An UNCTAD Review,* No. 5, 1984.
8. For example, the excessive role of the army in political life, or the need, in many cases, for armed struggle for independence against the colonial power, or the emergence of independent states with artificial boundaries which can only retain their territorial integrity through a heavy role for the army.
9. See István Kende, 'Local Wars 1945–1976', In A. Eide and M. Thee (eds.)

Problems of Contemporary Militarism. London. Croom Helm. 1980.

10. For a more detailed explanation see T. Szentes 'A New Emerging Pattern of International Division of Labour with Neo-Colonial Dependence. A Possible Strategy to Escape', *Peace and the Sciences.* Vienna, 1975. No. 2. or 'Socioeconomic Effects of Two Patterns of Foreign Capital Investments' in P. Gutkind and I. Wallerstein (eds), *The Political Economy of Contemporary Africa.* Sage, London, 1976.

11. For my critical comments see T. Szentes: 'The Strategic Issues of NIEO and Global Negotiations', *Second Congress of Third World Economists,* 1981, and 'The conception of a New International Order – is it a fashionable slogan or a feasible strategy?', *IPSA Round Table Conference*, 1982. Tokyo.

12. See T. Szentes, 'Global nature, origins and strategic implications of the world economic crisis: an Eastern European view', *Trade and Development: An UNCTAD Review*, No. 4, Winter, 1982.

6. East-West Rivalry and Regional Conflicts in the Third World

by **Raimo Värynen**

Introduction

International relations can be observed from either the top or the bottom; and the results are obviously rather different. A great-power perspective argues that international relations flow out of the domestic conditions of major powers and from their mutual relations, often characterized by tensions and rivalries. Great powers are assumed to be expansive – provided they are really great powers – and thus subject minor nations to their domination. An important difference is whether this domination is achieved through agreement on the spheres of influence between the great powers or obtained in a competitive fashion. In the latter case, peripheral areas become theatres of rivalry between the leading powers in the system.

The peripheral perspective is a diametrically opposed interpretation of international relations and focuses on the position of 'people without history', to use Eric R. Wolf's characterization. This perspective may have two variants. One may explore the peripheries as objects of international relations and focus on the impact of great-power policies on them. The other approach may stress that peripheries are not mere objects of international power games, but they have a measure of independence and can therefore shape, in part, the course of international relations. Certainly they are not able to lead the world, but they may be capable of injecting their own interests and values into these relations. This kind of a philosophy can be discerned, for instance, in the activities of the Movement of Non-Aligned Countries or the Islamic Conference Organization.

One of the virtues of the peripheral perspective is that the conflict dynamic in the international system is not attributed solely to the preponderance and expansiveness of great powers. Such a perspective indicates that there are in the Third World (semi) autonomous domestic and regional factors that are conducive to violent conflicts. A look into African history, for instance, reveals that war has been an important social institution there much before the advent of Europeans. Hostility to 'the other' was made to serve the cause of political identity leading to a situation in which 'intersocietal, intertribal, or regional relations were inevitably conceived as bellicose relations'.[1]

Certainly the intrusion of European economic interests, culture and military technology into the Third World changed patterns of war and increased their overall destructiveness. Colonialism did not mean, however, only the exploitation of the peripheries and the violent suppression of local resistance. It also gave rise to colonial nationalism and the subsequent process of decolonization. Even though important decisions shaping the structure of international relations were made within and between colonial powers, the spread of colonial nationalism and new productive forces provided launching pads for more autonomous development in the periphery.

The capitalist world economy penetrated through different historical sequences into the peripheral areas of the world. Penetration was naturally an uneven process and affected precapitalist societies in different ways. The spread of capitalism spurred – for instance by means of commodity production, local industrialization and migrant labour – the emergence of novel economic formations. The uneven nature of the penetration process meant that in some areas there was an opportunity for a more rapid and partially autonomous economic development, while in others change was prevented or distorted.

This point of departure has two important implications. First, the *heterogeneity* of the world peripheries is admitted. This is due both to their separate historical development and to their differential patterns of incorporation into the world capitalist and politico-military power structure. Each social formation, whether national or regional, is historically singular in the Third World; it is assumed 'to be the product of the interaction of a particular precapitalist production mode with a world capitalism which itself is changing'.[2] Second, international relations are characterized by several *discontinuities* reflecting both the uneven process of development in various regions of the world and the prevalence of ideological, cultural and other barriers between central actors.[3]

Methodologically these considerations stress a kind of duality; the international system and local/regional formations are analytically autonomous yet at once aspects of each other. Autonomous parts of the international system operate, in other words, in the context of a global system with which these parts are interacting both in a dependent and autonomous mode. This conception has an important implication for the theory of change in international relations: 'systems composed of complex parts may expect change to come not only from the evolution of the whole . . ., or from influences without in the form of the impingement of other systems, but also from development within the parts, whose movements are endogenously determined'. That is why it is relevant to know, in addition to the constellations of power between the great powers, the ways in which the parts of the whole, for instance regional subsystems, 'may transform themselves for local reasons but with important repercussions for the entire system of relations between strong and weak'.[4]

This essay aims to develop a framework for the analysis of interaction between regional political, economic and military processes in the Third World on one hand and the changes in the great-power relationship on the other. A premise of this endeavour is that the potential of regional power centres and regional socio-economic formations has selectively increased over time. Shifts in international economic and military power relations have gradually eroded the bipolar power constellation and contributed to the *fragmentation* of the international system. As a result, 'the diffusion of power in the contemporary system raises the importance of actors at the bottom of the power hierarchy for the functioning of the system as a whole'.[5]

A consequence of this macrotendency is the rise of *regionalism* in the Third World. It is manifested both in cooperative efforts, i.e. in the establishment of regional integration arrangements, and in the emergence of relatively permanent and complex regional conflict formations. These regional subsystems are shaped both by their internal dynamics and by the forces operating in the system as a whole. Their nature is then a result of these two separate but interacting sets of dynamics. I have argued elsewhere that the establishment of regional integration groups and the emergence of regional conflict formations in the world peripheries is a part of the new process of restructuring of the international system underway since the early 1970s.[6]

Regional orders in the Third World

Before embarking upon an analysis of the interrelationships between conflicts in the Third World and the development of great-power relations, some observations are needed on the conflict dynamics in the world peripheries. Following the methodological guidelines spelled out above we consider regional conflict formations as basic units of analysis. In the Third World conflicts are seldom transregional, but they occur between neighbouring countries or, at a minimum, between countries located in the same geographical region. This means, among other things, that such confrontations seldom remain bilateral, but other neighbouring countries easily become involved and convert them into multilateral conflict formations. The validity of this observation is testified by the dissemination of bilateral conflicts to the entire region in Indochina, the Arab/Persian Gulf and the Horn of Africa. The Central American case underlines how important domestic roots of conflict can be in pushing for escalation.

The selection of regional formations as a basic unit of analysis can be justified also for another reason. The economic and military presence of great powers in the Third World is somehow crystallized in them. The specific nature of the presence of one or more great powers cannot be disclosed without exploring its manifestations in individual regions. As pointed out earlier, the nature of linkages between the extraregional powers and the regional system as well as the impact of presence varies from one case to another depending on the nature of the regional order. Hence overarching theoretical formulations should be avoided before sufficiently detailed empirical studies are carried through on the regional conflicts and their connections with the world of great powers.

An analysis by Carl Brown of the Eastern Question in the 19th century can be used, with some qualifications, to highlight the postwar international system as well. The Eastern Question was characterized by a vulnerable regional system (i.e. the Ottoman Middle East) which was exposed to an expanding system (i.e. Europe). Even though the states involved differed in terms of size and social system, both regional systems were composed of a multiplicity of autonomous political entities. The study argues that, despite the signs of great-power bilateralism in 1956–81, the Middle Eastern system is now returning to a more normal pattern of multilateralism that was characteristic to previous stages of the Eastern Question. The vulnerability and multiplicity of state actors in the Middle East has been a constant feature of this regional system.

This feature is typical of other conflict formations as well. It does not prescribe, however, the manner in which the regional systems are otherwise ordered. There are at least three conceivable *regional orders* in the Third World. The first of them may be termed *regional anarchy* where there is no clear-cut ordering principle and where rules of the game have not been institutionalized. Such an anarchy is manifested, among other things, by changing alliances and the prevalence of the use of force between states involved. It is not probably an enduring order, but states of the region obviously seek for a less volatile and violent constellation of their mutual relations.

An alternative to anarchy is the order based on the influence wielded by a *dominant power*. In this case the region is hierarchically structured due to the uneven distribution of economic and military resources. Regional stability is ensured by the ability of the dominant power to control, and ultimately to coerce, those on lower rungs of the hierarchy. An order based on hierarchy and domination tends also to be unstable because such organizing principles mobilize opposition. It searches for a regional system which serves better the interests of those in subordinated positions.

The third model of a regional system differs from the domination model in that there are several relatively equal powers as in the anarchical model. A difference is that in the *balance-of-power* model there is an order that is based on countervailing coalitions and on their adjustment to changing realities. A merit of the balance of power is that the alternative rules of the game have been rather clearly spelled out both by scholars and diplomatic practitioners. A problem is that the balance conception is too mechanistic and does not pay attention to socio-economic changes and differences that underline intra-national and intra-regional conflicts.[7] The weight of this critical argument is added by the fact that, in the peripheral conflicts, political and socio-economic conditions may change fairly quickly and man-operated balances of power may breakdown (into a regional anarchy in the first instance).

All these three models of regional order stem from the consideration of the underlying distribution of power and interests embedded in it. The question is whether and how the relevant actors are able to manage changes in the power distribution and in associated interests. A different approach would argue that the distribution of power and its management is given too prominent a role, and more attention should be paid to the *dynamics of integration and cooperation* in the regions. Indeed, in many regions of the Third World, institutional arrangements and modes of cooperation are developed, collective decision-making is promoted and value commitments are made.

Probably regional arrangements of cooperation and integration will become increasingly important in the future. This may also mean that their ability to contribute to regional order and to the settlement of conflicts will become more effective. So far few, if any, regional arrangements have truly been able to develop such a capability; power games rather than cooperative arrangements have dictated the outcomes of regional conflicts. This is not to say that regional political institutions (e.g. OAU and ASEAN) or more *ad hoc* efforts (e.g. the Contadora Group) are without any significance. The point is rather that their influence on regional conflicts is more incipient than established. This is, however, the way to go as it provides an alternative to the models informed by power politics that we have outlined above.

Modes of great-power involvement

Involvement and intervention of great powers in the Third World must be accounted for both by the conditions in the metropolitan and peripheral environments, as well as by the state of the international system as a whole. The answer to the causes of involvement is again dependent on the perspective we have adopted. Consonant with the orientation of this paper is the argument that the circumstances prevailing in the target state and region figure prominently in the explanation of external involvement. These circumstances are obviously a necessary but not a sufficient reason for the involvement of great powers. A similar reasoning is reflected in the conclusion that interventions into the Third World are catalyzed by the 'sudden emergence of opportunities in the target environment' or by 'threats to the position of an external actor's clients and, by extension, to the perceived interests of the external actor himself'. These events ultimately 'alter the balance of costs and benefits upon which the external actor's policy-making is based'.[8]

This conclusion implies that conditions in the target of intervention do not suffice to bring it about. External actors must have motivations of their own to react to the 'altered balance of costs and benefits'. These motivations may be domestic or associated with the rivalries with other great powers, or both. While conditions in the target catalyze specific measures of involvement, the prevailing balance of incentives and constraints in the intervener's domestic system and in the international system regulate, often effectively, the resort to such measures. Thus the great powers are assumed to have a domestically motivated strategy of involvement in the peripheries whose implementation is dependent on the nature of the international order and on the circumstances in the periphery.

Both metropolitan and peripheral factors shape the frequency and mode of involvement. In the metropole, the rivalry between great powers is probably a more important reason for involvement than their domestic motivations, even though these factors cannot be easily disentangled from each other. Great-power rivalries are to a large extent results of incompatibilities in their ideologies and interests. These rivalries as such do not, however, bring about the essential preconditions for involvement in the Third World, but they are primarily of local/regional making. Thus the circumstances in the peripheries are independent causes for involvement that are continuously fed into the competition between great powers. Finally, the prevailing structure of the international system regulates the magnitude and direction of intervention. Thus in a bipolar system each great power is assumed to maintain order, by coercion if necessary, in its own sphere of influence, while competitive interventions occur in the 'grey areas' between these spheres.

To be more specific we may make a distinction between three modes of involvement by the great powers in the Third World. *Unilateral domination* occurs when a given great power has been able to establish its hegemony in the region. Such a situation may reflect either the existence of a *hegemonic power* which has gained ascendance in a given region because of its preponderance in the entire international system or the existence of such a regional dominance that is acknowledged by other great powers. The impact of unilateral domination is dependent on the type of regional order in which it is exercised.

Another theoretical possibility is *bilateral competition* between two great powers. In such a competition great powers are sensitive to the policies of each other and apparently follow rather closely the changes in the periphery. There is a dual purpose in this type of game; promote one's own position in the area and, to serve partly this purpose, to prevent the adversary from gaining from changes. Another duality involved is the inherent logic of escalation embedded in the great-power rivalries and the need to manage the crises in order to avoid the escalation to dangerous heights. Bilateral competition, which does not expand to all the regions as some of them will be unilaterally dominated in any case, is most probable in a *bicentric international system*.

The third possibility is then *multilateral competition* in which at least three major powers participate. The main difference between bilateral and multilateral competition is that, in the latter, there is the possibility of coalition formation and dissolution between major powers. Competition between several major actors in the world peripheries is naturally most

probably in a *multicentric international system.* Major powers constituting
it are, however, seldom of equal weight and this fact tends to modify the
nature of competition. Middle powers are obviously able to become
involved only in a limited number of regions and issue areas. They have
also a greater need to cooperate with the leading power closer to them in
terms of ideology and common material interests.

The recognition of *heterogeneity* both in the peripheries and in the
metropoles leads one to observe altogether nine alternative regional orders
or disorders in the Third World.

Table 6.1 Great-power involvement and regional orders in the Third World

	Unilateral domination	*Bilateral competition*	*Multilateral competition*
Dominant regional power	Sub-imperialism	Bilateral or multilateral competition for an alignment with the regional power centre	
Regional balance of power	External power as a balancer	Polarized balance of power	Complex balance of power
Regional anarchy	Divide et impera	Volatile regional order; efforts at polarized bloc formation	Disorganization

These alternative regional orders probably cover most real cases, even
though they may not exhaust all of them. They may be further grouped in
several different ways. The diagonal from the upper left down to the lower
right corner may be termed, for instance, the *order-disorder dimension.* On
this dimension the regional orders vary from *hierarchically* organized
systems, where the weaker units are subordinated to a dual pressure by
both the extra- and intra-regional power centres, to a largely *horizontally*
organized and competitive system in which, at best, a complex balance of
power can be established.

Different types of regional orders have a different propensity to shape
relations between the leading powers in a bipolar system. In general terms it
may be argued that the more there is competition between the leading
powers and the more anarchical and unstable is the regional order, the
more complications there will be in the management of great-power
relations. If this is true, the best world to assure stable relations between the
leading powers would be a hierarchically ordered system where spheres of
interests have been divided and potential conflicts are controlled by mutual
efforts at management. Such a world would be, however, at variance with
other values than the stability of great-power relations.

To better understand the *dynamics* of regional orders further theoretical insights would be needed. One perspective is provided by the *theory of structuration* which aims at integrating spatial and temporal components of action systems. According to Anthony Giddens, structures are 'situated practices' in the cross-sections of time and space routes or 'time-space edges' in which potential or actual social transformation may occur. Thus, to study the 'structuration of social systems is to study the conditions governing their continuity, change or dissolution'.

Structures exist independently of any particular action, but provide rules and resources for individual acts. Structures are, in other words, dual in that they both constrain and enable action. Actions may thus mobilize pre-existing structures and give rise to new ones. This involves the 'use of power as a necessary implication of the logical connection between human action and transformative capacity'. Structures enabling or constraining action may be, in the time-space dimensions, proximate or distant from the practical consciousness of actors. Structures vary, in other words, on the presence-absence dimension.

For Giddens 'locales' are physical settings associated with the operations of collectivities. Locales are, in turn, usually regionalized on a time-space basis. By 'regions' within locales, Giddens means 'aspects of settings which are normatively implicated in systems of interaction, such that they are in some way set apart, for certain individuals or types of individuals, or for certain activities or types of activities'.[9]

Seen from the standpoint of our research problem, the theory of structuration is suggestive rather than a definite guideline. One of its functions is to point out that the region should not be comprehended only as a geographical unit, but also as a bundle of actions in which both regional and extra-regional actors participate. Structures are changing on the time-space dimension, both constraining the activities and enabling their use for system transformation. The mode of transformation is apparently dependent on the manner in which regional and extra-regional actors meet each other in a given locale. The process of regionalization defines the specific way in which actors and their activities are 'set apart' from the overall international context. Regions are, in other words, territorially-based, yet action-oriented structures which embody rules and resources constituted by the action itself.

In the light of the preceding analysis two processes of structuration may be singled out specifically for further analysis. The first process may be indicated by the movement between the counterpoints of *hierarchy* and *emancipation*. In the process of emancipation a disorder may be a consequence, and perhaps an intermediate step towards a new order, of the opposition from the old order based on hierarchy. Another significant process of structuration is the movement between *unicentric* and *multicentric* systems in the relations between great powers.[10] By combining these two processes the following summary of theoretical remarks may be obtained:

Table 6.2 Main processes of structuration in international relations

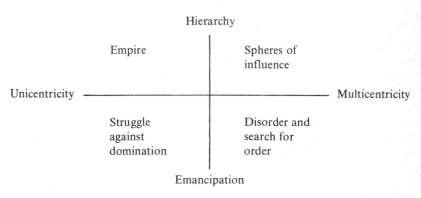

Hierarchy

	Empire	Spheres of influence
Unicentricity		Multicentricity
	Struggle against domination	Disorder and search for order

Emancipation

It may be argued that there is a dynamic, and even a dialectical, relationship between the counterpoints of these two dimensions: hierarchy encourages emancipation which in turn motivates efforts to restore hierarchy, and in a similar fashion there is a tension between uni- and multicentricity. The international systems are historically shifting in the field of forces defined by these two dimensions.

Before moving to explore these historical variations one should point out that the probability of great-power confrontations is lowest in bi- and multicentric systems in which the subordinated regions are divided into spheres of interests (in a unicentric hierarchical system the conflict between great powers is, by definition, impossible). The strengthening of the forces of emancipation in a unicentric system gives rise to a vertical conflict between centre and periphery. The most conflict-prone situation appears to be one in which there is a shift towards bi- or multicentricity in the centre and towards emancipation in the periphery. In such a situation the periphery is feeding its own conflict dynamics into the relations between centre powers which, in their turn, are not capable of managing effectively their mutual rivalries. It may be argued that the international system is now moving towards such a state.

This theoretical scheme is structuralist in that it focuses on the horizontal and vertical dimensions of the international system and on the dynamics of change embedded in them. The shifts between unicentricity and multi-centricity are assumed to reflect the processes of *power transition* in the centre of the international system. These processes are results of the combined and uneven development which is an enduring feature of the international economic system. Uneven development is a systemic pheno-menon, even though it is rooted in differential rates between technological and institutional *innovations* between nations.

The processes of power transitions in the centre are themselves causes of confrontations between major powers, almost independently of what is happening in the peripheries. Their management is, however, complicated by the tensions that may be injected from the regional conflict formations of the Third World. To understand this aspect of international change, one has to explore the determinants of how the *capacity for change* is accumulated in the peripheries. Usually it is a selective process benefiting only the few. It may be that the spread of economic and military capabilities to the peripheries starts during the period of unicentricity, but continues during the competition embedded in the shift towards multicentricity.

Competition in the centre seems thus to be associated with the selective emancipation of the peripheries. In the beginning at least the emancipation is political by its character as the substantive hegemony inherited from the era of unicentricity continues to restrain economic emancipation. Political rebellion and military unruliness in the peripheries tend to precede the material liberation of the peripheries. This may be an explanation why the political demands for the redistribution of economic resources in the global scale (NIEO) did not produce any tangible results in the 1970s. The international system is not yet 'ripe' for such a change, for the redistribution of material wealth.

To avoid a structuralist bias – i.e. the implication that conflict-proneness only depends on the disjunctures between uni- and multicentricity on the one hand and between hierarchy and emancipation on the other – additional variables should be incorporated into the analysis. One relevant variable is the nature of *political management* of great-power relations. The management systems may be characterized by the degree of their flexibility and by their capacity of restraint. In a flexible system of management, states may realign rather easily, while in an inflexible system it is based on sustained confrontation between two or more alliances. A management system is restraining when it has collective capacity to steer the developments in the desired direction.[11] The conflict-proneness would be reduced most effectively by a management system that combines flexibility and restraint, while an inflexible, unrestraining system is the worst conceivable alternative.

Transformations in the international system

In the late 1960s a major process of transformation started in the international system. In fact the postwar period can be divided into two parts. Their turning point occurred roughly in the period of 1968–1973 when the crisis of the postwar international order deepened. It can be argued that during these years both economic and political cycles diverted to different paths than those they had followed during the preceding quarter-century. This turn to a new international system has been complex and multi-layered. In the *productive mode* of transformation it was reflected in the redistribution of production capacity, ability to innovate and world markets of goods and capital. In the *monetary sphere* the shifts were more volatile, but symptomatic of the redistribution of economic capabilities and broader tensions between industrialized countries. In the *strategic mode* of transformation the East-West dimension is more important than in the productive mode. The strategic relationship of the United States and the Soviet Union was transformed in the late 1960s from US supremacy to rough parity. Yet, these two great powers retained their bipolar dominance vis-à-vis the other states without any interruption.

The period from 1945 to 1968 was characterized by *US predominance* in the productive and financial areas. By 1968 the competitive position of the US was, however, steadily undermined by the inflationary spiral which also threatened international free trade and the position of the dollar. Furthermore, the American alliance system had been overextended: the economic price of predominance had become too high. The toll had been further added to by the costs of military involvement abroad, in particular in Vietnam. To ameliorate the situation, the Nixon Administration acted unilaterally by devaluing the dollar in 1971 and by rejecting the system of fixed- exchange rates.

These decisions were 'an adroit manoeuvre to extricate the United States from the wreckage of its previous grand strategy'. The economic burden of US predominance was increasingly shifted to the shoulders of her allies. The premise in the new policy of the Nixon Administration was that the United States should retain her leadership. This would happen by devolving commitments and their costs to others, but maintaining the essential strings of control in her hands.

During the era of US economic predominance American military hegemony was by no means total. Even though the United States possessed for a few years the monopoly over atomic weapons, this supremacy could not be converted into all-embracing military dominance. This was largely due to the geographical spread of Soviet conventional military power. That is why parts of Asia and especially Eastern and Central Europe were largely outside US military control. This observation does not undermine, however, the point that the United States enjoyed a true predominance in international relations for 25 years after World War II. Economic hegemony can be maintained also by less than complete military control: 'The military conditions for economic hegemony are met if the economically preponderant country has sufficient military capabilities to prevent incursions by others that would deny it access to major areas of economic activity'.[12]

Even though the theory of *hegemonic stability* should be taken with a pinch of salt, it is probably right in arguing that the existence of an effective political leader in the international system provides it with an order. The preponderant economic power is able to institute such rules and norms in the system which are obeyed by others, either reluctantly or in their self-interest. Even though there have been repeated efforts to reconstitute US predominance, her decline in the productive mode has continued. As a consequence rules and norms of the previous international order have been gradually eroded. This means that the US ability to steer international economic and political relations has decreased.

In comparison to other centres of the capitalist world, Western Europe in particular, the US position has been in long-term decline. The socialist countries of Europe are also somewhat stronger in relative terms than they were in the 1950s, even though their growth prospects have been dim for some time now. In particular since the early 1970s new centres of economic power have emerged in the Third World. The rise of military industries in, and the transfer of arms and military technology to, the Third World indicates that military power in the periphery and its capacity for resistance is spreading. Despite this tendency bipolarity in the stretegic mode is still the rule, but in the productive mode there has been a veritable shift towards multipolarity. As a consequence the fragmentation of the old economic order is taking place.

During the period of US predominance the world was hierarchically ordered, even though the colonial powers tried to maintain their own international hierarchies. Yet, hierarchies in various issue areas were probably more concordant before than after the transition period of 1968–1973. This means that the transformation of the international system is reflected by two processes: the diffusion and diversification of power. *Diffusion* refers to the dissemination of economic and military resources, assisted often by transnational corporations, to the world's peripheries. *Diversification* means the emergence of new power resources, including new political and cultural motives of action.

As observed previously, the international military structure is still predominantly based on the duopolistic control of nuclear explosives and on mutually exclusive military alliances. They have not been, however, able to prevent the diffusion and diversification of power leading to the process of fragmentation in international relations. A similar conclusion is reached by Stanley Hoffman who points out that there is 'no longer one hierarchy based on geo-military power. There are separate functional hierarchies'.[13]

Not only has US relative preponderance declined in the productive area, but also the Soviet Union has faced greater hurdles than before. The growth of her economic and technological power in the world economy has decelerated. There was no similar sharp downturn in Soviet economic growth as there was in Western growth in the beginning of the 1970s. Rather the Soviet slowdown has been a gradual process that originated earlier than in the West. The slowdown has been probably due to the growing disjunction between the centralized system of planning and management and the demands of a modern economy. The present policy of economic and technological innovation in the Soviet Union aims at reversing the slowdown by making the planning system more effective and flexible.

There is also evidence that, in economic terms, the allies of the Soviet Union are becoming more of a liability than before. This is obviously due in part to the internal dynamics of development in the socialist bloc. (e.g.

Poland's indebtedness), but also a reflection of the global economic crisis. In the words of Valerie Bunce 'the dynamics of a regional hierarchical system and the dynamics of the world capitalist system in economic recession led to the semiperipheralization of the Soviet bloc in the global economy'.[14] This tendency has manifested itself in particular since the early 1970s onwards.

Conflicts in the period of US predominance

Wars have been a regular phenomenon in the Third World, and often industrial powers have participated in them. Until the late 1960s they were usually efforts at emancipation, by military means, from hierarchical subordination to the capitalist centres of the world. A compliance/rebellion relationship is still operating in centre-periphery relations and involves 'efforts by one more authoritative, or powerful actor to teach a particular outlook to a second actor'. The predominance of the US contributed directly to the adoption of a *world-order policy* that aimed at the containment of rebellions in the periphery. This meant simply that the United States became the leading *counter-revolutionary power* against the challenges posed by the forces of nationalism and socialism. The role of any counter-revolutionary power is to suppress forces of dissent and to look for allies to aid in such a policy. A central problem of the US government after the late 1940s was

> to find allies among the southern elites who were able to contain and direct the changes taking place in these lands and who were at the same time likely to be dependable participants in a world order where a range of American security interests... would be respected.[14]

The revolt in the periphery started almost immediately after World War II. The revolution in China, considered a 'loss' in the United States, opened the floodgates. As additional examples one can refer to the US role in Greece (1946–49), Iran and Guatemala (1954), Cuba (1961), Congo (1960–65), the Dominican Republic (1965) and Vietnam. The support to counter-revolution in these and other cases was intended to keep the peripheral economies open to her activities.[15] This has occasionally demanded resistance to Soviet policy when ideological incompatibilities have further fuelled the confrontation.

During the period 1945–68, the confrontation between the major powers was not solely between the United States and the Soviet Union. The efforts of France and Great Britain to maintain their old colonial systems and their own world-order policies rekindled disagreements and tensions in their relations with the United States. These disagreements were eased, however, by the gradual dissolution of the British and French empires. French resistance to US policy in the Third World has continued longer probably for the reason that Paris has tried to maintain an independent power position in international relations, while London has accepted more easily the replacement of British power by American. This had become apparent as early as 1946 when the United States realized the strategic importance of British air bases in the Mediterranean and in the Middle East. In particular, from such bases air strikes could potentially be directed at the Soviet Union.

The Suez crisis of 1956 illustrates how the American world-order policy operated. The Eisenhower Administration refused to co-operate militarily with the Soviet Union to pacify the situation in the Middle East. It also criticized heavily its allies, Great Britain and France, and effectively tried to check their military operations in Sinai. The motive was in part to deprive the Soviet Union of any opportunities for direct involvement in the crisis and hence strengthen US control of Middle East. Another motive, and it may have been shared with the Soviet Union, was to push the two West European powers 'into secondary positions in a region in which ... they had been the major external powers till quite recently'.[17]

This kind of a push reflected the desire of the United States to preserve the hierarchic world order in which her economic and military resources assured the leading position. The Anglo-French military operation in Suez had deviated from the rules of such an order which the United States sought to maintain within the Western alliance as well. US policy makers were critical of France and Great Britain because of their *parochialism*; they defended only their geographically and functionally limited interests which were usually inherited from the colonial period.

The United States, in turn, defined her role as *universal* in the manner every hegemonic power has done. With the Soviet Union becoming more active in the Third World, the United States could not focus on selected areas only, but she had to safeguard Western interests in all major areas of the world. This presupposed Western primacy, based on the US strategic arsenal, to deter the Soviet Union from spreading her influence further. Politically the Western powers were also expected to work in a co-ordinated manner under the US direction.[18] As a consequence, the policy of containment had to become global.

This was in fact no new idea discovered in 1956: a similar US approach had prevailed from at least 1950 when the Truman-Acheson leadership extended political and military commitments to Asia.[19] The extension of containment to Asia crystallized in the Korean War. This war 'institutionalized a set of operational premises' embodied in the NSC-68 document. These stated simply that the Soviet Union would resort to aggression if she was not checked by countervailing military power both in the global and regional contexts, first in Central Europe but also in various parts of Asia. That is why the United States must 'attend to the power ratio focused on the prime military-industrial regions', even though she should 'not neglect local imbalances in secondary and tertiary areas' either.[20] The Korean War was, in other words, interpreted as part of the global Soviet challenge and as a threat to US predominance.

This interpretation was not totally without foundation. The Soviet Union started to turn to the Third World in 1954 and by the early 1970s was a global power.[21] The growth of Soviet activity in the Third World after the death of Stalin elicited a new political response from the Eisenhower Administration. Initially the Soviet challenge was met by a military counterreaction, crystallized in the *Eisenhower Doctrine* of 1957 and in its application in the Jordanian crisis and the intervention in Lebanon in 1958. These events revealed, however, the clumsiness of military interventions and enabled the administration to understand that Third World circumstances were changing drastically. The Soviet Union could attract nationalists in underdeveloped countries by its socio-political model and economic aid. From 1958 onwards the United States tried to counterbalance this by also promising economic aid, by encouraging national and regional development planning and by making attempts to align with the forces of change.[22] A competition of the great powers by economic, ideological and even subversive means in the Third World became pronounced with the advent of nuclear stalemate.

Towards the end of the 1950s the United States came to rely less on direct military means. The network of previously established military alliances continued to exist, though. As a consequence, the policy of *containment had become globalized and militarized*, deviating from the guidelines proposed by George Kennan. He had argued in the late 1940s that containment should be pursued by resolute political and diplomatic means rather than by military ones; self-confidence was a keyword in his strategy. Furthermore Kennan stressed strongpoint defence, a focus on some central regions, instead of perimeter defence where all areas on the Soviet borders were accorded equal importance.[23]

The Korean War also contributed in the United States to the adoption of the view that disputes in the Third World were primarily provoked, steered and utilized for her own purposes by the *outside meddler*–the Soviet Union. Such an interpretation neglected complex local and regional factors and accepted a simplified view that Soviet meddling alone gave rise to these conflicts. The invalidity of this approach is well evidenced, for example, by the 1967 war in the Middle East in which the complexity of actions and reactions rendered the 'idea of a single master planner hopelessly simplistic'. In this crisis regional initiatives also 'outweighted those from outside throughout the crisis and, most important, at the crucial turning points'.[24]

Some, but only some, credibility to the theory of an outside meddler as cause of conflicts was given by the evolving expansiveness of the Soviet Union in the Third World. In the 1950s she backed China, established relations with Egypt and other Arab countries and courted such rather remote countries as Indonesia and Cuba. These moves were, however, so preliminary in many ways that they could not erode the US power position in the world. Most international conflicts until the late 1960s were manifestations of the compliance/rebellion relationship between peripheral states on one hand and the United States, or the former colonial powers, on the other.

Indeed, very few major armed conflicts until the end of the 1960s occurred between developing countries. The most notable exceptions were the Sino-Indian war in 1962 and the Indo-Pakistan war of 1965. Most wars were actually associated with the counter-revolutionary roles of the United States, France and, to a lesser extent, Great Britain. Such roles were, in part, justified by the gradually growing Soviet interest in the Third World.

The predominant power, viz. the United States, had in these circumstances three alternative strategies to *manage* international conflicts. One of them was to use the United Nations as a means of the American policy for world-order. This was very visible in the Korean war and in the Congo crisis of the early 1960s. In the Suez crisis of 1956 the UN resolutions sponsored by the United States were converted into standards with which the behaviour of her allies was compared. The ability of the United Nations to manage and resolve international conflicts started to decline from the early 1960s onwards. For instance in the Middle East crisis of 1967 the world organization was virtually powerless and its role was replaced by the bilateral efforts of the great powers to cope with the risks of escalation.

The diminishing influence of the United Nations can be accounted, among other things, by the decline in US preponderance. 'It is undeniable that the success of the United Nations until the early 1960s was due in large measure to American leadership, pressure, and support'.[25] The United Nations has, however, never been the sole US instrument of conflict management, but it has been combined with the direct handling of relations with the allies and with the Soviet Union. Direct relations with allies were especially important in 1956 when 'the American government brought influence to bear on the allies both through the United Nations and through direct contacts'.[26] In general it can be argued that the United States has systematically persuaded and pressured her allies to comply with her own policy interests. This has been probably more true for Great Britain, while France has been more enduring in preserving her counter-revolutionary role in the Third World.

In fact three different phases may be discerned in the relations between the United States and her allies in managing conflicts in the Third World. Until the late 1950s there was a mixture of rivalry between the United States, France and Great Britain because their traditional colonial spheres of influence were eroded by US expansiveness. Such a rivalry tended to increase regional volatility, particularly in the Middle East. The Cuban missile crisis and the Vietnam war reveal that, throughout the 1960s, the US wanted to manage either unilaterally, or in cooperation with the Soviet Union, the 'hotspots' of the Third World. The opinions and interests of allies were pushed aside which became costly, however, as the open conflict within NATO on the handling of the 1973 crisis in the Middle East shows.

Since the Vietnam debacle the United States has refrained from active involvement in peripheral conflicts but has endeavoured to maintain at least some management capacity in them. Due to the decline in her predominance and domestic restraints, the US would have needed the support and assistance of her West European allies in 'out-of-area' conflicts more than ever before. This support has not been easily forthcoming as the allies have wanted to keep NATO more as a regional alliance. In the present circumstances, the United States can neither compete with her allies in the same manner as in the 1950s, nor neglect them as was done in the 1960s, but their cooperation is rather secured on an *ad hoc* basis in each particular conflict.

The third dimension of conflict management is the *US-Soviet relationship* which is rooted in the common interests of these two great powers to avoid the escalation of confrontations as they might lead to large-scale destruction or, at a minimum, benefit third parties. Signs of conflict management and 'tacit coordination' between great powers were discernible already in the Suez crisis, but did not become really visible before the Cuban crisis of 1962. Without going into details of this crisis, it has to be pointed out that its experience, has, in terms of its management, been often idealized.

It has to be recalled that the US-Soviet relationship in the Cuban crisis was both geographically and politically asymmetric in favour of the United States and modified the end result accordingly. Even though the crisis probably contributed to the beginning of the détente period, it also motivated the Soviet Union to launch a major rearmament programme in order to eliminate the existing strategic asymmetry. This effort was based in part on the mistaken belief that it was this asymmetry that terminated the Cuban crisis in favour of the United States. Probably in this as well as in many other crises the balance of non-nuclear military forces and geographical conditions have affected the outcome in a more crucial manner than the strategic nuclear balance.

The impact of the nuclear factor should not, in other words, be exaggerated. Neither should one excessively believe in the rationality of crisis management. The decision-making of both great powers has contained irrational traits which have, in part, been due to the behaviour of individuals involved, but perhaps more to the underlying operation of large and complicated security bureaucracies. The experiences of the Cuban crisis suggest that it is close to impossible to keep such bureaucracies under effective control in times of crisis. A certain lack of collective rationality in crisis management derives from its inherent duality: an international crisis contains both threats and opportunities. The parties involved make simultaneous attempts to utilize opportunities and to contain threats. There is no ultimate assurance that moderation will win in such a situation. A relevant example is the US nuclear alert in the Middle East crisis of 1973 which was intended to dramatize the US resolve in the area and to convince the Soviet Union to refrain from any escalatory decisions. The Soviet Union, by and large, did so but she might well have responded in kind, and the situation would have considerably deteriorated.

The Cuban missile crisis gave rise to an enduring effort by the great powers to manage not only their direct mutual relations, but also peripheral conflicts affecting these relations. This effort has been only partially successful, and the incompatibilities in US-Soviet relations will ensure that this will continue. The great powers cannot manage their mutual relations without considering the regional conflict formations in the Third World. The Middle East crisis of 1973 is an example of the possibility that competition between great powers

in third areas may allow a highly motivated local actor to play one power off against the other and to pursue its own interests in ways that generate dangerous crises into which the superpowers are then drawn.[27]

The vertical accumulation and the horizontal spread, though slow, of *nuclear weapons* also underlines the need of great powers to stabilize the strategic equation in their mutual relations. In addition to that, it is also in their interest to prevent the initiation of nuclear war by a third party and its escalation to the US-Soviet relationship.

Conflicts and fragmentation in the international system

An overview

The international system is still predominantly bipolar, and will probably be so in the foreseeable future. *Bipolarity* can be regarded as a baseline model which is, however, under pressures of change. My previous theoretical considerations suggest that the declining predominance of the leading or even hegemonic power, a shift towards mutlipolarity and growing forces of emancipation all contribute to the fragmentation of international relations. As a consequence, extra-regional causation of peripheral conflicts become weaker and local cultural, ethnic, economic and political factors become more prominent as causes of armed confrontations. This means in concrete terms that, relatively speaking, more wars occurred between developing countries after 1968 than before it. It may also mean that the relative and even absolute rate of military intervention by the major powers into Third World conflicts has decreased.

Wars in the periphery appear to have two sources. The spread of power resources to the Third World has created a middle rung in the international hierarchy which has been often called the *semi-periphery*. An empirical study identified 29 semi-peripheral countries and observed that during the period 1970–77 as many as 62% of them had been involved in either civil or international wars. This was a much higher proportion than in any other group of countries. A systematic downward mobility by semiperipheral countries was especially conducive to war participation. In a declining semiperipheral country, economic stagnation alone can give rise to aggression, while among upwardly mobile countries economic growth is conducive to peace, particularly if the process of militarization is halted.

This suggests that economic development builds peace, or conversely that peace builds development.[28]

Semi-peripheral countries may adopt the role of a regional power centre. In this role it may act as a sub-imperialist agent or as an autonomous unit whom the great powers are courting. As a rule both semiperipheral and peripheral powers have become dependent on external suppliers of sophisticated arms and military technology. This has not, however, resulted in political subordination but often in the opposite; the external policy of (semi)peripheral powers, backed by their new military capacity, has tended to become more reckless.

This development is not confined only to the regional power centres, but also to smaller Third World countries. It has been observed that many wars in the South have been initiated by attacks of smaller countries against the stronger. An explanation of this counterintuitive tendency may be that the war initiators have been usually dictatorships where the decision to go to war has been made by a small clique as an effort to alleviate the pressures emanating from domestic instabilities. In the regional contexts, the result has been the dissolution of old power configurations and either a degeneration into regional anarchy or the establishment of a new regional order based on power balance.

The changing nature of warfare is reflected in the data assembled and analysed by Istvan Kende and Dieter Senghaas. The analysis can be divided into two periods, viz. 1945–68 and 1969–82. *In toto*, 34 interstate and border wars have broken out in the postwar period; 14 of them in 1945–68 (0.6 per year) and 20 in 1969–82 (1.4 per year). The rate of interstate wars has increased, in other words, with the fragmentation of the international system. A further change can be discerned by making a distinction between wars with and without external intervention. They were almost equally common in the first period (6 vs. 8 wars) but, in the latter period, the number of wars with outside interference remained constant, while those without intervention increased to 14.[29]

The number of intra-Third World wars has increased over time. In fact, wars between two developing countries, into which a major power intervened, decreased while both wars between Third World powers without external intervention and with participation by a third party from the Third World increased. These observations suggest that intervention by major powers has lost some of its significance as a mode of management of peripheral conflicts in which other Third World countries increasingly participate.[30]

A similar tendency may be discerned in civil wars into which altogether 58 interventions were made in 1945–68 (2.4 per year). During 1969–82, the number of such interventions decreased to 24 (1.8 per year). A similar comparison of the number of civil wars without foreign intervention yields the ration of 25 to 29 wars (1.0 vs. 2.1 per year). A closer look into types of external military intervention reveals that in 1945–68 only 8 out of 58 (14%) interventions involved a Third World power. In 1969–82 the corresponding share was 33%.[31] Other studies have concluded that the rise of Third World interventionism has been even more pronounced so that in 1970–77 an outside Third World power participated in practically every civil war.[32]

These developments indicate a gradual *decoupling* of core and regional subsystems in the military sphere. This observation is consistent with the interpretation that relations between the core and the periphery are increasingly governed by market rules, i.e. substantive economic aspects of predominance still exist, while the formal politico-military structure is increasingly challenged. This is evidenced by growing political and military instability in Third World regions.

One should not conclude, however, from the tendency of decoupling that peripheral wars cannot spread to Europe and to relations between great powers. Even though major powers are participating numerically in fewer wars in the Third World, their strategic stakes in some key areas are so high that escalation is still conceivable. The intensity of commitments matters, in other words, in addition to their sheer number. The Middle East and the Persian Gulf are usually regarded as regions in which the confrontation between great powers is particularly serious and from which the conflict might escalate into Europe. The actual involvement in peripheral conflicts is not the only aspect of great-power intervention. These powers are almost routinely conducting contigency planning for major regions of the world outlining their strategies in potential conflicts. If such conflicts break out the plans may be put in operation.[33]

Regional conflict formations

Earlier an effort was made to develop a typology of both regional political orders and the modes of great-power involvement. These typologies can be utilized to analyse the main structural processes in international relations. These processes are sparked off by the structural and political tensions between unicentricity and multicentricity on one hand, and between hierarchy and emancipation on the other. It is pertinent to stress again that there are regional variations in these processes. Even though the tension between hierarchy and emancipation is a global fact, the intensity of its manifestation is dependent on the specific historical phase in a given region in relation to the power structure of the international system. The fact of bipolarity, though eroding, does not mean that the mode of great power involvement in each region should be bipolar. On the contrary, it may vary from unilateral domination to multilateral competition.

Looking into major regions of confrontation, one can observe that there is a polarized balance of power in *South East Asia*. The United States and the Soviet Union are the main external actors sponsoring their own allies which are, in turn, in conflict with each other. It should, of course, be recognized that China is a major power in the region as well. That is why the South East Asian region is potentially a multipolar subsystem. During recent years Chinese policy has, however, complied so closely with overall

US strategy that it has not transformed the region into a complex balance of power.

The polarization between the Vietnamese coalition and ASEAN indicates that the regional order in South East Asia is not stable, but it contains a danger that the region may degenerate into a greater anarchy. Provided that the bipolar mode of superpower involvement remains, this would mean an increasingly volatile regional order that would start seeking for a new order. The efforts, though not fully institutionalized, between the Vietnamese coalition and the ASEAN to regulate their conflicts indicate that regional stability, based on polarization, can probably be maintained. The Kampuchean issue can hardly develop into such a stumbling bloc that a general war in the area will be unleashed.

The military and political involvement of the great powers in South East Asia probably sustains the regional confrontation. The rapprochement between the two regional blocs is obviously constrained by the interests of the greater powers, including in this case also China. It would be far-fetched, however, to argue that regional conflict is created by these powers; its roots are in the present and historical conditions of the region. It should be recalled, though, that the Vietnam war brought the great powers to the area and transformed the conditions in which the regional power game was occurring. In particular in Indochina it is difficult to say which specific forms the subregional order would have assumed if the great powers had not entered into the area as massively as they have in the last 25 years.

The South East Asian conflict does not have any prominent negative influence on US-Soviet relations. It is rather a part of their larger strategic rivalry in the Asia-Pacific region. It is obvious that the Asian factor is in general becoming more important in great power relations, in part because of its economic upsurge, the rise of Japan and China, and in part because of the spread of strategic rivalries to the region. It appears that the Asian-Pacific area is getting both more multicentric and witnessing signs of emancipation from strategic competition (Australia, New Zealand and the South Pacific Nuclear-Free Zone).

The experiences of the US-USSR negotiations over intermediate nuclear forces (INF) indicate that the situation in the Asia-Pacific region cannot be entirely isolated from European affairs. This development together with the signs of disorder/search for new order in the region may make the management of potential conflicts between great powers there more difficult. This possibility is accompanied by the fact that the mechanisms of conflict resolution in the Asia-Pacific region between the great powers are underdeveloped. Hence, intra-regional confrontations may rather easily have adverse effects not only on relations between the United States and the Soviet Union but also on their relations with China.

The situation in the Arab/Persian Gulf is based on a relative subregional balance of power between Iran and Iraq, supported by most Arab states. The United States and the Soviet Union are not the only relevant actors in the area, as France has played with her arms and technology supplies a not insignificant role. That is why the situation in the Persian Gulf hovers between the polarized and complex balance of power. There is without any doubt competition between the United States and the Soviet Union in the area. This is shown by the Soviet intervention in Afghanistan in 1979 and the Gulf strategy of the Carter Administration. Geopolitical imperatives have become dominant and the policy of containment has been reinstituted.

At the beginning of the Iran–Iraq war were signs that the great powers might choose opposing sides. The United States probably encouraged the Iraqi attack and the Soviet Union considered an alignment with Iran in spite of her treaty commitments with Iraq. It soon became clear, though, that an alignment with Iran was not feasible and the great powers came to favour a stalemate in the war. The risks of involvement had been too high because of the escalation potential of the crisis, and hence functioned as a kind of deterrent. Iraq has been provided, however, with enough support that she has been able to prevail in the war and to avoid the regional predominance of Iran. The Soviet Union has delivered arms to Iraq, while US support has been primarily indirect through her economic and military involvement in the Gulf Cooperation Council (GCC).

The continuation of the Iran-Iraq war can in part be explained by extra-regional factors such as the patterns of alignment and arms supplies. Its termination by extra-regional efforts seems to be, on the other hand, almost inconceivable. The antagonism of the conflict suggests that its resolution can be achieved only by the supremacy of one party or by local compromise. As the former option is undesirable and the latter unattainable, the external powers tend to opt for the continuation of the political and military stalemate.

The Middle East is the most complex of all regional conflict formations. Since 1973–74 there has been a strong effort by the United States at unilateral domination and at external balancing of the rivalry between Israel and the Arab countries. As a result, the Soviet Union has been pushed from the mainstream of the Middle East politics to a rather narrow pattern of alignments with Syria and Libya. Obviously her possibilities to wield influence in the region through these allies are limited. The US efforts at unilateral domination through Kissinger's shuttle diplomacy, Carter's Camp David Settlement and Reagan's peace initiative have reinforced the division between radical and conservative Arab governments.

This, together with the efforts of the Soviet Union, and to a lesser extent by the European Community, to restore its influence have sown seeds of disorganization in the Middle East. This is associated with the failure of the great powers to agree upon the mode of management of the Middle East conflict. This failure was manifest already in the settlement of the 1973 war which damaged US-USSR relations. 'Although it would be going too far to say that détente was dealt a mortal blow by the October war, the relationship between the two sides was never the same thereafter'.[34] The decline of détente started probably earlier than it has been usually realized.

The US policy of regional order in the Middle East has largely failed to produce any uncontested influence in the settlement of regional issues. This is shown by the decision to send and then withdraw the Multinational Force in Lebanon. The limits of great-power influence in the region have given more *Spielraum* to local governments and raised the spectre of disorganization. This spectre has provided an impetus to the search for a regional order by local forces. This is manifested in the recent initiative of Jordan, supported by the PLO and Egypt and encouraged by influential sections of political opinion in Israel, to initiate a subregional peace process leading ultimately to an international conference. In more general terms, it has been observed that

> while many Middle Eastern countries individually nurse expansionist or hegemonic ambitions, all of them collectively, by their preference for the weaker side and their readiness to shift alignments regardless of ideology, offer strong support for the status quo... The pattern of hostility, interaction and manoeuvre thus has its self-balancing features.[35]

The Southern African conflict comes closest to the pattern of sub-imperialism in which unilateral extra-regional domination, by the West, is associated with the existence of a dominant regional power, South Africa. The Frontline States and SADCC are not able to establish a regional balance of power and Soviet influence is not able to convert the Western unilateral domination into bilateral competition. In a long-term perspective such a regional order is probably the most explosive one, even though confrontation is likely to occur between the *apartheid* regime and the Black opposition. Because of the relative absence of great-power competition in Southern Africa, the potential of this conflict formation to disturb their mutual relations will probably remain limited.

The Central American conflict can be best characterized as a combination of unilateral domination by the United States and by a measure of regional anarchy. Such an order would easily lead to a *divide-et-impera* policy in which Nicaragua and any other radical state would be isolated from its neighbours. The policy of the Reagan Administration provides strong evidence of such a tendency. The support of the Soviet Union and Cuba, acting in part on her own, for Nicaragua and indirectly to the Salvadorean opposition inject a measure of extra-regional competition into Central America. This involvement is not, however, strong enough to create a true situation of bilateral competition, but gives a rationale for the predominant power to group her allies more closely together to defend the *status quo* against the forces of change.

This kind of a volatile regional order may inject a degree of unruliness to relations between the great powers. It is, however, more symbolic than real and hence the risks of escalation are rather limited. That is why the instability injected by Central America into the relations between the United States and the Soviet Union cannot be compared with that emanating from South East Asia and, in particular, from the Middle East.

In conclusion one may argue that the multicentricity and autonomy of regional conflict formations have increased since the 1960s. The Soviet Union became more active in the Third World in the 1970s, while the United States reduced her involvement after the Vietnam War. During the Reagan Administration she has again become more prone to interventionist policy. In general a shift from unicentricity to bicentricity, and even beyond, has taken place in the extra-regional control of Third World conflicts. Due to the hierarchical nature of international relations, a consequence has been the division of the globe into spheres of influence by the great powers. This tendency should not be exaggerated, however, but the forces of emancipation should be duly recognized. These forces have aligned more often with the Soviet Union than with the United States, but often also strive for independence from the great powers.

. A general tendency in the military sphere of the Third World has been the growing volatility which the great powers are not able to control effectively. This may increase the danger of conflicts in the Third World escalating into their mutual relations. The decoupling of the periphery from the centre works, however, both ways: the lack of control over events in the Third World may also mean that the great powers reduce their involvement there and hence curtail the dangers of escalation. More importantly, the great powers seem to have developed a number of safeguards by which conflict escalation can be regulated.

Such safeguards include stalemated conflicts, proxy confrontations and great-power consultations on regional issues that were started by Washington and Moscow in 1984. These and other safeguards do not, of course, mean that the great powers are withdrawing from the Third World. In some cases their modes of involvement are only changing. The great powers also continue to support their clients which are opposing the adversary or its clients. The safeguard strategy underlines, however, the efforts of the great powers to manage regional conflicts and to keep them within bounds in spite of their growing autonomy.

Notes

1. See Adda B. Bozeman, *Conflict in Africa. Concepts and Realities.* Princeton University Press: Princeton, N.J. 1976, pp. 202–204.

2. For a very useful development of this theme see Michael Bratton, 'Patterns of Development and Underdevelopment. Towards A Comparison', *International Studies Quarterly*, vol. 26, no. 3 (1982), pp. 333–372 (the quotation is from p. 341).

3. See Oran R. Young, 'Political Discontinuities in the International System', *World Politics*, vol. 20, no. 3 (1968), pp. 369–92.

4. Tony Smith, *The Pattern of Imperialism. The United States, Great Britain and the Late-Industrialized World Since 1815.* Cambridge Univ Press: Cambridge, 1981, p. 195.

5. Barry Buzan, *People, States and Fear. The National Security Problem in International Relations.* Harvester Press: Brighton 1983, p. 113.

6. See Raimo Väyrynen, 'Regional Conflict Formations: An Intractable Problem of International Relations?', *Journal of Peace Research*, vol. 21, no. 4 (1984), pp. 337–59.

7. Väyrynen op. cit. 1984, pp. 347–49.

8. See Neil Macfarlane, 'Intervention and Regional Security'. *Adelphi Papers*, no. 196. London 1985, pp. 30–32 and 54–55.

9. See, e.g., Anthony Giddens, 'The Time-Space Constitution of Social Systems', in *A Contemporary Critique of Historical Materialism*. University of California Press: Berkeley 1981, pp. 26–48.

10. See Nicole Bousquet, 'From Hegemony to Competition: Cycles of the Core?', in Terence K. Hopkins & Immanuel Wallerstein (eds.), *Processes of the World-System*. Sage Publications: Beverly Hills 1980, pp. 46–83.

11. See Raimo Väyrynen, 'Economic Cycles, Power Transitions, Political Management and Wars between Major Powers'. *International Studies Quarterly*, vol. 27, no. 4 (1983), pp. 402–406.

12. Robert O. Keohane, *After Hegemony. Cooperation and Discord in the World Political Economy*. Princeton University Press: Princeton 1984, pp. 39–41.

13. Stanley Hoffmann, *Primacy or World Order: American Foreign Policy since the Cold War*. McGraw-Hill: New York 1975, pp. 114–19.

14. Valerie Bunce, 'The Empire Strikes Back: The Transformation of Eastern Bloc from a Soviet Asset to a Soviet Liability'. *International Organization*, vol. 39, no. 1 (1985), pp. 1–46. See also Peter Summerscale, 'Is Eastern Europe a Liability to the Soviet Union?' *International Affairs* (London), vol. 57, no.4 (1981). pp. 585–98.

15. Charles Doran, 'Modes, Mechanisms and Turning Points. Perspectives on the Transformation of the International System', *International Political Science Review*, vol. 1, no. 1 (1980), pp. 44–45.

16. Smith, op. cit. 1981, p. 195.

17. See Carsten Holbraad, *Superpowers and International Conflict*. Macmillan: London, 1979, pp. 20–35.

18. Seyom Brown, *The Faces of Power. Constancy and Change in the United States Foreign Policy from Truman to Reagan*. Columbia University Press: New York 1983, pp. 99–107.

19. Norman A. Graebner, *America as a World Power. A Realist Appraisal from Wilson to Reagan*. Scholarly Resources Inc.: Wilmington 1984, pp. 165–83.

20. Brown op.cit. 1983, pp. 52–58. See also John Lewis Gaddis, *Strategies of Containment. A Critical Appraisal of Postwar American National Security Policy*. Oxford University Press: New York 1982, pp. 89–126.

21. Bruce D. Porter, *The USSR in Third World Conflicts. Soviet Arms and Diplomacy in Local Wars 1945–1980*. Cambridge University Press: Cambridge 1984, pp. 16–35.

22. Bartlett, *The Global Conflict 1880–1970: The International Rivalry of the Great Powers*, Longman: London, 1984, pp. 311–16 and Brown *op.cit.* 1983, pp. 124–29.

23. Gaddis op. cit. 1982, pp. 54–71, and Ernest R. May, 'The Cold War', in Joseph S. Nye, Jr., *The Making of America's Soivet Policy*. New Haven 1984, pp. 219–21.

24. Brown op.cit. 1984, pp. 198–204.

25. Ernst B. Hass, 'Regime Decay: Conflict Management and International Organizations,' 1945–1981. *International Organization*, vol. 37, no.2 (1983). pp. 229–32.

26. Holbraad op.cit. 1979, p.29.

27. See Alexander L. George, 'The Arab–Israeli War of October 1973: Origins and Impact,' in Alexander L. George, *Managing U.S.–Soviet Rivalry. Problems of Crisis Prevention.* Westview Press: Boulder 1982, pp. 147–48.

28. Raimo Väyrynen, 'Semiperipheral Countries in the Global Economic and Military Order', in Helena Tuomi & Raimo Väyrynen (eds.), *Arms Production and Militarization.* Croom Helm: London 1983, pp. 163–92 (esp. pp. 179–81).

29. The figures presented are based on the recalculation of data provided by Istvan Kende, Klaus Jurgen Gantzel & Kai Fabig, Die Kriege seit dem Zweiten Weltkrieg. *Deutsche Gesellschaft fur Friedens- und Konfliktforschung. Hefte 16.* Bonn 1982, and Dieter Senghass, Militärische Konflikte in der Dritten Welt. *Leviathan*, vol. 12, no. 2 (1984), pp. 271–80.

30. Even though the direct military interventions by major powers into peripheral conflicts has decreased, the use of force short of war has continued, even though it has hardly compensated for the decline in military interventions. An important feature is that the nuclear-weapon powers have not resorted to the strategic nuclear threats since the Middle East crisis of 1973. See Philip D. Zelikow, Force Without War, 1975–1982. *The Journal of Strategic Studies*, vol. 7, no. 1 (1984), pp. 29–54.

31. Senghass op.cit. 1984, pp. 271–80.

32. See Bertil Duner, 'The Many-Spronged Spear: External Military Intervention in Civil Wars in the 1970s'. *Journal of Peace Research*, vol. 20, no. 1 (1983), pp. 59–72.

33. For further analysis see Miroslav Nincic, *How War Might Spread to Europe.* Taylor & Francis (SIPRI): London 1985.

34. See George op. cit. 1982, pp. 139–54. It should be also recalled that the 1973 war also led to a major disagreement between the United States and her Western European allies of which in particular the Federal Republic of Germany prevented Washington from using their ports and airfields for arms shipments to Israel. In that way the Federal Republic, France and Italy underlined that military operations in the Middle East were not a part of the NATO obligations. In Henry Kissinger's opinion these allies 'wanted the option to conduct a policy separate from the United States and in the case of the Middle East objectively in conflict with us'. See Henry Kissinger, *Years of Upheaval.* Weidenfeld and Nicholson: London 1982, pp. 712–17 (the quotation is from p. 716).

35. Dankwart A. Rustow, 'Realignments in the Middle East.' *Foreign Affairs*, vol. 63, no. 3 (1985), p. 598.

7. East-West, North-South Conflict: Interrelationship: Western Europe's Role

by Lothar Brock

Introduction

Compared with the bleak state of conceptual thinking in the fields of peace and development in the mid eighties, the early seventies were days of remarkable vigour and vision. On the one hand, there was détente and the growing confidence that a viable and constructive co-existence between states with different social systems would be possible. On the other hand, new concepts for dealing with the problems of the Third World emerged, culminating in the institutionalization of the North-South dialogue. Thus it appeared that the politics of confrontation and direct or indirect coercion in both the East-West and the North-South arena would come to an end and be replaced by multilateral bargaining in the framework of conference politics.

In the late 1970s and the early 1980s, the situation and the public mood reflecting it changed completely. Whereas in the early seventies, it looked as if the struggle between East and West would be replaced as the number one problem of international relations by the struggle over a restructuring of the world economic order, the East-West conflict all too quickly came to the fore again and apparently was re-established as the dominant conflict formation.[1] There was a renewed and drastic cooling off of the East-West climate and a dramatic acceleration of the arms race, demonstrating the inadequacy of all previous efforts to establish effective arms control procedures. In addition, there was a complete stagnation of efforts to follow-up the great designs of the early 1970s concerning a restructuring of North-South relations, with concrete negotiations and workable agreements. While the idea of global negotiations was treated in a dilatory fashion and for all practical purposes has been discarded by now, agreements which *were* reached on certain issues like the integrated commodities programme did not attain practical relevancy.

Both tendencies, the renewed tightening-up of East-West relations and the stagnation of North-South deliberations, merged in an intensification of East-West quarrels over North-South issues, implying, as it seems, not only a reaffirmation of the East-West struggle as the dominant conflict formation but also a globalization of the East-West conflict. However, as will be shown briefly in the next chapter, the East-West conflict has been global in nature from the very beginning. What is new today is the fact that the globality of the East-West struggle has become more visible and has attained a new military quality. It has done so through the 'reassertionism' of US world politics under the Reagan Administration on the one hand, a more systematic engagement of 'real socialism' in the Third World on the political, economic and military levels on the other. In addition, the Soviet Union has attained new military capacities which match the US capacities for a global military power projection. This policy has brought about a latent military omnipresence of *both* superpowers in the world.

This observation does not imply that everything which happens in the Third World today can be defined in terms of the East-West conflict. There exists rather a growing contradiction between the institutionalization of the East-West conflict as a global military conflict and the increasing complexity of political, military, economic and social developments in the Third World. These developments simply do not fit any dualistic model of world politics and therefore cannot be understood as mere functions of the East-West conflict. Furthermore, the East-West conflict, for a good part, has turned into sheer power-rivalry between the two superpowers, though the latent military omnipresence of the superpowers should not be interpreted as omnipotence. (The drive for military omnipresence rather reflects a growing insecurity on the part of the superpowers concerning their ability to keep things in the Third World under control or to channel them in the 'right' direction.)

If the East-West conflict has been global in nature from the very beginning, one of the deficiencies of détente has been that it was not. So it seems that what is needed today in order to stem the tide of a further militarization of politics and of conflict escalation, is a truly global détente, implying – in the long run – cooperation or at least co-existence between East and West in the Third World instead of the present costly and dangerous confrontation. Global détente, while living up to the globality of the East-West struggle, would call for an approach to Third World problems which would recognize the complexity of these problems and thereby refute the dualistic conceptualization of world developments which enables the superpowers to legitimize any policy they pursue around the world as action in the interest of national security or world peace, freedom or anti-imperialism.

Under the conditions prevailing today, Western Europe has neither the ability nor the interest to opt out of the East-West conflict understood as a struggle between OECD-capitalism and COMECON-socialism. But Western Europe has a special interest in mitigating superpower rivalry and in reviving or reconstituting détente, both under economic and security considerations. At the same time, Western Europe, which is the most important regional grouping in Third-World trade and the biggest source of development funds, has a special interest in, and capacity for opening up new economic opportunities in the Third World in order to secure its own economic standing in the global competition with the United States and Japan. With a view to these interests, can we expect Western Europe to take up the task of global détente? Would Western Europe be willing in this respect to play a more independent role in world politics even at the risk of embarrassing the United States? Is there anything at all like a Western European view of the world which could serve as the basis for a policy of dialogue (instead of confrontation) on the East-West level concerning North-South problems?

This paper does not aspire to answer these questions but rather attempts to contribute to a debate which may eventually produce some answers or even workable suggestions. In making this attempt, the paper deals with the global role of Western Europe in the East-West context. 'Western Europe', in the discussion of the present situation in this paper, refers to the member states of the European Community (EC). In the historic part the term 'Western Europe' or 'Europe' is used in an unspecific but self-explanatory way. Neither Western Europe in general nor the EC countries are being viewed as one actor in world politics. Rather, part of the problem addressed in the paper is that we are dealing with multinational politics. Such multinational politics, on the one hand, offer special chances for innovative thinking. On the other hand, they hamper the decision-making process in the realization of innovative ideas even more so than the complex constellation of domestic political forces does in a big national actor like the United States.

Global dimensions of the East-West conflict

The formative stage

From the outset, East-West politics have been global politics: They have always affected 'out of area' developments (in the Third World) and have been affected by them. The historic roots of the global nature of the East-West conflict are easy to trace: First, the October Revolution, with which the East-West conflict began, took place at a time when the last blank areas of the globe had been divided up among the colonial powers. From this time on, inner European conflicts had global implications. This was dramatically demonstrated by the fact that the war that broke out in Europe in 1914, eventually turned into a world war. Second, the October Revolution took place in a country which, due to its geographic features, is multi-regional, stretching from Europe to East Asia and the Pacific. Therefore, any attempt by the new political forces in this multi-regional state to rearrange its relations with its neighbours had by necessity wide international repercussions. This was illustrated by the early manifestations of East-West rivalry in China during the 1920s.

Third, capitalism and socialism are, of course, universal concepts though their standing and stamina continue to depend on the organization of world politics in a nation state-system, in which the actors tend to pursue particularistic aims. The universalistic nature of capitalism and socialism has helped their protagonists to define their particularistic interests in terms of global needs and has led to the creation of a 'universalistic nationaiism' (H.J. Morgenthau) which feels challenged by its adversary in any location of the globe, however remote it may be.

The theoretical way to this perception of world developments was paved by Lenin who, by reformulating the Marxian perspective on the world revolutionary process, brought the Third World into focus as a battle-ground for the struggle between socialism and capitalism. Lenin advanced the idea that the October Revolution had created an international milieu, in which it would be possible to combine national liberation and social transformation as two mutually reinforcive elements of the struggle against capitalism in its imperialist stage. If capitalism in this stage of its development depended on the exploitation of the Third World, then a breakdown of capitalist exploitation in the wake of national liberation would unleash a chain reaction which would eventually also lead to revolutionary change in the capitalist centre. This is the understanding of world political and social developments to which the Comintern was committed.

Lenin was not very familiar with the conditions in different colonial or semi-colonial areas. And despite its highly developed sensitivity for contradictions, Leninist theory helped to introduce the zero-sum per-ception of political and social change in the world at large and particularly in the Third World, which implies that all change can be defined in terms of gains and matching losses of influence in the struggle between East and West. In the formative stage of the East-West conflict, this zero-sum view of the world was quickly modified by the progress of fascism, which called for new alliances. The respective adjustment of the policy of the Communist International again was a matter of global politics concerning the strategy of communist parties in both industrialized and Third World countries (especially Latin America). It was, however, only of a temporary nature as became clear at the end of World War II.

Post World War II institutionalization of global competition between East and West

At the end of the Second World War, there was ample reason to expect the advent of an American century. But the expectant mood made Americans all the more susceptible to disappointment. The general idea behind the prevailing American concept for the post-war order was to foster American economic, political and security interests within a cooperative international system as outlined in the Charter of the United Nations. In this system, the United States – in accord with the prevailing self-perception of American political tradition – would play the role of a leading power but not that of a hegemonic power.[2]

This concept ran into difficulties, because the initial agreement between the Allies to continue cooperation in the post-war period did not comprise agreement on the terms of cooperation in concrete matters. Because of the postponement of such an agreement, the system broke down before it started. American politics reacted by readily taking up the zero-sum perception of world developments which was strongly re-affirmed by Stalin's or Zhdanov's 'Two-Worlds' thesis and which offered the Americans an *explanation* of the turn of events, a *motivation* to do something about it and a *justification* for doing so. The respective policy was defined in terms of help to those peoples threatened by international communism (Truman Doctrine), while the Soviet Union saw herself in the role of a mere midwife assisting historic necessity to come to life as a forceful reality.

The ensuing struggle, which, like the famous Clausewitz dictum, was waged as the continuation of war with other means, went hand in hand with a retreat from collective security and a return to (selective) alliance politics on a global scale. Undoubtedly, the core-area of the struggle was Europe. But it was in a Third World area that the first regional alliance was formed – in Latin America (Rio Pact of 1974). It was in Latin America, too, where the transformation of an anti-fascist front into an anti-communist front made the quickest advances.[3] Also the areas bordering the Soviet Union and those from which the European colonial powers had to retreat, immediately became an object of East-West rivalry. The respective geographical area reached from Turkey via West and South Asia to China, Korea and Indonesia. In this area, the United States after the 'loss' of China, went to war to prevent further inroads of communism. In addition, the United States, partly in cooperation with the old colonial powers, installed a system of regional alliances which were to serve as southern bases for the containment of the Soviet Union. With the installation of the multilateral alliance system in Europe, Latin America and Asia, the East-West conflict was institutionalized as a global conflict from which only parts of Africa remained temporarily unaffected.

Escalation of the East-West conflict in the South

During the Cold War in Europe, there were continuous efforts on the part of East and West to keep up communication and to reach a certain understanding on how to prevent an escalation of the cold conflict into a hot one. This danger remained acute. In substance, however, despite the rhetoric of 'roll-back', Western policy towards the East in Europe, during the fifties, was already status quo oriented with the possible exception of German reunification. But this issue, too, was used much more as an instrument in the general East-West struggle than accepted as a task in itself. After the political rearrangement of Europe in the late forties, the real struggle between East and West over the political orientation of states moved to the Third World. This struggle was not preempted but invigorated by the 'Spirit of Bandung', which paved the way for the creation of the Non-Aligned movement.

Of course, there were a number of crises in Europe during the fifties – the GDR crisis in 1953, the Hungarian and Polish crises of 1956 and in Berlin in

1958. But these were crises of adjustment to the socio-political status quo. In the Third World, the status quo itself was changing rapidly within the context of decolonization. This change soon wielded a conflict potential which led to indirect and in some cases even to direct military confrontations between East and West. Thus, in the Suez crisis, in which the West was split (US versus France and Great Britain), the use of military force by France and Great Britain met with the threat on behalf of the Soviet Union to use missiles in defence of Egypt and the Nasser regime. If the Soviet Union had not been tied down in Hungary, the Suez situation could well have escalated to the point of a direct East–West military encounter in a most sensitive Third World region.

In the case of the Cuban missile crisis of 1962, the confrontation between the United States and the Soviet Union over the stationing of Soviet missiles in a Third-World country led to the brink of a third world war. This situation was, of course, of a special nature and could not have repeated itself easily at any other part of the Third World, since no other country outside the Caribbean Basin is strategically as exposed vis-à-vis the United States as Cuba is. But one can also state that no situation in Europe since 1945 (including the Berlin blockade) had ever taken such dramatic turns as the Cuban missile crisis did. For this very reason, the missile crisis, despite its specific features, gave a most important impetus for the general reorientation of East-West politics from cold war to détente.

The missile crisis did not, however, keep the United States from escalating their military engagement in Vietnam in the following years up to the point where the Americans became the major military adversary of the National Liberation Front and North Vietnamese. As a consequence, US military action in Vietnam became one of the main issues of East-West political fighting during the sixties and early seventies. But the Soviet government carefully avoided a further internationalization of the conflict beyond its own participation as a weapons supplier.

The era of détente

With a view to the timely coincidence of the initiation of the détente process on the one hand, and the escalation of American military action in Vietnam (including the bombing of North Vietnam) on the other, the question arises whether this escalation actually took place under the shield of incipient détente. It may well be that the easing up of the East-West confrontation in Europe was perceived to allow a regionalization of conflicts in the Third World despite the fact that such conflicts continued to be understood in terms of the universalistic antagonism between the Western world and communism. However, the American margin of action in Vietnam depended much more on the Sino-Soviet dispute which, in turn, helped to bring about the Sino-American *rapprochement*, allowing the Nixon/Kissinger Administration to play the 'Chinese card'. The Sino-Soviet dispute implied a tremendous complication of Soviet world policy and a modification of the whole East-West pattern of conflict, comparable perhaps, in form though not in substance, with the modification caused by the advent of fascism in the 1930s.

It was not entirely out of place, though, to have doubts about the meaning of détente for the Third World. The Moscow agreement of 1972 between the Soviet and US governments concerning their respective 'out of area'-conduct, could have been interpreted as a barter-trade by which American consent to the sanctity of the status quo in Europe was exchanged against Soviet consent to a continued predominance of Western influence in the Third World. This may have been the understanding of the Nixon/Kissinger Administration.[4] But, as it soon turned out, if this was the American understanding of the agreement, it was not that of the Soviet government. From an ideological viewpoint it would not have made sense anyhow, if the socialist countries had consented to freeze the distribution of Western and Eastern influence in the Third World, because such an agreement, under a Marxist perspective, would have amounted to a negation of the laws of history. The Soviet Union rather regarded détente as an expression of a turn of Western politics towards more realism. This was to imply that the West now switched from trying to beat socialism to adjusting to a world in which the anti-imperialist and socialistic forces were gaining ground. Détente was regarded as a factor helping these forces all over the world by creating among other things a favourable climate for more international solidarity and cooperation with and among these forces.[5]

The expression of such solidarity, however, through Soviet policy towards Angola, Mozambique, Ethiopia and Afghanistan, accompanied by a new anti-imperialist optimism, was not accepted in the West as a policy conducive to détente. As a result, the complete failure of East and West to reach a working understanding of the situation in the Third World and of the nature of the most acute problems of underdevelopment together with the shifting balance of East-West military potentials in favor of the East and the changing structure of Soviet armament, was a most important determining factor in the rapid demise of détente.

The demise of détente

Détente and the North-South dialogue for a short time nourished a new confidence that the most pressing world problems could and would be solved cooperatively and that East-West and North-South conflict formations would be transformed into a system of viable coexistence on a global level. But this vision quickly faded. The 'Vietnam trauma' in the United States had hardly reached its climax when it was superceded by the 'Angola shock' – the apparent surprise of Western governments that the Soviet Union, despite the Moscow agreement of 1972, aided liberation groups with a socialist orientation in the struggle over the liquidation of Portuguese colonialism in Africa. The 'Angola shock' was followed by growing inhibitions about the military presence of 'real socialism' (including Cuba) in Ethiopia after the fall of Haile Selassie, about the de-

Westernization of Indochina and about the new dimensions of Soviet armaments which established the capacity of the Soviet Union for global military power projection. Finally, the Afghanistan intervention in the context of the radical change in Iran, the new oil crisis and general disturbances of the world economy, helped to foster the political and socio-psychological climate which gave rise to a political fundamentalism which, after the change to Reagan, swept away what was left of détente.

Instead of a strengthening of the feeble but conceptually bold new approach to world politics symbolized by détente and the North-South dialogue, the world witnessed a resurgence of superpower rivalry, a return to the worst of zero-sum thinking, a stagnation of global development efforts, an unprecedented acceleration of the East-West armament process and the spreading of the arms race to the Third World.

What was the role of Western Europe in this lamentable development?

Western Europe in global politics

The Europeanization of the world and European retreat

At the beginning of world politics in the modern sense there was Europe. It was the industrialization of Europe which led to the establishment of one world, in which henceforth the political, economic, social and cultural developments of the different world regions would be more or less tightly linked up as parts of a global system of social reproduction. In other words, today's world system derives from the projection of the interests of European capital and European nation-states onto the globe. These interests, again, were determined as much by intra-European rivalries as by the demand for overseas markets and resources.

World War I was the culminating point of the Europeanization of the globe and the Second World War put an end to it. After World War II, contrary to Zhdanov's and Stalin's 'Two-Worlds' thesis, the one world, established by Europe, persisted. But the European states themselves were reduced to secondary actors. While Germany lost its identity as a political entity altogether, the other European states, too, became an object of world power competition, which many of them hitherto had taken part in. Of course, Great Britain and, to some degree also France, played an active role in delineating the contours of the post war-order as it was spelled out in the UN Charter. But it was clearly the American perception of the post-war situation which dominated what was henceforth to be understood as the *Western* position. This process was based on the economic and military disparities between the United States and the European states, which prevailed at the end of the war. It was enhanced by the accelerating dissolution of the former colonial empires.

The retreat from the colonies, which was forced upon the colonial powers by internal decolonization drives (abroad and at home) and which was helped along by the American open-door policy, symbolized more clearly than anything else that Europe, while remaining a major stage for the great political struggles of the day, had lost its function as the centre of gravity of world developments. To the extent that the old colonial powers continued to play an important role in world politics, they often did so by causing trouble in the process of their retreat from empire instead of contributing constructively to the solution of problems which they themselves had helped to create. This was demonstrated in the Suez crisis when France and Great Britain, far from supporting UN action to alleviate the crisis, escalated it by acting unilaterally and landing troops on the very day on which the General Assembly, under the 'Uniting for Peace' resolution, called for the removal of all foreign troops from the canal area and the Sinai.

Another example of the inability or unwillingness of European colonialists to accept decolonization as a historic necessity and to adjust to it in a constructive way, was the Algerian war. It was one of the bloodiest wars of the 1950s and was finally ended in the early 1960s by de Gaulle who had re-entered the political scene in 1958 by promising to keep Algeria French. In the 1960s and 1970s, it was again the persistence of European colonialism – this time that of the Portuguese under Salazar – which had disturbing effects on the international scene. It prepared the way for the counter-productive interaction of East-West and North-South politics which helped dismantle détente in the second half of the 1970s.[6]

The reassertion of Western Europe
The wartime destruction and division of Europe, as well as the forced and bloody retreat from empire, were only one side of the post-war development of Europe. The other was the re-assertion of Western Europe by way of integration. Initially this process was inward directed, spurred by economic advantage and the political drive towards overcoming war in Europe. It resulted not only in the speedy elimination of the colonial empires but in the reconstruction of Europe as an economic bloc which by its sheer economic weight had considerable importance for world economic development.[7]

The drive towards European integration was supported by the United States. But it also increased economic competition between the United States and the Common Market and led to a number of acute conflicts over protectionistic practices and over the question to what extent economic means including development aid should be used as a weapon in the East-West struggle. This way, European economic integration was gradually politicized through its potential or manifest external repercussions. This process of politicization of economic integration, during the sixties, was accompanied by a first round of quarrels over Western military policy-making within NATO, which ended in the withdrawal of France from military integration.

The politicization process received a big push by the efforts of the EC member countries to install the European Political Cooperation (EPC) as a partial compensation for, and a first step towards European political integration. EPC succeeded to play an important role in coordinating the policies of EC member countries in negotiating the Helsinki agreement on security and cooperation betwee the East and the West in Europe, which, in turn, was accompanied by an impressive upsurge of economic exchange on an all-European level and a qualitative intensification of East-West economic relations through the introduction of industrial cooperation.[8]

This success on the level of EPC within the context of East-West politics coincided with a reorganization of the relationship with the formerly associated Third World countries and part of the old British colonies through the Treaty of Lomé, which was hailed as a historic step towards a cooperative solution of world problems.[9]

At the same time, the EC countries, experiencing what was quickly defined as a threat to their economic security by the oil-exporting countries, started a Euro-Arabian dialogue with the aim of preventing further exposure to economic pressure within the context of the middle-East conflict.

The EC countries also ventured to formulate a comprehensive concept for an integrated approach to the whole mediterranean area and eventually intensified contacts and concluded agreements with the Maghreb-states, Latin American sub-regional state groupings like the Cartagena group and with ASEAN. They also issued declarations on various conflicts around the world like in the Middle East, Cyprus, Portugal, Southern Africa.

All these activities could be and were interpreted as a search for a 'European identity in the world',[10] as a sign that the Western European countries were on their way back to a global policy and that by doing so they were determined to play a relatively independent role – though adherence to, and the existence of, the Atlantic Alliance was never put into question.[11] To what degree did this search transcend the East-West interpretation of North-South politics which played an increasing role in US policy towards the Third World after 1975?

The end of détente and attempts to transcend the East-West dimension of North-South relations

As mentioned above, it was in the United States where a harsh critique of détente over Soviet policy in the Third World began to be voiced soon after the Helsinki agreement had been reached. But Western European policy-makers also demonstrated sensitivity towards Soviet policy in the Third World long before Afghanistan. This sensitivity reflected concern about:

- the political future of Africa in the light of Soviet and Cuban involvement in the last stage of the decolonization process and the relevancy of this involvement for strategically important areas like Southern Africa and the Horn;
- the future of the Non-Aligned Movement especially in the context of the 1979 Havana summit and Cuban attempts to establish the Eastern

interpretation of non-alignment as the official understanding of the Movement;

- Europe's 'supply security' with raw materials. As far as oil was concerned, 'supply security' seemed threatened by a further destabilization of the Middle-East region through the revolution in Iran, Soviet intervention in Afghanistan and also through the Iran-Iraq war.

Nevertheless, Western European policy concerning these developments and the whole issue of interaction between the East-West and the North-South conflict was not identical with that of Washington. As a matter of rule, there were attempts on the European side to prevent an overdramatization of, and overreaction to the Eastern role in Third World developments. Of course, the Europeans could not but agree that Soviet intervention in the Third World was a threat to what was left of détente. Thus, the then President of the European Council, Ruffini, summarized the position of the EC with a view to Afghanistan by stating that détente by its very nature is global and consequently indivisible.[12] But the concrete reactions even to Afghanistan, especially the two-phased plan for a political solution of the problems at hand which was forwarded in June 1981, by the European Council, demonstrated that the EC countries were very much interested in preventing further disturbances of East-West relations through Eastern engagement in certain countries or regions of the Third World.[13] To be sure, not only on the transatlantic level but also in Europe, there was a controversial debate on how to react to the politics of 'real socialism' in the Third World. In general, however, there certainly was more interest among EC countries in the divisibility of tensions than in the indivisibility of détente.[14]

Western Europeans, while appreciating American concerns, felt that they had more to lose by horizontal conflict escalation than the Americans. Consequently, in the EPC declarations and those of the EC Parliament referring to different conflicts with Eastern and Western involvement in the Third World, there was (and is) a tendency to point to the economic and social causes of such conflicts, to call for substantial conflict resolution which goes to the roots of the respective conflicts, to support intra-regional initiatives for settling disputes, and to modify the influence of the superpowers. For instance, in the case of Central America, the EC countries are supporting regional, non-military conflict resolution with the help of the *Contadora* group. Such regional conflict resolution, according to Western European understanding, should be supported through external economic aid and internal reform. As far as the EC is concerned, both external aid and internal reform are supposed to be brought about or intensified through a European-Central American dialogue in the context of a more active Latin American policy of the Community.[15] Of course, the 'Kissinger plan' for Central America and the Caribbean by taking up the concept of earlier Caribbean Basin Initiative, also strongly emphasizes the necessity to go to the roots of the turmoil in the region and to embark upon a programme of intensive economic aid and social reform.[16] But this part of the plan apparently had the function to legitimize more military action on the part of the United States or more support for military pacification in the region.

In contrast to this approach, (seemingly 'pacification first, development later, if still needed to keep things quiet') Western European declarations and resolutions on the subject stress the inadequacy of military measures and the counter-productivity of such measures as far as preventing intervention (on the part of the socialist countries) is concerned. Western Europeans do not view Central America so much as a test-case for the credibility of the West vis-à-vis alleged ambitions of 'real socialism' to foster world revolution. They rather prefer to look at the situation in its historic specificity and as a test-case for the possibility of combining social transformation and political democratization or for the credibility of the left's claim in Central America to pursue this end. In this context, Western Europeans draw upon their experience with the Portuguese revolution. In the case of Portugal, after the downfall of Salazar, it was not an attempted isolation of, but a critical or rather selective dialogue with, the forces of change which, according to the understanding of those active in the process (i.e. especially from the viewpoint of the Socialist International), helped to keep Portugal in the Western camp and paved the way for its final inclusion into the European Community.

This line of thinking manifested itself in the refusal of the EC to go along with the American trade and aid embargo against Nicaragua. Nevertheless, there is, of course, a considerable variety of attitudes towards US policy in the region. Some party groups within the EC parliament, especially on the left, and the Western European member parties of the Socialist International in general are willing to express strong opposition and to risk at least a modest degree of American embarrassment (as expressed by President Reagan's refusal, during his recent 'Bitburg-visit', to see Willy Brandt). Though, as a ruling party, the West German Social Democrats were careful not to upset the applecart, the European section of the Socialist International under Willy Brandt set up a committee for the defence of the Nicaraguan revolution and supports the Salvadorian *Movimiento Nacional Revolucionario*.[17] Among the ruling parties, the Socialists in France under the Mitterrand government are the most outspoken in formulating (and carrying through) an approach to Central American politics which pays little heed to the American definition of the situation. Thus, in 1981, France in a joint declaration with Mexico afforded quasi-diplomatic recognition to the revolutionary forces in El Salvador. Furthermore, France has delivered weapons to the Sandinista government in Nicaragua and ostentatiously offered Nicaragua help to remove the US-installed minefields off the Nicaraguan coast.

At the other end of the spectrum, we find Great Britain and Western Germany, the latter after the 1982 change of government. The official position of the West German government always was mellowed by considerations concerning the special ties to the United States in security matters. This was also the case under the Social Democrats. The present government of the Federal Republic, however, went beyond the traditional caution. It normalized diplomatic relations with El Salvador and stopped bilateral aid to Nicaragua (without preventing multilateral aid on the EC level). It has explicitly rejected the critique that aid was stopped because of the socialist orientation of the Sandinistas. Instead, the respective policy was justified with the argument that Nicaragua was intervening in the affairs of its neighbours. But these nuances just showed that the Christian Democrats are more willing to adjust to the US interpretation of the situation than were the Social Democrats.[18]

There is, therefore, no uniform European stand on Central America (or any other region of the Third World). But there is the attempt to offer Central America and other regions of the Third World a 'European option' which would widen the margin of action of the respective countries by helping to prevent an all-out projection of the East-West conflict onto the conflicts developing i the Third World.[19] Along this line, members of the EC Commission and of the EC Parliament have warned that the renewed tensions on the East-West level would withdraw attention from North-South issues and would further worsen the chances for concerted and effective efforts to solve some of the basic problems of underdevelopment. Commission member Pisani in this connection talked of the 'marginalization of the North-South dialogue' through the East-West conflict.[20] Against this danger, the European Parliament, after the Cancun coference of 1981, pleaded for a reaffirmation of the necessity and feasibility of transforming the North-South Dialogue into formal global negotiations which the developing countries had called for.[21] The arguments in favour of such negotiations were not so much expressed in terms of European economic interests as in terms of a close relationship between persistent underdevelopment and instability, as well as the likelihood of violent conflict on the international level. This was a language very much in accord with the analyses offered by the United Nations on the interrelationship between peace or disarmament and development.[22]

One year after the Cancun conference, however, it became clear that the EC saw little chance for concrete initiatives leading to global negotiations.[23] In its memorandum on development policy in October 1982, the EC Commission pointed to the difficulties standing in the way of global negotiations and underlined the necessity of immediate but specific or rather limited action.[24] The urgency of such action, in the view of the Commission, followed from the fact that the East-West conflict in its global dimensions could block the way for the developing countries into a meaningful future and that this could lead to unintended and uncontrollable consequences for all parties.

It was with a view to this observation that the special role of Western Europe was pointed out once more by the Commission. The East, so the memorandum argued, had confined its own policy on Third-World problems to the critique of Western colonialism and its long-term implications. Instead of assisting in the construction of an effective multilateral system for development, they had preferred to work on a bilateral level to foster their own interests in the way of military aid and ideological influence. As a result, Eastern military aid and ideological influence counteracted Western aid leading to the devastating consequence that the North-South dialogue was, in practice, replaced by East-West confrontation.

According to the Commission, the US under the Reagan Administration was almost exclusively interested in the East-West dimension of world politics. It preferred to exert influence through bilateral interaction instead of supporting collective action in the context of the North-South dialogue. In this way, it failed to put to work its enormous resources for overdue tasks.

In contrast to these policies and conceptions, the EC, so the memorandum argued, was very much interested in enhancing the stability of the international system. As a commercial and political power, the EC was not interested in conflict, but in regulating interdependence. In this respect, Europe and the Third World countries, according to the memorandum, are in one boat. They both profit from peace and suffer under conflict and war because they are likely to be their victims and/or serve as the battleground on which conflict and war are being fought out.[25] Is this mere ideology? Does this European view of present tasks have any substance or is it nothing but fine rhetoric?

Conditions favouring and limiting an independent role for Western Europe

The dynamics of inter-state politics and the role of Western Europe as a global actor

From the viewpoint of 'real socialism', Western Europe as a centre of world capitalism will always remain committed to the strategic aim of fighting socialism no matter where. While this may be logical, the practical relevancy of this logic is being modified by many factors. One of them derives from the dynamics of inter-state politics as such.

The modern world system which was established in the process of European industrialization remains a nation state system. To be more precise: the establishment of the modern world system went hand-in-hand with the creation of the nation-state system and fortified the latter. This was not in contradiction to a growing internationalization of production but rather interacted with it. The projection of the European nation-state system onto the globe has not been challenged by the advent of 'real socialism'. To the contrary, 'real socialism' is defined by its adaptation to the nation-state system. This adaptation, under Stalin, was perceived as 'socialism in one country'. Therefore, the East-West conflict from the very beginning has been an inter-state conflict. Or, to state the case in more general terms, the organization of social formations in a 'system of contending states' (Toynbee) has modified and continues to modify all social transformation processes by putting them into the context of a continuous struggle for the accumulation of national power. The one side of this accumulation process is national self-determination, the other hegemony.

Thus, under the specific conditions emanating from the Second World War, it was not only the universalistic antagonism between capitalism and socialism, but also the dynamics of the power accumulation process as such which led to the creation of a world order which was determined by the dual hegemony of the United States and the Soviet Union. This structure by its very nature implied a curtailment of the freedom of action of all other states, including the respective allies of the superpowers. Since freedom of action is one essential ingredient of self-determination, and since self-determination is a driving force of politics as long as the nation-state system exists, the bipolarization of the world, by itself, unleashed centrifugal countertrends, which did not abolish the antagonism between capitalism and socialism but modified the concrete meaning of this antagonism in international relations.

These centrifugal trends demonstrate a stubborn autonomy of the high politics of national self-assertion vis-à-vis the seeming imperatives embodied in global interdependence and universalistic value systems. However, since power inequalities between single states are transcended by power inequalities between regions, there is also a tendency to compensate these inequalities through 'group politics' on the international level, i.e. to coordinate and integrate national policies and to pool national resources in order to strengthen the competitiveness and bargaining position of the respective societies vis-à-vis third states.

From this viewpoint, the search for a 'European identity in the world' is limited but real. It is real because it reflects the general dynamics of inter-state politics. But it is also real in the specific context of present world developments. Thus, Western Europe with a view to the protracted world economic crisis and the destabilization of the global security system has a genuine interest to prevent horizontal conflict escalation under the global military power projection of the United States and the Soviet Union; it has a genuine interest in strengthening its position in the world economic system in the face of growing international competition and to open up new economic opportunities instead of limiting them through political considerations pertaining to the East-West conflict.

But the search for a European identity in the world is also limited. This is so for the following reasons: First, the dynamics of inter-state politics which are one of the causes of a differentiation of interests between Western Europe and the United States, at the same time constitute a grave obstacle for the formation of Europe as a single actor on the global stage. In accord with this observation, we have to remind ourselves that the search for a European identity was not only the expression of the necessity to combine forces in the global struggle for scarce resources (including influence and security). It was also an expression of the inability of the EC member countries to make substantial progress on the way towards the envisaged European Political Union. European political cooperation was introduced because overall political integration was way behind schedule, if not considered impossible for the time being. This situation was not only the result of a lack of political will to integrate, but rather of structural conditions reflecting the concrete divergencies of problems of growth and development among the Western European countries, the power disparities between the big and the small EC members, the complicated interplay between domestic and European politics in every one of the member states and also different political traditions and value orientations, which are, of course, still very much influenced by the historic experience of bloody intra-European rivalry.

The search for a 'European identity in the world' is also limited because, as a correlate to the divergencies of problems, potentials and interests among EC members, the policies of the latter towards the United States differ considerably. This has already been mentioned in connection with Central America. In addition, the existence of remarkable divergencies in the degree of cooperation and disagreement with the United States was demonstrated in the worldwide debates on a restructuring of the world economic order (in which Western Germany, France and Great Britain together with the US took a resolute position), the recent transatlantic debates on security matters, especially strategic questions and armament spending, the consent to, and critique of, Reaganomics and, most recently, by openly divergent views on SDI.

To sum up, the dynamics of inter-state politics in connection with specific economic and security concerns resulting from present world developments make it most likely that the search for a 'European identity in the world' will go on, but that this process will be very slow and in a piecemeal fashion. This general observation also holds true for the relationship of Western Europe with the United States. We may expect increasing conflicts of interest deriving from divergent security needs and from decreasing margins for compromise on economic matters. Such developments would further a policy of collective self-reliance both in the economic and the security field on the part of Western Europe.[26] But they are most unlikely to lead to an economic and military dissociation from the United States in the foreseeable future.[26] The following sections will try to substantiate this assumption.

The realignment of economic forces in the West
The Western Alliance was formed in a situation in which there was a striking discrepancy between the United States and the European countries in military as well as in economic potential. This situation has changed due to the quick reconstruction and post-war development of the European countries, but also due to a loss of dynamism of the US economy itself. In

this way, a reordering of economic power constellations within the Western Alliance occurred involving a relative economic decline of the United States vis-à-vis Western Europe.

At the end of the Second World War, the task for US economic policy was to put to work a vast productive capacity, which had been created during the war. Due to wartime destruction and trade restrictions, this capacity was matched outside the US by an equally vast need. Under the Marshall Plan, the US government helped to transform this need into an effective demand. Thus, a mutually re-enforcive spiral of transatlantic trade and European reconstruction was set in motion which functioned as an engine of growth for both sides.

Today, it is not a vast demand abroad to which the US economy is challenged to respond, but a tremendous productive capacity that has been built up in Europe as well as in Japan and in newly industrializing countries. The result is that the US is running a trade deficit of a previously inconceivable magnitude. In addition, the present Administration has embarked upon a programme of astronomical military spending resulting in unprecedented budgetary deficits. It could be argued that these developments imply a loss of economic leverage on the part of the US government vis-à-vis third states, making the attainment of American objectives abroad more dependent on political and military leverage. If this were the case, it would lead to new conflicts of interest with Western Europe because a continuing militarization of US foreign policy would increase the danger of a spillover of tensions from 'out of area' conflicts to Europe. Such undesired spillover could come about through conscious efforts (on the part of the United States) to influence Soviet behaviour in one region of the world (somewhere in the 'South') by applying pressure in another region (like Europe) or through the build-up of Western Europe as a logistic entity serving US global strategies without substantial influence of the Western Europeans themselves on strategy formulation and decision-making in concrete cases. In both functions, Western Europe is already being drawn into the global policy of the United States. As the controversy concerning the shipment of pipeline equipment to the Soviet Union has demonstrated, Western Europeans are quite aware of the conflicts of interest resulting from the fact that the economic costs of applying pressure on the Soviet Union in the context of the new US policy are much higher for them than for the United States itself.

Such conflicts do not, however, point to a general polarization of interests in the relationship between Western Europe and the United States. The United States remains an economic giant with a remarkable ability to influence European economic development both in a negative and a positive way. For instance, high interest rates in the United States have led to a drain of capital from Europe which in turn is considered by Europeans to be one of the causes of their economic stagnation. On the other hand, investment in the United States in connection with the high rating of the dollar has opened up export opportunities for European countries to the United States which, in some cases (like Western Germany) were by far the single most important source for a return to economic growth. This way the situation is ambiguous, leaving plenty of room for intra-European quarrels on what to do. With the same ambiguity the Western Europeans are confronted in the case of future technology policy and SDI. In the race for a new generation of technology (computers, bio-technology), the United States and Japan clearly lead the way, putting Western European governments under high pressure to consider closer cooperation with the United States as offered by the latter in the context of SDI. However, considering the ongoing attempts on the part of the US government to restrict the international flow of technological information in order to keep the Soviets from participating in Western achievements, it is most likely that technological cooperation in the context of SDI would help the Americans more to tap European capacities in this field than vice versa. In addition, it is much more costly to depend on civilian spin-off effects of military R & D than to achieve non-military technological advances by directly working on them. Therefore, it made sense that the Mitterrand government offered a European alternative to SDI, the Eureka-programme. But the prospects for a closer Western European cooperation envisaged in the Eureka-programme do not seem to be promising enough yet to convince all governments in Western Europe that they do have an alternative to the militarization of R & D under the leadership of the US in the context of SDI.

These brief observations, again, underline that there is an objective basis for the drive towards common action of EC countries vis-à-vis third states including their main ally, the United States, while, at the same time, there are serious limiting factors which will make for slow progress towards collective self-reliance of Western Europe. In this respect, reality is running way behind the visions of those who see Western Europe on the verge of neutrality or non-alignment.

Growing complexity of West-West politics and the economic and political differentiation of the Third World

There are still other factors giving substance to the search for a 'European identity in the world' and limiting it at the same time. First, there is the fast that the post-war reshuffling of the economic power constellation between the United States and Western Europe has been followed by the formation of an economic triangle, in which Japan has become the strongest cornerstone. There is no single European country that can match the Japanese economic potential today. But Japan has a decisive advantage even over the combined Western European economic potential accruing from the fact that the Japanese potential unfolds, just like that of the US, in one country. It is, therefore not hampered by the unnerving complications of multinational politics of the type practised in Western Europe. Furthermore, Japan is only part of a Pacific challenge to Europe, which has been building up for the last five or ten years. This challenge comprises the newly industrializing countries of the Far East. These countries have turned the incipient 'Asian drama' into something like a success story in comparison with other parts of the Third World like Africa and Latin America.[27] The impact of this success story is being enhanced by a Pacific bias in US politics under the dominance of West Coast interest and, to a certain degree, also by the growing importance of the Siberian-Pacific resources for the Soviet economy. These resources were opened up mainly with the help of European technology. But Japanese firms are advancing in this realm and may well help to give the flow of resources from this vast land a new direction – towards the East.

These converging developments may lead to the formation of a new centre of gravity to the world economy and world politics which would bring with it the danger of a final marginalization of Europe. The Pacific challenge, therefore, is of the utmost importance for the future of Western Europe. Meeting the Pacific challenge will absorb so much of public attention and practical skills, that almost by necessity the East-West conflict in the Third World will lose much of its impact on policy formulation vis-à-vis Third World countries in comparison to Western European economic interests in the context of the trilateral economic competition.

This tendency will be strengthened by the continuing differentition of political and economic interests and objectives which Third World governments pursue on the international level today. To be sure, there is at present a more systematic engagement of 'real socialism' in the Third World than there was ten years ago. But this engagement is not the expression of striking advances in the attempt to streamline the world in accord with the conceptualization of progress preferred by 'real socialism'. To the contrary: 'real socialism' just like the West has experienced the limits of its influence and power vis-à-vis Third World governments and societies.[28] The days of an easy going anti-imperialist optimism, which culminated at the Havana summit of the Non-Aligned Movement in 1979, are gone because it has become quite clear that socialism in Third World countries has as hard a time to survive with Western help as without it.

As pointed out above, reference to the East-West dimension of North-South relations in principal is justified due to the universality and globality of capitalism and socialism. But with a view to the ongoing political and economic differentiation within the Third World, within the OECD group and also among socialist countries and countries with a socialist orientation, reference to the East-West dimension of North-South relations involves a fair amount of ideology designed to justify intervention or other forms of forced interest aggregation as action in accord with the right to individual or collective self-defence.[29] The Western Europeans could, of course, try to foster their own interests in the Third World by defining them as part of the struggle between the two world systems. But first, as the experience of the past ten or fifteen years has shown, the socialist orientation of a Third World country does not at all infringe upon its interest to retain or even intensify its economic relations with Western countries. Socialism may even open up special chances for those who, like the Western Europeans in the face of increased international competition, are very much interested in growth and stability of international economic relations.

Second, for Western Europe, trade and economic cooperation with socialist countries has become a matter of unspectacular routine. With a view to this routine, it would not be very convincing to politicize economic relations with certain Third World countries on the ground that these countries pursue a policy of socialist transformation. Such a politicization of economic relations has much more to do with intra-Alliance politics than with actual developments in the Third World.

Third, within Western Europe, socialist political groupings play an important role but no role at all in the United States. The existence of these political groupings has made Western Europeans more willing to retreat from a monolithic interpretation of socialism and to accept the fact that there are not only many roads to socialism but also many forms of socialism and many forms of social organization that fit neither of the established categories.

In sum, it is very unlikely that Western Europe will eventually find it more profitable to return to a rigid, fundamentalist anti-communism than to try to broaden its relations with Third World countries regardless of their social order.

Global détente and the interest and capabilities of Western Europe: the record of the search for a 'European Identity in the World'

The main conclusion to be drawn from the preceding pages is that the reassertion of Europe and the search for a 'European identity in the world' are not expressions of a passing mood or a short-term irritation in Euro-American relations. They rather express long-term interests. East-West systemic competition is only one of various other settings, in which these interests are being defined. Among them are the dynamics of nation-state politics as such, the reshuffling of the economic power constellation within the OECD group, the formation of a Pacific challenge to Europe and a growing differentiation of interests and objectives pursued by Third World political forces on the international level. However, despite all the activities which have developed since the early seventies, the contours of a European identity in the world remain rather blurred and the record of achievements is mixed.

The search for a 'European identity in the world', on the official level, was viewed as an attempt to correct the former imbalance between inward and outward directed activities of the EC. In addition, the idea was forwarded that the search for such an identity could become a new moving force in the progress of European unification. This interpretation of the new outward directed activities did not go unquestioned. Especially in connection with the enlargement of the European Community (Britain, Denmark, Ireland), critical thoughts as to the nature of European integration and its functions for the member states and the outside world were being voiced. Such thoughts – on the academic level – climaxed in the thesis formulated by Johan Galtung, that the EC was 'a superpower in the making'.[30] This thesis implied that the EC was on its way to becoming a world power which, as such, would fortify the existing structures both in the East-West and the North-South, instead of helping to discard them.

The superpower thesis had some appeal especially in the academic community. But it soon turned out to be overstating or overdramatizing actual developments. Contrary to the expectations of those who hoped that the search for a European identity in the world would help to overcome the crisis of integration, this crisis deepened in the following years and hampered the search for an identity of Europe in the world. The failure especially of member states to come to grips with the problems of agrarian overproduction began to threaten the very existence of the Common Market. At the same time, outward-directed activities, while multiplying, were not very effective: the Euro-Arabian dialogue helped little in the way of establishing Europe as an effective actor. It began to fade in the early 1980s when oil lost much of its efficacy as an economic weapon. In addition, the global concept for the Mediterranean did not materialize and the European contribution to crisis management in the Third World at large remained marginal and was for a good part reduced to commissioning reports and issuing declarations with modest practical impact. Finally, there was a dramatic sobering up as far as the historic importance of the Lomé Convention and its quality as an example to the world for cooperative conflict solution was concerned.

Nevertheless, in principle there are a number of arguments pointing to the 'substantial rationality' (Karl Mannheim) of a continued search for a more independent role of Western Europe in the world. The first argument is one deriving more or less from the dynamics of power politics: a more independent role of Europe in world politics would, by definition, lead to a further multipolarization of international relations. It could thereby help to pave the way for the establishment of a new system of checks and balances in world politics which is urgently needed to cushion the global struggle for hegemony among the superpowers.

Second, Western Europeans are realizing today that the chances for isolating themselves from conflicts in the Third World are diminishing to the degree that superpower rivalry increases and the superpowers acquire the capacity for simultaneous military action in two or more world regions. Since superpower rivalry in the Third World does not manifest itself as such, but usually only in the context of concrete conflicts arising from conditions in the conflict area, the only dependable way to alleviate oneself from the danger of horizontal conflict escalation is to reduce conflict breeding conditions in the Third World. Under this perspective, Western

Europeans would have much to gain from a new global approach to détente which would accept social change in the Third World as such and not merely as a tactical move in the East-West struggle. Global tension-reduction, in the long run, would involve co-existence and preferably indirect or direct cooperation between the East and the West in the Third World. The chances for such a co-existence or cooperation at present are dim. But if there should be any advances on this way, they are more likely to develop among the European allies of the superpowers than between the superpowers themselves. Global détente in this understanding would enlarge the margin of action for self-determination in the Third World with a view to ideology as well as economic, technological and administrative capacities.

Notes

1. Klaus Ritter, 'The Dominance of East-West Conflicts', *Europa Archiv* 1985, pp. 1-10.

2. Daniel Yergin, *Shattered Peace. The Origins of the Cold War and the National Security State,* Boston 1977.

3. The Rio Pact of 1947 was the most visible expression of this transformation. Cf. *Inter-American Conference for the Maintenance of Continental Peace and Security.* Report of the Delegation of the United States of America, Washington, D.C. 1947; *Ninth International Conference of American States.* Report of the Delegation of the United States of America with Related Documents, Washington, D.C. 1948.

4. Cf. Henry Kissinger, *Memoiren 1968-1973,* München 1979, p. 182. German translation of the 1972 declaration on American-Soviet relations cf. *Europa Archiv* 27/1972, pp. D 289 sq.

5. Henry Trofimenko,'The Third World and the US-Soviet Competition: A Soviet View', in *Foreign Affairs*, Summer 1981, pp. 1981, pp. 1021 sq.

6. Cf. Alexander Dallin, 'Soviet Policy toward the Third World', in: *Vierteljahresberichte* (Bonn) No. 91, March 1983; Adrian Guelke, 'Southern Africa and the Superpowers', in *International Affairs 4, 1980.* J Seiler (ed.), *Southern Africa since the Portuguese Coup*, Boulder, Colorado, 1980.

7. In addition to the direct influence of the EEC on other regions' economic development, the EEC served as the example for effective regional integration.

8. Alfred Pijpers, 'European Political Cooperation and the CSCE Process', in *Legal Issues of European Integration*, December 1984, pp. 135–148.

9. Claude Cheysson hailed the Convention as 'unique in the world and unique in history'; *Frankfurter Allgemeine Zeitung*, February 1975.

10. Copenhagen Summit of the EC of 1973.

11. It rather was reaffirmed with special vigour by socialist governments and parties in France, Italy and Spain.

12. *EG Bulletin*[1], 1980, p. 9.

13. *Bulletin PE* 73862, July 6, 1981, p. 23.

14. Hans Adolf Jacobsen, Bedingungsfaktoren realistischer Entspannungs-politik, in: Deutsche Gesellschaft für Friedens- und Konfliktforschung (ed.), *Zur Entspannungspolitik in Europa.* Jahrbuch 1979/80, Baden-Baden 1980, p. 70.

15. Conference of European and Latin American States, San Jose, Costa Rica, September 28-29, 1984; German text of Communiqué in: *Europa Archiv* 2, 1985, pp. D 41 sq.

16. For a critical appraisal see William M. Leo-Grande, 'Through the Looking Glass. The Report of the National Bipartisan Commission on Central America', in *World Policy*, Winter 1984, pp. 251 sq.

17. Reimund Seidelmann, 'The Socialist International and Central America', in *Europa Archiv* 5, 1985, pp. 145 sq. Cf. Arnold M. Silver, *The New Face of the Socialist International*, Washington: The Heritage Foundation 1981, and Paul E. Sigmund,'Latin America: Change or Continuity', in *Foreign Affairs* 3, 1981, pp. 629 sq.

18. The German stand on Central America is determined much more by NATO politics than by actual developments in the area. With a view to this linkage, there was speculation in 1982 that the US had offered the Europeans a 'horsetrade' in the sense that the US would weaken their sanctions in the case of the Euro-Soviet pipeline deal against restraint on the part of the Europeans in their Central American policy and especially with a view to aid for Nicaragua. The existence of such an offer was denied by a speaker of the EC.

19. Heidemarie Wieczorek-Zeul, Member of the European Parliament.

20. In a debate of the European Parliament on the North-South Dialogue *Amtsblatt der Europäischen Gemeinschaften. Verhandlungen des Europäischen Parlaments,* Sitzungsperiode 1981–1982, Sitzungsberichte vom 14.–18. December 1981, pp. 126 sq. 147, 150 (statements by Poniatowski, Focke, Ferrero).

21. Katharina Focke stressed the crucial role of Europe in helping the global negotiations off the ground, ibid., p. 147–48.

22. Cf. Pisani, Focke, but also Berlinguer, ibid., pp. 127, 147 and 134.

23. Pisani himself already immediately after the Cancun Conference had been very open in expressing his doubts as to the possibility of inaugurating global negotiations in the foreseeable future. Ibid., p. 127.

24. Pisani Memorandum of 4 October 1982.

25. Ibid., pp. 13/14.

26. Cf. the opinion of former Chancellor, Helmut Schmidt, expressed in a recent speech at the Geneva 'Institut universitaire des hautes études internationales', that Western Europe even without US troops would be in a position to defend itself with conventional weapons against an attack by the Warsaw Pact, *Frankfurter Rundschau*, 9 March 1985.

27. Gunnar Myrdal, *Asian Drama*, New York 1968.

28. 'Soviet Geopolitical Momentum: Myth or Menace?', in *The Defense Monitor* IX, 1 January 1980.

29. This right (Art. 51 UN Charter) has been invoked both in the case of Soviet involvement in Afghanistan as in the case of US involvement in Central America and the Caribbean.

30. Johan Galtung, *The European Community. A Superpower in the Making*, London, 1981.

8.   A Keynesian Global Strategy for Employment and Peace

by Angelos Angelopoulos

A world economy out of control

Humanity confronts today a serious economic crisis. This crisis is characterized by enormous rates of unemployment, permanent inflation, high deficits in balances of payments, soaring interest levels, perverse fluctuations in exchange rates, steep drops in prices of raw materials, a large gap between rich and poor countries and a slowdown in economic growth.

Furthermore, there are many accompanying signs of social upheaval which result directly or indirectly from the economic crisis: political unrest, acts of anarchy and terrorism, repeated strikes and other profound disorders. These create a general anxiety throughout the world.

This anxiety becomes deeper because, despite the hopes that arose as a result of the application by governments of various remedial measures and adjustment mechanisms, the economic recession – outside of the United States and Japan – steadily progresses in almost all countries.

How can we explain this situation and determine what are the factors responsible for prolonging the economic recession and preventing the promotion of world economic growth?

Three great unsolved problems are mainly responsible for the poor state of the world's economy, for prolonging the recession, and for preventing economic growth.

The *first* is unemployment, which has assumed alarming dimensions. In the industrial countries alone, the number of unemployed has already gone beyond the figure of 35 million and the annual direct cost of this unemployment amounts, according to the OECD, to 350 billion dollars. It is expected that the number of unemployed will increase each year, particularly in Europe, in the period ahead. We must not forget that robots and office automation will progressively eliminate millions of today's jobs in the next decades. Technological progress is a permanent factor in the increase of unemployment. In the three years – 1980, 1981, 1982 – the production of industrial countries has been 2% higher than in the previous three year period, but with 15 million fewer workers. This situation demands a total revision of present economic and social policies for it is certain that the continuation of excessive unemployment will be a destabilizing factor in the world and will have serious economic, social and political consequences.

The second is the armaments race, which annually removes from the productive apparatus 700 billion dollars. The effects of this race have become more and more felt since 1980, when military expenditures began to increase faster than gross national products and at the expense of social outlays. According to American estimates, defence spending will increase between 1980 and 1984 by 41.5%, while spending for domestic programmes will decrease by 10%.[1] The permanent antagonism between the two superpowers is tending to transform the world's 'consumer and business economy' into an 'armament race economy'. Are we aware of the consequences of this deterioration?

The *third* problem, which endangers the foundation of the world's financial and banking system, is the over-indebtedness of Third World countries. I shall concentrate my remarks on this problem and propose an urgent solution.

The proposals are based on three postulates:

1. that the close and increasing interdependence in economic activity and international finance among all economies *requires* a global growth and development strategy encompassing all countries, industrial and developing.
2. that the prosperity of industrial countries is linked inexorably with the progress in developing countries and conversely. It is estimated that each increase by 10% of the imports of the developing countries causes an increase of 1% of the Gross National Product (GNP) of industrial countries, which further stimulates an additional increase of 3% in the exports of the developing countries.
3. that, as I shall explain later, the Keynesian theory – which helped to ensure full employment and raise living standards following World War II – can contribute to a solution of this problem, especially if applied on a world scale.

I shall now examine the requirements, effects and practicability of the application of my proposals.

The external debts of the developing countries today

Let us examine first the present situation with respect to the foreign debts of developing countries, and how they were created.

The developing countries, as a result of their economic backwardness, of the recession and especially of the oil crisis, have been obliged to incur external debt to cover the deficits in their payment balances. According to estimates of the International Monetary Fund (IMF), the total debts of the developing countries, which at the end of 1973 were only $97 billion, have increased to $329 billion in 1977 and to $812 billion at the end of 1984.[2] Table 9.1 shows the size and the distribution of this debt in the years 1977 and 1984.

Table 8.1 External debts of the developing countries: 1977 and 1984
($US billions)

	1977	1984
Developing countries:		
Total	329.3	812.4
Short term debt	51.6	97.6
Long term debt	277.7	714.8
By type of creditor:		
Official creditors:	111.0	254.4
Governments	79.1	166.4
International institutions	31.9	88.0
Private creditors:	166.7	460.4
Unguaranteed debt	55.1	112.3
Guaranteed debt	111.6	348.1
Non-oil developing countries:		
Total	280.3	710.9
Official creditors	97.6	235.0
Private creditors	139.6	387.8
	237.2	622.8

More serious, is not only the amount of the total debt, which is very large and represents 145% relative to exports and 38% of the aggregate Gross National Product (GNP)[3] of the developing debtor countries, but the extremely unfavourable conditions (interest plus amortization), which for the year 1984 alone obligate the debtor countries to pay an amount of $122 billion in servicing charges, which is a tremendous burden on their budgets and their foreign exchange balances.

This high annual service arises mainly because the greater part (more than the half : 57.5%) of these debts is owed to private lenders, particuarly to banks, and the greater part of these debts (about $460 billion) must be repaid within seven to eight years. It is indeed this private debt of $460 billion which constitutes the most important and most urgent problem that needs to find a rapid solution. These private bank loans have been granted under more unfavourable conditions concerning interest and amortization, as compared with the official debts to governments.

With respect to these private debts, amortization – that is repayment of capital – represents more than 60% of the total annual service. Thus it constitutes a great difficulty for the developing countries. For the period 1972 to 1982, amortization accounted for 62.5% while interest represented 37.5% of the debt servicing payments by developing countries.

The debts to governments have been incurred under more favourable conditions. According to the World Bank, the public debt interest rate averaged 7.8% for 1978 with a 16-year maturity and a grace period of 4.4 years, while the interest rate for private debts averaged 13.64% and the maturity 8.7 years. For this reason, my proposals concerning a solution to this problem concentrate on the private debt of the developing countries and not on the debts to governments.

The special case of Latin America

In Latin America the situation is worse. Here foreign debts to private lenders abroad amounted, at the end of 1983, to $305 billion. The table below shows the distribution of these debts by country as well as the annual servicing requirements in relation to the value of their total export receipts.

Table 8.2 Latin America countries
Foreign debts servicing and exports (1983)
(in $ billion)

	Debt	Service	Exports
Argentina	43.0	4.2	7.9
Brazil	94.0	10.2	21.9
Chile	19.0	2.0	3.8
Columbia	11.0	1.0	3.1
Mexico	90.0	12.0	21.2
Peru	13.0	1.2	3.3
Venezuela	35.0	4.2	16.2
Total	305.0	34.8	77.4

Source: IMF, *Trade Statistics 1984.*

From the above table, it may be seen that the servicing of the debt payments absorbs 45% of total export receipts – a very high proportion – and in certain countries, as Brazil and Mexico, more than 50%. If one takes into consideration also short term credits, the situation is worse. According to an estimate of the Morgan Guarantee Trust Company, four countries alone (Brazil, Mexico, Argentina and Venezuela) owed at the end of 1982 aggregate debts of $235 billion and these countries were obligated to pay in 1983 alone an amount of $112 billion for servicing (including short-term credits), which was equivalent to 47% of their total debts.

The situation will deteriorate in the coming years because the loans must be repaid in the next few years.

It is evident that such a repayment will be impossible to realize. For Brazil, for instance, the total debt service for the year 1984 represents 51% of its 1983 total exports, and for Argentina the figure is 57%. These proportions will be greater for the years 1985–89. Are the creditors aware of this financial situation? Do they know that the income per capita has dropped by 3% and, according to the last report of the Inter-American Development Bank, this drop was the most dramatic setback since the Great Depression, and brought living standards down to 1947 levels? Do they know that inflation in this region is more than 100% per year?

One must recognize that, for the creation of this 'debt crisis', all con-

Table 8.3 Projected Public Debt Service
(in $ billions $US)

	1985	1986	1987	1988	1989
Principal	29.805	33.898	33.643	33.800	29.471
Interest	20.677	18.012	14.842	11.178	7.859
Total debt service	50.482	51.910	48.485	44.978	37.330

Source: World Bank, *World Debt Tables, 1983*–84 Edition, Second Supplement.

cerned parties – banks, industrial and developing countries – are responsible:

The banks granted new loans and credits without examining the creditworthiness of the borrower, nor the use of the product of the loans. Having large amounts of funds at their disposal, they took a short-term view with the objective of obtaining immediate profits without thinking about the eventual risks;

The industrial countries sought to obtain greater exports not only, or mainly, for increased output of productive goods, but frequently for non-productive purposes, particularly armaments, and they encouraged the banks to grant the necessary loans. According to the Stockholm International Peace Research Institute (SIPRI), the Third World has experienced a tremendous increase in military expenditures. Their share in world military expenditure, which was, in 1971, 9%, increased to 16% in 1982 and is certainly higher today;

Finally, because the developing countries, instead of utilizing the funds received for productive purposes, devoted them to non-productive purposes and wasteful expenditures.

The proposals hitherto made by the international organizations and particularly by the IMF do not appear to provide an effective solution to the problem. Payments moratoria for one or two years for certain countries provide only a temporary illusionary arrangement without addressing the essence of the problem itself. Moreover, the requirements imposed by the IMF compound economic chaos by stimulating social destabilization and political unrest in many countries of the Third World.

To force developing countries to reduce their already low standards of living provokes a chain reaction, which ultimately leads to a defiance of foreign creditors. A sluggish world economy does not afford an opportunity for any significant increase in their exports, and the only possibility left to them is to apply the austerity policies required by the IMF, which results in a further reduction of their existing meagre imports. A diminution of the imports of the developing countries has, as an effect, a reduction in the exports of the industrial countries and in turn the deterioration of their economic situation. Is this a rational economic policy to apply?

Other agreements between debtor countries and banks do not provide a real solution to the long term economic problem. For example, the agreement with Argentina, although it adopts a more realistic orientation, does not lead to a basic improvement of the situation in that country where the inflation has increased from 434% in 1983 to 700% in 1984. Even the Quito Declaration and Plan of Action adopted on 13 January 1984, which proposed to link the payment of external debts to the level of export earnings on a basis of a 'reasonable percentage', is only a partial solution to the economic problems involved and moreover has not been accepted by the lending countries.

So, the debt situation of the developing countries is clearly untenable. It is inconceivable, by their past record, that Latin American countries will be able to pay over the five years (1985–89) $233 billion for debt service, an amount that represents more than 50% of their probable exports. It is unrealistic to think that such a payment is possible without a complete social and political destabilization of the debtor countries.

We must understand that the problem for the developing countries is a general structural problem and not a cyclical one. In order to solve this problem, the industrial countries, and specifically the banks, must help with a realistic plan that will be beneficial for all parties concerned. What this solution could be, we shall see in the next paragraph.

A plan to face the debt crisis and promote world economic growth

Let us now see how this problem could be overcome in the interests of all concerned: the lending banks, the debtor countries, and the industrial countries. In a recent book I submitted two basic proposals to avoid a general crisis in the international banking system and to revive world economic growth.[4]

The first envisages an immediate approach to the existing debt problem and the second a new long-term financing system. The first involves a suspension for a five-year period of the amortization of the capital of the existing debts of the developing countries. This amortization, which represents about 62% of the total annual service – an amount between $50 and $60 billion per year – would resume in the sixth year. The repayment of the capital will be resumed in the sixth year, and the entire remaining debt will be prolonged for a further period of fifteen years.

Interest during the grace period of five years would be paid to the banks – either at rates prevailing on the international market, or at a rate of 5% for the more slowly developing countries. In this case, the differences between the 5% rate and the rate prevailing on the market – which would probably be about 8 or 9% – would be added to the capital owed.

Neither arrangement would bring any real loss for the banks during the grace period of five years, as they would receive full interest.

During the extension period of fifteen years, interests should be paid also at the rate prevailing on the international market, with exception made for the more slowly developing countries, for which the interest rate could be lower – 4 or 5%.

The sums saved during the grace period of five years by the postponement of the amortization of capital, which could amount to about $220 billion, should be used exclusively for development projects, and the capital goods and services required would be bought from the creditor countries to which the amortization payments are owed.

This arrangement should be adopted and applied as a general arrangement for all debtor countries. It may be argued – as it is frequently in the United States – that no generalized or overall solution should be sought to the over-indebtedness problem since conditions are different for each developing country. This is true to some extent, but the argument disregards a very important psychological factor, namely that the adoption of the general principle of the postponement of capital amortization for five years for all debtor countries would create the proper climate of confidence which is a prerequisite for a new period of international, constructive cooperation. The particulars of the application of the plan could be negotiated separately with each individual developing country willing to accept the arrangement.

Perhaps the creation of a consortium of the big lending banks, in concordance with the main borrower countries, could facilitate the search for a practical solution. The present apathy, which is characterized by short-term solutions, made possible by provisional reschedulings, not only does not constitute a solution to the problem, but contributes to a larger complication and to the deterioration of the whole situation.

At the same time, over a period of five years, the industrial countries would grant new loans of a 25 year maturity to the developing countries under the following conditions:

1. The loans would be equivalent to 0.5 to 1% of the GNP of the industrial countries, that is loans totalling between $35 and $50 billion per year during the period of five years.
2. Interest on these loans would be at a 5% rate with a grace period of five years.[5]
3. The proceeds of these loans would be used exclusively to purchase capital goods and services from the donor countries.
4. A procedure would be established to ensure that these loans were used for productive projects in each borrowing country.

To safeguard the impartial character of the refinancing, it would be desirable that an international institution administer the financing and recycling mechanism between the industrial countries and the Third World. This institution could be the World Bank, as it already has the administrative apparatus and broad experience in dealing with developing countries. It might have to be reorganised somewhat or these financing functions could be added to its present structure. Furthermore, it might be possible to create a 'guarantee fund' to cover possible defaults on high-risk loans. On this point, an interesting proposal has been put forward by the former governor of the Bank of Greece, Prof Xenophon Zolotas, and submitted to the United Nations.[6]

The effects of the proposed plan would be beneficial to all concerned. Private banks would be able, through application of the proposed plan, to avoid a grave crisis resulting from the incapacity of the Third World debtor countries to pay the servicing charges due without any real loss for the banks themselves. For, as we have already pointed out, during the five-year grace period interest would be paid, either at rates prevailing on the international market, or at a special lower rate, with the difference between the special and prevailing market rates added to the capital owed for eventual payment. In other words, the formula would be the same as that for a long-term bank loan, in respect of which the creditor annually receives the interest due. The extension of the time of the amortization conforms with the usual conditions in the industrial countries for loans granted to private enterprises. In fact, governmental loans generally have a 15–25 year repayment period rather than the seven or eight years for private bank loans to developing countries.

If a solution to this problem is not found, the continuation of the present situation will inevitably lead to the bankruptcy of a number of banks that have furnished the greater part of this capital and to the cancellation of existing debts. It is perhaps useful to recall that, in the 5th century when the people of Athens were heavily indebted, the philosopher Solon, who was asked to advise a solution to the problem, introduced a decree called in Greek the 'Sisachthia', i.e. a law ordering the pure and simple abolition of all existing debts.

The developing countries would be able, through the above measures, to reduce the heavy charges on their budgets. They would also be able, as a result of the new long-term financing provided, to accelerate their economic and social development and increase the welfare of their populations.

With the application of this plan, the developing countries should have at their disposal during the first five-year period a total sum of $425 billion, of which $225 billion would result from the suspension of payments of the capital on existing debts and $200 billion as a result of the new financing granted.

It should be re-emphasized that one of the necessary conditions for the successful application of this plan would be that the developing countries would use the sums saved by the moratorium in a productive way, excluding unproductive and wasteful expenditures. The developing countries should thus be able to create an additional and strong aggregate demand for capital equipment and related services to the benefit of the industrial countries.

Industrial countries would benefit most from the application of this plan. Indeed, most of these countries are now confronted with a prolonged recession and steadily increasing unemployment, basically due to an insufficient demand. At present, demand in the industrial countries is mainly a 'maintenance demand' – to maintain the existing productive apparatus – and not a 'creative demand' capable of accelerating production, productivity and new capital investment. Entrepreneurs hesitate to make new investments for fear that their products will not be absorbed by the market.

It is, therefore, necessary to find additional markets able to absorb an increased production. If these markets cannot be found inside their economies, they must be found elsewhere. They can be found in the developing countries, which greatly need capital equipment and services to accelerate their economic and social development, but which do not now have the finance to acquire them.

The key to the solution of this fundamental problem is that we must create a mechanism that will permit a recycling of capital and goods between the industrial and the developing countries. The creation of new, effective demand in Third World countries could stimulate investment and employment in industrial countries. This is the essence of our plan. Taking into account, on the one hand, the economic needs of the countries of Asia, Africa, and Latin America in capital goods and services, and, on the other, the huge extent of surplus production capacity and unemployment in the industrial countries, it is really strange that such a plan has not been applied earlier.

A plan such as we propose for increasing demand for goods and services could be criticized on the grounds that it might increase inflationary tendencies in the donor countries. But this argument cannot be valid for the following reasons: 1) There is more than sufficient unutilized capacity to produce the additional goods and services required, and more than enough unemployed manpower. 2) Inflation is caused not by additional output of a productive nature, but rather by deficits due to spending on unproductive goods such as military hardware. Moreover, for the borrowing developing countries, the supply of additional productive goods would surely help combat the inflationary conditions that currently prevail in many of them.

Toward a Keynesian approach on a world scale for a new Marshall Plan

This plan would apply Keynesian policies on a world scale. The British economist John Maynard Keynes made an important contribution to economic growth and social progress in the Western industrialized countries for a quarter of a century, from 1948 to 1973. When his book, *The General Theory of Employment: Interest and Money* appeared in 1936, the effects of the economic crisis of 1929 were still vivid and very deeply embedded in the economic systems of all industrialized countries. A very high rate of unemployment prevailed. Keynes, in fact, foresaw the influence of the application of his theory on economic development. In a letter that he sent to his friend George Bernard Shaw on New Year's day in 1935, he wrote:

I believe myself to be writing a book on economic theory which will largely revolutionize – not I suppose at once but in the course of the next ten years – the way the world thinks about economic problems. . . . I know that you will not believe me at the present time. As far as I am concerned, this is not a hope which I express but a certainty.

And Keynes was right. His book was truly revolutionary, and his theory became the foundation of the economic policy of the Western countries. It helped to ensure, between 1948 and 1973, full employment in the industrial countries of Europe, a sustained economic growth, and an accelerating improvement in standards of living. As Kenneth Galbraith wrote in 1965 in his preface to the American edition of the *General Theory,* 'The Keynesian revolution was from a social viewpoint one of the greatest accomplishments of our times'.

In recent years especially, the question has been widely posed as to whether the Keynesian principles continue to be relevant in formulating national economic policy today, as they were during the earlier period when they were widely applied.

There are many factors – economic, social, technological, and political – that have led many economists to question the applicability of the Keynesian theory on a national scale, arguing that it can no longer ensure full employment and sustained growth without inflation. Of course, there are limits to the applicability of every economic theory under different conditions. Keynes himself recognized that his theory was not eternal, but argued that it gave to capitalism, as he said, 'thirty years of grace, of further life'.

There is no doubt that, if Keynes had lived longer, he would have adjusted his doctrine to the contemporary conditions and factors that have intervened in the interim and that have so dramatically altered the structure of society and of the world economy.

Indeed I believe that a readjustment of the Keynesian theory would permit its applicability on a world scale and could contribute, as Professor Lawrence Klein writes in the foreword to my book *Global Plan for Employment* 'to parlay the Keynesian medicine into another generation of high performance for the world economy beyond the turn of the century . . .'

The application of a Keynesian policy on a world scale means that the basic principles of this policy – namely the 'equalisation of savings and investments', the 'propensity to consume', the 'stimulation of investments', the 'distribution of wealth', and the 'intervention of the state' – would be utilized not merely within a national framework, but in an international context. As Keynes aimed at the creation of an effective demand of sufficient size to ensure full employment and improve the living conditions of low-income earners, through a new distribution of income on a national scale, so this proposed policy would be applied to the world economy as a whole. In other words, the Keynesian principles would be extended on a global scale to create a new aggregate demand in the developing countries, thereby helping to create new investments and jobs in the industrial countries.

In other words, a new Marshall Plan would thus be created, but on a worldwide scale. The objective of the Plan is to solve the problem of the overindebtedness of the developing countries and to provide at the same time a new long-term financing facility. In addition, this plan would eliminate one of the gravest debt problems in modern history, and lead to a fruitful cooperation between North and South.

Humanity needs an international manager capable of reviving economic activity, of promoting development and of ensuring prosperity and peace on a worldwide scale. In the realization of such a plan, Europe could play a prominent role, creating the appropriate climate for an international cooperation.

Indeed, Europe is destined to play an autonomous role between the superpowers and contribute to the reinforcement of détente. This policy could lead to a substantial reduction in military expenditures thereby releasing important resources, that will be utilized for the economic and social progress of all countries.

Notes

1. See: *U.S. News and World Report*, 12 December 1983, p. 87.

2. IMF, *World Economic Outlook*, 1984, p. 205.

3. IMF, op. cit., p. 206.

4. Angelos Angelopoulos, *Global Plan for Employment: A New Marshall Plan*. New York, Praeger, 1983.

5. In *Global Plan for Employment*, I proposed that these loans should be free of interest during the first five years. I think now that the debtor countries could pay an interest rate of 5%.

6. Xenophon Zolotas, *An International Loan Insurance Scheme: A Proposal*. Athens, Bank of Greece, 1978.

9. Peace and Poverty: Europe's Responsibility

by Louis Emmerij

The interrelationship between peace and development

What are the two greatest challenges of this century? Peace and security are, of course, our first preoccupation. If we cannot maintain these, we lose everything in an era of nuclear armament. It is not astonishing, therefore, that the problem of peace and security has attracted such overwhelming attention during the past few years and been given a high priority also in public opinion.

In a world which has become smaller because of the network of communications and the global international division of labour, international differences in income and lifestyles have become greater. It stood to reason, therefore, that for years the problem of poverty was considered the second greatest challenge of this century. In contrast to the problem of peace and security, poverty in the world has become a much lower priority item during the past few years. This has come about precisely at the moment when we have reached an economic, technological and financial situation which would make it technically possible to vanquish the poverty problem.

The paradox inherent in these two observations is that a relationship exists between peace and security on the one hand and poverty on the other: 'Poverty anywhere is a threat to peace and prosperity everywhere'. Why does the poverty problem no longer captivate the minds and the attention of people?

1. There is the fact that the new orthodoxy in financial and economic policies today again takes as a point of departure that it is economic growth that should be obtained at any price and so much less attention is paid to problems of income distribution, employment and poverty.

2. The more cynical outlook 'there will always be poor people' or 'we shall always have a poorest twenty per cent' prevails once again.

3. There is also a more technical and statistical discussion taking place. The concept of per capita income as expressed in US dollars has relatively little meaning in poor countries. Real purchasing power, production for consumption, the existence of the informal sector cause the actual situation to be less serious and tragic than the dollar-figures would insinuate, or so the reasoning goes!

4.   There is obviously a question of 'aid fatigue', not in the least because so much of the development cooperation effort has gone into ad hoc projects which were isolated events in the economy and society of the receiving country. Thus, this effort has not had structural effects. In turn this caused the poverty problem to increase rather than decrease.

5.   There is the problem of the very skewed distribution of income and wealth in the developing countries. There is often more conspicuous wealth in the poor countries than in the rich countries. This has as one of its consequences that development cooperation is being defined as the transfer of money from the poor in the rich countries to the rich in the poor countries.

The above points are sufficient reason to downplay the poverty problem in spite of, or maybe because of, the reappearance of relative poverty in the industrialized countries. This is true in spite of the observed fact that the employment problem and the question of poverty have not improved despite a long period of economic growth; on the contrary. For instance, the employment problem in developing countries still covers about one third of the active population. The number of people in absolute poverty is still on the increase. We needed the Ethiopian shock to realize that not even the food problem has been solved. The poverty problem is therefore still with us, increasing in volume, while the end of the tunnel is not yet in sight particularly in Africa and parts of Asia, and Latin America.

There is plenty of evidence in recent history to show how this poverty problem can become a threat to world peace. The example of Cuba in October 1962 is still fresh in most people's memory. More recent examples can be found in Central America, the Horn of Africa, Southern Africa, the Gulf, South Asia, etc. These are all countries or regions where poverty and/or political mismanagement stand at the base of problems of peace and security.

Poverty and peace are, therefore, closely interrelated. This does not mean, of course, that, as soon as poverty will have been banished, the problems of peace and security will be fully solved. This in spite of the fact that one could probably show that in about 30 to 50 years from now war will be much more difficult technically speaking – in the light of the growing interdependencies in the social, economic and technological fields. However this may be, when absolute poverty will have been reduced to its bare minimum, this by itself will reduce the chances that local problems will come up in the developing countries, and hence the threat of a general conflict will become less. Therefore, why not launch a campaign to wipe out absolute poverty within one generation in order to increase the chances of peace and security in the world? This would imply first and foremost the design of an economic and social development strategy which would focus on the satisfaction of the basic needs of the people within one generation. Europe's role in the realization and implementation of such a strategy could be vital. The next section indicates what such a strategy could look like.

Evolution towards basic needs

The origin

At first there was the paradox of high rates of economic growth that were paralleled by deteriorating trends in the employment situation and in the income distribution of developing countries. Indeed, the average rate of economic growth of these countries between the early 1950s and early 1970s amounted to around 5%, with several countries even reaching the 7 or 8% mark. An unprecedented high rate of economic growth historically anywhere. In spite of these very respectable rates of economic growth sustained over a long period, it became 'suddenly' clear towards the end of the 1960s that the employment situation was deteriorating in the face of the growing number of people looking for productive income-earning opportunities. Simultaneously, the awareness grew of a worsening in income distribution trends and the consequent increase in the number of people living in absolute poverty. These interrelated observations also apply to those developing countries whose rate of economic growth was far above the average.

The search for explanations started. The following summary of one of the diagnoses seems to me to give a plausible explanation. The economic and social development strategy which has been applied in the bulk of the developing countries since the end of the Second World War, and which is at the base of economic and social development planning and policies, can be traced back to the theoretical work of Arthur Lewis and Fei and Ranis.[1] In a nutshell, the approach inherent in this 'labour surplus model' amounts to the following. Within a country's economy two sectors can be distinguished: the modern and the traditional. The modern sector is supposed to be the engine of economic growth which will put into motion and move the entire convoy of economic and social development. The traditional delivers the cheap petrol for the engine in the form of labour which is present in abundant quantities. In this manner, unemployed and underemployed persons in the traditional sector move to the modern sector where they are all supposed to be productively employed in the rapidly explanding industrial and service sectors. Thus, planners and political decision-makers should fully concentrate on the growth and expansion of the modern sector. An important assumption of this extremely simplified version of the labour surplus model is that wages and salaries in the modern sector remain constant in real terms as long as the supply of labour from the traditional sector remains abundant.

But how did this situation develop in reality? In actual fact, the modern sector developed into a highly capital-intensive (partly because wages and salaries did not remain constant there), high labour-productivity enclave concentrated in a few cities – an enclave of steel and glass where a handful of people received incomes and salaries far above the country's average. In the meantime, the demographic horse continued its gallop, causing a population increase of 2.5-4.0% per year. At the same

163

time, because of the bright lights and high salaries in the cities, the rural/urban migration towards the urban-based modern sector became more and more important – further stimulated by ill-planned educational policies and expansion.

In retrospect, we can now say that the modern sector, because of its capital-intensive character and its high labour productivity, could and did develop very fast, but created much less productive employment than was anticipated. Because of the rapid population increase, the educational explosion and the much slower growth of the traditional sector, underemployment in the rural areas was transformed into visible and open unemployment in the urban sector which, in turn, led to the creation and expansion of the 'urban informal sector', as it is termed.[2]

This conventional development model was therefore based on the assumption that growth, with emphasis on the modern sector, was in itself *the* solution to development because, so the asumption went, the fruits of this growth would automatically, and *within an acceptable period of time*, spread to the less privileged sectors of the economy and to the poor segments of the population. This assumption has proved to be wrong. The economic growth based on this model concentrated on a few modern and capital-intensive branches of manufacturing and services and sometimes of agriculture which remained enclaves and which had a very small spread effect indeed. This small spread effect was also due to the fact that the modern sector of the poor countries was linked to the economies of the industrialized nations rather than to their own national *hinterland*. In this manner, it was possible to observe respectable growth indicators which, however, were hiding deterioration trends in the employment and income distribution situations. It is amazing that it was not realized at an earlier stage that the realistic solution would be an alternative development model focusing much more explicitly and *directly* on improving productivity and incomes in the low productivity sectors of the economy.

But what do we mean by the employment and income distribution problems? Although the notion of income distribution does not need further elaboration, it is worth clarifying what I mean by the employment problem. The employment problem has three major aspects. The first is, of course, overt unemployment where income is zero. This is partiuclarly dramatic but in reality, as a proportion of the overall employment problem, it is, on the whole and quantitatively speaking, relatively small. The most important aspect of the employment problem is the second, constituted of all those people who are not unemployed by any conventional criteria (on the contrary, they are often overemployed in terms of hours of work per day), but who only receive a poverty return for their labour. Here, therefore, we find all those people whose productivity is low, who are under-utilized and whose income falls below what has come to be called the poverty line. Finally, the third aspect might be called the psychological or frustration dimension of the employment problem. The most spectacular illustration of this aspect is the problem of the educated unemployed, i.e., people who could possibly find a job which, however, falls short of their aspirations and expectations through which they are led to believe they have an automatic right to a given status in terms of professional hierarchy linked to a given level of income.

The second, or poverty aspect, is clearly the most important but this does not mean that the others are unimportant. For young people to start their lives, whether they have had a certain number of years of education or not, with a frustrating round of job seeking may have important consequences on their subsequent actions. The low productivity and malutilization of many people in the labour force are obviously obstacles to a higher and better spread economic growth.

In order to face the employment problem as just defined, and given its origin in the conventional model of economic growth as summarized earlier, the search continued but now to identify alternative and more appropriate remedies.

Employment-oriented development strategies

An initial reaction to the above diagnosis was to concentrate explicitly on the creation of productive employment opportunities. Instead of taking as a starting point the rate of economic growth and deduce everything else, including employment implications from that, there should be a more balanced focus of attention, giving to the factor labour a much higher and a more explicit priority than had been accorded to it in the conventional development model.

Let me briefly pass in review a certain number of insights which we either gained or regained in the development problem during this phase of focusing on employment creation.

The first insight was to define more clearly both the dimension and the characteristics of the employment problem. This has already been presented above and is now widely accepted. But this was not so at the beginning of the seventies when most observers would leave out the whole poverty aspect of the problem and concentrate on open unemployment and specific aspects of underemployment.

It is the emphasis on the poverty dimension which, through income distribution, links the employment problem to overall economic and social questions. It is this same emphasis which has led many economists now to the conclusion that the overall rate of economic growth as an indicator for development is inadequate and that different weights must be given to increases in incomes of different social groups.

A second insight was arrived at by putting forward a quantitative relationship between the income distribution in a country on the one hand, and the employment problem on the other – a relationship which was different from the usual one most often hypothesized in economic literature, although there have always been exceptions. This conventional relationship was still dominated by the assumption that people with higher incomes also saved more and that therefore a skewed income distribution would be a good thing for higher savings, thus more investment, and so benefit economic growth and employment. There was not enough emphasis on possible negative aspects of a very uneven income distribution on the employment problem. Indeed, the high incomes frequently have a bizarre habit of leaving the country, savings are often placed abroad, a large part of the incomes are spent on imported goods and, if produced locally, on capital-intensive goods. Low incomes, on the other hand, are spent much more on locally-produced, labour-intensive goods. In this manner, the uneven income distributions we observe in many countries not only reflect the employment problem, but also *cause* it. This negative relationship has been underlined earlier but only during the 1970s have attempts been made to quantify the positive aspects of a given change in income distribution on the creation of productive employment opportunities. The results of these studies, although uneven, do tend to show that employment creation can become one of the more effective means of obtaining a less unequal income distribution, which in turn will further stimulate employment creation. For once we have an upward-spiralling circle rather than the better known vicious one.

A third and, to my mind, very important insight which is basic to the identification of an alternative development model, is the role to be played by the informal sector. I have already made reference to the concept of the urban informal sector earlier referring to the Kenya employment report. Basically this sector embraces activities that are characterized by: 1) ease of entry; 2) reliance on indigenous preferences; 3) family ownership of enterprises; 4) small-scale of operation; 5) highly labour-intensive technology; 6) skills acquired outside the normal school system; and 7) unregulated and competitive markets.

The bulk of employment in the informal sector, far from being only marginally productive, is, potentially at least, economically efficient and profit-making, though small in scale and limited by simple technologies, little capital, and suffering from lack of links with the modern (formal) sector. There is considerable evidence of technical change in the urban informal sector, as well as of regular employment at incomes above the average level attainable in smallholder agriculture. In most cases one can observe strong discrimination against the informal sector activities through such means as unrealistically high standards and licensing systems. It is the emerging view that most indigenous enterprises are small because of a structure of the economy in which policy measures favour the modern formal sector. Equally, or even more, important is the competitive advantage enjoyed by large enterprises, especially as a result of state measures reducing the cost of capital (duty-free imports of capital goods, relatively low rates of interest) and restricting competition (high tariffs; quotas; and building, health and safety regulations). It is not always certain whether many large-scale firms would be competitive relatively to small enterprises if they were required to compete without state favours.

Thus, a positive attitude on the part of the government towards the promotion of the informal sector is to be recommended. The strategy which could be put forward in this respect might embrace the following measures:

1. reviewing trade and commercial licensing with a view to eliminating unnecessary licences;
2. intensifying technical research and development on products suitable for fabrication in the informal sector;
3. attempting to increase government purchases of products and services obtainable from the informal sector; and
4. using large firms to train sub-contractors in the informal sector.

Whilst the conventional development model, based largely on the labour surplus theory, favoured an indirect approach towards development via the modern sector, the emerging alternative model favoured a *direct* approach which, without of course neglecting the modern formal sector, puts an equal amount of its 'eggs' into the hitherto neglected and low-productivity sectors. Some critics have maintained that such a development approach means perpetuating low incomes and poverty because of the very emphasis on the low-productivity sectors. Nothing could be further from the truth. Indeed, the choice is between, on the one hand, a strategy which favours disproportionately a small minority in the modern formal sector, while the majority of the population who cannot gain access to that sector eke out a precarious existence in urban informal and rural traditional sectors, and, on the other hand, a strategy which, given this situation, attempts to raise directly the productivity and the incomes of people in those low-productivity sectors. It is the latter approach, therefore, which is the more progressive and the more equitable. The point here is that the labour-surplus model has underestimated the length of the *transition period.* If in the foreseeable future the modern sector cannot absorb the entire economy, one must do something about the remainder!

A fourth insight we have obtained in the course of the 1970s is related to the link between education, training and employment. The strong emphasis on the quantitative link between the occupational structure and educational expansion can no longer be considered the most important one. The role and responsibility of education and training systems in employment and income distribution is not so much one of estimating the number of engineers or technicians required at a future date, but rather a question of structure and content of education. The formal educational system in most countries shows typical cannibalistic tendencies, in the sense that each level of education educates its products mainly for the next level, rather than for the world of work outside. Thus, the entire educational system is primarily geared to the minority climbing up to the top of the educational ladder, and not to the majority which drops out well before the end of the ladder is in sight. The aspirations and expectations stimulated and perpetuated in this manner cannot be remedied by a 'more of the same' approach, but only by changing the structure and content of education, linking it *qualitatively* to the immediate environment of the school in which the pupils and students have to spend the rest of their lives.

Another important question which is often forgotten by those who are obsessed by the planning of education and the expansion of secondary and higher education is: what happens to the 25 to 50% of the young people who either never go to school or who are very early drop-outs? This is one of the reasons why, in most developing countries, a re-allocation of resources is in order, in favour of basic education to cater more fully for the very young and to make sure that they get a minimum but complete educational base. In this connection it is also important to underline the importance of creating a link between formal and informal systems of education. Imaginative informal training centres must be set up which can pick up those who have fallen out of the educational boat or did not have a chance to get into it in the first place. There is much talk of an opposition between equity and efficiency: yet to re-allocate resources in favour of basic education and create second-chance informal institutions is both equitable and efficient.

I have selected a few examples only in order to show the direction of where development thinking was going. Obviously, the road was clear for the next step leading to the concept of 'basic needs'.

The original concept of a basic needs development strategy
Just think back to the situation faced, quantitatively and qualitatively, by those of us who about ten years ago had reached the stage in our thinking set out in the previous pages. Quantitatively, the situation was that about 275 to 300 million persons in the developing countries were inadequately employed, 550 to 700 million lived in severe poverty 500 million were chronically hungry and 1,500 million were illiterate. As mentioned already, despite two decades of rapid growth of national output in most developing countries, these indices of deprivation had clearly risen in absolute terms from 1950 to 1960 and again from 1960 to 1970. Moreover, in some developing countries there was evidence that sections of the poorest half of the population had become absolutely even poorer. Writing in 1985 the only thing that has changed is that people have grown tired of figures like those just quoted. The figures themselves continue to grow!

Back to the mid 1970s. We knew that between the early 1970s and the year 2000 the labour force and the population of developing countries would approximately double. Not only should productive employment opportunities be found for the approximately 300 million people then unemployed or inadequately employed, but for a total of 1,000 million including those who will be entering the labour markets of the third world over the following 25 years.

We knew, given our diagnosis, that there is nothing in the record of the past 20 to 25 years to support the contention that maximizing the rate of growth of national product within present output and distribution patterns can meet employment needs or eliminate absolute poverty in most developing countries over the foreseeable future. The exceptions are a handful of small countries where there is a high ratio of natural resources to population or where there was an extraordinarily rapid export growth rate. These cases cannot be generalized to most other developing countries, particularly not to the poorest among them.

We knew further that the option of reducing population growth is not relevant to the numbers requiring employment and release from absolute poverty by the year 2000. The majority of the people who would be alive then were already born and no reduction in birth rates could be fast enough or great enough to alter the size of the labour force much. Furthermore, historic evidence suggested that, among other things, a rise in income is one of the correlates of fertility decline. The implication of this is that a reduction in poverty may be a precondition for a reduction in the rate of demographic expansion.

So much for the figures. Qualitatively, it had taken some time until several of us realized that the danger in the elaboration of an employment-oriented development model was of the same order as the one inherent to the conventional development model with its over-emphasis on the rate of economic growth. Just as the latter is not an end objective in itself but rather a *means* to reach a certain number of societal and individual goals, so employment cannot be considered an end-objective, but is likewise a *means* to earn an income which in turn is necessary in order to satisfy a series of individual and societal objectives. In other words, the danger was that by introducing a priority focus on employment-creation, one might lose sight of the more important objectives in life. Thus, we were led to go to the logical extreme of our thinking as embodied in the previous pages, namely, that the creation of more and better jobs is not enough; that employment issues are linked to the wider issues of poverty and equality; and that it was in that wider context that the answer to the paradox set out at the beginning of this paper must be examined. And so a new objective for development strategies was set, namely *the satisfaction of an absolute level of basic needs for the entire population, including the poorest segment.*

By basic needs is meant, first, the minimum requirements of a family for items of private consumption, Adequate food, shelter and clothing obviously are included, as are household implements and furniture, and depending on the average income of the society, other goods and services might be added. Second, basic needs include essential services provided by the community at large, e.g. safe drinking water, sanitation facilities, public transport, health and educational facilities.

None of these things can be supplied unless there is adequate employment. The productive mobilization of the unemployed and seasonably unemployed plus higher productivity by the working poor are vital to achieving a level of output that is high enough to meet the two types of basic needs. Employment, evidently, is a principal means to satisfy basic needs. But the full utilization of the capacities and energy of the labour force is not just a means. Employment is also a source of pride, dignity and self-confidence. Thus, productive and adequately remunerated employment is a basic need in itself.

These, we considered the components of basic needs. They constitute the minimum objectives of a society, not the full range of desirable attributes. Closely related to basic needs, but separate, is the wish of people to participate in making the decisions which affect their lives. This is a subsidiary goal which, if achieved, would make the implementation of a basic needs strategy of development both easier and more effective in raising human welfare.

We went on to test the overall feasibility of reaching basic needs with the help of global projection models. For this purpose the key needs were defined in terms of FAO diet targets, nine to twelve years of education and UN minimum acceptable housing cost estimates. It was further assumed that the objective was to meet basic needs within one generation, which for the purpose of calculation was taken to be the year 2000. Finally, the poorest 20% of families was taken as the target group. There was, therefore, a production target (basic needs), a target group (the poorest 20% of households) and a time-horizon (one generation).

In bare outline the results of these calculations were the following.

If it is assumed that income distribution will remain essentially unchanged and that the proportion of basic goods and services to total output remains constant, then annual growth rates of output of 10 to 13% would be required in each geographical sub-region of the developing world, with the exception of China, if the basic needs of the fifth of the population with the lowest incomes were to be met by the year 2000. These required growth rates are more than double those actually achieved in recent years.

Several objections to these calculations could be made. 1) the data used in the models overstate the true cost of meeting minimum needs, if existing improved traditional technology were more widely used. 2) the value of housing and food produced by households for their own consumption is understated. 3) it is assumed that the present highly unequal access to public services will remain unchanged. On the other hand, in a growth-centred development strategy a shift to improved traditional technology is unlikely. Indeed, under such a strategy the traditional rural sector tends to stagnate. Moreover, the provision of public services tends to exacerbate rather than redress inequality in earned income.

If anything, the projections were too optimistic in their assumptions rather than too pessimistic. The assumption that the distribution of income received by the poorest groups remains unaltered under a growth maximization strategy is highly suspect. Rapid growth in most countries has usually led to a fall of the share of income received by the bottom 20% of households until after the achievement of average real per capita income levels above those projected for the Asian, African and lower income Latin American sub-regions for the year 2000. Exceptions to this generalization have involved radical initial redistributions of ownership of wealth and access to services – usually land reform and education.

If, on the other hand, emphasis was on meeting basic needs, including a change in employment patterns and a very large redistribution of income on the margin, then it would be possible with rapid growth rates of 6 to 8% p.a. to achieve basic needs targets for the entire population by the year 2000. However, the redistribution requirements out of the annual increments of income are substantial. The share of the lowest 20% in total personal income would have to double in only 25 years, i.e., rise from the present range of 1–7.5% to 9–15%. This would imply even greater equality of personal income than now exists in any of the the high-income countries.

Thus, on these assumptions it would be technically feasible to achieve the basic needs targets fairly quickly. In practice, however, it is doubtful that the political conditions would exist for such a radical redistribution from growth strategy to be sustained for 25 years. The above calculations are based on the assumption that there is no initial redistribution of income or wealth; all redistributions occur out of the additional output generated through the growth process. Hence the entire burden of redistribution falls on the margin.

We concluded that in some countries it may well be more feasible politically to have a substantial initial redistribution of assets and a more moderate redistribution from rising incomes due to growth. Economically, this is a preferable strategy in that the period required to meet the basic needs targets would be shorter and the level of consumption of the poor in every year prior to achieving the targets would be higher.

Returning to the present again, let me make it clear that it is on purpose that I have presented the main contours of the concept of basic needs only. I have done so to make it absolutely clear that it is redistribution of income and wealth that is at the centre of a basic needs model, at least as conceived by its originators. It is *not* a model that advocates *consumption transfers* in order to achieve basic needs. For sure, such transfers would raise the incomes of the poor initially, but because they have an adverse effect on the rate of capital accumulation, the average rate of growth of incomes would very quickly slow down in all sectors of economic activity. Nor is it a model that is only opting for a redirection of investment flows. Such *investment transfers* could be brought about by fiscal and other policies by governments; by changes in credit policies of financial institutions: or by a reorientation of foreign aid towards the poorest groups. Such a set of policies is equivalent to what I just now called a redistribution from growth. This is important and is also an ingredient in a basic needs model. However, on top of that the latter goes further by also incorporating the necessity of an *initial redistribution of assets*. Moreover, its starting point is not on income, but on achieving a set of targets in physical units for the hard core of the poor, which is taken to be the poorest 20% of the population.

The perversions of the basic needs development model

Let me start this section where I left off the previous one. It is, first, important to note that the starting point of the basic model is not a more or less abstract and arbitrary rise in the economic growth rate and of per capita income. On the contrary, the growth percentage is derived from the concrete, unsatisfied demands of the entire population with an emphasis on the poor segments.

Secondly, and I must repeat this, in a basic needs model income and wealth redistribution is an integral part of the socio-economic development policy package.

When in June 1976 the basic needs development strategy was discussed and ultimately accepted at the World Employment Conference, the United States and several of the EEC-countries (the German Federal Republic to the fore) were strongly opposed, although the Conference's action programme was accepted.[3]

It is therefore amazing to see that, less than a year later, especially the United States, suddenly heavily supported the concept of what they called basic human needs. In sequence to this complete *volte face*, the basic needs concept was also pushed to the front by OECD/DAC[4] and the rich countries even put it on the agenda at the last meeting of the North/South Conference in Paris.

This was enough to give the poor countries not only a probably welcome feeling of uneasiness about the true reason for this inconsistent behaviour, but also to make them oppose the basic needs model, at any rate at the level of international fora. Of course, the national élites who already were doing rather well by the present international order were not too keen on redistributing their incomes and wealth and, in doing so, losing part of their political power. They could, however, not very well vote against it in June 1976 because that would be tantamount to voting against motherhood. Every pretext was used to rid it of the more radical elements in this basic needs strategy and the discussion which is going on is so complex and so full of half-truths that everyone can find something to his taste in this international hotch-potch.

Let me quickly illustrate with a few examples the most pronounced fallacies about the basic needs strategy.[5]

Fallacy 1: A basic needs strategy is really equivalent to a series of ad hoc projects for the poor: The concept of basic needs as it grew out of the work summarized in sections 2 and 3 above had the ambition of replacing conventional development policy and planning. In other words, it was meant to be an overall social and economic development strategy, with emphasis on structural changes required to remedy the basic weaknesses of current models and policies.

Very soon, however, basic needs came to be interpreted as an *ad hoc* policy to bridge temporary difficulties during a transitional period. In other words, it was accepted that a number of difficulties could be encountered during a given period by prevailing development policies.

Such difficulties, however, were not seen as a reason to change the main thrust of the development model, but rather as an incentive to to something *in addition* and *next to* these policies. Basic needs was thus turned into a social welfare concept in the North-American sense. No wonder, therefore, that from many sides it was proclaimed that basic needs policies had been pursued and implemented for a long time. Was it not recognized everywhere that the emphasis should be on the poor? Had there not been many rural projects in many regions, integrated or not? Not a word was heard about income and wealth redistribution; not a word about the necessary structural changes and adaptations. Merely, a general pointing at projects which could be wiped out with one stroke of the conventional macro-economic pen.

Fallacy 2: Income inequalities are a *condition sine qua non* for economic growth: I touched already upon this point earlier in this paper. Indeed, in many textbooks to this day, it is stated that a high degree of income inequality favours savings and hence investments that are needed to guarantee continued economic growth. This chain of reasoning has been contradicted by the facts many years ago.

We know of course that the richer groups of the populations in the developing countries are saving, but they often take their savings out of the country. We also know that these richer groups have a consumption pattern that is concentrated on luxury commodities from abroad. In the case of the poor in developing countries, we see that for them to save and to invest are parts of one action. For instance, where they build their own houses and roads, no money is put in the bank, but free time is directly invested in the building of houses and roads.

It is therefore not surprising that, if one looks at the empirical evidence concerning the relationship between economic growth and income distribution, evidence of which is available for about 80 countries, we observe a perfectly spurious correlation. In other words, we observe countries with a high rate of economic growth and a very unequal income distribution, but we also observe countries with high rates of growth and a fairly equal income distribution and vice versa. The conclusion must therefore be that in matters of redistributive policies everything stands or falls with the specific mix of policy measures that is introduced and its timing.

Fallacy 3: The conventional growth model is good enough and there is no need to change that: Here the answer can be very brief. It is probably true that the conventional growth model would end up by satisfying the basic needs of everybody. The question is *when* this will occur. I come back to the crucial question of the length of the transition period. Clearly, the duration of that period has been grossly underestimated in the conventional development theory. The choice becomes then to either sacrifice several generations or attempt to identify an alternative growth model which sets out to satisfy the basic needs of everyone within one generation. To reject such attempts out of hand would be humanly unacceptable and politically irresponsible.

The answer is therefore not a *negation* of the fact that the present growth model could ultimately succeed in fulfilling the basic needs of everyone, but rather an *affirmation* of the fact that the present model would take far too long to be acceptable.

Fallacy 4: A basic needs strategy is equivalent to a zero-growth model: In conventional development thinking the major emphasis was put on economic growth while redistribution was seen as a more or less passive function of it. I have shown earlier that the basic needs model puts equal emphasis on growth *and* redistribution, both dimensions conceived as an integral part of the policy package. As so often when an attempt is made to set the balance right, people interpret it in terms of the other extreme.

Hence, the claim that basic needs is solely concerned with redistributing the cake and not with making it bigger...

Fallacy 5: Basic needs is only concerned with the poor: The fifth preconceived idea is that basic needs is only concerned with the poorest 20, 30 or 40%, and not with the rest. It therefore falls into the opposite extreme. In contrast to conventional development strategies, which over-emphasize the modern sector, the basic needs approach is only concerned with the poorest, and therefore would show many of the same weaknesses.

The starting point in the basic needs approach is, of course, to identify our target population, which are the poorest 20 or 30%, to identify and to quantify their basic needs. Once this has been done, it is necessary to work backwards, so to speak, to deduce consumption patterns for the entire population, settle the question of income distribution for the entire population, and then link that into the economy's production patterns. It is therefore not true that the basic needs approach, in terms of macro-economics, is only concerned w:th part of the population and that it neglects the rest.

Fallacy 6: Basic needs is opposed to the modern sector: The sixth preconceived idea – analogous but slightly different from the last – is that the basic needs approach would neglect the modern sector, would be terribly allergic to capital-intensive technologies, and totally in favour of labour-intensive technologies.

Perhaps the presentation is misleading, but it is not true that a basic needs approach would neglect the modern sector. It would indeed put relatively less emphasis on it, and relatively more on what we have come to call the 'urban informal' and the 'rural traditional' sectors. But it would surely be unwise not to use the modern sector as a creator of income to be channeled, much more than hitherto, to the urban informal and rural traditional sectors. Highly sophisticated industries can be stimulated, not to create *employment* but to create *more income* which, through taxation, can be channelled into those sectors of the economy which are labour-intensive.

To give an extreme example we could think of diamonds in Botswana.

Obviously, in a basic needs development strategy you do not leave them in the ground on the pretext that they have nothing to do with the basic needs of the poorest in the country. On the contrary, you dig them out and sell them at as high a price as possible. The point being that the income derived from these sales is channelled in such a manner as to be consistent with the objectives of the basic needs model.

Technology must be examined sector by sector. Each country has export products which must remain competitive on the world market. Very often this implies the use of sophisticated and capital-intensive technology. There is nothing intrinsically wrong with these technologies as long as their use is linked to stimulating the basic needs development approach.

In other words, the main criterion for investment decisions in the modern sector should now be its stimulating effect on the hitherto neglected sectors of the economy, through sub-contracting, for example.

Fallacy 7: Basic needs perpetuates dependence on rich countries: The seventh preconceived idea is that the approach is not radical enough, and that it perpetuates dependence on industrialized countries. It therefore does not go far enough in terms of substantive elements. This argument is put forward by those who believe that the basic needs model would imply more or less eradicating the modern sector which, they would say, is also inconsistent with self-reliance.

In my mind, a basic needs approach is at least one step further towards collective self-reliance. I think that the production patterns involved in a basic needs approach are such that they will tend to enable developing countries to trade much more among themselves. An examination of the present trade patterns of developing countries reveals that two-thirds of their trade is with industrialized countries. Only 25% is among themselves. Industrialized countries are much more advanced on the road to collective self-reliance than are the developing countries; but the two-thirds dependence of the latter could be reduced through a basic needs approach.

Fallacy 8: Basic needs is used as a stick behind the door by the industrialized countries: As indicated above, there have been certain manoeuvres by the industrialized countries that *could* be interpreted as if they first wanted to discuss the internal affairs of the poor countries *before* discussing the new international economic order.

To my mind, and I attach some importance to this point, so-called international decisions and objectives must be discussed *simultaneously* with national decision-taking and objectives. What has been lacking too often in the discussions on a new international order has been the fact that the national prerequisites and consequences of such 'international measures' have never been made explicit.

Since practically all decisions are still, whether we like it or not, nationally based, the lack of clarity in that respect has been the main reason for the absence of substantive advance made towards changes at the international level. Those of us who take the claim in favour of a new international order seriously, must be ready to face the implications of this claim back home in our own countries. Putting these national problems and policies explicitly on the negotiation table would not only make things clearer and more transparent, but might also lead to more rapid progress.

Conclusion

Coming back to the interrelationship between peace and socio-economic development, it will be clear that the introduction of a more equitable set of economic, financial, social and cultural development policies in the Third World is not the be-all and end-all for securing peace. But it goes a longer way on the road towards peace than the growth-maximizing strategies ignoring the inequalities they entail. Think of Iran in the 1960s and 1970s, for example, and the sequel to the policies pursued then as witnessed today in the 1980s.

Most important, therefore, is for Europe to stimulate and encourage such changes in the developing world rather than putting obstacles in the path. We know that countries which move from a growth-maximizing to a more human-centred development policy, will enter a transition period during which balance of payments problems may arise. Such countries will, therefore, need special care and assistance which is rarely forthcoming and rendered in time.

Europe has a special responsibility here which requires an independent worldwide economic, financial and monetary policy on her part. It is time that the economic and demographic superpower which Europe really is, finds reflection on the political world scene. Europe must act – if necessary on her own – in the interest of world peace.

Notes

1. W. Arthur Lewis, 'Development with Unlimited Supplies of Labour', *The Manchester School*, May 1954; and John Fei and Gustav Ranis, *Development of the Labour Surplus Economy – Theory and Policy*, Homewood, Illinois, 1964.

2. For a clear explanation of this concept, see *Employment, Incomes and Equality – A Strategy for Increasing Productive Employment in Kenya*, ILO, Geneva, 1972, Chapter 13. See also Louis Emmerij, 'A New Look at Some Strategies for Increasing Productive Employment in Africa', *International Labour Review*, September 1974.

3. ILO, *Employment, Growth and Basic Needs – a One-World Problem*, Geneva, 1976. For the result of the Conference see ILO, *Meeting Basic Needs Strategies for eradicating mass poverty and unemployment, Conclusions of the World Employment Conference 1976,* Geneva, 1977.

4. See the yearly reports of OECD/DAC since 1977; OECD, *Development Cooperation – Efforts and Policies of the Members of the Development Assistance Committee*, 1977 Review, 1978 Review and 1979 Review respectively, Paris, 1977, 1978, 1979.

5. What follows is an adaptation of my 'Facts and Fallacies concerning the Basic Needs Approach', in *Les Carnets de l'Enfance/Assignment Children*, Unicef, No. 41, January-March 1978.

Part 3: Beyond the Cold War: Europe in Search of a New Role

10. Transcending the European Model of Peace and Development

by Björn Hettne

International security and peace based on the European-originated nation state and the inter-state world system have come under increasing attack. Similarly, the Western model of economic development has been increasingly criticized and its continued relevance in the contemporary world questioned. Invariably, however, both these critiques proceed separately and lack any awareness that peace and development are inextricably linked together. After all, political and military imperatives associated with the processes of nation-building and industrialization have been dominant in the development of the international system. In their evolution, peace and development have reinforced each other; hence to transcend one entails transcendence of the other.

At present, Europe has reached the limits of this mainstream model of peace and development; in fact, the model has become more and more of a problem . New social movements on the continent such as the Green Party in West Germany and the Ecology Party in France have already begun to define an alternative model stressing different conceptions of the role of economic growth, the nature of international security, and the functions and dangers of the nation state.

This essay will discuss the problems of the peace and development model currently prevailing in Europe, and those forces leading more and more people to question them. It will then proceed to consider the processes that might lead to their transcendence and replacement, at least on the European continent. The paper concludes with an appraisal of the chances of actual reform in Europe occurring in the short term.

The nation state and the state of anarchy

The dominant approach to international relations is still to consider the international system as a form of 'anarchy:' in other words, a system composed of autonomous nation states without any central or overall authority. It is important to note that this view is a historical product which took shape during a particular phase in European history, roughly beginning with the Peace of Westphalia in 1648 that, some scholars assert, 'transformed the imperial model of international relations, a stateless model, into a practical irrelevance' [Mansbach et al., 1976, p. 12]. By the time Napoleon put an end to the shaky Holy Roman Empire in 1806, the state-centric paradigm was already dominant. Today we find it difficult to conceive of a Europe—indeed, even the world—without nation states.

The nuclear weapons crisis in which more weapons bring less security, and the schisms in NATO over recent years show that the logic of the European security system is falling apart. Notions such as common security are useful in pointing to the madness of further armament but fail to inculcate any awareness that the world's security problems are inherently embedded in the logic of the inter-state international system.

At the same time it is also becoming more and more difficult to conceive of a future for Europe, and the world, as long as it remains organized in an inter-state system. Theoretically, it should be possible to modify some of its features so as to 'retain the benefits of complex organization while reducing the role of the state in providing a framework for organization' [Strayer, 1970, p. 4]. Politically, however, this is not the case. The old Imperial Model cannot provide a solution since its realization would mean further centralization and possibly wars. But the structure of an even older stateless system in Europe affords some clues in its combination of strong local autonomy (the feudal village) with translocal institutions (culture, religion and trade). With the centralized state being increasingly challenged on several fronts, an obvious first step is to strengthen the organizational levels above and below the state, without necessarily abolishing it altogether. To be sure, nationalism is a very real and tremendous mobilizing force, but people do feel other commitments beyond identifying with a state. Indeed, not only are there different forms of coexisting identifications, they also change over time and in response to events. For example, the formation of states in Europe certainly did suppress other competing loyalties (whether local or universal), but did not eliminate them. The peoples of Europe are still more numerous than the states of Europe, and new loyalties, responsibilities, and identities have developed.

Of course, to stress state-formation and nation-building as historical processes is also to say that it is difficult to specify a definite date when a particular state was formed. A state has been defined as 'an organization employing specialized personnel, which controls a consolidated territory and is recognized as autonomous and integral by the agents of other states' [Tilly, 1975, p. 70]. However, it seems more fruitful to consider these criteria relatively, so as to make it possible to speak of a process of gradual increase in 'stateness' with reference to a particular political unit [ibid., p. 34]. To this extent, the 16th century was a time of rising stateness for Europe, culminating in the 17th century during the era of Absolutism. In the Third World, particularly in Africa, this phenomenon is more recent, though it is not advisable to read the history of Europe into the future of other regions. The relativist view of stateness is useful also because it allows for the consideration of *decreasing* stateness, i.e., the disintegration of the state.

Any nation-building project comprises among its most important elements the exclusive political-military control over a certain territory, the defence of this territory against possible external claims, and the promotion of its legitimacy within this territory. Such a project requires an economic surplus which can be broadly categorized into three funds: a security fund, an investment fund, and a welfare fund. How these various funds are allocated depends on the phase of nation-building and the various challenges facing it during a particular phase, but a continuous neglect of any one of these funds will weaken the entire project.

The main task of the armed forces is to defend a state from external threats, while the police forces are responsible for internal security. This division of functions may be seen as one dimension of state-formation; in fact, to a large extent, the growth of the police forces and the armed forces were parallel processes intimately related to it. Where there was strong resistance, the military also became heavily involved in the maintenance of internal security. Because of conflicts with other emerging states and internal unrest, the process of state-formation was often quite violent. People therefore learned to conceive of their 'own' state as a protector and the rest of the world as 'anarchical' and a threat to their security. Since then state-formation has become a global process, and the state a universal phenomenon. A less violent, though not necessarily peaceful, way of increasing the power of the state is 'development'. This process is understood here in the conventional sense of economic growth, institutional modernization, industrialization, technological development, commercialization of agriculture, urbanization, bureaucratization, and the monetization of the national economy so that a financial base to support the state is created. The expansion of the investment and welfare funds will make the state more acceptable to the citizens, that is, increase its legitimacy. At the same time, the choice of development strategy will create new conflicts, since different models of development affect different groups differently.

There are more or less three distinct development strategies within the Western tradition: the Liberal Model, the State Capitalist Strategy and the Soviet Model. They are variations on the basic paradigm, expressing different historical possibilities and constraints. They differ mainly with regard to means, but are basically similar as far as their objectives are concerned, especially given their strong emphasis on industrialisation.

The *Liberal Model* comprises, very broadly, the British development experience following the industrial revolution. Its main features include reliance on market forces, gradual industrialization beginning with light industries, private investment from high profits and low wages, and technological advancement which necessitates capital accumulation and expanding markets. Emulating this development path, however, became increasingly difficult with the emergence of a capitalist world economy predicated on a hierarchical division of labour among the participating countries. While other countries sought to duplicate Britain's success, other means had to be found if they were to catch up with the 'workshop of the world'. They could not follow the rather slow *laissez-faire* process of development but needed, for example, to industrialize quickly because of the distinct military advantages it afforded. Significantly, the theories of development of classical political economy were considered by the latecomers to be development ideology. Those countries industrializing later during the 19th century were usually protectionist and relied on state power to facilitate capital accumulation. The general rule seemed to be that the later a country began to industrialize, the greater the need for state intervention.

It was this perceived need for rapid industrialization that led to the adoption of the so-called *State Capitalist Strategy* of industrial development in continental Europe. Different states were active to varying degrees but invariably all needed a strong state to speed the process of industrialization. Of course, similar state-fostered modernization as a nationalistic reaction to perceived threats from industrially more advanced countries (rather than being endogenous and immanent) arose not only in Germany and Russia but also in non-Western countries such as Japan after the Meiji Restoration. This strategy typically took the form of an attempt to enforce development in primarily agrarian economies. A good example is the policies of Count Witte in 19th century Russia. Witte was influenced by the German economist Friedrich List, who saw industrialization as necessary for economic and security reasons (the 'modernization imperative'). List, however, never abandoned his basically liberal outlook [Von Laue, 1963]. According to List, it is advantageous to participate in the international division of labour as soon as state-fostered industrialization has been implemented, but not before the establishment of certain strategic industries.

The *Soviet Model* was essentially a continuation of the state capitalist policy of pre-revolutionary Russia, although the ideological inspiration and the political context were obviously different. In the famous economic policy debates of the 1920s, several options implying different development paths were discussed. In the end, the modernization imperative as dramatized by the military threat from Germany took precedence. Accordingly, the state promoted industrial development, as per the state capitalist strategy, albeit without the use of market mechanisms this time.

Since Stalin's economic policies were geared toward modernization and industrialization, their ideological bases aside, both the Liberal and Soviet strategies can be considered expressions of the Western paradigm of development. Modifications of economic policy in the post-Stalin era have only underlined this further because contemporary Soviet society is characterized by a consumerism basically similar to that prevailing in the West.

But what is striking when the Western development strategies are compared is the important role given to the state in contrast to the prevalent free market ideology of development. With the *State Capitalist*

Strategy, the state became responsible for capital formation and investment in strategic areas where spontaneous demand was lacking. And in the *Soviet Model*, the state completely replaced the market mechanisms, and later experiments with profits and prices have not substantially altered this picture. These state-oriented strategies have been especially attractive for the 'modern elite' in the Third World. Indeed, it is the more state-centred manifestations of European mainstream development which were often merged with the development ideology of the ruling elite in underdeveloped countries.

Clearly, this dominant role of the state is a basic feature of the Western model of development. And an important reason for this basic similarity is the military needs-related character of industrialization strategies. Even in the case of Britain, the 'first industrial nation', the pattern of industrialization was significantly influenced by the 150 years of warfare that preceded the 'take off' [Mathias, 1969]. When the 'latecomers' industrialized, their military needs were even more pronounced and the role played by the state in the early stages even more important. Industrialization was basically an *imitative* process, repeated from one country to another. But contrary to conventional modernization theory and orthodox Marxism, these similarities in the pattern of economic growth indicated not inherent tendencies towards 'modernity' but political and military imperatives for industrialization. Thus, the stubborn populist resistance against Witte's industrialization programme in Russia was substantially weakened after its humiliating defeat in the Russo-Japanese War of 1904 [Mendel, 1961]. And in the United States, the traumatic Civil War marked the dividing point between its agrarian and industrial epochs.

In the era of the Great Wars, between 1689 and 1815, Britain was the dominant participant in international economic and political rivalries. The European absolutist states that emerged during this period were 'machines built overwhelmingly for the battlefield' [Anderson, 1975, p. 32]. Because of the constant warfare and the requirements of huge armies in the 17th, 18th, and early 19th centuries, military demand for standardized output increased and hastened factory production [Sen, 1984, p. 103]. The difference between supplying large standing armies with food, equipment, clothing, etc. and the maintenance of decentralized feudal troops was, of course, enormous. More specifically, the impact of military needs affected not only demand but also organization and technological change. According to Sen, the advancement of organizational methods occurred on two levels: first, the mass character of military demand stimulated the rationalization of the production process; and second, the army itself provided a model for industrial and social organization [ibid., p. 111]. There is, after all, a similarity between economic growth controlled from above and military organization.

Besides the violence associated with its modernization and military imperative, the European Model of Development is also inherently unstable in the way it moulds the structure of international trade. Since the politico-military impulse leads to the reproduction of similar structures of production, and the strategic sectors are geared for export for economies of scale, there is a definite surplus capacity created. From the ensuing economic rivalry, it is a logical if not necessary step to trade wars and military wars. As a matter of fact, protectionism rather than free trade has been the predominant economic policy for those states that have been allowed to have their own say. International regimes characterized by free trade necessitate a stable economic order in which one dominant state—Great Britain and the US are two historical examples—decides upon the rules of the game. In consequence, the weakening of hegemonic power implies more uncertainty and more conflict, perhaps even war.

Significantly, recently there has been a renewed interest in the cycles of war. In large part, this is because of the depressing and alarming likelihood that, due to developments in military technology, the next war in the cycle will spell the end of human civilization. Without being deterministic, however, it is legitimate to ask what problems the present security arrangement may face in the future. The basic issue here seems to be changes in hegemonic power, i.e., the capability of a great power or a bloc of powers to impose their order upon the world system. According to the cycle theories, it is the displacement of hegemonic powers that give rise to major wars [Modelski, 1978]. In addition, D. Senghas has written about hegemonic drop-out contests: Spain and Portugal were replaced by the Netherlands; subsequently, England entered a hegemonic contest with France; towards the end of the 19th century, Germany and the United States emerged as challengers; and today the Soviet Union is challenging the United States. However, he believes that 'we are presently living in a time in which it is possible to interrupt the hitherto existing cycles of major wars and periods of hegemonic peace; e.g., we are living in a time of structural change which implies considerable dangers for peace as well as chances for a new international order' [Senghas, 1973].

The modernization imperative in the Third World

State-formation in the Third World parallels in many ways the experiences of Europe. It is important to stress, however, that modernization is not an inherent attribute of history but the outcome of a specific global power structure during the historical phase of state-formation and nation-building begun in Europe. Rather, the modernization imperative here can be defined as the external and internal pressures on the state of a less developed society to increase its productive capacity in order to survive and to consolidate the political system, thus avoiding the fate of either being swallowed by other states or breaking up because of internal conflicts. Since the conventional way of assuring security is to accumulate arms and strengthen the military establishment, there is a strong military interest in modernization. But security arrangements are costly and competition between allocations to the security fund, on the one hand, and the development funds (investment and welfare), on the other, will emerge.

Hence that more and more resources are currently devoted to arms purchases is very significant. Such a tendency usually implies strong pressures on the economy toward export orientation and dependence on external markets, which amplify the general tendency of the modernization imperative toward 'violent industrialization'. Local conflicts are used to legitimize importing the European Model of Peace and Development and are, in turn, reinforced by global conflict. The Cold War was a starting point for the diffusion of arms and military technology; up to the mid-1960s, arms transfers from the superpowers were mainly in the form of military aid to allied and friendly nations. After the mid-1960s, however, there was a marked shift from aid to trade, and from second-hand material to more sophisticated weapons. At the same time, the number of suppliers grew as the United States and the Soviet Union were joined by France, Germany, Great Britain, and Italy. Indeed, from the mid-1970s onwards, the number of arms suppliers in the Third World increased as well [Ohlsson, 1982].

Quantitatively, most of the developing countries have relatively small arms imports. Yet in spite of, or perhaps because of, the fact that more countries started from fairly modest military establishments after the breakup of the colonial system, it is in the Third World that the most dynamic arms market is now to be found. The development imperative has led developing nations to tailor development and other expenditures to allow for arms purchases, often at the expense of needed services.

Put differently, if the development of nation states is necessary for 'progress', the African peoples in particular are paying a heavy price. According to *South* [Jan. 1985], twenty-five of the fifty-one members of the OAU are under military rule. Ninety coups have taken place since 1960, the armed forces number 6.2 per 1,000 (to be compared with the Third World average of 3.4), arms imports between 1976 and 1980 amounted to $55.5 billion ($26.5 billion in the rest of the Third World), and more than 3.5 million people have been killed in uprisings, civil wars, and massacres. In spite of all this suffering, the African nation states do not seem to be on firmer ground today than when they emerged after decolonization. In Asia, ethnic heterogeneity is somewhat less pronounced but the nation states are also facing serious problems and may disintegrate. Pakistan was divided once—and it may happen again. Lebanon has for all practical purposes ceased to exist as a state. Sri Lanka seems to face division or civil war. And in India, Prime Minister Indira Gandhi became yet another victim of 'communalism', mainly due to her desperate efforts to save an overcentralized nation state ruled from Delhi. Are these temporary obstacles in the way of the modernization project or could it be that the era of 'demodernization' has set in?

Transcending the European Development Model

If the reality of European development has been violent industrialization, its ideology is much brighter. From the Greek philosophers to more recent development theorists, the European conception of development has been identified with growth: immanent, directional, and irreversible growth. In more recent times, growth also came to be identified with 'progress' and, with the birth of development theory, 'modernization'. The Marxist tradition is no exception to this evolutionist bias, which also carried a paternalistic attitude toward non-European cultures on their way to 'modernity'.

But there has been a 'counterpoint' tradition arguing for the inherent superiority of small-scale, ecologically sustainable, and decentralized patterns of development challenging the 'mainstream' paradigm. While not widely accepted, this counterpoint tradition is revived and strengthened in times of crisis for the dominant paradigm. Hence the current interest in 'another development' within development theory [Hettne, 1982]. Instead of specialization and maximum exchange in accordance with what economists have termed 'comparative advantage,' the emerging alternative tradition stresses maximum self-reliance for each natural economic unit or ecosystem, which does not necessarily coincide with the nation state. Needless to say, such a position denies the main premises of the Mainstream Model which is derived from European economic history. Accordingly, if this alternative approach to development is to have any relevance for Europe, then the European Mainstream Model must be transcended.

The removal of regional inequalities and pockets of backwardness was one of the overall aims of the European Economic Community (EEC). However, nothing has been achieved in terms of regional harmonization, partly because of the enormous dimensions of the problem, but also probably due to lack of theoretical understanding of polarized development. The early architects of the EEC not only saw growth as inevitable, they were also much too optimistic about the equalizing effects of growth. Perhaps it is this vision of progress that is the problem.

For spatial inequalities in Europe and at the world level to be addressed seriously, a more realistic vision would be the one derived from the counterpoint tradition: a more self-reliant Europe in cooperation with the Third World, and with new patterns of internal cooperation. I prefer to talk about 'new patterns of cooperation' rather than 'self-reliance,' because the latter concept is ambiguous and often misunderstood to imply some kind of autarchy and an attitude of non-concern for the external world. It may not be the intention of those who currently use the phrase, but the relatively large consensus about self-reliance as a thing well worth striving for makes one suspicious that self-reliance may mean different things to different people. As a matter of fact, self-reliance was adopted by most European countries in following the industrialization path carved out by England. In that context, self-reliance meant the setting up of strategic industries with a strong military component and at least during a period of transition, a protectionist policy vis-à-vis other countries. And in the Third World at present, this is usually the case when the importance of 'self-reliance' is emphasized.

Lest there be any uncertainty, self-reliance is not used to suggest isolation or autarchy. Rather, self-reliance must be conceived as a symmetric pattern of cooperation expressed on various territorial levels, and this obviously cannot come about without some coordination within and among the nation states. Therefore it is necessary to formulate a general principle of territoriality rather than to conceive development simply in terms of specific levels or regions. This principle becomes evident if we examine the distinction between 'territory' and 'function' [Friedman and Weaver, 1979].

According to the dominant *functional* principle, development is an abstract process of growth related to an artificial *'national* economy'. Beyond this abstraction is the concrete socio-economic 'world' that most people identify with and depend upon. When this identification is disturbed and threatened by the effect of 'modernization', conflicts between sub-state regions and the central power structure often occur over the goals and means of development. Smaller territorial units, however, lack autonomous power in the functional system. The revitalization of territorial life would therefore not be possible without a transfer of power to local communities, while the state level takes the function of coordinator. It is also necessary to strengthen territorial units larger than nation states, for example, the European continent, and ultimately, decision-making at the global level as the only way to protect the global ecosystem and achieve sustainability. This is because nation states that specialize and become efficient at exploiting certain ecological niches tend to continue this activity regardless of the signs of danger, an unfortunate result of that particular blindness associated with the promotion of growth in a functional system with little regard to what happens to specific ecosystems.

Territorial and functional forms of social integration both complement and contradict each other. The problem is therefore how to decrease the dominance of function over territory, and how a 'recovery of territorial life' can be brought about. To some extent, this already takes place when peoples react individually and in (local) groups to the crisis of the world economy. The point, however, is to make the territorial principle part of a planned transition.

For example, the European Mainstream Model is a rationalization of the interests of groups that have a central and dominant position in the functional system – mainly big business, politicians, and the bureaucracy (i.e., the power structure behind the European common market project). The power of those who dominate the controlling heights of the functional system has been taken more or less for granted until recently. Protests and disobedience from local leaders who accept the radically different perspective of territorial systems were considered as essentially criminal. But there is presently a revival of 'localism' where politicians experience conflict of loyalty between their respective party line and a contrary position more consistent with the interests of local constituents. Political parties traditionally follow the logic of the functional system: economic growth mainly with reference to the national system, but there are non-local parties with little contact or influence outside their territorial system (i.e. specific local community). Apart from those rather heterogeneous local groups, a 'green' type of national party is also emerging which denies the functional principle as a national development logic. All these challenges seriously threaten the functional system which must grow continuously in order to compensate for dislocations, imbalances, and strains created by the very process of growth. Because the conventional remedies often worsen the situation, the current crisis has indirectly strengthened the counterpoint opposition to the European Mainstream Model. Without political change there is no possibility of the European model being transcended. A new territorial economic model presupposes a change of the European collective consciousness, which involves new ideas and models of economic organization and the success of new social movements. As will be argued later, this can happen only with a convergence of political processes arising in the 'first', 'second' and 'third' worlds. Thus Europe cannot change without changes in the rest of the world, and conversely, its changes will have an important impact on the rest of the world.

The current state of European economic development, or rather non-development, has contracted the number of markets available for the Third World. This problem is further aggravated by desperate protectionist efforts to keep dying traditional industries alive. Indeed, such protectionism is not only evident between Europe and the Third World, but also within Europe itself, undermining the whole European Community enterprise which was originally devised in a very different era of growth and technological optimism, when the Mainstream Model was in full bloom. Steady economic growth is no longer the norm, and the institutions of the Mainstream Model do not function as they were designed.

A new international economic order can obviously not be a conscious creation by governments and international bureaucrats. But there have been certain attempts to build a new economic system in Europe and to introduce changes into the world economic system. There is a process of change as a result of the competition between conflicting projects such as 'the new superpower', 'Fortress Europe' and the 'Green Europe.' The relative success of these different projects will have varying consequences for the Third World and for world peace.

Of course, the main force in Europe is still 'the community' which from January 1986 will consist of twelve countries. With each enlargement, the coherence of the EEC suffers. The inclusion of Spain and Portugal took eight years of negotiations and the final agreement was actually hailed as proof that the EEC is a 'living reality with a future' [*International Herald Tribune*, 30–31 March 1985]. As far as the smaller and weaker countries are concerned, the reasons for joining differ—from Ireland's wish to balance England's dominance, to Spain and Portugal's struggle for democratic consolidation. The dreams of Europe being the 'new superpower' are probably confined to West Germany and France.

Increasing heterogeneity from expansion means less strength (and force) in external relations, but more internal options and, above all, a huge domestic market. Thus Fortress Europe, which is conceived as covering as much of Europe as possible, is at least somewhat more viable than the superpower project. To the extent that Fortress Europe also means a politically independent Europe, it may also be a force for peace, or what André Gunder Frank calls a 'Pan-European Entente for Peace and Jobs' [Frank, 1983]. Of course, this would be preferred to the anarchy of nationalist protectionism or to selective transnationalization creating or reinforcing economic dualism. These developments would be most unfortunate because a destabilized Europe would be a source of conflict in itself. But the real problem with the fortress project is, apart from the obvious lack of internal coordination, the isolationism it engenders. As the word 'fortress' strongly suggests, inasmuch as 'underdevelopment' is merely a result of 'dependence', the seclusion of the centre would be a precondition for development in the periphery, but the problem, as it is now realized, is not so simple. Besides, a European withdrawal will simply leave new regions open to the United States and Japan.

The 'Green' project or 'Alternative Movement' may not be a very good bet at the moment, but it is nonetheless presented as a solution to many ills, among them underdevelopment in the Third World. Its strength depends on the crisis further developing and the extent to which Europe is immune to fascism. It is somewhat disturbing that the potential political base of the Greens today is more or less similar to the (brown) political base of the fascists in the 1920s and 1930s. One important difference, however, is the strong intellectual component in the Green movement making it cosmopolitan rather than parochial and chauvinist. Its cosmopolitanism is evident in the great interest shown in an idea commonly referred to as the mini-NIEO (New International Economic Order). This is a selective cooperation between a group of developing countries with the purpose of implementing some of the main features of the original NIEO [Hveem, 1980]. In the originally Norwegian but increasingly Nordic research project concerned with an alternative future for the Nordic countries, it was emphasized that the goal of self-sufficiency among the Nordic countries should be combined with alternative bilateral trading ties to selected underdeveloped countries in accordance with the mini-NIEO concept. Certainly, the Alternative Movement has no monopoly on this concept. On the contrary, it is drawing a lot of attention from aid organizations and foreign ministries, particularly in Norway and Finland.

There are, of course, many serious difficulties with the mini-NIEO plan. But this is not the place to elaborate on them. Suffice it to say that an Europeanized Europe, self-reliant at various levels and whose economic policies are geared toward the region, is quite compatible with the planned, selective, symmetric cooperation implied in the mini-NIEO concept. In any event, that the concept of the mini-NIEO (leaving aside the question whether the term is adequate) is gaining popularity in Europe is very significant. First, it presupposes a closer regional cooperation on the part of both the industrialized and underdeveloped countries. Second, it is a cooperative relation rather than an aid relation, indicating at least an intent toward a more symmetrical relationship. And third, it offers the possibility of structural change not only in the underdeveloped but also in the industrialized countries. The new social movements are all more or less manifestations of the counterpoint to the European Mainstream Model, reacting to emerging problems with the industrial system, the welfare state, and the inter-state system. The problems are many and of different kinds, and so are the political reactions. Thus they are usually issue-oriented: for alternative security, for alternative lifestyles, for alternative production, for environmental protection, for solidarity with the Third World (often specialized to the extent of different continents and even different countries), for women's liberation, and for regional and ethnic emancipation. Increasingly, there is a growing recognition that these problems are linked and that the only lasting solution is to find another way toward security and development. Accordingly, it is appropriate to speak of an Alternative Movement, although there are obvious difficulties in articulating the specific alternatives save to look for new ideas of development and security arrangements from a critical evaluation of the European Mainstream Model.

An alternative security for Europe

The concept of alternative security departs radically from the conventional understanding of security as national security concerned with military threats and consequently relying on military forms of defence. Alternative security is neither exclusively linked to military threats, nor does it acknowledge the nation state as having the first claim to security. It asks four basic questions: what is to be secured, against what, by whom, and with what means?

The most basic question is obviously whose security should be guaranteed, and here *peoples* and their cultures should take priority over *states* and borders. Military threats must, of course, not be forgotten but relevant issues here are defence by whom and with what methods. Defence has become a highly professional activity within the Mainstream Model but a civil society aspiring toward sustainability, invulnerability, and legitimacy must find more appropriate forms to protect its self-reliant path of development and its autonomy vis-à-vis the external world. There is thus need for a more comprehensive defence model in which civilian based defence is given a significant role, and at the same time military defence is made defensive rather than offensive.

Non-military threats are basically of three kinds: 1) concerning the relationship between society and nature (the problem of sustainability); 2) the way society itself is organized (the problem of vulnerability); and 3) the relationship between government and its people (the problem of legitimacy). Of course, these issues are very much related but they can nevertheless be separated analytically and made the subject of ecological, socio-economic, and political investigations.

Sustainability

Lester Brown has focused attention on four problematic areas from the perspective of sustainability: the lagging energy transition, the deterioration of major biological systems, the threat of climate modification, and global food insecurity [Brown, 1977]. Although the current depressed world economy has reduced the demand for energy, the transition to new energy sources is still a necessity. Both nuclear power and coal face sustainability problems of their own, but the development of renewable energy sources has been a slow and frustrating process. Concomitantly, the deterioration of the four biological systems—oceanic fisheries, grasslands, forests, and croplands—is a very serious problem because their 'carrying capacities' will be increasingly exceeded. Ever-renewable resource bases are shrinking. Climate changes because of both long-term cyclical processes and human activities (deforestation, pollution of the atmosphere, etc.). The impact of even minor increases or decreases in temperature may have catastrophic effects on the productivity of various ecosystems. A transfer of cropland from subsistence production to cash-crop production and a shift from a variety of indigenous food crops to imported food crops like wheat and rice has created global food insecurity. A major disturbance in the production centres, due to flooding or drought, will bring hunger and famine to many parts of the world.

Recently the relationship between environmental degradation and conflict has drawn the attention of researchers and activists. For example, an Earthscan report [Briefing Document 40] argues that diminishing natural resources have become an important cause of violent human conflicts both between states and within states. This link is not surprising since changing environments provide the contexts in which varying types of conflicts emerge but the actual cause-effect relation has not been the subject of systematic research. The problem of environmental refugees in Africa, the Indian subcontinent, Central America, and the Caribbean, the desperation of nomads and indigenous forest people deprived of their habitat, and the ungovernable cities in the Third World are cases in point that show the undeniable interconnectedness among environment, conflict, and security.

These ecological threats to human security are clearly related to the mainstream paradigm of development and can only be countered if this paradigm of development is reconsidered. In addition, sustainability cannot, however, be achieved in any single country as ecological problems do not respect national borders. To this extent, the doctrine of national security presents a serious obstacle to a rational solution.

Invulnerability

A second important security risk, exemplified by the vulnerability of modern industrialism, is inherent in the way societies are organized. There are many aspects of this vulnerable 'modernity': dependence on foreign trade, large scale technology, extreme urbanization, excessive centralization, bureaucratic control, to name only a few. A vulnerable society will, furthermore, opt for an offensive defence. It will tend to 'export its wars' and fight them in other countries because its own system is too brittle to withstand the impact of a war and offensive weapons are needed to secure raw materials in other parts of the world [Galtung, 1982, p. 89]. Thus, the type of society and the type of defence go together. An invulnerable society is itself an asset from the perspective of security.

The problem of vulnerability can be related to different aspects of society as well as different levels of society. Its distinction from sustainability is not sharp; often, sustainability and invulnerability go together and support each other mutually, just as unsustainability and vulnerability can be seen as two dimensions of 'maldevelopment'. To think of a society that is sustainable and vulnerable (or invulnerable) would be a highly theoretical exercise. What then is the difference? We have already noted that sustainability refers to the relationship between society and nature whereas vulnerability refers to social organization. To this could be added that the former problem is a secular undermining of the system, whereas the latter manifests itself in sudden crises. Still, we cannot separate the two altogether. For example, the oil crisis in the early 1970s developed because of a sudden shortage of supply due to political reasons, but it is also a manifestation of the long term exhaustion of oil as a dominant energy resource in Western industrialism. While the latter problem led many to question the sustainability of Western industrialism (and the 'modern project' in the Third World), the former revealed the extreme vulnerability of production and transport systems in the industrialized countries. The change from oil-supported industrialism to production systems based on nuclear energy may reduce vulnerability in some respects, while adding new problems—protection against sabotage and handling of nuclear wastes—and still not addressing the problem of sustainability.

Legitimacy

The social and economic aspects of vulnerability are strongly interrelated, but the problem of *political* vulnerability, or legitimacy, arises regardless of the level of societal complexity and should be dealt with separately. We can think of highly vulnerable societies with legitimate regimes, at least until their vulnerability is exposed in more or less dramatic crises, which then provide reasons for social protest and political decay. So far, such tendencies are more widespread in less 'developed' societies, often sparked by the behaviour of ruling elites. However, the problem of legitimacy is relevant for every political organization, whether the society in question is industrialized or not.

Both the mode of production and the mode of political organization have a direct bearing on the psychological dimensions of security and welfare at the level of the individual. It is sometimes forgotten that perhaps the most serious form of vulnerability, from a security perspective, is a lack of interest and willingness on the part of the people to defend their country. There was no lack of nationalist sentiments in the last two world wars but history has also examples of societies that were destroyed because few 'citizens' actually cared very much.

There are two qualitatively distinct crises for the nation state: where the two development funds (investment and welfare) are exhausted and the state degenerates into a security or police state; and where the high level of education and welfare, the results of successful nation-building, is expressed in transnational identifications and concerns held by a reasonably large segment of the population. Local identifications will be strengthened in the first case, in the second, global or transnational. In both, the state will react with repression since the contradiction represents a fundamental threat to the nation state as the normal and dominant form of political organization.

Alternative military defence

In working toward a definition of alternative security, we have dealt with three prerequisites: ecological sustainability, social invulnerability, and political legitimacy. Obviously any security policy must also contain the actual forms of defence. If the struggle is usually military and violent, the alternative would logically be non-military and non-violent. Such a defence policy would rely less on military weapons and more on societal institutions and, above all, the determination and capability of the civilian population to resist invasion and occupation. Since participation in civilian resistance is necessarily voluntary, the legitimacy of the political regime is of prime importance. Non-military forms of defence would destroy less of what is to be protected—people, environment, institutions, culture, and ways of life. Furthermore, they might have a positive effect on the aggressor, which a conventional defence would not.

There is an impressive array of historical examples of more or less successful civilian struggles against invaders, occupants and usurpers [Sharp, 1973]. On the other hand, the technology of warfare is developing rapidly and it is sensible to question the relevance of civilian-based defence in the event of a major war between the blocs, which will probably become nuclear. A civilian-based defence can do little against a nuclear attack, but that holds true also for most military forms of defence. But a country with a civilian-based defence policy, and without nuclear weapons, would be far less likely to be targetted by nuclear powers [Sharp, 1982, p. 48]. Similarly, a process of disarmament toward more defensive defence policies, in which a civilian-based defence component must be crucial, would reduce present international tensions, and the likelihood of nuclear war.

To be realistic, it is doubtful that many elements of alternative security can be realized in the short term since they relate to structural characteristics which change very slowly. A sudden change in security policy is thus not politically viable and can be counter-productive. A more suitable approach will combine a defensive weapon system with non-conventional forms of struggle such as guerrilla warfare and civilian resistance. This approach is obviously not the same as non-violence, which logically would be the ultimate alternative approach, but it does not exclude non-violent action either. To a large extent, the actual forms of defensive struggle must depend on the specific circumstances.

Nuclear deterrence, the present paradigm of military defence prevailing, is offensive. A good argument can be made that it is this 'offensive' (in both senses of the word) quality of military thinking that explains much of the arms race, since no balance and stability can be found between offensive weapons systems. In fact, the offensive strategy contradicts the very idea of balance. Consequently a change toward a more defensive defence would also imply a more stable, if not balanced, situation and greater security for all—'common security' in the terminology of the Palme Commission. This perspective should be of particular relevance for European countries.

Only very small steps have been taken toward alternative security. In order to facilitate and reinforce the necessary ecological and structural transformations, it is important to develop suitable forms of struggle. These forms should be applicable to decentralized societies with a high degree of local autonomy, they should be manifestations of the psychology of self-reliance, and they should be consistent with the values of self-reliant development. The process has to be slow, since changes in economic, social and political organizations are also involved. The new structures and the new forms of struggle must be developed simultaneously and be mutually supportive. Alternative forms of struggle would not be very efficient in an extremely centralized, specialized, and professionalized society with a low level of political mobilization and ideological consciousness. In short, the way a society is organized and the choice of development model are important dimensions of a strategy for peace.

A Europeanized Europe

It was in Europe that the nation state and the Mainstream Model of Peace and Development originated, but the whole world is now carrying the burden of its obsolescence. As such, Europe has a moral obligation not to just preach alternatives to others but to practise them.

In the current European situation, both peace and development are being debated and their relationship somewhat confused since the two debates are carried out in rather different contexts. Without denying the relevance of the debates in their own terms, important dimensions could be elicited by relating them under the 'peace and development' umbrella. Mainstream patterns of development create vulnerable economic and social structures and necessitate offensive methods of defence. However, Europe, although vulnerable, is no longer capable of exporting its wars. It is in the unfortunate position of being both a vulnerable society and the chosen theatre for superpower confrontation. The only way out of this dilemma is through some kind of European delinking: a Western Europe less dependent on the US, and an Eastern Europe more independent of the Soviet Union, and the two Europes coming closer together. For this to happen self-reliance is necessary, but without alternative security, self-reliance will remain a distant dream. This is a controversial position and, in fact, there are at least three different approaches to peace and development.

The *Conventional Model* pictures the world as an inter-state system, each state being a sovereign unit and constituting a national economy. For each state, the rest of the world is an anarchy both in terms of the free play of market forces and in terms of the lack of overall political order. Economic competition and efforts to maintain a balance of power thus characterize the behaviour of nation states.

The *Reformist Model* contains three crucial elements. First, the level of armament must be lowered, but with the balance of power maintained. Second, the resources released by disarmament should be transferred to the developing countries so that the purchasing power of these countries is increased. Third, the growing demand resulting from the massive transfer of resources will generate growth and employment in the crisis-ridden industrial countries.

The *Alternative Model*, in contrast, is a fundamental reinterpretation of current peace and development concepts. According to this model, development is the creation of a sustainable society that fulfils basic human needs and where the relationship between society and nature is non-exploitative. Such a society would also be more secure, in the broader sense of the term. It would be self-reliant, less vulnerable, and ecologically balanced. Even in terms of the more restricted concept of security, the Alternative Model would be less provocative and more conducive for disarmament.

The first model is the traditional (or 'mainstream') European approach to peace and development. However, serious dysfunctions have emerged and the global system it organized seems to be breaking down. The Reformist Model tries to tackle some of these symptoms: excessive armaments, economic stagnation, rising unemployment, and polarization of rich and poor between and within the nation states. So far, these attempts have not succeeded. Rather this basically social democratic position is becoming increasingly marginalized. Many would call this position 'utopian' today. Would it be less utopian to call for a transcendence of the European Mainstream Model, as is the argument of this paper? There are several possible European scenarios and their relevance differs according to one's perspective. It is, thus, difficult to be very specific about current trends in Europe.

Beyond bloc politics

The Cold War is the most powerful force behind the present organization of the world. It is strong enough to destroy the world. Most peoples and states would benefit from the demise of Cold War ideology, especially the Europeans whose continent has been so senselessly divided by it. They have good reasons to ask themselves, what is the function of the cold war? One answer is that provided by the British historian and peace activist, E.P. Thompson, who sees the bloc division as a case of 'bonding-by-exclusion.'

'Rome required barbarians, Christendom required pagans, Protestant and Catholic Europe required each other. The nation state bonded itself against other nations. Patriotism is love of one's own country: but it is also hatred or fear or suspicion of others' [Thompson, 1982, p. 19].

Both the United States and the Soviet Union need very strongly an external threat. The threat of the *Other* is the main argument for maintaining discipline among the allies and control over their spheres of interest in the Third World. As with all ghosts, the Cold War ghost will disappear if the light is turned on, but the ruling elites in the two superpowers will not let this happen. When popular disgust and disbelief accumulates and threatens to get out of hand, a summit meeting is organized, publicized by the mass media as a turning point in the Cold War. Hope returns but then the lesson about who really runs the show is learnt again. As if to keep the show going, both sides display their arrogance in the Afghanistans and Nicaraguas, to be exaggerated and dramatized, or excused and talked away as the case may be. Clearly, the role of misinformation, disinformation, and non-information in keeping the Cold War going should not be underrated. Thanks to ignorance, the tribal instinct that makes the Cold War acceptable is given free expression.

In the United States, general understanding of and interest in the rest of the world seems relatively low and the political culture more primitive in comparison to Europe, at least after the political centre moved away from the eastern states. That is one of the reasons behind the crisis of Atlanticism: Europeans simply do not understand the United States any more. This process of drifting apart is certainly an important reason behind the new Europeanism. European tribalism is now adapting to new circumstances, and the 'we' and the 'others' are going through a reidentification process. This is a trap we should be aware of, although European tribalism in the present context may be more conducive to peace than the Atlanticist dogma. As Thompson puts it: 'We must begin to put

Europe back into one piece' [Thompson, 1982]. That is the only way to move beyond bloc politics.

However, Europe must not close itself to the rest of the world but play a much more active role, possibly in cooperation with the Non-Aligned Movement. This would mean some kind of 'neutralistic' stand, allowing room for substantial flexibility, in recognition of differing security interests [Albrecht, 1982]. Thus, the Europe emerging beyond bloc politics will be both more united and more diverse because the removal of Cold War obsessions will undoubtedly leave room for other kinds of conflicts such as ethnic revival and traditional national animosities that form part of the European heritage. Positive peace may not be around the corner even if the immediate threat of universal destruction is reduced. A more autonomous Europe may base its security on nuclear defence, a strengthened conventional defence, or a transarmament programme where the whole concept of security is radically redefined. This 'utopian' solution may, paradoxically, be the only realistic way to secure peace. If Europe as a third force in world politics should opt for nuclear defence, the nuclear arms race will be completely out of control. But a strengthened European conventional defence is too costly, will increase its dependence on the superpowers and, when the destructiveness of a conventional war is considered, hardly more acceptable to the peace movement. Alternative security must therefore be based on a new foundation of economic and political relations.

Toward third system politics

What are the forces that will move Europe from the Conventional towards the Alternative Model of Peace and Development? Since the nation state and the transnational corporation—the First and Second Systems—form part of the problem, one hypothesis is that the solution would probably be found in the Third System, i.e., peoples' movements and other emerging networks and decentralized structures reacting to the crisis. Can social transformation at the macro-level (national and global) be the result of micro-processes, social movements that are based on the territorial principle and organized around very different and usually local issues?

First, it is important to recognize that the conventional distinction about levels of society usually made by social scientists—micro, mezzo, macro, or local, national, international—are analytical simplifications, abstractions that do not exactly reflect real social processes. They contain systematic biases which induce us to underestimate the aggregate effect of dispersed and localized phenomena, such as Third System politics.

Second, there is a dynamic interplay between the functional macro-system and the territorial micro-system. The emergence of Third System politics, both in the West (including the socialist countries) and in the Third World, is related to the world economic crisis, which in fact is a crisis for the functional system. When it turns out to be increasingly dysfunctional, people who suffer from unemployment, marginalization, and the destruction of their habitat react and take their future into their own hands. As they increase their autonomy and scope of action, the functional macro-system becomes further reduced and crisis-ridden, in turn giving more room to local initiatives. From this dialectical point of view, the change in established power structures may come sooner than the present distribution of power suggests.

Third, while the issues in Third System politics vary due to local differences, they are quite similar at a deeper level. Here one may speak of a clear tendency toward convergence. The new social movements in the industrialized North, usually led by post-materialist elites, often refer to long forgotten populist, anarchist, or utopian socialist thinkers and explicitly give expression to counterpoint values. The new movements are also consciously transnational but in some cases, such as the regionalist movements, also consciously sub-national. Thus, the levels *below* and *above* the nation state are becoming increasingly relevant. In both cases, vested interests in the nation state are threatened. We do not know yet how serious this threat really is, but it is quite obvious that the European peace movement has revealed some basic contradictions in the behaviour of nation states. Whereas the traditional peace movement believed in improved inter-state relations and a supra-national negotiation machinery, the new peace movement is beginning to see the nation state as part of the problem. The new peace movement is more movement than organization, it is more concerned with people than with states, it associates peace with a stable and sustainable society (positive peace) rather than with a situation of non-war (negative peace). Thus, there seems to be a convergence between the peace movement and other so-called alternative movements.

To what extent do they have support from the grassroots in the Third World? The types of anti-systemic mobilization in the Third World differ in scope from local communities to civilizations and thus also threaten the nation state from below and from above. They would, on the whole, also support counterpoint values rather than mainstream values. However, the issues are not exactly the same. The environmental problems are focused, but the crucial problem is the survival of peoples depending on different ecological niches, and not merely the question of pollution. Similarly, the perceived physical threats are not so much related to the possibility of a nuclear war but more to the daily political repression, ethnic conflicts, and civil wars.

The problem of marginalization is relevant in both North and South, but in the industrial North the experience of marginalization in its current form is recent. As long as the idea of full employment was adhered to, marginalization was thought of as a criterion of underdevelopment; it has, however, been known to Eastern Europe as 'under-employment,' the phenomenon of quasi-work. Unemployment presently has passed the level of 10 per cent in many West European countries, and few people believe that full employment will ever be possible to achieve again.

Thus the marginals in both the North and the South constitute a potentially strong social force. Still, their possible ideological orientation is hard to foresee. They will grow in number as the present crisis continues and will certainly add to the strains on the system. They may support different political movements and organizations—red, green, brown—or they may be manipulated by the system in support of reformist solutions. On a deeper level, one could nevertheless speak of a thematic convergence related to the incapacity of the nation state to provide solutions to perceived threats.

Yet for organizational convergence, to build coalitions for social transformation, there is a real problem about creating horizontal channels of communication and vertical organizational links, not only because of the fragmented position of the new movements, but also because of the necessity of avoiding the old trap of First System macro-organizations exploited by elites for elite interests. New forms of organization must be found and this seems to be understood by many groups both in the North and the South. Their relation to the formal party system has been and remains a key issue, since the illusion of capturing state power to some extent persists.

Concluding Remarks on Voluntarism

The Earth cannot sustain a fully 'modernized' and 'developed' world society, and the social arrangements between and within the 159 nation states are frightfully unstable. Thus the search for alternatives is essential and we must believe that there is some scope for rational choice and constructive action, preferably on a pan-European level.

On a rather general level, a European identity now seems to be taking' shape, just like the various national identities formed in the past. This does not preclude divergent views on many issues. On the contrary, it is quite normal that an emerging 'likemindedness' on the continental level will also give rise to dissent. What happens is that the typical contradictions within the states manifest themselves on a European level. The concrete content of Europeanization will therefore depend on the balance of forces in the different states and regions at each moment. There is thus an emerging transnational likemindedness but not necessarily reflecting a European monolith. Both class/party perspectives and region-specific perspectives will continue to differ and there are still strong Atlanticist pockets. Security policies are in a flux. However, in this era of uncertainty there are latent possibilities for Europe to take on the role of a global actor in the promotion of peace and development. A modest optimism is therefore called for.

The least one can demand from Europe is not to make things worse. The potential role of Europe as a third superpower competing with the others for markets and influence would, if realized, have made things worse. At present, that does not seem to be a probable development, considering the problems within the EEC. Europe could also make things worse if the current critical situation develops into more serious internal tensions and crises of legitimacy that affect the very delicate European security system: viz., a situation that may lead to war with all the expected repercussions on the rest of the world, including nuclear winter. That must also be avoided. Provided Europe avoids these pitfalls, how can it make things better? Obviously by trying to reduce East-West tensions that are manifested in its tragic and artificial division. While division is an institution of the Cold War, concretely expressed in the Berlin Wall, closing the gap may in itself be interpreted as a security risk by each of the superpowers since the Europeanization of Europe implies reduced superpower control and, by definition, a movement toward the other camp. This is exactly the dilemma faced by the democratic movement in Eastern Europe, and to some extent it is also a problem for the left in Western Europe, not to mention the peace movement. Stability must not be mixed up with the status quo, but any change in the security system must be slow and cautious, and should be seen as a process of transarmament. Furthermore, changes in the security system must be supported by changes in the economic system, due to the necessary relationship between type of defence and type of society as well as the consequent contradictions between alternative security and the Mainstream Model of development. As I have tried to argue in this paper, the latter is inherently violent and will ultimately defeat all attempts at disarmament (which of course must remain the final goal).

So far I do not think my argument has been too controversial: popular disgust with the status quo, the need for alternatives in development and peace, the necessary links between type of defence and type of society, and the progressiveness and viability of a Europeanized Europe (provided it is a slow process with adequate modifications of the security system). Where people tend to disagree, however, is whether or not radical alternatives will be possible if political realities and the implications of various alternatives for peace and development in other regions are carefully considered.

On this point I should like to point out that utopianism, defined as an emotional or opportunistic attachment to an unrealistic project, may characterize conventional as well as alternative models. The Conventional Model of peace and development is, according to more and more people, utopian because of its long term unviability, as indicated by the current crisis and threatening holocaust. This is due more to inherent contradictions of the model than to lack of political support. On the other hand, the alternatives, what I have called the Reformist and the Alternative Models, may be more viable but are accused of utopianism because of the lack of political support. However, the issue of security has become a problem of general concern and a broadening debate in the last five to ten years which means options will increase and that, furthermore, it will be increasingly difficult to separate the issue of peace from the issue of development. It is significant that in both alternative solutions these two issues are inseparable. The Reformist Model sees disarmament as a precondition for development, whereas the Alternative Model sees security as an integral part of a new pattern of development.

References

Albrecht, U. 'Western European Neutralism' in Kaldor, M. and D. Smith, (eds) *Disarming Europe*, Merlin, London, 1982.

Anderson, P. *Lineages of the Absolutist State,* New Left Books, London, 1975.

Bayley, D.H. 'The Police and Political Development in Europe,' in Tilly, C. (ed.), 1975.

Brown, L. 'Redefining National Security,' in *Worldwatch Paper No. 14*, Worldwatch Institute, Washington, 1977.

Frank, A.G. *The European Challenge: From Atlantic Alliance to Pan-European Entente for Peace and Jobs,* Spokesman, Nottingham, 1983.

Galtung, J. *Environment, Development and Military Activity: Towards Alternative Security Doctrines,* Universitetsfôrlaget, Oslo, 1982.

Hettne, B. *Development Theory and the Third World,* SAREC Report R2, Stockholm, 1982.

Hveem, H. 'Scandinavia, the Like-Minded Countries and the NIEO,' in Laszlo, E. and J. Kurtzman (eds) *Western Europe and the New International Economic Order,* Pergamon Press, New York, 1980.

Mansbach, R.W. et al. *The Web of World Politics: Non-State Actors in the Global System,* Prentice Hall, Englewood Cliffs, NJ, 1976.

Mendel, A.P. *Dilemmas of Progress in Tsarist Russia: Legal Marxism and Legal Populism*, Harvard University Press, Cambridge, MA, 1961.

Modelski, G. 'The Long Cycle of Global Politics and the Nation-State,' in *Comparative Studies in Society and History,* Vol. 20, April 1978.

Ohlsson, T. 'Third World Arms Exporters: A New Facet of the Global Arms Race,' in *Bulletin of Peace Proposals,* Vol. 13, No. 3, 1982.

Sen, G. *The Military Origins of Industrialization and International Trade Rivalry,* Frances Pinter, London, 1984.

Senghas, D. 'Conflict Formation in Contemporary International Society,' in *Journal of Peace Research*, No. 3, 1973.

Sharp, G. 'Making the Abolition of War a Realistic Goal,' in *Development*, 1982:2.
—— *The Politics of Non-Violent Action,* Porter Sargent, Boston, 1973.

Strayer, J.R. *On the Medieval Origins of the Modern State,* Princeton University Press, Princeton, NJ, 1970.

Thompson, E.P. *Beyond the Cold War,* Merlin, London, 1982.

Tilly, C. *The Formation of National States in Western Europe,* Princeton University Press, Princeton, NJ, 1975.

Von Laue, T.H. *Sergei Witte and the Industrialization of Russia,* New York, 1963.

11. Transforming the State. An Alternative Security Concept for Europe

by Mary Kaldor

Introduction

The present period is characterized by what appears to be an intensified struggle for power. This struggle is manifested, on the one hand, in an accelerated arms race and a renewed Cold War between the United States and the Soviet Union and, on the other hand, in the economic crisis and the ensuing competition, primarily among capitalist countries, to determine the terms under which national economies participate in the world economy. Those engaged in studies of economic and political cycles in history predict that the present conjuncture is likely to lead to global war. But today global war would mean the extinction of humanity.

This is what is meant by civilizational crisis. If we are to avoid this catastrophe, a social transformation is required in the way States relate to each other and indeed in the nature of States which could be as momentous as the transformations which brought forth the empires of antiquity or which gave rise to capitalism and the nation-state system in or around the 15th century.

This chapter explores some of these arguments and how they apply to the situation in Europe. I want to suggest that there is currently an opportunity for profound change in Europe, and that the new social movements, especially the peace movement, could play a potentially catalytical role in bringing about changes with global, indeed possibly civilizational, ramifications. The focus of this paper, however, is on the possible changes in Europe: the global consequences are implied.

Long political and economic cycles

E.H.Carr observed that cyclical theories are typical of societies in decline.[1] Recently, there has been a spate of literature about long political and economic cycles and a rediscovery of earlier literature dating from the previous period of decline, Schumpeter and Kondratiev, Quincy Wright and Toynbee.[2] The evidence that emerges from this literature does appear to be rather convincing. Over the last three or four centuries, there do appear to have been roughly 50 year cycles in economic activity, although these might be described, as Trotsky[3] and others prefer, as stages since each cycle was characterized by a different set of industries, demand structure, labour process, class composition etc, and the dating of the cycles, in my view, is not very precise. Each cycle especially during the last two hundred years can be roughly divided into four phases: recovery, boom, recession, depression. Moreoever, several writers argue that these economic cycles roughly correspond with long political cycles.[4] Every hundred years or so (115 years according to Toynbee), a new hegemonic world power has emerged as a result of an intense military struggle. In the intervening period, it is possible to observe a pattern of general peace, followed by minor wars, followed by intensified rivalries, resulting in renewed global or major war.

The interpretation of these cycles, as is to be expected, varies considerably. Here I do not propose to describe or assess the various explanations, but rather to concentrate on those analyses that seem most relevant to the current period. Theories about economic cycles are much more developed than theories about political cycles. Among Marxists there is an important school of thought that explains the different phases of the economic cycle in terms of the mismatch between State and economy. Boom periods are periods of harmony in which the State guarantees the conditions for rapid accumulation. Crisis periods are periods of disharmony in which State policies become a fetter on accumulation. In particular, a contradiction arises from the national organization of the State and the global organization of the economy. States raise their revenues from within national boundaries and are, therefore, primarily interested in domestic accumulation. When strong States try to protect domestic accumulation at the expense of global accumulation, an economic crisis is the result.

Wallerstein and others place considerable emphasis on the fact that the capitalist economy is characterized by a competitive inter-State system rather than a single empire, so that global hegemony can shift from one State to another and thus allow for revitalization of the system as a whole.[5] Their argument is that one State takes on the role of guaranteeing global accumulation, preserving the conditions for free trade, access to resources, new markets and so on. This State establishes its hegemonic position through successful domestic accumulation; however, as the focus of global accumulation shifts away from its national territory, it uses its hegemonic position to protect domestic accumulation and, hence, becomes a fetter on the global economy. A struggle among core States, i.e. States in whose territory accumulation is concentrated, then ensues, probably involving war, resulting in a new hegemonic or world power.

Several writers add a technological or industrial dimension to this argument. Successful accumulation is based on a few leading sectors and key factors of production. The hegemonic State tends to favour these sectors and factors of production which retain their privileges even after accumulation has shifted into new sectors and new factors of production. A more sophisticated version of the argument centres around technology paradigms or technology regimes which represent an interlinked series of innovations expressed in patterns of production, locations of investment, forms of transportation, styles of consumption, skills and so on.[6]

This type of analysis would explain the current situation in the following terms. The United States established its hegemonic position as a consequence of two world wars, based on its success in Fordist mass production techniques, automobiles and other consumer durables as leading sectors, oil as a key factor of production, and so on. Today, the focus of global accumulation has shifted to Western Europe and Japan towards new leading sectors, particularly information technology, based on the microchip as a key factor of production. The current economic crisis can be understood in terms of the American attempt to protect domestic accumulation and privileged sectors that are now declining in relation to other sectors. As the crisis deepens, an intensified rivalry among core States for control of the global conditions for accumulation can be expected.

The argument has been expressed somewhat schematically and, for simplicity, I have not situated the argument within the context of core-periphery or North-South relations or domestic class struggle. This is because I want to draw out a different aspect. As an explanation of the economic crisis, the argument is extremely useful because it draws attention to the important role of the State. The weakness, however, is the discussion of the State which, in my view, is somewhat mechanistic. The State is seen as being primarily functional to the economy, even if it is the national economy rather than the global economy. The State does, of course, sometimes behave dysfunctionally especially in a national context but this is, as it were, punished through various forms of struggle, especially war.

Apart from the fact that this approach to the State is somewhat ahistorical – it does not explain how the State came to assume this function nor why some States adjust more easily to economic changes than others – there are two more serious problems. First, within this theoretical framework, it is very difficult to analyse the nature of socialist States. A typical approach is to treat socialist systems as nation-states captured by anti-systemic forces unable to bring about fundamental changes because of their national isolation in a global system. The main contribution of socialist States is thus to provide space for other anti-systemic forces in the world, although this may sometimes come into conflict with national interests in protecting their own positions. According to this analysis, there is a fundamental struggle going on between capitalism and socialism, expressed in the East-West conflict. This is superimposed on and more fundamental than the inter-imperial rivalry, expressed in the West-West conflict. An alternative, generally less favoured approach, is to treat the socialist States as core competing States. This approach implies that the East-West conflict is simply another example of inter-imperial rivalry.

Neither approach seeks to explore the role or nature of socialist systems in terms of the internal structures of those States, especially the Soviet State. Second, and related, is the fact that the analysis tends to be deterministic. The only alternative to another global war, the only way out of the civilizational crisis, is the capture of State power by anti-systemic forces on a global scale. The fundamental cause of war and economic crisis is seen as the capitalist mode of production. Changing the mode of production could be brought about through political struggles in both North and South which were successful in challenging global hegemony. Since success in this endeavour does seem remote, at least in the short run, although many writers express optimism, it seems difficult to be other than pessimistic about the prospects for mankind.

In what follows, I forward tentatively some elements of what would be required for an interdependent analysis of the State and long political cycles, how the economy impinges on State crises or the causes of war, rather than the other way round. This is not to suggest that politics is necessarily in command, as, say, realist analyses of political cycles, like Modelski, would have it.[7] Rather, the argument is that a focus on the State would complement the current focus on economies and provide a more sophisticated understanding of the linkages between political and economic cycles. What such an analysis does, however, call into question is the Marxist proposition that a given social formation can always be defined in terms of its mode of production. I believe this proposition is, in fact, a product of capitalism since the characteristic of capitalism was the separation of economic and non-economic spheres of activites. It was the consequence of the wage relationship. The very categories economic and political are much less meaningful, say, in the context of modern socialist societies.

An independent analysis of the State might build on this distinction. A very important insight is provided by State theorists in Britain and West Germany (Picciotto and Holloway, Offe, Habermas) who treat the State not as an institution but as a set of social relationships.[8] These social relationships are distinguished from the capital relationship in that they constitute non-economic forms or, to use Offe's term, they are decommodified. The free market, the wage relationship, requires that non-economic forms of coercion are separated off from the sphere of material production even though these other social relationships may be and indeed are required to guarantee free market conditions. These social relationships are concentrated, though not exclusively, in the State households, for example, represent a very important non-State, non-profit, set of social relationships. The problems then becomes how to analyse the internal logic and laws of motion of this set of social relationships.

To put it another way, the State accounts for a very large part of social activity, which is outside the market sphere of activity. This social activity should be viewed not as an homogeneous entity, an instrument which serves the market sphere of activity, but rather as a sort of society, a subsystem of the social formation. What distinguishes this sphere from the economic sphere is partly the nature of what it produces. The economy produces material goods, while the State produces social, political, judicial or military services. But more important, since the above is not a hard and fast distinction in any case, there is a difference in the relationships of production and reproduction. The economy is characterized by market relations in which exchange between users and producers is determined on the basis of prices and in which profit becomes a kind of signal for adjustment. The State, on the other hand, represents a whole set of non-market relationships ranging from consensus, based on democracy and representation, to various forms of ideological and physical coercion. Both voting behaviour, at one extreme, and victory or defeat in war, at the other extreme, are signals for adjustments in relationships and in State activities.

Two points need to be borne in mind. First, in analysing these relationships we have to take into account the process of reproduction. Hence the State is interested in promoting accumulation within national territory because domestic accumulation provides the resource base for the reproduction of State activities. But equally important the social relationships that constitute State activities take the form of specific structures of reproduction – the organization of bureaucracy, the balance of relations between parliament, the armed forces, the department of defence, and so on – which may constrain the State's ability to act in its institutional self-interest. Second, we are concerned not just about the domestic social relationships but also about relationships between states which similarly consist of a range of different non-economic forms. A coercive international relationship which might consist of foreign military intervention or pressure from a multinational institution like the IMF, again, might contradict institutional self-interest in, say, domestic accumulation.

An approach of this kind exposes the difficulty of assuming that the State can be used as an instrument for social transformation. Because the State constitutes non-market relationships and can intervene in market relations, socialists have tended to assume that capture of State power and State intervention in the economy can usher in a more advanced mode of production, (whatever we mean by advanced). But this depends very crucially on the form of social relationships that constitutes the State. A militarized authoritarian State relies on more primitive forms of coercion than the wage relationship and, indeed, this argument forms the basis of the liberal critique of Statism.

In what follows, I examine some of the ways by which we might explore the military dimension of State relationships within this analytical framework. I define warfare as being socially organized physical coercion against a socially organized opponent. By and large, this means that warfare takes place primarily between States. This is also true, to some extent, for civil wars since civil wars can be defined as violent conflict in which the State faces a socially organized domestic opponent, which could be described as a proto-State. Warfare is distinguished from repression in that the latter consists of socially organized physical coercion against individuals. The military can be described as the institution of war preparedness, the social organization for warfare. Two important characteristics of the social relationships that make up the military dimension of the State can be observed.

First, the main form of exchange, or realization, ie war, is discontinuous. Or to put it another way: in every social relationship involving exchange, some form of commensuration is required. Commensuration is the mechanism through which resources are reconciled to requirements. The market is one obvious form of commensuration in which the appropriate quantity of resources is assessed with numerical precision. War is the way in which the military as a social organization reconciles resources to requirements, how it decides how much is enough? In between wars, the way in which resources are mobilized for warfare depends on subjective assessments about what might happen in a future war. These assessments are shaped by past experience and by institutional self-interest. Both these factors tend to imply inertia, a tendency for tne military merely to replicate themselves, in their past image. For this reason, in peace-time, a militarized State, i.e. a State in which the military dimension is an important and influential component of the overall social relationships that consitute the State, tends to be rather rigid, resistant to adjustments or unresponsive to social, technological and economic changes.

Second, insofar as the State represents a continuum of social relationships, the more coercive relationships tend to prevail when consensual relationships fail. This argument is akin to Gramsci's analysis of Caesarism or Marx's analysis of Bonapartism,[9] although it is not necessary to go as far as to presuppose military domination of the State, merely to propose that in periods when social compromise, expressed in democratic forms of State relationships, is weakened, a shift takes place towards greater reliance on repressive apparatus or military institutions, the more coercive forms of social relationship. This point is particularly important in the international context, in understanding the shift towards the military element in relationships between States.

If our concern is to avoid war, then the central question is whether it is possible to bring about adjustments in the inter-State system, by shifting away from coercive relationships towards less rigid more consensual relationships. In other words, can we bring about adjustments in the inter-State system which could reestablish some form of social harmony, without war? Such a shift would be momentous. Moving beyond physical coercion in inter-State relationships is as significant as was moving beyond physical coercion in domestic production relationships. The next section considers these possibilities in terms of analysis of current military organization and concepts of warfare.

The role of deterrence

Just as each economic cycle can also be described as a stage, since it is characterized by a different set of production relationships, so each political cycle is also characterized by a different inter-State system, comprising a specific hierarchy of nation-States, one or two hegemonic powers and a specific set of relationships or institutions for managing the inter-State system. We can observe certain unique features of the post-war inter-State system in comparison with previous systems.

First, a number of international institutions were established to develop mechanisms for reaching international consensus. Even though these institutions were largely dominated by the United States, the fact that they were presented in an international form was a contrast to previous periods. This was particularly true for economic institutions, like IMF, GATT, EEC, OECD, etc which can be contrasted to the role played by, say, the Bank of England. The United Nations had its roots in the League of Nations, of course, but was far more significant in the post-war period, as was the role of international courts. Even military alliances can, to some extent, be viewed as mechanisms for developing compromises or consensus within a coercive framework as opposed to more direct forms of military coercion.

A second feature of the post-war system was the emergence of independent nation-States in the periphery. While it is true to say that core relationships were characterized by an inter-State system rather than a single empire, core-periphery relations were, by and large, characterized by competing empires. Independence allowed greater space for manoeuvre on the part of peripheral States and at the same time, introduced a new set of integrative relationships between core and periphery States. It can be argued that independence potentially represented a greater flexibility in inter-State relationships. Nevertheless, it is also the case that the new States were heavily militarized and the transfer of military technology and military institutions was an important component of these relationships, introducing considerable rigidity.

A third feature of the post-war system was the role of the Soviet Union. The post-war system can perhaps more properly be described as a bipolar system, although, of course, in a global sense, US hegemony was far more powerful and pervasive. The Soviet Union created a parallel inter-State system that to a large extent, had opted out of the world capitalist economy. Nevertheless it would be wrong to present the Soviet Union as a challenger to US hegemony, rather as a component of the post-war system. To analyse the nature of the Soviet system is beyond the scope of this paper, but it is worth noting that it is a system which has eschewed the profit forms at least domestically, but has not developed consensual or democratic forms of social relationship in either the economic or political sphere. The heavy reliance on physical coercion both domestically and in relation to other socialist States has also entailed a considerable rigidity in the system and resistance to change. To mount an effective challenge, States must exhibit certain structural characteristics that enable them to offer solutions to problems of stagnation or crisis or social turbulence, or to put it another way, to re-establish harmony; it was certain progressive (if you like) features of the British State at the turn of the 19th century or the American State in the early 20th century that enabled their ascendancy. The Soviet Union, as a competitor, can offer space to, say, anti-systemic movements in peripheral countries but this, in my view, is strictly limited by its own interest in survival and its own position vis à vis the United States.

Rather, the existence of a parallel system can be seen as a way of upholding the American role and of providing a permanent undesirable contrast and, hence, external enemy. The United States has a similarly legitimating role for the Soviet Union. In other words, the East-West conflict is seen not as a struggle between capitalism and socialism nor as a form of inter-imperial rivalry, but rather as an external manifestation of the internal for the Soviet Union. In other words, the East-West conflict is seen not as a struggle between capitalism and socialism nor as a form of inter-imperial rivalry, but rather as an external manifestation of the internal contradiction of each system. In the Western case, for example a major internal contradiction is the inter-imperial rivalry between the core capitalist States. The East-West conflict is a struggle between two systems but neither system actually represents an alternative to the other. On the contrary, the existence of both is needed to maintain both.

The world order concept for managing the post-war system was nuclear deterrence. Nuclear deterrence differed from previous world order concepts in that it also contained the notion of avoiding war. Hence, it was described as a security concept. If we think of a security concept as meaning the avoidance of war, a world order concept can be viewed as a concept designed to preserve or to manage a particular set of inter-State relationships. Previous world order concepts, say balance of power theories, did not include the notion of avoiding war. They were concerned with maintaining power relationships; indeed, the occasional war was an accepted element of the concept of balance of power.

Unlike previous balance of power concepts, deterrence works not so much through the direct application of military force but as a form of ideological coercion. (This may be one reason why the deterrence concept is less developed in the Soviet Union because relations with other socialist States have entailed great use of direct military intervention.) In fact, the transnationalization of military activities through the alliance system has effectively, although not completely, removed the use of direct military force as an element of inter-imperial rivalry. Deterrence can be thought of as an imaginary war. In military exercises, the deployment of troops and weapons systems, in the rhetoric of leaders and in the scenarios of military planners, a war is fought out daily in our imagination. This imaginary war takes place in Europe and bears a marked resemblance to the Second World War. In the West, it starts with a Soviet blitzkrieg across the North German plains and Europeans are dependent upon superior American technology for their defence. Nazism is conveniently transmogrified into Communism. This permanent state of neither war nor peace reminds us of our dependence on American hegemony and of the need for collective defence and for unity in the face of external danger. During the debate about Cruise and Pershing missiles, it became very clear that deployment was necessary, in the view of the West European and American elites, in order to display NATO unity and that unity was considered more important than domestic public opinion. Hence the alliance becomes a mechanism for preserving a unified set of positions among core States, for preventing the kind of domestic challenge that might be mounted against the prevailing world order, for suppressing inter-imperial rivalry. George Orwell anticipated the role of deterrence in *1984*, although he was mainly talking about domestic relations and did not include the relations between core States.

> The war, therefore, if we judge it by the standards of previous wars, is merely an imposture. It is like the battle between certain ruminant animals whose horns are set at such an angle that they are incapable of hurting one another. But though it is unreal it is not meaningless. It eats up the surplus of consumable goods, and it helps to preserve the special mental atmosphere that a hierarchical society needs.... In the past, the ruling groups of all countries, although they might recognize their common interest and limit the destructiveness of war, did fight against one another, and the victor always plundered the vanquished. In our own day, they are not fighting against one another at all. The war is waged by each ruling group against its own subjects and the object of the war is not to make or prevent conquests of territory but to keep the structure of society intact. The very word "war" therefore has become misleading. It would probably be accurate to say that by becoming continuous war has ceased to exist.... A peace that was truly permanent would be the same as permanent war.[10]

The contradictions of deterrence as a world order concept *and* a security concept become apparent as the prevailing world order comes under challenge. With the shift of the poles of accumulation away from the United States, it becomes harder to maintain consensus among core States. Precisely because the US, in various ways (interest rates, commercialization of aid, non-tariff barriers, etc), uses its hegemonic position to protect domestic accumulation, there are more and more disputes among core States. Consequently, there is a tendency to shift away from consensual relationships, towards more coercive relationships. Hence the American emphasis not just on economic coercion, but on the Cold War, deterrence, the military build-up.

The problem is that the utility of the imaginary war as a form of ideological coercion is limited precisely because it is imaginary, because it must not become real. Deterrence contains this paradoxical idea expressed by Orwell, that war is peace, that by imagining war, by demonstrating mutual vulnerability, war can never actually take place. Deterrence is, in fact, self-deterring. The demonstration of military power in imagination is only effective as a way of maintaining international hierarchy if people believe in its potential reality. This is what underlies the development of nuclear warfighting concepts, the attempt to find some way of using American military power to maintain the current world order. When President Reagan talks about escaping deterrence, in the context of Star Wars, he means that he wants to be able to use American military power. In other words, the Americans are attempting to reduce, although not entirely eliminate the security element of deterrence and make more conceivable an imaginary military struggle for world order which they win, or have already won. In other words, deterrence already contains an in-built self-limitation against war – extreme forms of coercion between core states were restrained after the Second World War. But as pressure mounts to shift towards more extreme forms of coercion, that self-limitation is eroded. Herein lies the danger of global war.

The role of military technology

Nuclear deterrence is a form of inter-State relationship but it also has to be reproduced. In order to analyse how the contradictions of deterrence unfold, it is important to take into account the process of reproduction. What we describe as the arms race is, in fact, a continual upgrading of military technology. Neither quantities of weapons systems (except for nuclear warheads) nor the absolute size of military budgets have increased significantly. What has changed is the performance characteristics of individual weapon systems speed, payload, accuracy, etc. And this represents an increase in the technical resources devoted to developing and producing weapons systems which, in turn, is reflected in rapid increases in the costs of individual systems.

In my view, this technological development cannot be explained in terms of the demand for weapons. Precisely because there is no form of commensuration in the absence of war, there is no way of judging the utility of any given technological development. On the contrary, utility tends to be judged in relation to the last major form of commensuration, i.e. the Second World War. Historically, the military sector has been characterized by conservatism and inertia. This is one reason why the imaginary war bears a close resemblance to the Second World War. Moreover, military institutions, with institutionally determined preferences, were largely created in the Second World War. Of course, there have been other wars in peripheral regions, the Middle East or Vietnam, which have undoubtedly influenced military technology but it is usually argued that these experiences are not relevant for deterrence, an imaginary global war fought in Europe, i.e. a struggle among core States for world order.

It is sometimes argued that the importance of science and technology was the great lesson of World War II and so it is not surprising if military men emphasize the importance of technology. But one has to ask why this particular lesson was learned. An even more important lesson, in my view, was the importance of quantity and of mass production techniques, but this lesson, at least in the West, is not remembered with such avidity.

In my view, these technological developments can only be explained in terms of the role of private enterprise in producing military technology. In this sense, military technology represents an interesting hybrid between coercive State forms and profit forms. An understanding of military technology provides an example of direct intervention in the economic cycle. Because armament companies are competitive and profit seeking, they *have* to compete technologically in order to survive. Because there is no form of commensuration, there is no form of saturation. It is possible for companies to continue development and production to the limits of their technological capabilities and/or the limits of military budgets. Hence, technology is developed far beyond the stage that in other sectors, where use is more or less continuous, would be judged sufficient. Typically, military technology is characterized by sharply diminishing, perhaps even negative, marginal returns, i.e. a huge investment produces a very small improvement in any given performance characteristic.

This is a contrast to other forms of State sponsored technology which, sooner or later, have to be used. Civil nuclear energy is languishing in the United States, for example, because as a form of electricity generation it was less efficient than other sources and because of public concern about safety. The military sector is, as it were, immune to such sobering influences. It is not called to account as are other social or economic activities.

The importance of the role of private enterprises is suggested by comparison with previous historical periods or with the Soviet experience. With the exception of the Anglo-German naval arms race in which private shipbuilders played an important role, there was very little pressure historically for technological change in peacetime and, for the most part, armaments were produced in State-owned arsenals. Likewise in the Soviet Union, it can be argued that technological change is externally induced via the arms race. The predilection of the armed forces and the armament enterprises is for quantity rather than technological change.

The contradictions of deterrence, of the imaginary war, are also, therefore expressed through military technology. There is something in the arms economy argument that military spending is a form of waste. However, the emphasis on forms of commensuration offers an alternative definition of waste in place of its traditional definition as a commodity that does not reenter the production process as a capital or consumer good; this definition is in any case only relevant in a production-dominated analysis of society.[11] Rather waste can be defined as a product which has no mechanism for defining utility. In the absence of war, military technology is a perfect form of waste. Military spending is suitable for boosting public expenditure because it cannot be subjected to tests of utility. To argue, however, that military spending can be used as a Keynesian instrument to increase income and employment in the short-run, is *not* the same as saying that military spending is good for accumulation.

Current military technology is based on a military paradigm established in the Second World War. Even though it may make use of modern technologies like the microchip, it inhibits the application of these technologies for other purposes, either because of the absorption of technological resources or because of the distorting effects of the military paradigm on the technology itself. Hence, it can be argued that military technology inhibits the diffusion of a new technological paradigm, i.e. the application of new technologies to new uses, which is needed either for the development of a new stage of accumulation, i.e. a new economic cycle, or for the satisfaction of need. Or, to put it another way, military spending entrenches the political and economic structures of the existing system. In particular, military technology, especially within alliance frameworks, is a way of reasserting US economic hegemony because of the relative militarization of the the US State. The demand for example that European enterprises participate in Star Wars research is a way of orienting European economies towards the technological areas in which the US has a comparative advantage, i.e. improving the terms on which the US competes in the world economy. Precisely because this technology is to be shaped by the American military paradigm; the long term consequence is likely to be a continued slow-down in global accumulation, increased inequalities between nations and classes, etc, and increased rivalry among core States.[12]

There is thus a parallel between the ideological coercion implicit in nuclear warfighting doctrines and the economic coercion that underlies the reproduction of nuclear warfighting technologies. Both contribute to growing disharmony both among states and between the international state system and the global economy.

The European peace movement and alternative security concepts

In the last five years, the peace movement has grown dramatically, especially in Western Europe and Australasia. (The peace movement had developed much earlier in Japan.) In Britain, for example, the Campaign for Nuclear Disarmament now has over 400,000 members and is larger than the Labour Party. Certain signficant characteristics of the new peace movement can be described. First, the peace movement has largely developed in competing core States. Second, the peace movement has largely developed in those countries with fairly developed welfare States, i.e. an important non-militarized segment of State activity. Third, the social composition is largely drawn from the professional classes, who have grown both absolutely and relatively as a share of the population, as a result of the welfare State and the science intensity of new technologies.

Peace activists are doctors, social workers, teachers, lawyers, journalists, and computer programmers.

These people are not opposed to the State; on the contrary, their livelihoods often depend on the State. But they are frustrated by the lack of responsiveness of the State to social need, the difficulty of influencing State activity. Although many people joined the peace movement because of fear of nuclear war, the danger that the imaginary war might become real, it is also true to say that underlying this fear was a disillusion with politics. In Europe, particularly there was a sense that States had been coopted by the structures of deterrence and this prevented the proper functioning of democracy. In the campaign against Cruise and Pershing, this disillusion became conviction. The missiles did not just represent a symbol of American nuclear warfighting strategies; they represented an imposition of sovereignty. The fact that it was impossible to stop deployment indicated very clearly the shortcomings of the democratic process – the way in which the relationship with the United States overrode domestic political relationships. Fear of nuclear war was essentially a fear of not being able to control politicians.

Thus, it is possible to argue that the historic role of the peace movement is to bring about a fundamental transformation of the social relationships that constitute the State and the inter-State system away from reliance on physical coercion towards more democratic State forms, just as the historical role of the labour movement was and is a transformation of economic relationships. The elimination or reduced reliance on physical coercion is ultimately based on nothing more than social norms and the acceptance of an international code of behaviour. These social norms are already implicit in the concept of deterrence. Nobody actually expects a war in Europe, especially not within the two alliances. The task of the peace movement is to ensure that the notion of war avoidance is accepted by all core states and does not require the build-up of military technology or the threat of war to sustain it. On the contrary, the military build-up and the threat of war are required to sustain power relationships and their utility in this role is limited precisely because of the desire by all parties to avoid war. The peace movement has to challenge beliefs about deterrence in order to undermine further the utility of direct or indirect forms of military coercion, while strengthening the social constraints on war.

In the specific European context, a process of demilitarization would imply a more equal relationship between Europe and the two superpowers. This would also mean a weakening of the privileges of the technological paradigm of the fourth Kondratiev and hence more space for creating a more harmonious relationship betwen state and economy. At least as far as European states are concerned, it would also weaken the influence of international as opposed to domestic relationships on state behaviour and enable a greater responsiveness to domestic social need. In specific terms, this could mean, for example, a shift in state priorities, from military spending to welfare and environment, or from emphasis on oil and nuclear energy to energy conservation or renewable energy sources – although this would, of course, depend on what changes in domestic state relationships were required by or linked with international changes. Potentially, the new forms of state responsiveness could also provide, on the one hand, an alternative to market forms and hence an alternative to accumulation as the motor force of society and, on the other hand, an alternative to physically coercive forms so that social disharmony has to be managed without war and repression. It would mean greater flexibility and hence the possibility of establishing more harmonious social relationships so that the conditions for satisfying need, which may or may not involve accumulation, do not produce the subsequent conditions for crisis.

To put it simply, democracy could replace both the market and repression. The State would regulate market anarchy according to social need and not arbitrary state priorities. This would mean a change in the form of State relationships. Although the practical implications would require much more elaboration, such changes might include decentralization of state activities, i.e. greater regional or municipal roles in economic planning, accountability of state institutions, i.e. patients to control hospitals, or consumers and workers to control enterprises, and so on.

To some extent, the demilitarization of inter-State relationships has already been achieved within Western Europe and especially among the Nordic countries. The task of the peace movement is to extend that process to the whole of Europe and to broader global relationships, both with the hegemonic powers and with peripheral States. Such a process implies that the current system of bipolarity, of Soviet and American hegemony, is not replaced by a new polarity, a new hegemony, but by new forms of democratic regulation of inter-State relations; the embryo of such forms already exist in current international institutions. To achieve this, greater internal democracy is also required.

Unlike previous anti-systemic movements, the peace movement does not view the State as an instrument for carrying out its objectives. Or to put it another way, the peace movement does not aim to capture State power. Rather the peace movement aims to change the nature of State power, to change the form of social relationships that constitute the State so that the State is responsive to popular demands. Whereas previous successful anti-systemic movements found themselves constrained by the nature of the State and inter-State relations so that they were unable to carry out fully programmes of social transformation, the peace movement aims to constrain State power. The way in which the US anti-war movement succeeded in forcing a right-wing government to end the war in Vietnam is an excellent example of such a strategy. A current example is Denmark, where a conservative government, against its own inclination, has had to act as a dissenting voice within NATO.

The peace movement does not displace the historic demands of the labour movement. It should be noted that one of the consequences or perhaps functions of the post-war system was the separation of democracy and socialism. Socialism was treated as the non-profit form and, because of the Soviet experience, dubbed as militarised statism. Democracy was linked with the preservation of profit forms. If the aim is to go beyond both physical and economic forms of coercion, then these mis-identifications have to be removed, and this means the elimination of Cold War mentality.

There are certain similarities to the peace movement in human rights movements in both the Third World and in Eastern Europe and in the women's movements. These movements are struggling against the militarization of the State, which in turn is an important component of inter-State relations. Both Solidarity in Poland and human rights movements in some Third World countries acquired a mass base and yet insisted on their independence from State institutions, their concern was to change the role of State power in their societies rather than to capture State power.

The success of the peace movement project is conceivable in Europe. (There may well be similar opportunities in the Pacific.) This is because the European States are the main core challengers to the present hegemonic powers. For a whole variety of reasons which include the internationalization of military institutions through the alliances, the contradictory nature of deterrence, and the change in the nature of European States in the post-war period, these States cannot offer a military challenge to American and Soviet hegemony. Currently, European elites in particular find themselves in a contradictory position. On the one hand, they require a world order concept and a hegemonic State to guarantee the conditions for a global accumulation. On the other hand, they consider that the US is abusing the role of guardian of global accumulation. They emphasize the security aspects of deterrence by opposing American war fighting concepts; yet they cannot accept that war fighting concepts are a logical outcome of deterrence as a world order concept. They seek military and strategic alternatives to nuclear deterrence – greater emphasis on conventional weapons or the Europeanization of deterrence. Yet, again for a variety of reasons, these concepts are unlikely to gain a domestic consensus. It can be argued, although I will not elaborate, that a parallel though not at all identical situation exists for the East European powers. It is precisely because of this odd combination of strength and weakness that an alternative security concept aimed at eliminating or lessening the role of physical coercion in inter-State relations is conceivable. Such a concept is based on acceptance of social diversity and tolerance of pluralistic systems, and the notion that physical coercion or ideological coercion based on the threat of physical coercion is unacceptable as a means of suppressing social change. Such a concept would mean, for example, that State intervention in economic processes is clearly distinguished from military intervention; economic protectionism would have to be respected or opposed through a process of negotiation and compromise.

Essentially it is a concept for managing economic and social change without catastrophic political upheaval, but it contains, within it, the prospect of civilizational change. It is a liberal concept rather than a revolutionary concept but it is informed by the objective situation. It is achievable through an interacting process of demilitarization and democratization which has already begun – in the growth of international institutions, the security element of deterrence, the emergence of the welfare state, and so on.

This alternative security concept is *not* a world order concept, or at least it is a world order concept based on sovereignty, self-detemination and international cooperation instead of hegemony. Whether this could be adopted on a global level depends to a large extent on the balance of existing constraints on both war and hegemonic power. These constraints include the theoretical commitment to war avoidance and, in the US case, the democratic possibilities for restraining the exercise of global power. If an alternative security concept were initiated in Europe, could it strengthen those security elements that already exist in the United States and the Soviet Union? Or would it precipitate the actual use of military power? In conditions of conflict, do forms of social relationships necessarily degenerate?

Notes

1. E. H. Carr, *What is History?*, London: Penguin, 1975.

2. Wright, Quincy, *A Study of War*, Chicago: University of Chicago Press, 1942; Toynbee, Arnold J., *A Study of History,* London: Oxford University Press, 1961; Schumpeter, J. A., *Business Cycles: A Theoretical, Historical and Statistical Analysis of the Capitalist Process,* 2 vols, New York, McGraw Hill, 1939; Kondratiev, N. 'The Major Economic Cycles', *Review of Economic Statistics*, 18 November 1935.

3. See R. B. Day, 'The Theory of Long Waves, Kondratiev, Trotsky, Mandel', *New Left Review*, 99, Sept-Oct, 1976.

4. George Modelski, 'The Long Cycle of Global Politics and the Nation-State', *Comparative Studies in Society and History. An International Quarterly*, Vol. 20, No. 2, April, 1978; George Modelski, 'Long Cycles and Strategy of US Economic Policy', in William P. Avery and David P. Rapkin (eds.), *America in a Changing World Political Economy*, New York and London: Longman, 1982; Hopkins, Terence K., and Wallerstein, Immanuel et al, *World Systems Analysis: Theory and Methodology,* Beverly Hills CA: Sage, 1982.

5. Immanuel Wallerstein, *The Politics of the World Economy. The States, the Movements and the Civilizations*, Cambridge: CUP, 1984; Christopher Chase-Dunn, 'International Economic Policy in a Declining Core State', in Avery and Rapkin, op cit, fn4.

6. Giovanni Dosi, 'Technological Paradigms and Technological Trajectories. The Determinants and Directions of Technical Change and the Economy', in Christopher Freeman (ed.) *Long Waves in the World Economy*, London and Dover, N. H.: Frances Pinter, 1984; Carlotta Perez, 'Microelectronics, Long Waves and World Structural Change', *World Development*, forthcoming.

7. Modelski, op cit.

8. John Holloway and Sol Picciotto, *State and Capital. A Marxist Debate*, London: Edward Arnold, 1978; Claus Offe, *Contradictions of the Welfare State*, London: Hutchinson, 1984; Jurgen Habermas, *Legitimation Crisis,* Boston, 1975.

9. Antonio Gramsci, *Selections from the Prison Notebooks*, London: Lawrence and Wishart, 1971, see pp. 219–233; Marx K., 'The Eighteenth Brumaire of Louis Bonaparte', in *Marx Engels Selected Works*, London: Lawrence and Wishart Ltd., 1968, pp. 94–166.

10. George Orwell, *1984*, London: Penguin Books, 1954.

11. P. Baran and P. Sweezy, *Monopoly Capital*, London: Penguin Books, 1966; M. Kidron, *Western capitalism since the War*. London: Penguin Books, 1967.

12. This argument is spelled out in Mary Kaldor, 'The Atlantic Technology Culture' in Richard Falk and Mary Kaldor (eds.), *Dealignment for Western Europe?*, forthcoming.

12. Economic Aspects of the Policies of Peace and Security

by Alfred Bönisch

Economic relations between countries of different social systems are shaped necessarily by the objectively existing conditions, primarily the international division of labour, and provide an important link within the system of international relations. In particular, they are subject to the correlations between economy and policy, i.e. political factors, aside from military and ideological ones, have a definite influence on these economic relations.

In the last few years, socialist States have taken great pains to expand international economic relations. Two major factors have been responsible for this:

1) consolidation of the process of political détente and its further development;
2) stimulation of one's own development.

The second factor is subordinate to the first, since at present the primary concern is to prevent nuclear war. All possibilities have to be utilized to safeguard peace, including various kinds of international economic cooperation. Such examples as the anti-Hitler coalition illustrate the fact that

> despite the existence of different social systems, different ideological and political views the States can jointly act in an effort to materialize their basic coherent interests ... In the face of the danger of a nuclear war, with neither side being victorious or defeated and realizing that neither side would be able to argue out the different views on the further development of our world it appears to be the more important to persistently remind people of it.[1]

Nowadays, as in former times during the struggle against fascism, the widest possible range of activities is required to safeguard peace. The German Democratic Republic, for historical, political and geographical reasons, has a specific interest in realizing this aim. The GDR is advocating security policy measures on various levels, e.g. the establishment in Central Europe of a corridor free from nuclear weapons, the exercise of confidence-building measures and the renunciation of the use of military force in relations between the members of NATO and the Warsaw Pact.

The challenges of the scientific-technological revolution call for the unity between policy and economy, for efforts by all regions and nations to secure normal conditions for existence and development on a world-wide basis and to speed up the solution of acute global problems. Proceeding from this standpoint, it is more necessary than ever before to take account of a kind of common concern for the world economic system 'irrespective of the different approaches, the different mechanisms and principles adopted by individual participants in this economy and system'.[2]

The Final Act of the Conference on Security and Cooperation in Europe emphasized,

> that the participating States, *aware of the differences in their economic and social systems* (my emphasis) are convinced that their efforts will contribute towards developing cooperation in the fields of trade, industry, science and technology, environment as well as in other fields of the economy and towards consolidating peace and security in Europe and throughout the world and that cooperation in these fields would promote economic and social progress as well as the upgrading of living conditions.[3]

From an economic perspective, this paper is concerned with problems of armament, disarmament and the safeguarding of peace which are of political and scientific relevance.

Armament and the functional mechanism of the economy

Armament and disarmament have to be seen as complex phenomena in conjunction with political, economic, military, ideological and other processes or manifestations. Without doubt, however, the relations between *armament* and the *economy* are of special importance and thus will be discussed in greater detail, primarily from the perspective of the functional mechanism of the economy.

The following important questions arise in relation to socialist and capitalist countries:

1) what amount in terms of cost of armaments can be sustained by the economy? Already, in times of peace, high military spending is a heavy burden on the economies of many countries;

2) what consequences do enormous arms expenditures have on *economic regulating mechanisms* and how is it possible to cope with these consequences?

3) what is the influence of current spending on *employment, economic growth* and the *development of prices?*

Let us first consider these questions by looking at the economic situation in Western industrial States. In view of high unemployment and high arms expenditure, the interaction between employment and armaments is heatedly discussed in capitalist countries.[4] Representatives of the arms industry even today speak out in favour of the allegedly great employment effect of armaments. But among scientists it has been increasingly stated that through arms production the employment effects are lower than in civilian production.

Indeed, for several reasons, arms production has an unfavourable employment effect:

1. Labour intensity is relatively low;

2. The capital intensity of arms production rises and the costs of fixed capital increase rapidly. Since the effects inherent in investments on capacity expansion are extremely high, armament expenditures have to expand persistently in an attempt to maintain the level of employment;

3. Arms production is discontinuous rather than continuous and, as soon as a production series runs out, there are often no connecting orders available.

When discussing the problems of armaments and employment, it is necessary to distinguish between the relatively low employment effects of armament, on the one hand, and the very fact that, on the other, unemployment under capitalist conditions is notably a *cyclical* and *structural* problem, but principally the consequence of the economic system. The bourgeois view that investments create jobs has a certain justification in the light of the expanded reproduction of capital, but it is only relatively applicable to armaments. In addition, the accumulation of capital has never had the main aim of retaining or creating jobs, but rather of increasing profits. Often, this is tantamount to an elimination of jobs. The creation of jobs during the cyclical upswing and massive unemployment during the cyclical crisis are the accompanying features of the accumulation of capital. Today capitalism is no longer in a position, not even during a cylical upswing, to compensate for the massive redundancy of workers, employees and intellectuals. This has been shown by developments since the mid 1970s. Since investments are largely used for rationalization, their effect on making labour redundant rather than compensating for them is stronger.

For measures to control massive unemployment to contribute to a reduction in armaments, they would have to be coupled with qualitative growth, a reduction in worktime, a democratization of the economy, the expansion of co-determination and democratically controlled economic planning. The idea is not to put any arbitrary State programme of job creation into reality, yet a programme which, at the same time, serves to save energy and to use non-polluting technologies. The funding of such a programme by means of reducing arms expenditure would be an effective contribution towards détente and disarmament.

It would even be possible to establish a direct link between the policies of disarmament and development if arms spending were cut by ten percent and the funds, thus released, used for development aid. The shipyards could launch fishing vessels and seawater desalination plants instead of submarines and destroyers and could hand them over to the developing countries. Presently, arms production is coupled with political factors. This stems mainly from the increasing political controllability of many economic processes under present-day capitalism, characterized by the existence of a close interrelation between private monopolies and the imperialist State, since the economic mechanism fails to control the economic problems. Thus the dialectics between economy and policy assume a new dimension that has to be taken into account when assessing armament.

When judging armaments under capitalism from an economic point of view, the following can be said:

1) there is no sphere where state expenditures create so few jobs as in the armament sector. As a result, the effects of initiative and multiplication are negligible. Military and arms spending is a particularly expensive instrument for stimulating an economy-wide growth of demands and it endangers even civilian jobs;

2) as a rule, additional arms production does not primarily mean a re-use of idle production capacities, but rather the build-up of new armament facilities. With these facilities being established, it is the capital-goods industry which shows a higher capacity utilization. However, capacity utilization will again fall as soon as the buildup is over. From this moment, the crisis-moderating low increase in demand within the entire economy caused by arms spending is replaced by a crisis-intensifying increase in the economy-wide supply of additional armament capacities;

3) In the case of a non-utilization of capacities, it is possible that a drastic increase in armament orders may lead to bottlenecks of supply for certain raw materials (cobalt, chromium, titanium, aluminium). If, in such a situation, rearmament is pushed through as a priority measure, strategic materials and technological knowhow will be withheld from civilian use. Then production and productivity would fall in the civilian sector, not because of any absence of demand, but due to lack of production facilities. It should also be noted that, despite high and rising arms spending, the number of jobs in armament production is even reduced;

4) the inflationary tendency arising from the price strategies of armament trusts and from supply bottlenecks is intensified by the need for another increase in State debts so as to maintain the State level of demand. Since the resources used for arms do not enter the economic reproduction process, yet they are lost within the general economic offer in foodstuffs and capital goods as well as infrastructural services, disproportions emerge between the stock of money and the amount of goods in favour of the stock of money. Thus the tendency towards inflation is intensified.

In analysing the correlation between economic growth and armaments, it is required to consider the functional mechanism of the economy. Only then will it be understandable why there are opposing views on this subject. Bourgeois economists proceed on the assumption that armaments produce profit, contributing to the growth of enterprises and stimulating the economy. This idea, correct from an entrepreneurial point of view, is, if applied to the national economy, incorrect. This has implications for the evaluation of the problems of growth.

Under capitalism it is possible that armaments may stimulate the economy for a while; when viewed, however, in the longer perspective, they do not bring about any appreciable growth effect, only a high waste effect. Their role is especially important in the process of *depreciation* of capital. Since capitalist production leads generally to crises of over-production (bankruptcies, unsaleable products, etc.), armaments have to be grouped with this process. As armaments destroy capital, when socially considered, they reduce the pressure exercized by the overaccumulation of capital on its utilization. This waste of capital is organized by the State and it has to be financially borne by the majority of the people in the form of taxes and rates. Today, even in capitalist countries, it is widely held that arms production weakens the economy, because the countries with the highest arms spending show a relatively unfavourable development of labour productivity.[5]

Arms production leads to parasitic consumption, it raises the disproportionality of the capitalist reproduction process and, to a great extent, distorts the structure of the national economy because of the change in the material composition of the GNP. Its major effect is that it inhibits the development of productive forces, squanders material resources, leads to a reduction in real incomes for many working people through inflation and tax increases and accelerated indebtedness.

For these reasons a reduction in arms spending is necessary. Since the mid 1970s, this problem has been under discussion especially in connection with the conversion of arms production into civilian production. The American economist Melman was one of the initiators of this discussion.[6] His most significant, yet valid, statement was that the US economy is fast developing into a 'wartime economy', thus becoming more and more unstable. Hence, his view is – and this view has since been frequently repeated – that a conversion of wartime production into civilian production is indispensable.[7]

Armament conversion is mostly defined as a 'conversion of arms production, military installations, administrations and personnel into civilian purposes and activities'.[8]

The need for such conversion is recognized by an increasing number of people in imperialist countries because the arms race accelerates inflation, squanders scarce raw materials, degrades the environment and jeopardizes man.

> Armament conversion would be feasible without any grave losses of jobs and investments. By the way, it is a conversion of production that becomes necessary not only because of disarmament: every technological novelty introduced into the economy is comparable to a conversion. Modern industry is continuously developing new products and new production techniques. Adjustments are also made for legislation, promoting the technological change by labour safety and labour reeducation, by providing funds for adaptation to new structures, etc. If

armament conversion proceeds smoothly rather than abruptly, the adaptive measures in the economy will be less coercive than those caused by the oil shock in the past few years.[9]

Armament conversion has always been embedded in the dialectics of policy, economy and ideology. However important the demolition of ideological inhibitions and prejudices is for armament conversion, the creation of the politico-economic and technical preconditions is equally important for the conversion and, finally, their translation into practice.

The demand for conversion has to be viewed against the broader political background of the struggle waged for arms control and disarmament, for such a conversion can be reached only step-by-step if influential forces in society support vigorously such a conversion by way of, say, a reduction in State armament spending.

Armaments also have a highly negative effect on socialist countries because the economy is deprived of material and financial resources urgently required for development. In addition, planning the socio-economic development is rendered more difficult. In this context, it should be emphasized that there is no social group within socialist society interested in arming and profiting from it economically. The socialist countries, for political and economic reasons, stand for a reduction in armament production and a conversion of funds thus made available into civilian production. They support proposals made in the interest of a conversion and, specifically because of the dangers of atomic war, think it necessary to expand economic cooperation with capitalist and developing countries, realizing that this is the road that promotes the political process of détente and facilitates the transition to military détente. The aim of cooperation is also to upgrade the living standard of people and to advance the personal development of all citizens. For these reasons the socialist countries are not the initiators of the qualitative arms race and, in line with their security interests, are endeavouring to limit or diminish arms production in quantity and quality. The recent proposals by the USSR point in this direction.

International economic cooperation as an instrument for the stabilization of peace

Socialist States, in the interests of the preservation of peace as well as in their own economic interests, attach great importance to the intensification of international economic relations. The major motivation for international economic cooperation is the need to implement the policy of détente and to make use of the benefits to be derived from a division of labour with capitalist industrial countries.

The CMEA-countries, in pursuit of the further shaping of inter-systemic economic cooperation, take account of the importance of foreign economy for national economic growth which increases with the intensively extended reproduction and the change in international conditions. The CMEA-countries view their economic cooperation with capitalist industrial countries primarily as a complementary source for the multiplication of their national income. Priority is accorded to relations within the framework of CMEA for these relations are the foremost requirement for their active participation in the international division of labour. This requires developing economic relations with the capitalist industrial countries in the 1980s – in consideration of the objective processes in world economy and world politics as well as on the basis of equality of rights and mutual benefit. In this context, the character of the world market and world economy plays a decisive role: the world economy exists as a controversial unity of the two world economic systems: socialism and capitalism. The increasing utilization of the international division of labour by each individual country is a specific aspect of the present time. To ignore it would mean to allow for a considerable loss in efficiency for the national economy. Influential imperialist forces have again and again been trying to prevent socialist countries from participating in the world-wide division of labour.

The 1970s showed the great importance of economic relations for promoting peaceful coexistence. In this period an expansion and deepening of the political process of détente was achieved, together with an expansion and intensification of economic cooperation. Notwithstanding the development of economic cooperation, however, an effective complementation of economic and political détente by military détente was not achieved. By contrast, the importance of the military aspects was even enhanced. The economic aspects were allocated or subordinated to them by the ruling forces of imperialism. No moves were made in the direction of disarmament which could have been coupled with a utilization of military capacities for civilian goods produced in the interest of an exchange of commodities and the transfer of technologies between East and West. Instead, economic relations were increasingly gripped by confrontation and the economic war against socialist countries.

Undoubtedly, in the economic relations between systems there is a dialectical relationship between economy and policy. But, on the one hand, favourable political relations are not bound to lead directly to intensified economic relations. Nor, on the other hand, need a political confrontation necessarily and immediately influence negatively economic relations between States, although, in the long run, a deterioration in the climate of cooperation will be unavoidable.

The economy is not at all unilaterally influenced by policy and, vice versa, policy does not obediently follow the economy. There is no automatic dependency between economy and policy. Both are relatively independent. Although policy, as the joint expression of the economic interests of the ruling classes in socialist and capitalist countries, is the determining element in international relations, the economic interests play their own independent role, elicited ultimately by the tendencies of development of productive forces and the processes of internationalization.

East–West economic relations are largely determined by the correlations between economy and policy. If confrontation is predominant, they will be obstructed, but, if political détente prevails, they will be persistently influenced in their tendencies. It is only under the impact of constructive political solutions, including the budding processes of military détente as an expression of the peace-promoting goodwill of all people involved, that East–West economic relations can be durably and positively developed. This shows that the political conditions providing primarily the framework for political confidence have to be highly valued for the future of East–West trade.

International economic relations must not be allowed to be misused for political purposes. The imposition of trade embargoes, disruption of credit lines and the blockade of technology exports should be avoided because they stand in the way of reaching reciprocal benefits.

Socialist countries pursue the goal to stimulate qualitative factors of growth and, for this reason, they stand up for an effective and predictable international economic cooperation. They practise different forms of economic cooperation: in production, compensation, on third markets, scientific cooperation, 'mixed corporations'. With the further development of the contractual and legal formulation of foundations for East–West economic relations, a new functional mechanism was established for them, as was evidenced by the formation of mixed governmental commissions for cooperation in economy, science and technology, in special working groups within the framework of these mixed governmental commissions, in joint chambers of commerce, economic councils, etc.[10]

In analysing economic relations between East and West since the 1970s, several important findings have to be mentioned. Under the impact of the political process of détente, a fabric of connections for constructive economic cooperation had emerged, providing an essential requirement for the material structure of peaceful coexistence and for its evolvement, above all, in Europe. Cooperation between East and West has been of enormous benefit for all involved. This is illustrated by the dynamic growth of turnover over the years, the rising priority of East–West economic relations in foreign trade of the partner involved, the wide application of new forms and methods of cooperation and by the new functional mechanism and the diversified contractual regulations concluded in favour of and on economic cooperation. In spite of all the progress, there is still a great number of unresolved problems. They comprise the unsatisfactory structures in commodity exchange as well as the imbalances in mutual relations.[11]

The complicated correlations between policy and economy affect all trends and forms of this cooperation. The cooperation on third markets is of a form that developed under propitious political conditions in the 1970s. This cooperation reflects the aspirations of partners to put their interests into reality for mutual benefit, with the involvement of the interests of developing countries.

In maintaining economic relations between partners from socialist and capitalist countries, a level has often been reached which presses for a *long-term* shaping of cooperation. Thus, the benefits offered by the international division of labour can be better utilized.

In the first stage of cooperation on third markets, the GDR

provided the requirements indispensable for cooperation between States. Provisions were laid down in adequate government agreements with important European capitalist States, with Japan, but also with a number of developing countries, such as India. The banking syndicate agreements were another field of agreements signed between GDR foreign trade enterprises and firms of western industrial states. This is the concrete side of government agreements and they often include also agreements on cooperation on third markets. These were the foundations on which the first results were achieved and experience gained. The first projects were put into practice primarily with firms from such countries, as Austria and France. Between the GDR and France a government agreement was concluded as the basis for this cooperation on these markets. Proceeding from the inter-governmental agreement on economic cooperation between the GDR and Austria a syndicate agreement was signed between GDR foreign trade enterprises and VOEST-Alpine, providing also for cooperation on third markets.[12]

Cooperation on third markets developed especially with those West European firms which had already gained experience from bilateral cooperation with socialist countries. Concerted action on third markets requires confidence in the efficiency and reliability of the partner. The existence of mutually complementary economic structures also plays a role in exports. However, export structures are subject to changes, they are related to internal economic processes as well as to marketing opportunities. Therefore, it is necessary to watch these dangers carefully with a view to drawing conclusions for the further shaping of cooperation even on third markets.[13]

The possibilities for East–West cooperation have not been exhausted. Its continuity, however, requires a decrease in the confrontational course pursued by the leading imperialist circles to provide a political background for the further shaping of relations. The aims of the CMEA-countries are continued development of their national economies and further economic integration. Their considerations focus on the better utilization of the qualitative factors to be derived from these commercial relations (higher effectiveness, improved export and import relations, etc.).

A new aspect to the international division of labour has emerged within CMEA in the form of the 'socialist international division of labour'. It encompasses the planned development of labour divisive relations on an equal footing in science, technology, production and investments for mutual benefit between socialist national economies. These relations, instead of the exploitation of individual countries by their partners, make use of the voluntary step-by-step rapprochement to social labour productivity on a high level, with the partner countries consciously entering into stable, complex and contractual relations between their economic reproduction processes. This is achieved with the aim of a reciprocal satisfaction of the demands and an increase in economic benefits.[14]

The socialist international division of labour is objectively passing through different stages of maturity on account of the qualitatively new development processes of productive forces and the socialist production relations in the formation of developed socialist society. This process began in the 1970s with the advent of intensively extended reproduction. It will be intensified further in the 1980s and 1990s on the basis of decisions arrived at by economic consultations.

In the long perspective the idea essentially is to create a system of socialist international division of labour which, in all its manifestations, corresponds to the comprehensively intensive economic reproduction. This makes it necessary that the *entire* process, – i.e. its material and value-oriented effects, the forms and trends of international division of labour, economic management and planning and its inter-governmental co-ordination, the commodity-money categories employed – of economic, scientific-technical and investment activities within CMEA – shall be supplemented in line with the intensive economic reproduction, reaching thus a better solution to the current social and economic tasks by resorting to a concerted mastery of the scientific and technological revolution.[15]

Expansion of economic relations with the developing countries on a democratic basis

The demand of the developing countries for the establishment of a New World Economic Order is a fundamental problem of our time. It is supported by socialist countries for it is indispensable because of their basic approach to practising universal equal foreign-commercial relations. Principally, the idea was, and is, to consolidate the developing countries economically by expanding trade relations and avoiding international conflicts. The economic policies pursued by the GDR have been determined by this deliberation in the past few years.

From 1970 to 1982 the foreign-trade turnover of the GDR with developing countries rose more than five-fold. Thus, it grew more rapidly than the total trade. At the time of the foundation of the GDR, developing countries had a 0.3% share within its total foreign trade, but this rose to about four percent in the 1960s and 1970s and, in 1982, reached 5.8% (cf. Table).

Proceeding from the 30 main trading partners among the developing countries with which in 1970 the GDR contracted a total volume of some Mark 1.6 billion, or 85% of its trade with developing countries, and in 1982 some Mark 7.95 billion, or 94%, we obtain the following picture in terms of territorial distribution: The essential changes occurred in relation to the African countries

Foreign trade of the GDR with developing countries, effective prices, basis: convertible mark, share in %

	1960	1970	1982
Share of developing countries in GDR foreign trade	0.3	4.0	5.8
Share of developing countries in GDR foreign trade with non-socialist countries	16.9	14.2	17.1

Source: *Statistisches Jahrbuch der DDR 1983*, Berlin 1983, p. 236.

south of the Sahara. In 1970 these countries with a share of only 1.4% in GDR foreign trade with developing countries hardly played any role at all, but in 1982 their share had risen to 12.4%. The most important trading partners within this group are Mozambique, Angola, Nigeria and Ethiopia. The Arab countries have all along assumed an important place. These countries in 1970 had a share of 39.5% and in 1982 a share of 44.8%, taking the greatest share in GDR foreign trade with the developing countries. Iraq became the biggest trading partner in this region. Growth rates above average were reached with Syria and Algeria. The share of Asian countries in 1970 was 20.8% and in 1982 21.7%. The most important trading partners of this region are Iran and India.[16]

In 1982, Latin American countries had a share of 15.3%, mostly with Brazil, Colombia and Mexico.

Under modern complicated foreign trade conditions, it is necessary to develop new forms of international commercial relations and to raise the benefit from the international division of labour for the GDR. The long-term orientation towards expansion of GDR's foreign trade relations with developing countries makes it necessary to observe continuously the tendencies and objective processes in these markets and to draw the conclusions for foreign trade. Against this background, it is also necessary to follow more closely the tendencies in foreign trade developments with several countries. Thus, the developing countries Algeria and Mexico are of great interest for the international commercial relations of the GDR. Within their regions, they belong to those countries that already experienced a dynamic upswing of foreign trade with the GDR. Between 1970 and 1984 foreign-trade turnover with these countries rose sharply.

In future it will be necessary to take practical steps to extend and deepen economic cooperation with developing countries on an equal basis for mutual benefit. This will include:

1) conclusion of long-term trade and payments agreements as well as agreements on scientific and technical cooperation;
2) assistance provided for the development of the domestic resources of these countries, especially industry, and promotion of the public sector of industry;

3) assistance for the development of agriculture in Asia, Africa and Latin America and for the solution of the food problem;
4) greater purchases of traditional and new products from these countries, primarily finished and semi-manufactured goods;
5) organization of multilateral industrial cooperation with the participation of socialist countries;
6) assistance in the creation of a modern scientific and technical infrastructure, of modern systems of public education and science as well as in the training of national cadres.

Disarmament is necessary because the arms race obstructs the solution of global economic problems, erodes confidence between countries and wastes enormous natural and human resources. These resources will be required to overcome hunger and poverty in the developing countries.

Conclusion

1) After World War II, there was a speedy increase in economic internationalization. Individual countries made use of the benefits derived from specialization in a world-wide division of labour, they utilized the exchange of technology, information, commodities and services. Economic relations between socialist and capitalist countries can only be brought about if both sides have an advantage. An exchange of technology for mutual benefit rather than one for unilaterial advantage has to be the dominating element in international economic relations.
2) Under the impact of the scientific and technological revolution, there is no longer any country that alone could follow equally all the lines of scientific and technological development. Dynamics, complexity and the complicated character of scientific and technical progress, the global problems involved in the supply of raw materials and energy, the conservation of the natural environment and the control of poverty are compelling causes for intensified cooperation and a new quality in international economic cooperation. However, the international economic relations can be developed for mutual benefit only within the framework of peaceful coexistence, a line of policy without any reasonable alternative.

   All forms of the policy of embargo pursued by certain circles in capitalist countries are the expression of a well-calculated policy of confrontation and are aimed at impeding international economic cooperation.
3) The most important task of the industrially developed countries of Europe is to support developing countries in their efforts to attain full sovereignty over their resources and to recognize them as full and equal partners in the solution of international problems.

4) It is becoming more and more urgent to pay great attention to the problem of the conversion of armaments within East–West cooperation.

> This is part of the aspirations for arms control and disarmament and is directly related to the promotion of East–West economic relations. In addition, it is a highly complicated problem and certainly it has a great number of intermediate links. Here the idea is not only to convert arms production into civilian production which constitutes an internal problem in the countries concerned. But the point is to connect this theme with the international exchange relations. This is associated with the question of confidence building as well as with the security interests of countries. It is also related to the questions of funding, the priorities of budgets and to the kinds of subsidies and to many other problems. A cutback on arms spending could release essential means for the promotion of trade and cooperation, not only between East and West, but also with the developing countries.[17]

5) The GDR and other socialist countries must in future also work towards the creation of common sense and a realistic approach in international relations. To this end, the dialogue on economic questions has made an invaluable contribution. Important goals of the socialist countries in terms of a policy of peace and security are:

a)   consistent development of the alliance within the socialist community on the basis of the contracts concluded. Consolidation and increase in the international influence of socialism by means of its further display and utilization of its benefits;

b)   persistent activities for the safeguarding of peace, for the cessation of the arms race with the aim of defending and expanding political détente in an attempt to stabilize it, and to make it irreversible primarily by the measures of military détente and disarmament;

c)   development of multilateral cooperation with Africa, Asia and Latin America. Support of the struggle for a New World Economic Order on the basis of the equality of rights. Expansion of relations with capitalist countries and intensification of contacts and agreements with the aim of deepening cooperation in the interest of peace and for mutual benefit.

Notes

1. E. Honecker, *Eine welthistorische Tat: die auch das deutsche Volk befreite.* Neues Deutschland, 23./24, 3, 1985, p. 4.

2. A. N. Bykow, *Realistische Zusammenarbeit statt Konfrontation: Wissenschaft und Frieden.* Wien, 3–4/1984, S. 135 ff.

3. Konferenz über Sicherheit und Zusammenarbeit in Europa in Helsinki vom 31.7–1.8. 1975, Schlußakte, *Jahrbuch Internationale Politik und Wirtschaft.* Berlin, 1976, S. 504 f.

4. See U. Albrecht, P. Lock, H. Wulf, *Mit Rüstung gegen Arbeitslosigkeit.*

Hamburg, 1982; 'Burdens of Militarization', *International Social Science Journal* Vol. XXXV, No. 1, 1983, UNESCO, Paris.

5. J. Kuczynski, *Erinnerungen und Erfahrungen: 60 Jahre Konjunkturforscher.* Berlin, 1984, p. 185 ff.

6. S. Melman, *The permanent war economy.* New York, 1974.

7. A. Bönisch, *Politökonomische Aspekte des Kampfes um Frieden und Abrüstung.* Deutsche Zeitschrift für Philosophie, 12, 1983, p. 1353.

8. G. Zellentin, 'Möglichkeiten der Rüstungskonversion', in H. A. Pestalozzi, *Frieden in Deutschland,* München, 1982.

9. Ibid, p. 277.

10. G. Scharschmidt and W. Spröte, *DDR an der Seite der Entwicklungsländer im Kampf um demokratische Umgestaltung der internationalen Wirtschaftsbeziehungen,* IPW-Berichte, Berlin 9, 1984, pp. 20–21.

11. Ibid.

12. J. Nitz and P. Freiberg, 'Probleme und Perspektiven', in Ibid., p. 80.

13. Ibid., p. 125.

14. See P. Sydow, *Intensivierung und sozialistische ökonomische Integration,* Berlin 1985.

15. Ibid.

16. G. Scharschmidt and W. Spröte, op. cit., p. 25.

17. M. Schmidt, *Politische und ökonomische Aspekte der Ost-West-Wirtschaftsbeziehungen in den 80er Jahren.* Wissenschaft und Frieden, 3–4, 1983, p. 1 ff.

13. In Search of Peace and Security: The Potential of Neutrality

by Josef Binter

Introduction

In spite of the so-called balance of terror and an 'almost-no-war' situation in Europe for 40 years, the world as a whole has witnessed a dramatic upsurge in the use of military force. The concept of deterrence by nuclear weapons not only threatens to destroy exactly what is to be preserved but also stimulates the greatest destabilization by an unprecedented global arms race. The 'peace' through military deterrence based on pact systems should merely be understood as a 'gain in time', which must be urgently utilized in the search for political solutions and alternatives.

There are a number of models, strategies and scenarios proposed by peace research and the peace movement, where the concept of neutrality, in a narrower or wider sense, is playing a crucial role for conflict resolution and the establishment of peace. This paper aims to review and discuss some of these proposals. Furthermore, it tries to provide a general analysis of the neutrals' profiles and practices in contemporary world politics. Where the actual behaviour and policies of the present neutral countries are concerned, there are high expectations with regard to their contribution to world peace. Are these expectations, that also coincide with the self-image of some European neutrals, at all justified? A historical analysis of the concept of neutrality shows no agreement as to whether 'neutrality and peace' are at all compatible or even mutually exclusive. Nevertheless, a review and analysis of the actual role and behaviour of the neutrals in the international system reveals their great potential to contribute to regional and global security and peace.

The concept of neutrality: definition, features and characteristics

In spite of its long tradition in the international system, neutrality still appears as a very amorphous concept. Today, most people might share an understanding of the word neutrality that is similar to the traditional Swiss legal definition: neutrality is the act of sitting still while others fight. To some, neutrality implies impartiality, while to others it means nonbelligerency. It was been applied in many forms during the last three decades, but no comprehensive theory of neutrality either as a legal system or as political strategy exists. Neutrality generally describes the posture of a state vis-à-vis a conflict–usually a military conflict–between other states and means in essence the non-participation in ongoing wars. Neutrality can also be defined as the attitude of 'impartiality adopted by third states towards belligerents, such attitude creating rights and duties between the impartial states and the belligerents'.[1]

As a system inscribed in international law, neutrality evolved with the emergence of sovereign national entities in modern history. For a long time in the middle ages, neutrality was thought to contradict official moral standards and was in principle rejected. This attitude has persisted and was reflected in the famous remark by John Foster Dulles that 'neutrality is immoral'. Also Soviet theory, which long repudiated impartiality in class struggle, did not approve of the doctrine of neutrality until the early fifties. Today neutrality, comprehended as the actual and existing neutrality manifested in the international positions and policies of the European 'neutrals' (Austria, Switzerland, Sweden and Finland), is recognized both by East and West and seen largely as an instrument of reconciling incompatibilities in difficult conflict situations. When neutrality is seen as the 'status and policy of non-participation on either side in an ongoing war' then different types can be distinguished.[2] For instance, the time factor fosters a distinction between temporary or occasional neutrality declared with regard to specific war situations, and permanent neutrality as a matter of principle on a lasting basis. From a legal point of view, one may differentiate between neutrality inscribed in law and recognized in treaty arrangements or the *de facto* neutrality unilaterally introduced into foreign policy with international acceptance by tradition.

Although international lawyers' and politicians continue to argue over variations in its concept and meanings, three basic categories of neutrality have gained acceptance:

The first, often called temporary or common neutrality, is invoked when a state refuses to participate in a specific war. This kind of neutrality has a long tradition. Whenever war broke out, states not immediately involved could decide whether to fight on the side of one party or to stay out of it. Those who did not enter were 'the neutrals' and international law required them to conduct their relations with the belligerent states under a special set of rules, the 'laws of neutrality'.

The second category is a form of permanent neutrality based upon a unilateral political decision that can be changed by the state. This is the situation for Sweden where the concept of neutrality remains an unchallenged mainstay of Swedish policy, whereby no commitment is made in peace-time that would interfere with Sweden's fulfillment of obligations as a neutral state and its peace-time policies attempt to sustain the confidence held by the rest of the world in Sweden's determination to remain neutral in wartime.

The third category of neutrality may be termed permanent neutrality on a legal basis. A permanently neutral state is one that had its neutrality guaranteed by outside powers or is bound by deed or agreement under international law, as is the case with Austria. As a political principle, permanent neutrality was adopted by Switzerland in 1674, but it was almost 150 years later in 1815 before the Congress of Vienna recognized the permanent neutralization of Switzerland. In 1907, the Hague Peace Conference dealt in some detail with the right of neutrality. According to the agreed definition, a country having decided in favour of non-participation in a war between two states, assumed certain rights, such as inviolability of its territory and some duties, such as the withholding of military support from belligerents. These rights and duties are partly codified in international treaties and partly based on customary law. Therefore, a permanently neutral state is, by virtue of an international treaty or a binding unilateral declaration, under a legal obligation not to participate in any future war.

The obligations a state has to undertake to stay neutral in war-time can be summarized as follows:

● A neutral state must not provide belligerents with military support nor allow states involved in a war to engage in military activities in its territory;
● More than temporary neutral states, a permanently neutral state having declared its intent to stay neutral once and forever and not to participate in any future wars, should abstain even in peace-time from acts and engagements which could involve it in wars or would prevent it from applying the laws of neutrality to the belligerent parties, in case war occurred. Thus, it seems to be very clear that a permanently neutral state must not launch a war of aggression, join any military alliances or permit the establishment of foreign military bases on its territory, nor should it enter into economic arrangements which would prevent it from applying the laws of neutrality to the belligerent parties, in case war occurred;
● In addition a permanently neutral state has to show its readiness to defend its independence, territorial integrity and neutrality with all means at its disposal;
●Last but not least the concept and practice of permanent neutrality also entails the so called 'policy of neutrality', its objective being to strengthen its neutral status in the eyes of other states and to enhance the credibility of permanently neutral states to live up to the expectations of the international community.

The three 'classical' neutrality models discussed above have the following characteristics in common:

● non-participation in a war between two or more states;
● non-adherence with military alliances;
● no foreign military bases;
● no unilateral launch of war.

Further discussion in this paper will show how these main features of neutrality contribute to conflict resolution and to the establishment of peace. Apart from the different models of neutrality as a permanent legal status or as a temporary or permanent diplomatic, political and military posture, a number of other models can be discerned, that share some of the general features and action patterns related to 'neutrality', and are currently being discussed under the label of neutrality in connection with conflict resolution, alternative security and peace proposals. These include:

Neutralization

This term is quite frequently used in English-speaking countries in reference to the case of permanent neutrality e.g. neutralization meaning the status of one whose political independence and territorial integrity are guaranteed permanently by a collective agreement of great powers, subject to the condition that the neutralized state or territory will not take arms against another state, except to defend itself, and will not assume treaty obligations which may compromise its neutralized status.

In most other languages however, 'neutralization' means the imposition of demilitarization or limitations of sovereignty and implies a foreign-imposed status and a lack of initiative on the part of the respective country with regard to the act of establishing its neutrality.

Demilitarization

The term demilitarization is many times confused with neutralization, but is clearly different, meaning the deprivation of organized military force to the inhabitants of an area. This military measure, however, does not legally and politically regulate the actions of other states towards that area or 'neutralize' that area politically.

Neutralism

This concept is–in quite different contexts–often used but rarely defined. So, for instance, in political quarrels on the policy of neutrality it may have a depreciatory sense, suggesting 'indifference' in the struggle between good and evil. Secondly, the term 'neutralism' is also used in the context of the non-aligned movement, although it is not liked or accepted by the non-aligned countries themselves. Even if a 'neutralist posture' of the non-aligned is obvious, in the sense that they dissociate themselves for various reasons from the worldwide struggle for influence between the two superpowers, those states want to be non-aligned only with reference to the East-West antagonism. They do not want to be neutral in all military conflicts. Thirdly, neutralism has been brought into discussion as a strategy of the Western European peace movement. It is regarded as a special case of non-alignment with respect to the East-West conflict and the related Cold War. In contrast with the neutrals, these 'neutralists' do not consider themselves as tied to the classic law of neutrality. In the event of war they consider any option open to them. In general, this approach would rather pursue gradual measures to dissociate from great power rivalries in peacetime, than a fixed, inflexible posture. Currently, Western European neutralism aims at the diminution, if not dissolution, of post-war alliances in Europe; it will be discussed later in more detail among other peace proposals related to neutrality.

Non-alignment

In contrast to neutralism as a pattern of behaviour for foreign policy, the non-aligned countries perceive their status as a common political doctrine with certain goals and principles.

The concept of non-alignment should not be confused with neutralism, insofar as it is predominantly a concept for Third World countries, based on their development problems. The emergence of the non-aligned group has a particular anti-colonial background. The group's desire to steer away from involvement in the Cold War and the East-West conflict is rooted in the belief that for developing countries a conflict between industrialized powers is of secondary concern.

To summarize, the most evident common feature of the different types of neutrality valuable for peace in the 'narrower sense' is non-participation in a military conflict, whereas the common feature of models within the 'wider context of neutrality' is non-participation in military alliances.

The next section describes various 'neutrality related' proposals, plans and models for establishment of peace and conflict resolution, and then the third section reviews and assesses the actual roles, policies and contributions of European neutral states in regard to peace and security.

Neutrality as strategy for conflict resolution

Currently, neutrality as a legal status or policy is exclusively practised by European countries. The European neturals, by taking themselves out of the strategic equation in Central Europe, have no doubt greatly contributed to post-war peace and stability in Europe. The question may be raised, therefore, if and to what extent neutrality can be a model for solving conflict situations in other trouble spots of the world. So far, not too many studies on the applicability of neutrality for the avoidance or settlement of international conflicts have been undertaken. It behoves peace research to take up this issue, to reflect and give some thought to the status and policy of neutrality as a possible alternative strategy for small countries situated in sensitive strategic areas and threatened by war and violence.

The main idea behind the proposals discussed below is to remove a state from an area of destructive regional and global competition and remove it from international controversy by the obligation to abstain from military and political commitments to other states. The anticipatory application of neutrality would thus prevent the outbreak of violent clashes or terminate hostilities in which neither side can hope to gain decisive advantage at the existing level of conflict.

Currently, there are several states and areas that can be considered as potential candidates. One such geographical region would be Indochina, where patterns of external intervention especially curtail the prospects of stabilizing the international politics of any one of the area's states without regulating the instabilities of the whole region. Other opportunities may be seen in keenly disputed territories, like Palestine, where the contesting forces and the area's legitimate inhabitants might accept neutrality to regulate the conflict among the external forces and to offer practicable self-determination to the people involved.

Marek Thee's study of Indochinese wars led to the conclusion that neutrality was and is the historical solution for conflict in this region.[3] Traces of that concept can be found in the Geneva Agreements of 1954 and 1962 and the Agreement of the Neutrality of Laos. According to Marek Thee, the key problem in that area is 'security'. While the continuation of the actual great power linkages to the conflict can only result in its escalation, the adoption of a policy of neutrality by the three Indochinese countries promises to defuse tensions in that area. In that course, a neutral posture by Vietnam devoid of military ties in its relations with the Soviet Union would calm China's fears of being faced with a pincer move and threatened militarily from the direction of the historically most sensitive 'soft underbelly' in its south, while a neutral Kampuchea would soothe Hanoi's apprehensions about a hostile Kampuchea in China's service with a revival of territorial revindications as a source of a protracted conflict. Vietnam could then proceed to evacuate its military forces from Kampuchea.

Along the same lines the permanent neutrality of Afghanistan following the 1962 declaration of Neutrality of Laos might well serve the historical interests of Afghanistan, the security of the Soviet Union and the concerns of all states within the powerfield of that conflict.

In one of his recent books Mroz[4] discusses neutrality as one option for resolving security threats in the Arab-Israeli conflict. In an exploration of attitudes toward potential resolution scenarios conducted among Israelis and Arabs, he notes that a neutral Palestine state was one of the few ideas frequently mentioned by Palestinians, other Arabs and some Israelis.

Mroz mentions neutrality as one of those compromise positions that might meet the basic security fears of every party of the conflict, but should be freely accepted and not imposed. In this regard, for the Palestinians it is an option only if they can choose neutrality on their own will during an exercise of their right to self-determination. The process of establishing neutrality has to be tailored to the process of self-determination. A certain parallelism to the Austrian case can be observed in this context, in so far as the Austrian declaration of permanent neutrality is closely linked to the State Treaty that regained Austria's full sovereignty and independence.

According to Mroz, as one of the main advantages to the Palestinians, the concept of neutrality would address both the question of Palestinian sovereignty and the concerns over the security of its neighbours, including Israel, whereas one of the main advantages of this concept for the Israelis would be Palestine's declaration of neutrality as a signal commitment by the Palestinians to live in peace with their neighbours.

So, can one conclude from these proposals that permanent neutrality or neutralization can serve as a world wide panacea for conflict re resolution and peace establishment? To what extent is it possible to export this European model overseas and have it solve other trouble spots of the world? On the one hand, the ex-colonial world provides a number of settings of small vulnerable states burdened with sustained violence due to inconclusive competition from outside for dominant control. Such states or territories could be removed from international controversy and interstate competition by the obligation to abstain from military and political commitments, thus ensuring that they cease to be a source of conflict.

On the other hand, for neutrality as a means of stabilizing a crisis area certain factual conditions must exist: that is 'neutralization' can come about only if the interests of the states concerned are sufficently convergent and the forces of rival powers are in relative balance. For some European scholars, also some endogenous conditions have to be met for 'functionable' neutrality e.g. a stable society, a broad national consensus, a responsible government, etc., that make it hard for neutrality to be applied in any but a Central European territory with relative utility in a specific situation.

On one hand, what can be more contributive to peace than the permanently neutral's solemn declaration not to start a war of aggression or become involved in any war, that even coincides in its contents with the famous League of Nations repudiation of war in 1928? On the other hand, is it nowadays logically possible to 'neutralize' all states, without ensuing destabilizing alterations and reorganizations of the international system to the extent that more and more states are removed from international participation? All those questions need further investigation.

Even if neutrality has been a policy so far practised exclusively by countries belonging to the western social system, there are no rational reasons why this policy could not at least be tried on other parts and ideological systems of the world. From this point of view, the traditional neutrality model in the strictly military sense, that includes ideological freedom and choice of social system, is not at all unthinkable for a socialist country like Nicaragua. Perhaps there would be much less animosity against this country if it were openly and reliably removed from the superpowers' military contest.

Finally, another concept for regional security tracing back to the 19th century practice of 'neutrality' is worth mentioning. It is the so-called 'Zone of Peace Concept'[12] whose roots can be found both in Inter-Asian Relations where the SEATO countries declared themselves an 'Area of Immobilization' and the UN Assembly Resolution of 1971 declaring the Indian Ocean as a 'Zone of Peace'. The concept is somehow related to that of non-alignment and springs from the needs of lesser states to escape victimization as a result of the superpower conflict, and, in many cases, means the initiation of unilateral disarmament without requiring endorsements from other states. The zone of peace concept and 'neutrality' have one aspect in common–moving territories from being sources of conflict.

In the self-perception of the 'Zone of Peace' initiators there are important differences between 'neutralization', meaning the status of permanent neutrality, and the 'zone of peace' concept. Whereas with 'neutralization' greater powers impose their specific interests 'downward' on weaker states and to some extent infringe on their sovereignty, the 'zone of peace' concept, if successful, seeks to extend an 'upward' influence on other states as a unilateral and joint policy of the weak and vulnerable states that reject superpower victimization and living under the balance of terror.

But, does it really matter globally whether insignificant nations establish isolated zones of peace? By itself an isolated zone of peace may at best provide temporary relief, and an association of 'zones of peace states' wields little international influence. Even more, when looking for the most suitable areas, one might realize, just as in the case of 'neutralization', that exactly those states caught directly in the margins of superpower conflict are not likely to become suitable candidates. Before focusing on actual profiles, policies and potential roles of European neutrals, it is necessary to point out two European related strategies with relevance for neutrality:

Western European neutralism
'Neutralism', along with other concepts which are variously labelled disengagement, nuclear free zone, etc., are mainly discussed in the search for alternatives to the current defence and deterrence dilemmas that face Western Europe, because it cannot be defended with nuclear weapons in actual warfare, which thus voids the concept of deterrence since, in fact, nuclear protection would destroy exactly what is to be preserved. According to Albrecht[5], the basic notion of all these alternative concepts is simple: the direct confrontation of forces along the line of division of Europe should be diminished by partial withdrawals of certain military units, and European states should put greater momentum into efforts to bring actual policies more in line with national interests. By the decoupling of the deterrence system, neutralism offers opportunities of a de-escalation in military buildup transcending the traditional 'two pillar' strategy of European security by arms increases and détente.

As one of the alternative postures discussed under the label of 'neutralism', 'disengagement' demands a reorientation of military alliances but not a reshaping of the two blocs nor their dissolution. It calls for a reduction of armaments in a given area and the elimination of certain kinds of armaments, notably nuclear weapons. This kind of nuclear 'zero-option' would, in the same sense as a neutral state, offer the two antagonistic great powers a balance of their mutual security interests outside their own territories. More than simple disengagement, Western European neutralism aims at the diminution or even dissolution of the bloc-system. Its protagonists favour a dissociation from great power rivalries already in peace-time and aim at a nuclear-free-zone in Europe that opts for a neutralist path in its external relations. In their view, neutralism is the best policy for medium and small powers.

New European peace order

The concept of neutrality also plays an important role within models of a new European peace order as proposed for instance by Lutz.[6] The focus of his proposals lies within a continuation of the basic idea of common security into the idea of a European system of collective security as envisioned by the UN Charter. His well-elaborated concept comprises phases, individual steps and graded measures towards realization of a regional European system of collective security, with unilateral disarmament, nuclear-weapon-free-zones, relaxation of bloc integration and finally 'neutralism' as one of the last steps towards the transition to the dissolution of military blocs.

Along with the phasing out of the blocks, Lutz envisages a complementary parallel buildup of a new European order based on the idea of collective security, with the temporary 'neutralization' of former pact states only acting as an intermediate and transitory step, since in the long term, neutrality and collective security are regarded as mutually exclusive.

The contribution of neutrality to world peace and the role of European neutrals

As for the actual contribution of neutrality to world peace and the role neutral states can play, perceptions and assessments have widely differed throughout history, mainly depending on the historical circumstances and constellations of forces. So, for instance, whereas John Foster Dulles despised the immorality of neutrality, Woodrow Wilson half a century earlier praised the neutral state as 'best equipped for action in the interest of peace', as 'a nation beyond others to exhibit the fine poise of undisturbed judgment, dignity of self-control, efficiency of dispassionate action that keeps herself fit and free to do what is honest and truly serviceable for the peace of the world.'

The neutralism of the United States as espoused by Wilson and others, which led to a more and more isolationist posture of 'idly standing aside' in the thirties, was heavily criticized by scholars of that time. In his book *Neutrality and Peace*, Politis[8] termed neutrality mainly as a function and counterpart of war, doomed to lose its importance in the course of the historical development and the collective striving to eradicate war and build up a system of collective security. An overall historical analysis suggests that a potential positive function of neutrality is possible only at a certain time and under certain constellations. The views of some contemporary Austrian scholars do not give a clear-cut picture either. Some emphasize that the gain function and target of Austria's neutrality is to ensure its independence and inviolability and deny a relevant contribution to peace, whereas, for others, neutrality per se, in the sense that it is applied conflict resolution, already provides the main features contributive to peace.

It is another contested question whether neutrality only delimits and balances conflicts, or really solves and overcomes them and contributes to the 'dissolution' of conflicting interests. Using Galtung's terminology, it seems that neutrality rather fits into the concept of 'dissociative' conflict resolution. In another recent analysis Zemanek[9] concludes that neutrality as a mere function of power does not enable neutral states to play any relevant role, an argument that mainly relates to the legal status of neutrality, but does not take into account the actual policies, profiles and practices of neutral states in the international system. By looking at them a bit more closely however, one can draw the following sketches on the actual and potential roles of European neutrals in respect to peace and security.

Neutrality contributive to regional stability: There seems to be an overall agreement on the stabilizing role of neutrality in Central Europe. The neutrals' main contribution to peace in Europe, and thereby to international peace, lies in the disengagement of forces and the interruption of direct military confrontation in that area. European neutrals, by taking their countries out of potential conflicts and establishing a neutral belt between the two military blocs, not only prevented a conflict spillover from one to the other but also created zones of regional stability in a 'cold war' atmosphere. Such zones of relaxation might radiate beneficial effects far beyond their borders.

Neutrality contributive to loosening up inter- and intrablock structures: Neutrality in the sense of pursuing a policy of national interest and not a policy furthering bloc interests or interests of other states outside Europe, is a 'healthy sign of pluralism and democratization of international relations'.[10] As a Hungarian scholar once expressed it, the 'fact that Hungary does not face a rigid capitalist country as a neighbor makes it certainly easier to pursue its nationalist interests.'[11] As such, neutrality, maybe once rooted in the Cold War, has a great relevance for peacetime Europe; as a symbol against the so-called 'bloc-logics'. The European neutral and non-aligned nations ensure that the European continent is not fully divided into spheres of influence and totally covered by bloc structures and give evidence that bloc-type policy is not the only option left to ensure independence and security. Thus, neutrality has become a legitimate and permanent political option in Europe. As Raimo Väyrynen sees it, the 'desire for dealignment is not just a specter but a political force, though still largely unorganized'.[12]

Neutrality's potential for mediation, peace keeping and good offices: Even if the European neutrals lack political weight for active mediation, as not aligned states, by virtue of their independence position they are able to perform useful functions such as the use of their diplomatic and technological proficiency in order to help major parties to find solutions and make independent contributions whenever desirable and possible, so for instance with joint initiatives of the N-N Group in the CSCE-Process. Just as in the case of providing troops for UN peace-keeping actions, the neutral and non-aligned 'unobtrusive disposability' in regard to military verification (verification measures undertaken by neutrals or training provided in neutral countries) could be a main contribution to the success of the Stockholm Conference on Confidence Building Measures and Disarmament in Europe.

The neutrals contribution to disarmament and the extension of a nuclear-free-zone in Europe: In principle, neutral states hold a unique position in regard to disarmament and arms control. Since they are neither militarily nor legally committed to any power bloc interests, it seems to be easier for them to take a more independent and detached view, and thus not only to act as a bridge and deadlock breaker but also to reveal and express unpleasant truths and spearhead exemplary initiatives. As most neutrals have a comparably lower level of armament than bloc countries, they have a vested interest in arms control, because a global arms freeze of any kind would automatically modify the military power differential between neutrals and blocs to their benefit.

In spite of this convergence of moral potential and real interests, that would be the case in regard to disarmament initiatives, there are no overtly active policies of neutrals in regard to arms control and/or the creation of a nuclear weapon free zone in Europe. That is why there is a strong feeling in the international peace movement that neutrals should play an even more prominent role by demanding their participation and intervention as a 'third party' in the so far only bilateral arms control negotiations.

Regarding the extension of nuclear free zones in Europe, it seems that already now Sweden's and Finland's neutrality not only bolster the stability of the so-called 'nordic system', but also by practically representing a nuclear-weapon-free zone actually enable Norway and Denmark to stay denuclearized at least in peacetime. Also in this context, the unique position of Ireland is worth mentioning. Although it is not fully perceived as neutral in the 'narrower sense' its factual non-alignment as the only member state of the European Community which is not also a member of NATO–thus representing a zone of reduced armament–is of high political and military significance.

Last but not least it has to be mentioned, however, that concrete initiatives by the neutrals, who themselves already represent a nuclear free zone with a defensive military structure, towards actual dis- or transarmament measures of their neighbours, have until now been missing. So far, maybe against better knowledge, the neutrals, too, seem to be entangled by the myth of 'military balance' that prevents any sensible appeal to unilateral dis- or transarmament as the first step to global disarmament.

Neutrality contributive to strengthening of international institutions and mechanisms for conflict resolution and participation: Doubtless, the peaceful development of the international system is of utmost importance especially to small and unprotected states. It is the strength and universality of internationally accepted norms that protect small neutral states rather than mere military force, and it is multilateral international organizations that provide mechanisms for their global participation instead of imposed alliances. Thus, the interests of the global system as such do, to a large extent, coincide with those of a small neutral country, so that 'not burdened with any particular bloc interests, small and neutral powers are able to be conscious of the universal interest'.

Neutrality and alternative defence: An analysis of the security profiles of European neutrals reveals an overall defensive military structure that also reflects their special status as non-aligned countries forbidden to start any war of aggression.

This means that neutrals may have a pilot role in the change of strategies and military postures towards a more defensive orientation as one step of confidence building. So it might be their task to give an example to overcome armament pressures and use their moral weight to pursue others to follow suit!

Neutrality and solidarity: The neutral's contribution to an ethics of international relations and to 'positive peace': The increasing convergence of global and state self-interests due to growing world-wide interdependence is naturally better perceived and more easily understood by small neutral states than by superpowers. Even more, the neutrals still have to counterprove the widespread perceptions about the 'immoral neutrality of idly sitting aside' and bolster up their image and identity by setting higher than normal 'moral' standards in their international relations by representing an exemplary model and showing solidarity e.g. in their engagement as 'like-minded countries' for world development, their humanitarian refugee policies or arms export regulations.

The North-South conflict has so far remained, at least in Europe, an economic and non-military conflict. Although Western European neutrals, as industrialized western economies, cannot be regarded as neutral in this conflict, it still seems that they better understand the problems and even support some of the demands of the developing countries, maybe even because they themselves have increasingly become economically peripheral within the North.

Neutrality and peace movement: Whereas the new Peace Movement rose first in bloc-countries with clear and pressing issues e.g. missile deployments, the Peace Movement in neutral countries developed later, primarily concentrating on the situation in neighbour bloc countries, such as the NATO rearmament in Germany. The question increasingly raised after the deployment of new missiles in East and West is whether the concept and status of neutrality entails any potential for a new Peace Movement strategy. Could it create spaces for creativity and advance? For many it seems as if some aspects and features of neutrality could be used more constructively. The neutral states' independence of the bloc system could further activities on a non governmental and popular level, since from a global point of view the 'national self-interests' of these small states are more in line with the objectives of global movements than bloc countries and superpowers.

Conclusion

It seems to be a matter of course that, in a martial world, in spite of the outlawing of war, where collective security mechanisms have so far failed, where deterrence has proven to be most destabilizing and the adherence to bloc alliances has not increased security, the main features of neutrality such as the pledge to start no war of aggression gain increasing attraction. A realistic analysis of the world situation would approve of the relative utility of neutrality in a specific situation and under specific circumstances, but would deny its general applicability. However, the world's current critical condition calls for a search for alternatives, breaking of taboos and opening of conceptualizations. Furthermore, the neutrals themselves have to adapt their practices and profiles to changing circumstances and new challenges such as nuclear warfare, the growing instability of 'military balance' and the peace movement. Facing these new challenges, the neutrals' policies should go beyond the traditional levels. So, for instance, with joint initiatives for nuclear-weapon-free-zones, a change of military strategies and the restructuring of the bloc-system. On the other hand a lot of military conflicts concerning non-aligned states could possibly be solved by opting for some features similar to permanent neutrality within the non-aligned movement.

The traditional concept of neutrality is changing from a purely legal status, related to war, to a more political concept and strategy to preserve regional and global peace, to support social change and to stimulate the democratization of international relations. Will the neutrals respond to these challenging expectations? And will peace research?

Notes

1. L. Oppenheim and H. Lauterbach, *International Law*, Vol. 11, 1952, p. 653.

2. John E. Mroz, *Beyond Security: Private Perceptions among Arabs and Israelis*, New York: Pergamon Press, 1980, p. 140.

3. Marek Thee, 'Towards a New Conceptualization of Neutrality: A Strategy For Conflict Resolution in Asia', *Occasional Paper Series, No. 9,* Center for the Study of Armament and Disarmament, California State University, 1982.

4. Mroz, op. cit, pp. 136–163.

5. Ulrich Albrecht, 'Western European Neutralismus', *Bulletin of Peace Proposals*, 3, 1981, pp. 259–69.

6. Dieter Lutz, 'A New European Peace Order as a System of Collective Security', *Journal of Peace Research*, 21, 2, 1984, pp. 169–180.

7. Woodrow Wilson, 'Appeal for Neutrality', *Message to the US Senate*, August 1914.

8. Nicolas Politis, 'Neutrality and Peace' *Carnegie Endowment for International Peace, Pamphlet Series*, 55, 1935, pp. 3–56.

9. Karl Zemanek, 'Austria's Policy of Neutrality: Constants and Variables', in Laxenburg Papers, *The European Neutrals in International Affairs*, 1984, pp. 17–23.

10. Lázló Valki, 'Neutrality: A Hungarian View', in Ibid, p. 106.

11. Ibid.

12. Raimo Väyrynen, 'Neutrality, Dealignment and Political Order in Europe, paper delivered to the *World Congress of the International Political Science Association,* July 1985.

14. The World Economy, International Relations and the European Challenge

by Andre Gunder Frank

The Second World War started in Central Europe, as did the first and several wars before that. It is possible that another war may start there, but this does not seem likely despite the postwar building of political blocs and the increasing build-up of military defences in Europe. Two traditional enemies in Europe, France and Germany, have been through three major wars in the last century and several before that, but, ironically they have now become apparently secure, if not entirely trusting, allies. Ex-Chancellor Schmidt of West Germany even proposes the unification of their conventional armed forces, and President Mitterand of France has broached the subject of a French nuclear defence of West Germany, although the thought of any reunification of West and East Germany still generates fears in France and in quite a few other places in Europe. Yet another war in Europe – even between East and West – is not now likely to start in Europe, or to be about European issues. More plausibly it may start somewhere in the Third World and escalate into another European and world war. The main reason for this is the development of economic relations within Western Europe and between Western and Eastern Europe as parts of the process of world economic development since the last war.

Another irony lies in the fact that, at the end of that war, Central Europe (now called Eastern Europe) was intentionally transformed by the Soviet Union into a political buffer zone controlled largely by itself. This zone was set up to prevent influences from the West reaching the Soviet Union and most particularly, to protect it from another military threat. (What used to be called Central Europe came to be called Eastern Europe, east of the Elbe – the traditional dividing line between Western and Eastern or Central Europe since the 15th and 16th centuries.) What is ironical is that this ex-buffer zone has now become a transmission belt of economic, political, social, ideological and other influences and relations between the West and the East. That is to say, Eastern Europe now occupies a position and increasingly plays the role of intermediary between West and East, especially between Western Europe and the Soviet Union. This is just the opposite of what post-1945 Eastern Europe was designed to do.

The Soviet Union, of course, intended to be substantially dominant in Eastern Europe for a long time, and is still regarded as such. It is often thought that for anything to change in Eastern Europe, the Soviet Union has to initiate, or at least, permit it. Ironically, the reality is just the opposite: it is Eastern Europe that initiates economic, political, ideological, or social changes – Poland is a recent example observed by all. Increasingly, circumstances beyond its control, especially economic developments, oblige the Soviet Union to accept these changes and will eventually oblige the Soviet Union itself to change as a result.

The Soviet Union and its Warsaw Pact military and Comecon economic allies are supposedly under the Soviet thumb, on the one hand, and supposedly friendly allies on the other. Yet ironically the Soviet Union increasingly uses its military power to blackmail its Eastern European allies to extend political and, in some cases, economic concessions to the Soviet Union on pain of losing Soviet military protection or actually experiencing Soviet military force as in Hungary and Czechoslovakia, or suffering the threat of such force, as in Poland. The two statements are not contradictory: change is initiated in Eastern Europe, and the Soviet Union tries to limit that change through blackmail; but its power to blackmail is increasingly limited.

During the 1970s the socialist countries increased their economic integration into the world capitalist market. This was intended, on the one hand, as a way out of their internal economic difficulties, and, on the other, as a way to take advantage of the changes in the international division of labour that developed during the 1970s. But this economic integration and increasing reliance on the market – first and foremost in Hungary, now also increasingly in Poland and elsewhere in Eastern Europe, recently most spectacularly in China, but also in Vietnam and Cuba, and foreseeably in the Soviet Union – far from being a simple solution to their old problems, becomes itself a major source of new problems, (for instance, in Poland, as we will see later).

In the second World War the Soviet Union and the United States were allies against Nazi Germany. Ironically, the allies have become the major enemies, perhaps enemies of convenience, as by analogy with marriages of convenience, they were once allies of convenience.

The Americans claim with considerable correctness that the Soviet Union is economically very weak relative to them, so it does not pose an economic threat and does not offer much economic competition. The Soviet Union also does not pose an ideological threat and offers little or increasingly less ideological competition. Even its political challenge is relatively limited. So the Soviet Union requires military might not only for its defence, but because it provides its only basis for any political influence in the world.

The United States formed an alliance with the Europeans after the war and, again ironically, its recent enemy, Germany, became its main ally in Europe. On the other side of the world, the same happened with Japan. But, increasingly also, the relationship between the United States and its Western European allies is analogous to that of the Soviet Union and its allies in Eastern Europe. Although the United States remains economically more powerful than the Europeans, its relative economic and political power has been declining. So, as the Europeans become increasingly independent, the United States, like the Soviet Union, also relies increasingly on its military power, particularly on its so-called nuclear umbrella, to blackmail its West European allies in order to extract economic and political concessions from them.

Thus, to a significant degree, the Soviet-US conflict or the East-West conflict, of which of course the Soviet-US conflict is the main example, is also a conflict of convenience for both superpowers in that it provides each with a cover for intrasocialist east-east conflicts for the Soviet Union and for west-west conflicts across the Atlantic Alliance for the United States. The Soviet-US conflict is, in part, a matter of convenience to each of the superpowers, because it helps them, indeed they need it, to exert pressure on and to blackmail their respective allies. In that sense, to put it in an extreme form, the best enemies are in a sense each others' best friend because they need each other's enmity to deal with their own friendly allies. Of course, the Soviet bogeyman is also used in the United States and inside the West for internal political purposes; and, ipso facto, the imperialist bogeyman is used in the East for a whole series of political, economic and other domestic purposes.

The US became dominant, or hegemonic, after the Second World War, and its German and Japanese enemies have become the main pillars of the Atlantic and Pacific Alliances; but, at the same time, they have also become the principal economic competitors of the United States. For some years West Germany has displaced the United States as the principal industrial exporter in the world, and the growing Japanese challenge to the United States is well known. This is a reflection, again perhaps ironically, of the fact that the so-called 'American century', Pax Americana, lasted only a quarter of a century. A century ago Britannia ruled the waves under Pax Britannica. How long she did so is subject to interpretation, but the really top-dog position of Britain was during that long economic expansion between 1850 and 1873. After that, Britain's power began to decline, relatively during the 1873–1895 economic crisis; and absolutely in the 1930s, when it was replaced by America's. This was to be the beginning of the American century, but that also lasted less than a quarter of a century. The decline of American hegemony had started by 1967. Politically, it was manifested by the 1968 Tet Offensive in Vietnam and ultimately the loss of the war in Vietnam. Economically, the relative US decline was expressed by the rise of Western Europe and Japan as economic competitors and challengers. Moreover, there is an important connection between these two. The war in Vietnam, and the expenditures that it involved, benefited the American economy in some ways in the short run, but eventually became prejudicial to it and to America's place in the world economy. First, the deficit expenditure of so many new dollars undercut their value and forced the United States to devalue the dollar after cutting it loose from gold in 1971. In 1973, the dollar was also de-pegged from European and Japanese currencies, so that the post-war Bretton Woods monetary agreement and US financial dominance unravelled.

Another way that American military expenditures have been partly beneficial but substantially prejudicial to the US is that, while it spends a high proportion of its GNP on military hardware, the Europeans and the Japanese do not; instead, they spend on civilian technology and now outcompete the Americans. All through the 1960s the rate of growth of productivity in Europe was nearly twice that of the US, while Japan's was nearly twice that of Europe and nearly four times that of the US. An irony, indeed a contradiction, is that the Americans are now pressing both the Europeans and even more so, the Japanese to spend more on armaments – read 'American armaments'. The American Nato commander General Bernard Rogers' air-land battle plan of relying more on conventional weapons and less on nuclear ones in Europe is, first and foremost, a proposition that the Europeans should buy American conventional weapons, which are much more expensive than nuclear ones. The Americans also want the Japanese to spend more money on arms, beginning of course with American arms, so that they will spend less on the technology with which they are increasingly outstripping the Americans. Ironically, they now keep twisting Japan's arm to change the American-imposed constitution, which prohibits possession of nuclear arms and an army with offensive capabilities. If the Americans succeed, of course, the Japanese will spend more money on arms, but it may soon be on their own arms. So the Japanese will increasingly escape from American blackmail, namely their nuclear supremacy. So here too the Americans are damned if they do and damned if they don't.

The US and Japan are allies, but increasingly also competitors throughout the world, including in China. Again, ironically, there is on the one hand, something of a political Washington-Tokyo-Bejing axis, while on the other, the Japanese and Americans are competing economically for the Chinese market. Even Ronald Reagan has gone to Bejing and signed a major deal for the sale of nuclear reactors. It may be ironically noteworthy for environmentalists, who are not particularly enthusiastic about nuclear power, that not a single nuclear reactor has been sold in the United States, and hardly any elsewhere in the West, in the last ten years, while the Chinese and socialist market and, to some extent, the Third World market, is now an attractive proposition in this respect.

Another irony – perhaps hardly anybody even considers it ironical anymore because we have come to accept it – is that the world's two major socialist states are each others' principal enemies and that one of them is an effective ally of the United States. Not so many years ago, the principal danger of war came not from intra-capitalist war but intra-socialist war between the Soviet Union and China. Then, of course, there was intra-socialist war, the Chinese invasion of Vietnam 'to teach it a lesson', in the words of Deng Xiaoping, and the Vietnamese invasion of Cambodia. There

Pol Pot and company had introduced the most far reaching changes. They had abolished money, and really de-linked from the rest of the world. Pol Pot now says that socialism, let alone communism, is not on the agenda in Cambodia or Kampuchea for the rest of this century. The only thing really on the agenda is to get the Vietnamese out. So Pol Pot has made an alliance with Son Sann and with Prince Sihanouk. Here we have a few more ironies – in this case of 'socialism'.

Whatever else Washington and Moscow may disagree on, an important irony is that the one thing upon which they do seem to agree is that this movement, which some call national liberation and others call the opposite, is advancing by leaps and bounds. Concretely, both Washington and Moscow count fourteen different countries in the Third World that, between 1974 and 1984, have become either socialist or what the Soviet Union calls socialist-oriented, or, as the Americans claim, have fallen under Soviet domination and, to use the old terminology, been lost to the Soviets. The Americans think this a very bad thing and the Soviets a very good thing; and both think that this is a process which will continue. The Soviet Union thinks this process must be supported and promoted; and the Americans want to contain this process and under Reagan, they even want to roll it back. The Kissinger Commission report on Central America makes it terribly clear that the issue in Central America in the eyes of the Reagan administration, is not North-South and not internal responses to internal problems, but an East-West problem. There are few other people who concur with that point of view, which seems at odds with all the evidence.

Another irony, of course, is that it is precisely American policy in Central America, and most specifically in Nicaragua, which is forging an alliance between the Nicaraguan Sandinistas and the Soviet Union, which would not exist if the Americans were not pursuing that policy. The same thing happened when Vietnam, after 1975, wanted immediate so-called normalization of relations with the Americans, with diplomatic recognition, economic aid and foreign investment, especially in oil. It was the Americans who said, 'No, none of that'. The Americans responded negatively in part on their own account, but also, in part, because they were blackmailed into this policy by the Chinese. Again ironically, the Chinese said to the Americans in 1975, 'You have to choose between Peking and Hanoi.' The Americans chose Peking and abandoned Vietnam to the Soviet embrace. The same is now being repeated in Central America, although not at the behest of the Chinese. Of course, this policy does not favour the Chinese anti-Soviet interests either.

But the main irony of the Washington-Moscow agreement about the supposed pro-Soviet socialist/anti-American imperialist progress of totalitarianism/liberation is that much of this supposed progress/regress is belied by the facts. These fourteen cases are well known: in Indo-China: Vietnam, Laos and Cambodia; in Africa: Angola, Mozambique, Guinea-Bissau, Cabo Verde and Sâo Tome, and also Zimbabwe and Ethiopia; in

West Asia: South Yemen, Iran and Afghanistan; and in the Caribbean and Central America, Nicaragua and Grenada. But first, the ones that have become socialist are not very many and their socialism has been, all things considered, a bit disappointing both to the people and their leadership there and to many elsewhere who supported the National Liberation struggle, especially the heroic struggle in Vietnam. Secondly, what the Soviets call socialist-oriented, those countries that are not yet socialist but supposedly on the road to it, are not travelling very far or very fast along that road. None of them have cut, or even tried to cut, their economic and political relations with the West, and those that went a little way along that road in the mid-70s, have stopped and backtracked in the opposite direction in the early 1980s. A stellar example is that of Mozambique, which under very severe pressures – economic, political, military, and because of the drought – signed a pact with South Africa. David Rockefeller was in Mozambique for three days to look at investment opportunities. He said some time ago, referring particularly to Angola, that a lot of places that call themselves Marxist are not really so and, even if they are, it does not matter as long as they are responsible and can be dealt with, that is to say, it is possible to make money with them. Moreover, the main export of Angola is oil from Cabinda, and that is guarded by Cuban troops. Most of the oil and Angola's diamonds and coffee etc., are exported to the West. So another irony is that there has really been no attempt on the part of Angola to cut its ties with the West. Indeed, ironically, the Soviet Union has repeatedly insisted that Angola should not cut its ties with the West, because the Soviet Union does not want another Cuba there (although also ironically, Cuba is defending the regimes in Angola and Ethiopia). In Zimbabwe, which was also liberated through protracted guerrilla struggle, progress toward socialism or even away from dependence on the West, or indeed on South Africa, has not been any greater. Its Prime Minister, Mugabe, has declared that he is not only a practising Marxist, but also a practical one! So all these regimes are well on the road to neo-colonialism on the Kenyan or Ivory Coast models, though probably without the relative successes of these countries prior to their present crises. The other ex-Portuguese colonies, Guinea-Bissau, etc. are best left altogether unmentioned in this regard, other than to observe that the politically and ideologically most advanced socialist movement of Africa, which was led by Amilcar Cabral, has failed completely to build the kind of society he had fought for.

So, as a start, these fourteen places are not all that they are claimed to be either by Moscow or by Washington. Then, in reckoning, nobody ever seems to mention what has happened on the other side of the balance. First and foremost, the Sino-Soviet split, and then the de-Maoization of China. The Washington-Bejing-Tokyo axis has even caught up Ronald Reagan. Secondly, Egypt; thirdly, Somalia; and fourthly now Grenada have changed sides. In Grenada it happened with American military intervention but the murder of Bishop certainly provided a pretext, at least in Fidel

Castro's judgement. Moreover, we have to ask ourselves seriously how many Grenadas (under Bishop) and Sandinista Nicaraguas does it take to counterbalance one China? Quite a few, by any balanced reckoning, which seems to be out of fashion in Washington and Moscow. So, on the one thing that the Americans and the Soviets really agree about, they are both wrong. Another irony!

These observations among others suggest the further irony that much of the East-West conflict, especially that between Washington and Moscow, is a smokescreen for North-South conflicts. We have already observed that the East-West conflict is used by both superpowers to press harder bargains and even to blackmail their respective allies. One of the areas in which Moscow and especially Washington do so is on North-South issues. The examples are legion of US pressure on its European allies to back up, or at least condone, its policy, earlier in Vietnam, and now in Central America, as well as all the time in the Middle East, on the supposed grounds of the need to combat a Soviet communist threat. The successful pressure by the conservative United States President Reagan on the Socialist President Mitterand of France to intervene militarily in Chad is again another recent example.

However, the East-West conflict also provides a welcome if not necessary, pretext for direct superpower intervention in the Third World to further their own interests in the North-South conflict. US intervention in Central America under the Reagan Administration is only the most recent example of a long list that stretches back through Grenada in 1983, Lebanon in 1983 (and in 1958), to Vietnam, Laos and Cambodia; Chile from 1970 to 1973; Santo Domingo in 1965; and many other cases too numerous to mention. The argument is always the same, to combat or prevent Soviet communist intervention or takeover; and without this pretext the American intervention would lack the necessary 'legitimacy'. Perhaps the most revealing aspect of this irony is that the Soviet communist bogeyman is used in Washington to drum up Congressional and public support for ever larger military expenditures, the vast bulk of which are not for nuclear and other arms directed at the Soviet Union, but for conventional arms specifically designed for use in and against the Third World. The United States rapid deployment force is only the most conspicuous tip of the iceberg of this United States military force for direct intervention and other shows of force in the Third World. Without the convenient availability of the Soviet communist enemy, neither this United States military expenditure nor this policy of intervention to keep the neo-colonial Third World in line, and especially to keep the United States backyard in Latin America subservient, could be politically justified.

A further irony, however, is that maintenance of this capitalist economic neo-colonialism of the United States does not even require most of its political intervention, for the dependent Third World countries have few real alternatives. Those they have are largely closer economic and political relations with American rivals in Western Europe and Japan as

255

long as the Soviet Union and Eastern Europe remain unable to offer adequate trade and industrial alternatives. Of course, this means the continuation of the irony of using East-West conflicts to intervene in West-West rivalries. The same East-West conflict, moreover, also plays a significant role in the domestic class struggle within each of the countries of the West and the South, where the supposed communist and the Soviet bogeyman are used to legitimate virtually any policies of the ruling classes and to strengthen their bargaining power against the interests of the majority of the people. Of course, the usefulness of the communist scare at home then exposes America's allies to its use against them by the United States abroad.

Is it any different in the East? Perhaps. But there can be no denying that the allies of the Soviet Union are also under pressure to accept its foreign policies in the Third World in the name of combating the common US-led imperialist enemy. Moreover, the Soviet intervention in Afghanistan was a clear case of defence or promotion of the interests of the Soviet Union or of its Russian ruling class against the threat of a Muslim movement that might spread into Muslim areas of the Soviet Union itself.But this threat was backed up by the US imperialist enemy and its CIA, against which Soviet intervention is supposedly necessary. Soviet aid and trade in the Third World, much of which is often on terms that are no better and sometimes even worse than those of the West, is also justified by reference to the imperialist enemy. Soviet and allied social control at home and abroad, as recently in Poland, is, of course, also fortified by reference to defence against imperialist subversion. So the East-West conflict is also used to promote Northeastern interests in the South and to defend the status quo in the East. The irony of using the East-West conflict for other purposes works on both sides.

The real place and role of the socialist economies of the East in these developments is ironical indeed, if it is compared to their spokesmen's theoretical hopes and ideological claims. Just before he died, Stalin claimed (in *The Economic Problems of Socialism*) that by then there were two separate and different economic and social systems in the world, one capitalist and the other socialist. His successor, Khrushchev, belied part of this claim by inciting the Sino-Soviet split in the socialist 'system', and he introduced 'goulash communism' in the Soviet Union with the promise to 'overtake and bury the United States' economically by 1980. The Soviet Union introduced timid economic reforms in the mid 1960s and some of its East European allies, especially Hungary, introduced bolder ones in economic organization and policy. But the hallmark of the latter was the increased role of market prices and increasing integration into the world market, including the progressive introduction of world market prices in the domestic economies of Eastern Europe and especially for their trade among each other. The aforementioned massive import of Western technology followed in the 1970s.

None of these industrial policies, or central economic planning in the 'command' economies of Eastern Europe and the Soviet Union, have produced all of the intended results, and some have had quite a few unintended ones. Since the mid 1960s, the rate of economic growth has declined from each five year plan period to the next (except for the forward jump in Poland from 1971 to 1975, which had the severest negative consequences a few years later). Plans have been underfulfilled in practice year after year, especially in the Soviet Union, and planned growth targets have been lowered for the subsequent year and missed again, until the 1982 target was the lowest since Stalin started planning in 1928. In the early 1980s, economic growth slowed down to zero in the Soviet Union and became negative in 1981 and/or 1982 in Czechoslovakia, Hungary, and Poland. The latter's national income declined by one fourth through negative 'growth' rates of 2% in 1979, 4% in 1980, 14% in 1981 and 12% in 1982. In the face of this experience, it can hardly be claimed that central planning is a sure fire method to formulate and implement economic policy, and still less so in the face of the world economic crisis.

Ironically, it turned out that 'independent' policies of 'planned' goulash communism required the import of Western technology to ease the transition from extensive growth (stuffing more raw meat into the goulash sausage machine) to intensive growth (improving the productivity of the machine) in order to be able to produce and afford more goulash. Moreover, the import of this technology, and the imported technology itself, made the socialist East more and more dependent, not only technologically, but financially, economically, politically, socially, ideologically and culturally on the capitalist West. The world capitalist economic crisis then exacerbated this dependance or its manifestations in the East. Western inflation and other manifestations of the crisis were imported wholesale. As the socialist economist, A. Köves, points out in italic emphasis in the Hungarian *Acta Oeconomica* (vol 21, No. 4, 1978, pp. 301, 302, 306) ironically 'the share of trade with the West grew in general also in the total trade of CMEA [Comecon] countries', 'the objective process of development demands that economic policy should give preference to export orientation at the expense of import substitution' and 'in other words', increased participation in the international division of labour, opening towards the world economy, was put on each CMEA country's agenda by the requirements of domestic social and economic development'. The requirement of this increased international participation is the strongest and has the most far-reaching domestic consequences precisely – and ironically – in the field in which the socialist economies were supposed to offer the most independent alternative and the strongest development policy, that is technology. But as it turns out, technological development and the development of technology are a sub-product of world economic development and the long cyclical process of capital accumulation on a world scale. Far from having escaped from this process through socialist planning, the socialist economies of the East turn out ironically to be integral parts and integrated processes of this world economic development. Moreover, although they have pulled ahead of many Third World countries, the advanced socialist economies still remain dependent on, and increasingly behind, the most technologically advanced sectors of the capitalist world economy. Far from burying the United States in 1980, the Soviet Union has lagged further behind and is now being bested by Japan.

Certainly the socialist countries no longer pursue any active policies to help, or even to applaud, the erstwhile prospect of capitalism burying itself in the ashes of its own crisis and then being succeeded by socialism. Soviet Premier Chernenko, addressing a commission charged with drafting the Communist Party programme to be presented to the next party congress, proposed that Kruschev's 1961 prediction of the impending triumph of communism over capitalism should be eliminated from the programme since capitalism 'still possesses quite substantial and far from exhausted reserves for development' (Tass report in *International Herald Tribune*, 27 April 1984). Although Chernenko maintained his faith in the ultimate victory of communism over capitalism, his (and his predecessors' and colleagues' in other socialist countries) practice in the meantime was to pray for and advocate the recuperation of capitalism from its present crisis. In the words of Chernenko's predecessor, Leonid Brezhnev 'because of the broad economic links between capitalist and socialist countries, the ill effects of the current crisis in the West have also had an impact on the socialist world', and in the words of his colleague Todor Zhivkov, the president of Bulgaria, 'it may be hoped that the crisis which is raging in the West may come to a rapid end, since it affects and creates uncertainties for the Bulgarian economy'. Thus, ironically, the leaders of the socialist 'alternative' to capitalism are waiting for the crisis of capitalism to end as soon as possible, so they can get back to business as usual. However, while they wait, world economic and technological development that is now passing through a crisis of regeneration is (perhaps again ironically) likely further to diminish, if not to eliminate, the importance of the East-West political division of the world much more than the North-South economic division, which it is likely to accentuate still further.

Recent developments in transatlantic and intra-European relations

In recent years, the tendencies outlined above have continued to develop in the same directions, despite some political attempts on both sides of the Atlantic and of Europe to retard or reverse them. Some political and journalistic highlights of the continuation of these tendencies were editorial headlines such as 'When Allies Diverge' (*International Herald Tribune*, 30 November 1983) and 'The Atlantic gets wider' (*Financial Times*, 3 January 1984). The third ranking official in the US State Department forecast the shift of the center of gravity of US foreign policy from the transatlantic relationship toward the Pacific basin, and particularly Japan... as the Pacific and clearly Japan are consistently taking on a more important role, at least in terms of the world economic situation... The US... and our NATO allies, dealing more and more with their immediate difficulties, have tended to some degree imperceptibly to move further apart. (*International Herald Tribune*).

Since 1980, some 85% of the growth of American imports has been from the Pacific area, rather than from Europe and Africa.

In the meantime, 'the Atlantic gets wider' because, according to the *Financial Times* (3 January 1984):

on the more material questions of defence and economics, however, it is by no means clear that we are bound by a common interest. The American shield now looks, to a significant and vocal minority, more like an American threat.... The European governments should take a lead in seeking more constructive means of adjustment... Russia's self-confessed economic weakness is, in fact, an important opportunity for the West, as the European business community has always recognized, but it will take courage to speak up for constructive contacts.

So President Reagan's closest ideological and political ally in Europe, Prime Minister Margaret Thatcher, condemned his invasion of Grenada as illegal, immoral and politically unacceptable, and turned around to make a state visit to Hungary and then to pay her respects in Moscow on the occasion of the funeral of Andropov because, as she said, beyond all ideological and other differences with the Soviet Union and Eastern Europe, a European dialogue with them is necessary. For her West German conservative colleague and ally, Chancellor Helmut Kohl, even more than talk appears necessary. He put his money where his mouth is and gave a state guarantee to a one billion mark credit to East Germany, which was negotiated by none other than the arch-conservative Franz Joseph Strauss of Bavaria and which is to be administered by a Bavarian bank. The British Labour Party's opposition leader, Neil Kinnock, is calling for an Assembly of Europe with attendance also by non-members of the European Economic Community and closer economic links as well as more political dialogue between Western and Eastern Europe.

On the other hand, in Southern Europe the Socialist Party governments or heads of government in France, Italy, Spain, Portugal and Greece have adopted 'a pragmatic line (whose) realpolitik comes before ideology, as the New York Times (*International Herald Tribune* 5 December 1983) has acutely observed. This "realism above everything else" has in no way changed the pro-American alignment... or endangered U.S. military interests'. On the contrary, the French Socialist Party President Mitterand has been more Atlanticist than his conservative predecessor and has led the European field in following President Reagan, with the other socialists Craxi, Gonzales, Soares not far behind. Demonstrably and symptomatically, and contrary to their conservative colleagues in Britain and Germany, none of them are at Andropov's funeral in Moscow. Of course, none of these Socialists, unlike Mrs. Thatcher and Mr. Kohl, are quite beyond reproach from their domestic opposition for possible pussy-footing with Communism or the Soviet Union; and all of them still need maximum political leeway to impose the economic austerity measures at home without quite admitting it. Maintaining their best Atlantic behaviour in foreign affairs, therefore, shields them a bit on their still exposed right flank. But once they too have done their necessary job of imposing austerity at home and this becomes plain for all to see, even these socialist party heads of government – if they survive that long – may be able politically to afford to join the North European move to more Europeanist positions and policies.

These political and journalistic highlights are only the tip of the iceberg reflection of continued economic, strategic, political, social and ideological shifts of the continental plates underlying the Atlantic and Europe. 'When Allies Diverge' was the title of an editorial commenting on an opinion poll that demonstrates that

> what comes through clearly is a very big and important difference between how Americans view their security, and the prospect of war, and how the European allies and the Japanese see the situation ... The American vision of the world today is not really that of the allies. Policy divergence follows the perceptual gap. The situation is getting worse. The alliance is in trouble because its institutions of common action no longer rest upon a foundation of agreement on what the threat is, how grave it is and what should be done about it. ... There lies the problem. (*International Herald Tribune*, 30 November 1983).

The international opinion poll by the Atlantic Institute-Louis Harris found that, during the year 1983 alone, popular confidence in cooperation with the United States fell by 25% in Western Europe as a whole and by 35% in West Germany, where the desire for continued dialogue and contacts with the Soviet Union increased as a response, especially among conservatives, to displace relations with America as the first concern. In Italy and the Netherlands the trend was similar, albeit less pronounced; and in Japan, where there was no comparable poll the previous year, 'contacts with the Soviet Union (33%) were clearly preferred over all other options'. Only in the United States was trans-Atlantic security deemed more important than the year before, and there it clearly reflected the sharp rise in the fear of war; which is shared by West Europeans, but which expresses itself in increasingly divergent policy options on the two sides of the Atlantic. One third of Italians support unilateral nuclear disarmament, and the British Labour Party has turned against the Trident submarine and other nuclear defence options. The West German Social Democratic party, under the leadership of whose then Chancellor Helmut Schmidt the idea of placing the new American Pershing II and Cruise missiles in Europe was first launched, reversed completely and, at their October 1983 congress, voted overwhelmingly against this stationing, leaving Schmidt with a minority of only 6 votes in favour of deployment.

Yet even Schmidt has warned that the 'egoistic economic policies' of Washington are now a greater danger to the coherence and political stability of the Atlantic alliance and could soon ruin it (*International Herald Tribune*, 16 January 1984). For their part, the Americans continue to press the Europeans to spend more money on conventional (read American) weapons for NATO and their own defence, while the Europeans increasingly argue that they can ill afford such increased military expenditures and certainly do not have the dollar foreign exchange to purchase them in the United States, which already sells five times as much arms as it buys in NATO. Thus, Henry Kissinger notes that Americans and Europeans are 'lulled by complementary illusions'; European leaders still want to make believe in the credibility of the by now threadbare American nuclear deterrent, while American officials seek to sell more conventional weapons to Europeans who want to cut military spending (*International Herald Tribune*, 19 January 1984). A former Kissinger aide, William Hyland, goes further and says that 'serious, thoughtful people in the United States' now doubt the value of staying in NATO; and 'an important American general, known for his extravagant talk, took bets that the United States will quit the alliance by 1990 – just six years away – in revulsion against the Europeans' (*International Herald Tribune*, 18 January 1984). It was the Europeans, both West and East, who were most insistent at the European Security conference in Madrid (the continuation of the process started in Helsinki) that the proposals for the establishment of 'confidence building measures' at the 1984 conference in Stockholm be taken seriously; and it is the Europeans who most insist that Stockholm and Vienna be used to renew superpower negotiations for arms control that were broken off at Geneva. The appointment of Britain's Lord Carrington (who was a former 'wet' softie in Mrs. Thatcher's conservative cabinet) to succeed the . Atlanticist hawk Joseph Luns as Secretary-General of NATO has also been viewed as an indication and instrument of strengthening a more independent European voice and resisting the tough American anti-Soviet line within the Alliance (*Time*, 16 January 1984).

The often underlying conflicts of economic interests between Europe and America have also continued to grow and to generate renewed complaints and clashes. 'You don't print money anymore, you import it,' Helmut Schmidt told the Americans who are running not only a $200 billion domestic budget deficit that drives up interest rates and attracts European money, but also a nearly $100 billion foreign trade deficit, which the US can afford only as long as the dollar is high and remains the world's principal reserve currency. In furious reaction, the French Finance Minister, Jacques Delors, has already proposed that Europeans consider some kind of curbs and penalites against the export of West European capital to the United States which he estimates at some $150 billion during the past year. These foreign funds permit the Americans to engage in their extravagant defence and other expenditures with the money of other people, whose resentment of this is fed by their own thereby increased austerity. At the same time, the United States has further restricted the import of European (and Japanese, Brazilian, etc.) steel; and the Europeans threaten to retaliate with import restrictions on American petrochemicals and other products of heavy industry. The Americans, with the powerful farm lobby getting up steam, continue to complain about European (also powerful farm interests) subsidisation and protection of their agriculture; and the Americans threaten to retaliate by raising the tariff on European wines, which compete with the growing California wine industry. European trade with the Soviet Union and Eastern Europe, and especially European government credit guarantees and subsidies of this trade, which is vital for both parts of Europe, remains a major and growing bone of contention with the Americans, who continue to try to use the CoCom (Coordinating Committee on East-West trade in strategic goods) in Paris and US multinationals' licensing for technology to tie the European hands. The European response even by a British Conservative Party minister and others is to reject American 'extraterritorial' legislation and rulings and to assert British and European sovereignty and independence in matters of intra-European trade.

Prospects for East-West Pan-European rapprochement

Renewed recognition of the need for and desirability of increased trade and other peaceful relations within Europe, and particularly between Eastern and Western Europe, continues to grow in all parts of Europe. The abovementioned one billion mark credit and negotiations about an additional one are indications and instruments of this rapprochement. So are other bilateral contacts between West and East Germany, including a cordial meeting in Moscow between their respective heads of government, Kohl and Honecker. The latter has stressed several times that the deployment of new American missiles in West Germany need not poison good intra-German relations in other areas of common interest. Indeed the *Washington Post* (*International Herald Tribune*, 22 February 1984) reports that 'East Germany becomes the strongest advocate of détente and cooperation with the West, spurred by public discontent with the economy and anxiety about nuclear weapons.... For the East Germans more profitable relations hold out the promise of a relaxation of years of rigid austerity measures'. The other side of this coin is that American spokesmen, and also some in France, have voiced concern that the West German peace movement is little more than a smokescreen for German reunification, which some continue to regard as a threat in both West and East. Moreover, the retaliatory deployment of new Soviet missiles in East Germany has drawn the open opposition of Romania and supposedly the quiet chagrin of some political currents in Czechoslovakia and in the German Democratic Republic itself within the Warsaw Pact.

The concern with domestic problems and intra-European détente, which Chernenko displayed publicly in the ceremonies and receptions of European leaders for the funeral of his predecessor Andropov, are evidence of some basis for increased and improved intra-European relations. So are the continued pressures for and steps toward economic and administrative reform in various countries of Eastern Europe. At the same time, the crisis-generated pressure for greater Comecon integration in Eastern Europe and the Soviet Union does not necessarily pose an alternative but may offer a complement to East-West trade, since many intra-Comecon exports, especially those from Eastern Europe to the Soviet Union, are based on technological and other inputs from Western Europe. Therefore, the recent crisis-generated decline of East European imports from the West and the use of their resulting trade surpluses to start paying off the accumulated debt to the West, can provide the basis for more stable future East-West European economic and other relations over the long run. Analogously, the continuing, and indeed growing, obstacles to West European economic integration within the EEC and its expansion to include Spain and Portugal (need not) be an indication that an even larger Europe to include the East is necessarily illusory. On the contrary, more East-West European economic ties and political dialogue even through a criss-cross network of bilateral relations throughout all of Europe, can be a means of overcoming or at least bypassing some of the obstacles to integration within a smaller Western Fortress Europe – and such a re-emergence of pan-European relations can be a major step towards defusing the growing threat of nuclear war.

This expansion of the EEC as it would in effect be, is stirred on by the West-West dissension within the Atlantic Alliance and NATO and the no doubt different but complementary economic and political difficulties that are emerging with Comecon and the Warsaw Pact countries, as well as a potentially common European interest in a stable solution to the crisis in the Middle East and the steady flow of oil to all of Europe, not to mention the desire for peace and arms limitations in Europe. All this could perhaps provide the political and economic basis for a major international and national political realignment and an alternative regional or economic bloc strategy. Western and Eastern Europe could form ties to the Middle East and perhaps Africa, and there are common interests which could lead to the political and economic rapprochment of Western and Eastern Europe. Moreover, the growing conflicts within both the Atlantic Alliance and the Eastern bloc and the underlying economic and political weakening of both the American and Soviet 'superpowers' relative to their respective economic and political allies on either side of the Elbe could render important political and economic forces in each of the present four major regional groupings (Western Europe, Eastern Europe, the United States and the Soviet Union) able to consider an alternative East-West European economic and political rapprochement.

When there is a real mutual economic basis for the amalgamation, or at least rapprochement, of the two systems, as there is between the EEC and the CMEA, and the alternative is the possible nuclear destruction of both, there is more than enough reason to make the political effort. Significantly, this political effort is one in which important economic and political interest groups, and the peace movements within Western Europe could for once join each other in a common cause. Of course, mutual economic interests do not provide or guarantee political agreement. They only offer an economic basis to enhance the chances of success of any political effort. Each of the present allies of Eastern and Western Europe may have, at the very least, lesser evil reasons for acquiescing in such a politico-economic realignment, particularly if their vital interests are safeguarded in the process. The USSR would have a reduced economic and military burden. The mere weakening or breaking up of NATO should offer the Soviet Union a significant enticement to go along with such a European rapprochement.

For its part, the United States would find the apparently inevitable loss of its hegemony in Europe increasingly confirmed, but would be freed to draw its economic and political attention increasingly away from Europe and the Atlantic and to turn them preferentially to the Pacific, including parts of Latin America and Asia in whose direction powerful forces are drawing or leading important American political and economic interests anyway. If there was any 'Soviet threat' it would be turned more towards Asia and the Pacific where it could be checked through a further development of the Washington-Tokyo-Bejing axis and their possible politico-economic collaboration in the Asia Pacific region.

Important economic and political interests in the United States, related especially to newer technologically more advanced industries and the expanding 'sun belt' states in the South and West of the country, have for some time been pushing for a Pacific Rim strategy to replace the old transatlantic European ties.

The *New York Times/International Herald Tribune* of 26 January 1982 carried a long article by W.W. Rostow, a former National Security Advisor to Kennedy and Johnson (and whose brother was arms adviser to Reagan). Rostow calls for East-West détente in Europe. He asks, above all 'Why should Germany not be unified? Why should the European continent be littered with American and Soviet nuclear weapons?... What is needed now... is to allow Europeans, in both East and West, to organize themselves more as Europeans... to achieve the abiding Soviet dream of a Western Europe cut off from the military support of the United States. They would be supported by a few Americans who have long hankered to cut West Europe loose'.

In conclusion, it appears that the natural course of world capitalist development and its renewed structural crisis are undermining the economic basis of the Atlantic Alliance and generating ever sharper political dissension within it, also about the strategic issues of relations with the Soviet Union and its allies in Eastern Europe. These in turn, also in part because of the world economic crisis, are facing increasing economic political problems of their own. The combination of [these] Western and Eastern political and economic problems poses serious dangers for the stability and peace of a world based on the bipolar Mutual Assured Destruction (MAD) and nuclear parity face-off between NATO and the Warsaw Pact. But the same politico-economic forces that pose this danger also offer the opportunity – the Chinese ideographs for crisis are a combination of those for danger and for opportunity – to forge a new multipolar balance of power, including a possible Pan-European political economic entente to again stabilize the strategic balance, at least in the European theatre. Moreover, this possibility can become a more practical proposition in so far as the combination of the economic crisis in the West and in the East, and the effect of undermining the economic basis of the Atlantic and Soviet-East European Alliances, also provide a new economic basis for the tactical, if not strategic, cooperation of the peace movement(s) and powerful politico-economic interests. This could permit at least grudging acceptance or even support of the former by the latter) in Europe (West and East) and even the acquiescence in the same by influential forces in the United States and the Soviet Union. The implementation of such global (political economic) realignments would not eliminate East European and Third World dependence any more than alternative realistic proposals would. Compared to the in any case untenable status quo and other alternative policies, however, the proposed world realignment centering on a Pan-European entente would offer greater hope for the achievement of important and widely shared desires: maintenance of world peace, or at least avoidance of nuclear war, greater possibilities for economic growth in Western Europe, wider opportunities for national independence and political liberalization in Eastern Europe, and increased political bargaining power and room for manoeuvre for socialist and nationalist liberation movements in the Third World.

15. A Culture of Peace or Exterminism: Socio-cultural Alternatives

by Miroslav Pečujlić

One fact above all others determines human existence and hangs over humanity like the sword of fate: the perpetual danger of man's self-destruction. This of itself changes our comprehension of history, of man and his world. The entire problem of human emancipation acquires new content and forms. The simplified picture of history as a continuous evolution from its lower to higher stages changes utterly. The nuclear confrontation has entered our existence threatening to destroy everything we have, everything we know, everything we are. Our present knowledge is like Newton's simplified picture of the world compared to the modern theory of relativity. We are, consequently, in need of a theoretical framework which will express this critical aspect of our transition from the 20th to the 21st century:

a) the causes of this faceless and ominous *dramatis personae* under whose looming shadow today's world is being shaped;

b) the new emancipatory – peace potential of unprecedented intensity and depth being opened by our age.

The category *exterminism* (the tendency towards man's self-destruction), the brilliant theoretical innovation of E.P. Thompson, we accept but, at the same time, we supplement it with another epoch-making novelty, *radical emancipatory potential*. Instead of one category, we propose a theoretical couple – *civilization of exterminism – radical emancipation*. These are not merely two tendencies; it is the very duality of the contemporary world. The civilization of exterminism and the civilization of greater solidarity, freedom and peace. One horizon is empty and closed, the other is open and crowded with creative possibilities. On one side stand the powerful forces, new militarism raised to the level of planetary destruction, a pathology of domination (power), a pathological type of modernization. Opposing it stand the objective-subjective foundations of a 'culture of peace'. The objective basis consists of a gigantic production power which man has mastered and which can eliminate scarcity and misery. The subjective basis, new human subjectivity, consists of the promotion of new human abilities, the driving forces of new civilizational development.

Its other side is reflected in new values: *'universal emancipatory needs'* – aspirations for greater solidarity, freedom and peace, aspirations to make men and women not only the objects but the subjects of modernization as well as to give them the power to change the world. The planet is the birthplace of this new social energy that is expressed in mass-scale social movements, peace movements taking a central place among them.

The acute danger of a nuclear holocaust has not one, but a whole series of sources. An anatomical picture of this *entity* reveals two different groups of causes feeding upon each other and developing into a *deathly war spiral*. The new, frightening wave of armaments is the direct cause. It is the *determinant*. But, simultaneously, it is a consequence of deeper causes, an entity of antagonistic social processes which give rise to a permanent tendency of destruction. The more profound causes, the *'superdeterminant'*, is the civilization of exterminism. This complex whole contains a series of different aspects: the pathology of domination (power), and the pathological type of development, of modernization and its crisis. It is a supra-systemic phenomenon; the contamination spreads to all types of social systems, although it does not mean their symmetry. Gramsci's words still hold good: 'The crisis consists in the fact that the old is dying and the new cannot be born; in this interregnum a great variety of morbid symptoms appear'.

New militarism is both a consequence of this social entity and a factor which, for its part, significantly jeopardizes, and prevents, transformations which have become a condition for mankind's survival. This leads to the 'deathly spiral of war':

1) 'New militarism' is the direct cause of the planet's possible destruction;
2) the crisis of the civilization of antagonism is the deeper cause of new militarism;
3) the new armament programme has an adverse effect on social transformations which are necessary to maintain the peace.

Consequently, a breakthrough from this lethal antinomy, the opening of a path to 'a culture of peace' also includes several dimensions. One of them involves the struggle for disarmament, détente and the gradual abolition of the military blocs. But the peace cannot be secured without changes in the 'superdeterminant' as well, without profound transformations on the world social scene geared towards a different type of development. The struggle for peace is also multidimensional.

The role of Europe on both sides of the equation: war–peace is of fateful significance. It is the decisive actor on a stage which is being hurriedly set, the stage of 'limited nuclear war'. Europe also provides a vast potential for the creation of a 'culture of peace'.

New Militarism

War is the central feature of antagonistic civilization. But novelty above all other novelties is represented by elevating the means of warfare to the level of power capable of destroying the planet. The neutron bomb, with its 'awesome' ability to destroy only people not things, the new incredibly powerful and precise cruise missiles, the Pershing II and SS-20, have a potential which is equal to one and a half million bombs of the kind dropped on Hiroshima. We are on the threshold of space warfare, 'star wars'.

War is no longer simply an epiphenomenon. It is becoming an active cause. The *mode of producing war* has its own means of production and production relations, its subjects – owners and managers – the *technocracy of death*. It shapes the technological base and economic life of society. It affects the type of state which provides its framework, the type of authoritarian state of national security which is based on the citizen's utter submissiveness to the state, and the state's utter submissiveness to the bloc. The ideology of war is rooted in a picture of a diabolical enemy – inhumane monster – the sole culprit and cause of all ills and dangers. The arms race is acquiring its *own, autonomous dynamics and objectives;* production of the means of warfare is subject to the laws of *expanded reproduction.* There is no point of balance at which it will stop of its own accord or be stopped by its propagators. Reciprocity, 'the balance of nuclear terror', can never be achieved: their missiles call for ours, which in turn call for theirs.

Three factors have been responsible. The new destructive power of means of warfare are also expressed in fateful changes in philosophy and morals, in military doctrine (strategy); from the strategy of deterrence to acceptance of what was once unimaginable: limited nuclear war. But, limited nuclear war in Europe would, in practice, inevitably lead to a generalized atomic holocaust. This is so because the European theatre is not internally symmetrical: it comprises, on the one side, no more than the periphery of the American strategic military complex, but, on the other, it represents the metropolitan heart of the Soviet strategic military complex. Thus, even if a perfectly equal number of 'theatre' missiles could be defined and controlled in each zone of Europe, the fact would still remain that those on one side could strike at the entire strategic defences of the other. Precisely because of this 'asymmetry', the only way forward for Europe is the total dismantling of the two nuclear theatre systems.

Meanwhile, a second, and no less important, mutation has occurred. There has been a sudden multiplication of the circle of producers of nuclear weapons making the situation even less controllable, so proliferating the risks of local conflicts setting off a global war. This military tendency has found a new social and material basis since the oil crisis. For, within the underdeveloped world as a whole, those countries which command valuable natural resources have finally become able to profit substantially. But this unexpected wealth has not been directed to real development, it has found a natural outlet in military expenditures in the Third World, which have unleashed new local conflicts.

The logic of crisis as well as the autonomous development of means for producing war have led to this change. The guiding notion, hitherto, was that of deterrence: each side sought security in its own capacity to respond to any attack by physically destroying its adversary. Whoever contemplated unleashing an atomic war could be certain of signing his own death-warrant too; there was no sense in further multiplying nuclear weapons. Recently, however, the novel opportunities opened up by the sophisticated technologies of the electronic revolution and space research have seen the emergence of a new philosophy of nuclear arms. The objective of this doctrine is the capacity to destroy the military forces of the adversary and so 'render him harmless'. It commits its adherents to the logic of the preemptive strike; and it plunges them into an unlimited race to acquire new weapons systems before the adversary can do so. Deterrence, instead of constituting a limit to rearmament, becomes an uncontrollable stimulus to the constant renewal of armaments consigned to obsolescence.

The causes of possible war are not just of a rational nature. The very fact that a pluralism of causes exists indicates that the effects with which each actor individually calculates will not occur. The calculated risk is an illusion. The danger of war does not lie only in rational interests, therefore, we can sleep peacefully because no élite will do anything that will lead to its own self-destruction. The very nature of modern nuclear weapons leads to to an unprecedented historical fact: the decision on humanity's life or death would have to be made within a space of five to seven minutes and by a very small political-military élite. And now we come to the crux of the problem: in these few fateful minutes, who will decide whether or not to use nuclear weapons? Who weighs the decision on the life or death of hundreds of millions of people or the complete destruction of mankind? The decision-maker does not rely upon the will of the people but upon anonymous and totally computerized, automated systems endowed with a mechanical will, created for total devastation.

The Crisis of Modernization

New militarism does not arise in a social vacuum but within a broader social context. It is incited by a crisis in a type of civilization development, a crisis of a type of modernization – modernization without emancipation – that dominates.

Events of a true historical magnitude are represented in a post-industrial revolution, which, like the double-faced god Janus, is highly contradictory. A deep restructuring of the entire techno-economic base of society is like an earthquake that throws up a new terrain; for the subterranean structure on which our social organization is based, now is itself changing. Man is conquering new worlds; industrialism is giving way to the post-industrial revolution-atomic energy, the computer, informatics, biology revolution – which is taking shape along radically different principles.

Production will be based on the wondrous wealth of energy sources. Gene splicing, the most powerful skill acquired since the splitting of the atom, will enable us to create a new revolution in agriculture. In the 'information society' that is taking shape, computer technology will be the innvoative technology that will constitute the developmental core. An immense part of human endeavour will be linked to information. Both Adam Smith and Marx's 'labour theory of value', born at the beginning of the industrial economy, must be corrected with a new 'knowledge theory of value'. The new wave of civilization primarily relies upon human capacities, the full utilization of capabilities of each individual and endogenous creativity of each society. It offers new prospects to the development of the developing countries, as well. The new productive potential has the power of making an old dream come true – doing away with poverty and misery.

But, as if by some fateful magic spell, the new sources of productive power – as opposed to their great liberation potentials – serve to subordinate people and entire communities. The expanding gulf between the highly-developed 'centre' and the 'periphery' is entering a new period, heralding a division of worlds, the formation of a number of completely different and parallel civilizations (social formations):

a) a few oases of highly-developed *societies* which are entering an era of *post-industrialism*, candidates for mastery of the world (technocratic, authoritarian post-industrialism); b) dependent *old and new industrial* societies; c) *agrarian-industrial* societies; d) a so-called *fourth agrarian world.*

Growth inside this historical pattern turns into a new form: *domination and dependence,* which significantly limits the possibilities of an individual choice of strategy and becomes *development of under-development*. In the 21st century, many parts of the world will constitute industrial societies, many presently undeveloped countries will develop into newly industrialized ones, but completely dependent on the post-industrial masters of the world.

The blast furnace in which this 'remodelling of the world' would be realized is the great crisis accompanied by a giant reorganization, *restructuring* of world production. Changes in the international division of labour are followed by the destitution of entire branches of industry; conventional unprofitable and dirty industries are moving to less developed countries. Old types of mass manufacturing industries: automobile, steel, rubber, textile – the backbone of traditional industrialism – are in crisis. Meanwhile, the highly-developed centre becomes the sole mainstay of the branches of the future. The other countries at the base of the pyramid of victims can only imitate and play the role of mere executors of routine work.

A second mechanism establishing the new world division between the command centres of post-industrialism and dependent industrial and agrarian societies, can be found in *debtor modernization*. Its major effect is the giant re-distribution of wealth on the world scene which has created the financial basis for large-scale technological restructuring and for an abrupt post-industrial revolution in the centre.

Upon entering the orbit of dependent modernization, an 'iron-bound' sequence begins:

1) the initial point is the existence of a legitimate aspiration – the necessity and yet inability to achieve rapid industrial development exclusively on the basis of one's own resources; 2) modernization is planned by completely neglecting endogenous resources; it is based upon a complete import of all its component parts, and large irrational spending of loans; 3) falling into 'debtors slavery'. The main invention leading to it is the move from fixed to changing interest rates. Usurer's interest rates are becoming a historically new form of pouring in the surplus of value. But the scissors open up one notch more. The prices of raw materials, the greatest treasure of the developing countries, are plunging drastically; the exports cannot win the race against mounting debts; 4) the strengthening of authoritarian tendencies in society, extracted by the need to discipline the labour force, and to pacify the population. Debtor modernization leads to collapse, impoverishment, to economic nationalism, commercial and financial wars, renewed religious wars, and military conflicts. 'The debtor bomb' has been set.

Those disastrous effects of the 'decade of development' represent only one pole whose other side is the irrational, parasitic model of consumption at the 'centre'. This is a model which cannot be maintained as it clashes against social and natural boundaries. By the constant launching of new status goods, the system creates more unsatisfied, rather than satisfied, needs. The shortage has not been caused by insufficient productive capacities, but was produced by society; a social shortage is created, the social limits of growth have been reached. Highly developed countries represent a minority of the world's population but they consume 90% of world energy and raw materials.

The process cannot be maintained without violence, militarism is its artificial lung. The atom bomb and computer are marching side by side across the planet. But even Europe does not escape all negative consequences.

Western Europe is a powerful competitor for world dominance, but also a strong candidate for the new dependent society as well. From 1870–1950 the US rate of productivity growth exceeded Europe's by 60% and Japan's by 70%. Starting in 1950, the situation was reversed, and US productivity growth now lags well behind Europe and Japan.

The Share of World Industrial Exports

	1950	1977
England	22.5	9.3
U.S.A.	27.3	15.9
West Germany	7.3	20.8
Japan	3.4	15.4

The renewal of hegemony is effected through the sector in which US capital enjoys absolute superiority in high technology and fundamental research through the war industry.

Furthermore, the unity of the conservative crisis-solving project and the new militarism is threatening to destroy the most valuable achievements of Western civilization: the 'welfare state', the intellectual heritage of the enlightenment and national independence and democracy. By heavy blows directed against individual and social welfare, the balance of forces has been changed. For a whole epoch, public expenditure was a flywheel of growth and employment. Today, we witness the crisis of the welfare state amidst chronic inflation running hand in hand with increasing military outlays. To maintain their level, it will be necessary to dismantle the welfare state; to achieve this political repression will be necessary.

Europe also is faced by limited national sovereignty and reduced democracy. Both blocs have confined decision-making on nuclear weapons to hidden apparatuses, far from the eyes of the public, or the control and influence of public opinion. Important obligations have been taken and acknowledged by the NATO and Warsaw Pacts relating to nuclear strategy and installations, obligations concealed in simplified agreements. In the name of 'military secrets' the rights of parliaments to decide on war and peace are *de facto* negated. Does democracy imply the right of the people to decide on this problem or not?

One of the causes of the new militarism and wars can be found in the politics of hegemonistic state interests on the side of the other block as well. Here, we are facing a highly ambivalent, twofold relationship toward emancipatory movements. On the one side, military and economic support is offered to liberation movements exposed to outside intervention from the West. On the other side the face of hegemonism appears in the desire to subordinate liberation movements to egoistic state interests, or to reduce the autonomy of states to that of an outer defence belt of a superpower. The socialist countries are themselves falling into the logic of hegemonistic relations, especially in the military field. Even the fatal prospect of wars between them is now becoming a reality.

The past years have thus seen decisive events in the other camp, the East European countries, at present hit by economic crisis and the effects of

Average annual growth rate in USSR		Gross industrial output		
			1971–75	*1981–85*
1933–1937	16.1%	Bulgaria	9.2	4.7
1951–1955	11.9	Czechsolovakia	6.7	2.6
1976–1980	4.3	East Germany	6.5	3.9
1980–	3.8	Hungary	6.4	2.4
		Poland	10.4	4.8
		Romania	13.0	4.7
		East Europe	8.7	2.1

rearmament. It is the ground on which the specific 'authoritarian historical compromise' is eroded as well. There is no doubt that these countries have achieved exceptionally dynamic industrial growth; a once backward economy transformed into a modern economy. All research shows that all of this has catered to the basic existential needs more than in other societies at the same level of economic development. It has opened prospects for employment and education. On that ground a specific 'historical compromise' is reached: a combination between an existence guaranteed by the state, and a subordination to the state power apparatus, which is the general employer of hired labour. But the compromise that has been grounded upon high rates of economic growth, is now endangered; growth rates of output and productivity have fallen significantly.

The gulf between the two Europes is greater in the new sectors of high technology. It is above all the result of structural processes. The existing economic mechanism in Eastern Europe does not provide sufficient economic incentives for a transition from a model of simple and extensive to complex and intensive growth, from industrial growth achieved through the expansion of the workforce to growth achieved through the adoption of the new techniques. This arises from the rigidity of overcentralized administrative systems, the lack of individual initiative and the absence of autonomy of producers, production units and institutions, which is a decisive factor in achieving a rapid leap to a higher scientific-technological level. A second major cause is the over-emphasis on heavy industry and arms. The contradiction between re-armament and socio-economic development is deepening; a society like the USSR whose per capita income is a third of that of the USA has traditionally had to sustain a military burden comparable to that of its adversary. This discrepancy was in the past tempered by the fact that national income was itself registering constant and steady growth. But, from the moment that growth rates start to decline in the USSR as well, such a disproportionate military effort cannot be continued.

The system has tried to postpone the maturation of these contradictions by opening itself to trade with the West. The outcome was a kind of double-entry historical bookkeeping. Its positive side has been to break out of the artificial isolation and establish natural connections between the two parts of Europe. But, since it was not followed by economic reform at home, and was affected by a debt crisis – bloc debt to the West grew ten-fold, from eight to 80 billion US dollars – it did not succeed in checking and reversing the economic decline. The time is ripe for a new approach on both sides of Europe. Disarmament that offers the convincing guarantee for durable peace, and the reduction of the economic burden could be decisive to overcoming the crisis of modernization. If Europe responds by aligning itself with new aggressive postures, it is all too probable that everything will end tragically.

From the culture of war to the culture of peace

Just as the causes of war are manifold, so too is the struggle for 'the culture of peace' multidimensional. One of its dimensions is the elimination of the direct 'determinant' – from disarmament to the gradual abolition of the military blocs.

The road to the 'withering away of war' takes many parallel directions. First, the control and reduction of, especially, nuclear arms. Second, substitution of aggressive preparations for war with a radical alternative popular nationwide defence not based on nuclear missiles, including non-military forms of self-protection, combined with military defence aimed exclusively at protection from aggression. However, a final break with exterminism requires a more radical, if gradual, move embracing the programme of complete disarmament. Third, a key moment in the strategy of peace is a commitment against the world's division into blocs, and renewing proposals for abolishing the blocs. 'An initiative by the Russell Foundation suggests a procedure according to the principle of 'multilateral unilateralism': while the general goal of a nuclear-free zone from Poland to Portugal is maintained, each country enacts unilateral disarmament. Only then can a transition from an escalation of arms to an escalation of disarmament be achieved. Unilateral disarmament is seen as appropriate to end the arms race as balanced disarmament is suited to secure its continuation. A unilateral initiative for disarmament is needed to break the spiral leading to war.

The 'culture of peace' can flourish in an environment different from the 'culture of domination'. An attack on the 'superdeterminant' constitutes the other dimension of the struggle for peace. That refers to the transformation of the world economic order and development model from the civilization of exterminism towards a civilization of greater solidarity and emancipation. The more so since the demystification of new militarism exposes a great but simple secret: major armament programmes do not so much serve as preparations for victory in future wars but for victory in present peace. Their hidden function is to preserve the status quo; if the enemy did not exist, it would have to be invented, otherwise the tower of domination would collapse. Neither side has anything to gain from war, while both sides profit from the existence of a permanent external threat, a kind of necessary ritual, masking real social conflicts.

The values of peace, freedom and greater solidarity have become universal needs. They are no longer individual aspirations, mere intellectual constructions. They are long-range emancipatory projects for changes in the world order and development model. They have collective and mass-scale protagonists and strategies which promote them.

The rupture strategy

Secession from the world market is the first condition for authentic development. Is integration in the world economic system really necessary, at least for the Third World countries, when we know that it is based on the division of labour which is to blame for the inequitable distribution of income and consequently for the growing gap?... Basically, this means supporting autarchy, not in an effort to question the advantages resulting from better organization at a world level. But, if the international system cannot be changed, then autarchy is the best solution, in spite of the limitations and negative aspects it may carry with it. For most Third World countries secession today means: an end to production of raw materials which are mostly processed in metropolises; an end to industrialization which works for foreign markets, which is expensive and which leads the development process into a stalemate; abandoning industrialization which did not help meet the needs of the impoverished majority. [Mary Kaldor]

The target of the rupture strategy is not xenophobic nationalism, but fundamental changes in international relations of domination and inequality. But it may be an expression of the tragic discrepancy between the depth and accuracy of its diagnosis and the medicine proposed. It is idle to believe that true progress can be achieved without the use of the giant scientific-technological potential that has been created. The secession theory constitutes a warning that dependent integration carries in it the seeds of explosive conflicts.

The strategy of regionalism

The unification of mankind is not carried out in a single manner; there is a multitude of forms, regional integration being central among them. Plurality of regional entities will come into being. They will be strengthened as the reaction against the unyielding position of the centre. But, there is a crucial question: if simultaneous transformation of the world economic order is absent could it lead to:

a) reproduction of old vices, the relationship of domination established within the regions, under the leadership of the great overlords who offer protection, but at the price of abandoning independence; b) the legitimate tendency of regional integration can move into the other extreme: from open systems of 'closed regionalism'. Regions become a closed monolith, impenetrable walls of protectionism, waging economic, and perhaps not only economic, wars with the rest of the world.

The project for a New World Economic Order

The strategy of modernization and of emancipation is expressed in a series of crucial programme declarations adopted by the UN and its agencies, and by the non-aligned movement. Even a superficial glance shows an impressive evolution. The core idea began with those of the Group of 77 countries (1964) and was elaborated by Non-Aligned countries. It was embodied in the International Development Strategy (1970), as well as in the Lima target (1975), UNCTAD Integral project for raw materials etc.

The main normative foundations lie in the Declaration on the Introduction of a New International Economic Order (1974).

We solemnly state that we are resolved to relentlessly work on the introduction of a new international economic order which will be based on equitable relations, sovereign equality, mutual dependence, the communality of interests and cooperation among states. In order to abolish inequality and existing injustice, to bridge the evergrowing gap between the advanced and developing countries and to secure present and future generations quicker economic and social development, peace and justice...

These norms did not become a reality. It is only one, yet powerful, tendency within the framework of world society, an emancipatory tendency whose active subjects are the Third World countries. It is advancing against fierce resistance on the part of the highly developed world; or it may be viewed as a forced concession to the order which the American representative called 'the tyranny of the majority'. However, in the North there existed a strong minority current which farsightedly understood the imperative need for changes, and the existence of common North-South interests. For the more radical part of the world community, the new project was a democratic 'constitution' for the world economic community. For them it compared in significance with the ideas of 'liberté, fraternité, egalité' in the creation of modern societies.

The new development model
The philosophy of progress has undergone many changes but the only changes that really constitute progress are those which present a gain in terms of the essential qualities of human existence. That means at least: a) that the fruits of technological growth should not benefit tiny elites and privileged countries, but develop man's productive capacities instead of reducing them to a cheap labour force, b) it should expand the possibilities for the endogenous creativity of each society; c) it should strive for the preservation and renewal of natural resources.

The new development strategy would have a number of important components:

1. It would seek as a first priority to remedy basic needs – foods, shelter, clothing, health and education;
2. It would utilize human abilities and knowledge towards attaining collective self-reliance as an important lever of development;
3. A balance between labour-intensive and capital-intensive technology, a combination of human resources and the scientific and technological heritage of the 'centre';
4. Public funding for development, and not primarily for the repayment of enormous and unjustifiably high interest rates which totally negate the possibility of real development. It would induce support for the Brandt Commission's call for a World Fund for Development.

Disarmament and development

At the core of the 'development problem' lies the fact that resources spent on arms reduce the level of resources available for development.

The resources spent on development are shamefully small because the resources spent on armaments are high. Between 1945–75 there were 119 wars (civil and international) involving 69 state territories and the armies of 81 states. The expenditure on arms has increased 30 times in the past 80 years. It is ten times greater than the amount spent in World War I and three to four times greater than for World War II.

World military expenditures account for about two-thirds of the gross national products of all Third World countries. The amount corresponds approximately to the joint income of three quarters of the poorest inhabitants of the Third World, and almost coincides with the GNP of Latin America, while it is twice as large as the GNP of all African countries. Between 1960–76, cumulative military spending in the world totalled 3,325 billion US dollars, compared to cumulative economic aid to the less developed nations for the same period of 162 billion dollars. The costs of a ten-year programme which would satisfy basic needs in food and medical services in the developing countries would not even account for half of annual military expenditures; in 1972 there was five times more money spent on military research than on medical research. More money is spent for military purposes than for education; a modern tank costs about two million dollars, a sum which could secure 1000 classrooms for 30 thousand pupils.

Arms expenditures create an enormous budgetary deficit (200 billion dollars in the United States in 1984) which produces high interest rates, which, in turn, damages the prospects for development.

In the 1970s, there were some 23 million people under arms, or 36 million if we include those organized in para-military forces; in turn, they were backed by another 25 to 30 million civilian staff, a grand total of between 61 and 66 million.

Militarization particularly includes corporations in technologically leading branches: aeronautics, electronics, nuclear technology, industrial computer and information systems, and chemistry. Here we find an exceptional concentration of scientific potential, and a mass of highly educated and gifted personnel. The militarized apparatus of production is the first and foremost laboratory for scientific revolution; from it were taken scientific methods of research, the complicated use of computer technology in large management systems. They are closely connected with strategic research projects within the universities. The lion's share of state funds is directed to the corporations intensively engaged in military programmes. In the 1960s, the USA allocated 86.6% of research funds for military research and development, space exploration and nuclear physics research, and only 3.2% for the economy, while Japan oriented 75.4% of these resources towards the economy and only 16.5% for military purposes. In USSR the military industry and research enjoys the highest priorities.

The extraordinary economic support for the third scientific-technological revolution in military-industrial sectors reduces technical innovations in other sectors of industry. But this curious marriage between the post-industrial revolution and the military mode of production carries the greatest danger. If the main bridge towards the society of future is such a symbiosis, then its outcome may well be the *post-industrial military civilization*, as opposed to *post-industrial libertarian tendencies*.

The armament industry is surrounded by a particular set of mystifications which provides a false picture, a kind of 'military fetishism'. We often hear arguments that the production of arms is important for the economy and employment in the North. This is a misconception. Although it is true that the military industry stimulates growth and employment, it is certainly not irreplaceable. Investments in the arms industry create less work places than investments in other industrial branches and public services. Greater research should be geared towards the possibilities of transforming the production of armaments into production for civilian purposes. The thoughtful alternatives for gradual conversion from production for war into production of socially useful products lies at the heart of the matter.

Social protagonists
The analysis reveals the increasing contradictions within the dominant model of development. But, simultaneously it is discovering many vital points of common interest between Europe and developing countries.

> Irrespective of the extent of the differences between North and South, the two regions also have common interests. Their fates are tightly linked together. The quest for solutions is not an act of charity, but a pre-requisite for collective survival. Perhaps, part of the problem could be illustrated by the development of some currently industrialized countries during the 19th and the beginning of the 20th century. A long and permanent learning process was necessary before it became generally accepted that higher wages adequately increase the buying power of workers, so that the entire economy is set into motion. The industrial countries should now be interested in broadening their markets in the developing world. This will have a noteworthy impact on the possibilities of employment...The North can only expect to export more if it makes its own markets more accessible. *(North-South Report)*.

Life itself furnished the arguments. By the second half of the 1970s, it was becoming apparent that for the first time the more developed nationals had become more dependent upon the less developed, and therefore could no longer regard all proposals of the Third World as irrelevant or inimical to their interests. Less developed countries doubled their exports to the more developed between 1970 and 1980. More important, the less developed provided a market for nearly a quarter of the exports of the more developed by 1980. Western Europe in particular had come to depend upon the less developed for nearly one-third of its export sales. The importance of this trade for employment is eloquently illustrated by the fact that every 20th worker in the USA works on production for exports to the Third World, while in the Federal Republic of Germany one out of every six workers is dependent on exports.

But the importance of the Third World cannot be reduced to the role of markets. Its emancipatory potential cannot be reduced to a rebellious 'ocean of misery' without anything to be lost. The better, peaceful solutions of the tremendous existential problems of mankind cannot be built on domination. It is tantamount to destroying or blocking enormous hidden creative potentials that only the pluralism of cultures can activate. The new renaissance of world society necessitates active participation by all cultures with deep historical roots and civilized values. Let me try to single out a few such 'cultural circles'. The first is traditional knowledge, experience and skills. Secondly, there are values, at the heart of which lies a philosophy of life which is less imbued with the instrumental-exploitational attitude to man (towards himself and towards others), but rather tries to achieve greater harmony within man. This is an orientation towards self-development. It is a philosophy of life which is less imbued with extreme possessive egotism and selfish competition. The third involves a different attitude to nature, one that entails less ruthless exploitation, and more cultivation, of nature. These values coincide with the coming post-industrial civilization, although at a much lower technological level. At the same time the confrontation with western culture can help them to overcome some negative and unfruitful aspects of their tradition, which constitute the powers of social inertia.

Europe should also show its other face, release its latent potential. If the Europeans could strike through the chain of armaments and find a third way, they would bring tremendous political and material reinforcements to the strategy of non-alignment and afford more space to Third World nations to pilot their own course of development independently of either bloc. But any new relationship with the Third World presupposes a qualitative change in our own type of development. To make an alternative presupposes an advancement of its own unity.

The historical protagonists of a 'culture of peace' cannot be reduced only to states, to governments. Government negotiations still remain within the framework of a 'balance of nuclear terror'. Disarmament, as a matter of life or death, cannot simply be left to governments, management groups which either propagate this danger or are too weak to withstand it, without large social movements which will give them the strength they need. Under the present global situation, any establishment objectively becomes a transmission, transmitting the influence of international supradetermination. The system in an individual country cannot resist global coercion unless it has, under the wing of its own society, powerful social and cultural movements aspiring to a different pattern of development, ecology, peace, etc. The political system itself cannot bring salvation if social forces lack autonomy, if there is no autonomous activity on the part of people seeking alternatives, endogenous creativity, constituting a social force enabling greater freedom of choice. Large scale autonomous action by social movements which are not the vassals of their governments passively waiting for the decisions taken only from above, is the premise for advancement in the long march for peace. This of course, does not mean to say that the establishment may not participate in progressive changes. Social movements may be transformed into movements of societies, the vast majority of people aspiring for some universal needs, such as peace. The danger of war and crisis introduces the polarisation into the sectors of the dominant social groups, strata, elites – the new differences between the conservative social bloc with interest in expansionistic military industrial complex, and the old leading groups of owner-managers tied to large consumer production sectors, and proponents of 'historical compromise' of the previous period. Similar social differentiation takes places in all types of social systems, although in specific forms connected with the character of social structure.

The danger of human extermination quickly forms an awareness of the need for an alternative. Bombs can be dropped from the sky but a solution for peace must come from the ground. Human consciousness is being aroused as the revolting peoples' strength. On the march is an age of sweeping social peace movements which are not advocates of a pacifist utopia but which rather offer a realistic response. The strength of this response will depend upon a host of factors, one of them being fateful: the ability to unite the struggle for peace with the engagement for socio-cultural alternatives, new ways of development, universal existential needs, greater equality and freedom (democracy). It is the crucial test.

Intellectuals too have responsibilities and roles in promoting those values in these early stages. They are the couriers who must take the messages across the frontiers of ideologies, and they must find their own routes; they cannot await any 'high command to tell them what to do'.

Index

ABM system, SDI and 61, 65
Abrahamson, James 62
Afghanistan 134, 137, 256; as neutral 240
Africa: military rule in 187; Soviet-Cuban involvement in 136
aid, arms reduction funds for 223
Albrecht, Ulrich 242
Algeria, GDR trade with 231
Algerian war 135
alliances, with past enemies 250-1
Altman, F. 52
Andreyev, Y.V. 7-8, 39
Angelopoulos, Angelos 9, 150
Angola 133, 154
Anti-Ballistic Missile Treaty (ABM) 60-1; SDI and 63, 65-7, 70, 73-4
Arab-Israeli conflict 122, 240-1
arms control 202, 274; negotiations, SDI effect on 70, 73; neutrality and 245
arms conversion 225-6, 233
arms industry 94, 214, 278
arms race 18-19, 97-8, 151, 196, 213, 232, 268-9; stimulated by nuclear deterrent 235
arms trade 187
Atlanticism 2, 5, 201
Austria, neutrality 244

Bahro, Rudolf 5
basic needs 169; development strategy 168-71, 174, 276-7/income redistribution in 171-2/modern sector in 174-5/perversions of 172-6/Western attitude to 172, 175-6
Betkenhagen and Wessels 52
Binter, Josef 10-11
biological systems, deterioration of 193
bloc politics 198-9
Bönisch, Alfred 10, 221
Brandt Commission 3-4, 9
Brezhnev, Leonid 258

British air bases abroad, USA and 114
Brock, Lothar 9, 127
Brown, Carl 104
Brown, Lester 193
Brucan, Silviu 7, 15
Bunce, Valerie 113

Cambodia 253
Campaign for Nuclear Disarmament 215
capital-labour antagonism 89-90
capitalism: cause of war and economic crisis 207; Third World penetration by 102
capitalist-socialist conflict 129-30
Caribbean Basin Initiative 137
Carr, E.H. 204
Central America, US military action in 137-9
Chernenko, K.U. 258
China: geopolitical strategy 34-5; reforms 23-4; Soviet relations with 121, 132-3; US relations with 121, 252-3
class: interests, in international affairs 16, 18; struggles, Soviet menace as pretext for 256
Clement, H. 52
COCOM 46-7
Cold War 16-17, 29, 198; cooperation preceding 90; effects in Third World 88-9, 91, 95; ideological change in 31-2; mentality, elimination of 218; sheltering Europe 27
colonialism 88, 102, 113, 134-5
Columbus project 75-6
Comecon (CMEA) 24, 226-7, 230, 233; debt to West 50; increasing trade with West 229, 257-8; rapprochement with EEC 263-4LL; summit conference 46, 53
Comintern 130
compensation projects 50-2

consumerism 98
crises: economic 150-1, 206; in Europe in 1950s 131-2
Cuban missile crisis 116-18, 132
cyclical theories of society 204

de Gaulle, Charles 18
debt crisis, Thired World 151-8, 271; plan to meet 155-60
decolonization 134-5
defence, civilian-based 195-6
Delors, Jacques 261
demilitarization 238
détente 39-40, 58-9, 96-7, 117, 148; decline in 122; demise of 133-4, 137; economic 45, 53, 228; global 128-9; objectives 132-3; Third World and 96-7, 133
deterrence: contradictions of 213-14; mutual 27; peace movement and 216, 218; role of 210-13; SDI role 62-4; stimulus to arms race 269; *see also* nuclear deterrence
developing countries: foreign trade 175; socialist states' trade with 230-3
development: in agrarian economies 184; basic needs, *see* basic needs; capital-intensive 163-5; comparative advantage 188; decade 271; disarmament and 277-8; economic growth model 173-4; employment-oriented 165-9; European projects 1-6; liberal 183-4; military needs and 185, 187; new model 276; peace and 1-6, 181; regional interest 278; self-reliant 188-9; Soviet 184-5; state capitalist 184; territorial 189-90; Western model outmoded 181; *see also* European development model
disarmament: development and 277-8; economic benefit 273; 'multilateral unilateralism' 274; unilateral 242-3
division of labour, world pattern of 98
Dulles, John Foster 236, 243

East-West conflict 90, 127-8, 206; between contradictory systems 211; cooperation preceding 90; global dimensions of 129-34, 131-2; global effects 97-8; North-South conflict's interaction with, *see* North-South conflict; probability 109; Western Europe's role 129; *see also* Third World, E-W conflict's effects on
East-West confrontation: Middle East 120, 122-3; replacing North-South dialogue 140; South East Asia 120-1
East-West economic cooperation 227-9, 232-3; arms production conversion and

233; barriers to 228; detente and 227-8
East-West economic gap 24
East-West economic relations 21, 39-49, 221; differing opinions on 47; linkage strategy 51-2; new forms of 50-2; treaties on 47-9; US attitude to 50
East-West German relations 3, 59, 249
East-West intermediary, Eastern Europe as 249-50
East-West pan-European rapprochement 262-5
East-West rivalry: Asian-Pacific area 121; increasing 147; in Third World 110, 114-15; Third World regional systems and, *see* Third World; US economic dominance 111
Eastern Europe: debt to West 273; as East-West intermediary 149-50; economic integration with West 250; economic problems 272-3; liberalization 7, 13, 17, 37; planning in 98; reforms 24-5, 256-7; unfavourable influence on developing countries 96
ecology 193; parties 181
economic: crises 150-1, 206; cycles 204-5; expansion 29-30; gap, East-West 24; growth 163, 165, 173-4, 252/Soviet bloc 272-3; importance of Europe 15; policy, poverty and 161; reform, Soviet bloc 256-7; relations, interdependence strategy 41/*see also* East-West economic cooperation/relations; reorganization 31-2; stagnation 29-30; strength, superpowers' 19-20
education, role in employment problem 167-8
Eisenhower Doctrine 115
Emmerij, Louis 9, 161
employment-oriented development 165-9
energy sources, renewable 193
Eureka project 74, 144
Europe: arms expenditure in 222-3; basic needs development strategy role 176; conventional defence of 199; crises of 1950s 131-2; development projects, peace and 1-6; disengagement concept 242-3; economic importance 15; Fortress Europe project 4, 190-1; global politics 134-6; independence from superpowers 197, 199; medium-range missiles in 57, 216, 260; neutrality in 239, 244-6; new European peace order 243; non-alignment in 55; nuclear-free 243, 245; Pacific economic challenge to 144-5; peace movement 238/alternative security concepts and 215-18;

predominance in science 15; reducing
E-W gap 202; role in solving debt crisis
160; role in war or peace issue 267-8;
SDI and 9, 22, 71-6, 144, 215; search
for identity 140-2, 146-8, 201;
Stockholm Conference on Confidence
Building Measures and Disarmament in
245; as superpower 3, 147, 190-1, 201;
supply security problem 137, 142; world
role 87; *see also* nation state; security,
European; Third World, Europe's effect
on
European Defence Community (EDC) 58,
60
European development model 184, 196-7;
alternative 202-3; conventional 202;
military needs and 185; peace and 181,
197-8; reformist 202-3; transcending
188-92
European Economic Community (EEC)
135, 188; agricultural policy 147;
enlargement 33, 147, 190-1, 263;
rapprochement with CMEA 263-4
European Political Cooperation (EPC)
135-7, 142
European Security and Cooperation
Conference 222
European unity, possibility of 32-3, 36-7,
37-8; Soviet attitude 37
Europeanization of world 134
exports, shares of world 271

Far Eastern development 23
fascism 130
Fei, John 163
feudalism 182
food production insecurity 193
Fortress Europe project 4, 190-1
France 18, 76; Central American policy
138; colonialism 113-14; reactions to
SDI 3, 74
Frank, André Gunder 11, 191, 249
free trade 186
French-West German relations 3, 59, 249
fundamentalism 96

Galtung, Johan 147
German Democratic Republic (GDR):
attitude to SDI 74-5; Central American
policy 138-9; foreign trade 229-31;
French relations with 3, 59, 249; peace
movement 21; relations with West 262;
security measures 221; Social
Democratic policy 138
German reunification 28-9, 131, 262, 264
Giddens, Anthony 108

Global Interdependence Project 3-4
government attitude to informal sector
166-7
great powers: confrontation probability
109; involvement in Third World
105-10; political management of
relations of 110
green parties 4-5, 190-1

Haig, Alexander 42
Helsinki Security and Cooperation
Conference 40
Hettne, Björn 10, 181, 188
Hoffman, Stanley 112
Holme, Hans-Henrik 8, 55
Howe, Sir Geoffrey 73-4
human rights movements 218
Hyland, Willliam 261

Iklé, Fred 62, 69
income distribution 173; unemployment
and 166; world inequality 98
income redistribution in basic needs
development strategy 171-2
Indochina neutrality solution 240
industrialization 184-5; violent 187
inter-state relationships 208-10;
demilitarization 217
interest rates 271
intermediate nuclear forces (INF) 20-1, 57,
121, 216, 260
international: behaviour models 1-6;
economic relations 232-3/peace
stabilization through 226-33;
institutions 210
International Monetary Fund (IMF), debt
crisis and 154
international order: alternative 191-2, 197,
199; conventional 197; reformist 197-8;
single state dominance for 186; *see also*
New International Economic Order
international system: fragmentation 118;
power transitions 109-13
Iran-Iraq war 121-2; Soviet-US rivalry and
122
Ireland, non-aligned 245
Islamic Conference Organization 101
isolationism 96
Israeli-Arab conflict 122; Palestine
neutrality solution 240-1

Japan: economic potential 144-5; foreign
trade 23; US relations with 33

Kaldor, Mary 10, 11, 104, 272-4
Kampelman, Max 69
Kampuchea 240, 253

Kende, Istvan 119
Kennan, George 115
Keynes, J.M. 158
Keynesian global strategy: for employment 159-60; Third World and 151, 160
Keynesianism 4
Keyworth, George 65
Kissinger, Henry 261
Kivikari, U. 44
Klein, Lawrence 159
Kohl, Helmut 74, 259
Korean War 114-15
Köves, A. 257
Kristol, Irving 22

Latin America 131; external debt crisis 153-5; socialist economic relations with 231-2; US military actions in 22
Lebanon 123
Lenin, V.I. 130
Lewis, W. Arthur 163
liberal development 183-4
liberalization in Eastern Europe 7, 13, 17, 37
List, Friedrich 184
Lomé Treaty 136, 147
Lutz, Dieter 243

Mansbach, R.W. et al. 182
manufacturing expansion 29
Marshall Plan, new global 160
Marx, Karl 209
Marxism 99n6, 185, 188, 205, 207
Melman, S. 225
Mexico, GDR trade with 231
Middle East 104, 118; E-W confrontation 120, 122-3; nuclear alert in 1973 117; US strategy 22
militarization 97, 277-8; of Western technological research 144
militarized authoritarian state 208-9
military: alliances 210-12, 235; defence, alternative 195-6; exercises 211-12
military expenditure 151, 277; benefits of reduction of 160, 223; economic effects 222-5; inflationary tendency 224-5; US 143, 261; US pressure on allies to increase 252, 261
military pacts, ideology and 18
military technology 213-15
missiles: medium range 20-1, 121/in Europe 57, 216, 260
Modelski, G. 207
modernization crisis 269-76
monetarism 4
Mroz, John E. 240

Mugabe, Robert 254

nation state: alternative to 181; development crises in 195; formation 182-5; international anarchy with 181-6; power structure in 189-90; real socialism and 140; vested interests threatened 200-1; wars and risings in 187
neutral countries, peace movement in 247
neutralism 238-9, 242-3
neutrality: concept 235-8; contribution to world peace 243-7; immorality charge 246; permanent 236-7; political 241; as strategy for conflict resolution 239-42
neutralization 238, 242
New International Economic Order (NIEO) 96-7, 98-9, 110, 190-2, 275-6
Nicaragua 123, 138, 253
Nitze, Paul 65, 66
non-alignment 97, 101, 131, 136-7, 199, 238-9; European 55
North Atlantic Treaty Organization (NATO) 212; conflict on Middle East 116; dissension within 264; flexible response strategy 73; Third World and 92; US attitude to 261
North-South, new social movements in 200-1
North-South conflict 96; E-W conflict's interaction with 88-9, 92, 98-9, 127-9, 133, 145-6, 255-6/Europe and 129; economic 98; European attitude to 137-40
North-South dialogue, E-W confrontation replacing 140
nuclear: arms reduction 66; decision-making, democracy and 272; deterrence 67, 69, 196, 211, 213, 218, 235; disarmament, unilateral 260; missiles, intermediate 20-1, 57, 121, 216, 260; war 202/limited 268
nuclear war threat 266-9; alternative 280; causes 267, 269; radical emancipation alternative 266
nuclear weapons 117-18; INF 20-1, 57, 121, 216, 260; proliferation 268; threat to Europe 21
nuclear-free zones, European 243, 245

oil crisis 194
Organization for Economic Cooperation and Development (OECD) 47, 50
Orwell, George 212

Pacific Rim strategy 34-5, 36-7
Pacific tripartite axis 264

Paleologue, E. 52
peace: culture of 274, 279-80; development
    and 181; and development projects,
    European 1-6; social movements and
    280
peace movement 21, 59, 64, 200, 204;
    alternative security concepts and 215-18;
    deterrence and 216, 218; new 247
peace zone concept 241-2
peaceful coexistence 2-3, 5
Pecujlic, Miroslav 11, 266
Perle, Richard 65
planning, central 98, 112, 257
Poland, Solidarity's struggle 32
political cycles 205
political development, post-war 16-18
Politis, Nicolas 243
population control, poverty and 169
poverty 161-2; economic strategy to
    abolish 162-5; threat to world peace 162
power, world, cyclical theory of war for
    205
protectionism 4, 98, 186, 190

Ranis, Gustav 163
Reagan, Ronald 19, 21-2; on SDI 60-2,
    64-5, 67, 213
regionalism, world 275
Reinikainen, V. 44
repression 209
Rockefeller, David 254
Rostow, W.W. 264
Russell Foundation 274
Russian Revolution 129-30

science, European predominance in 15
SEATO area of immobilization 241
security 5-6; alternative concepts 218-19/
    peace movement and 215-18; ecological
    threats to 193-4; European 55-6/
    alternative 192-8/dependence on
    superpowers 56-8/independence
    movement 58-60/SDI and 79-80/
    superpower guarantee of 56-8;
    legitimacy of regime and 194-5; military
    defence 195-6; superpowers' 55;
    vulnerability 193-4; Western allies'
    differences on 260-1
self-reliance 188-9
Sen, G. 185
Senghaas, D. 119, 186
Shröder, K. 52
social control in East 256
social projects 1
socialism 90; in one country 140; Third
    World 90, 137, 145-6, 253-5; in Western
    Europe 259-60
socialist states 206; arms industry in 226;
    international division of labour 230-1;
    international economic cooperation and
    226-33
socialist-capitalist conflict 129-30
South Africa, conflict in 123
Soviet bloc: economic growth 272-3;
    hegemonistic relations within 272;
    semiperipheralization of 113
Soviet system 210-11
Soviet Union: 20th Party Congress 31;
    26th Party Congress 40, 45-6; attitude
    to possible European unity 37; central
    planning 112; China and 132; credit
    relations with West 47, 49-50;
    development model 184-5; Eastern
    Europe blackmailed by 250-1; economic
    discrimination against 48-9; economic
    reform 256-7; foreign policy 39; foreign
    trade 1960-84 42-3; gas pipeline to West
    21, 45-6, 51; growth in power of 112;
    nationalism within 36; rearmament 117;
    social unrest possible 36-7; trade with
    West 41-5, 47-9, 53/US attitude to 40-2,
    46-7, 50; *see also* East-West relations;
    great powers; superpowers; Third
    World
state 207; militarized authoritarian 208-9;
    socialist 206; transformation towards
    greater democracy 216, 219; *see also*
    inter-state relationships
state capitalist development 184-5
Strategic Defense Initiative (SDI) 21, 32,
    60-1, 213; defence coverage 76-9;
    European attitude to 8, 22, 71-6, 144;
    European participation 215; European
    security and 79-80; French concern
    about 3, 74; goals 61-6; presentation of
    68/to allies 68-71; as research 64-5;
    technology 66-7
strategy prevailing over ideology 16-17
Strayer, J.R. 182
structuration processes 108-9
Suez crisis 114, 116, 132, 135
superpowers 91-2; dual hegemony 141;
    European security dependent on 56-8;
    ideological leadership by 32-3; interests
    in Europe 27-9; internal disorder
    possibility 35; military omnipresence
    129; relations with partners 16-18;
    rivalry 19-22, 147; security 55/risks 5;
    strategy 39; *see also* Cold War; East-
    West conflict
Szentes, Támas 8, 87

technological progress 144, 269, 278; international consequences 270-2
technology: exchange 232; Soviet bloc imports 257
Teller, Edward 63
Thatcher, Margaret 4, 72-3, 259
Thee, Marek 240
Third World: aid through military savings 96; anti-democratic leftist regimes 93; autarchy 275; capitalist penetration 102; change in, zero-sum perception of 130-1; conflict dynamics 103-5; conflicts under US predominance 113-18; cultural values 279; debt problem 151-60, 271; détente and 96-7, 133; East-West competition in 22; East-West conflict's effects on 88-9, 91-3, 127/ foreign trade 93/military 91-5/political 92-3, 97/security 91/socio-economic 90-1, 93-5, 97-8; East-West conflict's escalation and 131-2; East-West rivalry and 103, 114-18, 120-4, 147-8; economic development 117-18; economic stagnation 118; emancipation and E-W rivalry 110; Europe's effect on 87, 96, 102/ militarization 94-5/new world economic order and 99/security 88, 90-1/socio-economic 88-9, 91, 94-6; exports problem 190; foreign trade 278-9; great-power involvement 105-10/ regional power and 106-7; income inequalities 173; influence on international relations 101; integration and cooperation dynamics 105; liberation struggles 130; likely area of next world war 249; Marxist view of development in 99n6; militarization 91, 93, 112; military expenditure 154; military intervention in 92-3; modernization imperative 186-7; national liberation conflicts 89-90; NATO and 92; polarization of regimes 92-4; political changes in 92; poverty in 162, 164, 168-9; regional alliances 131; regional anarchy 104; regional conflicts 103/causes of 115-16, 118, 119, 121/ danger of escalation 124/E-W rivalry and 114-18, 120-4/numbers of 119-20/ semiperipheral 118/US-Soviet management of 117-18/Western differences on 116-17; regional dominance or balance of power 104; regional power centres 119-20; regional systems and E-W rivalry 103; revolts due to rivalry in West 94; socialism 90, 253-5/real 137, 145-6; socialist states'

trade with 230-2; socialist-capitalist struggle in 130; unemployment 163-5, 168; US intervention 255-6; US-European differences on 137-40; *see also* development; North-South conflict, interaction with E-W conflict
Thompson, E.P. 198-9, 266
Todman, T. 69
Toynbee, A.J. 204-5
traditionalism 96
Trilateral Project 3

unemployment 150, 200, 223
United Nations, US use of 116, 130
United States: attitude to East-West trade 40-1, 46-7, 50; as counter-revolutionary power 113; disagreements with colonialist Britain and France 113-14, 116; economic decline 30, 142-3, 251; Europe drifting away from 198-9; Far East relations 15; global containment policy 114-15; international predominance 111, 206, 211/conflicts under 113-18/economic 111-12; intervention in third world 255-6; Japanese relations with 33-5; military expenditure 143, 261; neutralism 243; nuclear guarantee to Europe 57-8, 74; power in decline 19, 30, 251; pressure on allies 116/to increase arms spending 252, 261; social unrest 35; ties with Europe weakening 258-60; West European differences with 137-40, 142-4, 261-2; Western Europe blackmailed by 251; *see also* great powers; Strategic Defense Initiative; superpowers; Third World
UNU peace and security conference 6-7, 28
US-Japan-China triumvirate of future 34-5, 36-7

Väyrynen, Raimo 8-9, 101, 244-5
Vietnam 133-4; as neutral 240; war 111, 116-17, 121, 132, 217, 251-3

Wallerstein, Immanuel 7, 27
war: causes 209; for hegemony, cyclical theory of 205; prospect of global 204; threat of, as ideological coercion 212-13, 215
Weinberger, Caspar 61-2, 65, 70, 72
West Germany, French relations with 3, 59, 249
Western consumerism 98
Western Europe: capital exports to USA 261-2; closer links with East 259-60; consumer society 95; differences with

USA 137-40, 142-4, 261-2; economic
    revival 142-3; emancipation from US
    supremacy 17; neutralism 242-3; role in
    E-W conflict 129; socialism in 259-60;
    trade with socialist countries 146
Western European Union (WEU) 58-60
Wilson, Woodrow 243
World Bank 156
Wörner, Manfred 74-5

Zemanek, Karl 244
Zhivkov, Todor 258
Zimbabwe, political future 254
Zolotas, Xenophon 156